DATE DUE

3-24-09	
5-4-09	
10-28-14	

Water-Based Tourism, Sport, Leisure, and Recreation Experiences

Water-Based Tourism, Sport, Leisure, and Recreation Experiences

Gayle Jennings

AMSTERDAM • BOSTON • HEIDELBERG • LONDON
NEW YORK • OXFORD • PARIS • SAN DIEGO
SAN FRANCISCO • SINGAPORE • SYDNEY • TOKYO

Butterworth-Heinemann is an imprint of Elsevier

Butterworth-Heinemann is an imprint of Elsevier
30 Corporate Drive, Suite 400, Burlington, MA 01803, USA
Linacre House, Jordan Hill, Oxford OX2 8DP, UK

∞ Recognizing the importance of preserving what has been written, Elsevier prints its books on
acid-free paper whenever possible.

Library of Congress Cataloging-in-Publication Data
Application submitted.

British Library Cataloguing-in-Publication Data
A catalogue record for this book is available from the British Library.

ISBN 13: 978-0-7506-6181-2
ISBN 10: 0-7506-6181-X

For information on all Butterworth-Heinemann publications
visit our Web site at www.books.elsevier.com

Printed in the United States of America
06 07 08 09 10 11 10 9 8 7 6 5 4 3 2 1

Contents

Preface

Water-Based Tourism, Sport, Leisure, and Recreation Experiences grew out of an interest in providing a volume of writings that addressed a broad range of water-based experiences conducted in, on, and under a variety of water based settings: fresh, estuarine, marine, as well as frozen. The water-based experiences presented herein are not exclusive; there are other forms, but the ones presented are the most popular in industrialized nations at the turn of the twenty-first century. The book aims to complement other specifically focused works related to water-based experiences, such as cruise ship experiences, marine experiences, and snow experiences. It also serves to supplement and enhance discussions presented in more generic works related to sport and adventure experiences. Moreover, the book essays draw together the related fields of tourism, sport, leisure, and recreation, as well as to identify the connectivity among these fields, rather than to polarize discussions by assuming field-specific perspectives. As a result, *Water-Based Tourism, Sport, Leisure, and Recreation Experiences* serves to commence and continue a dialogue linked to water-based experiences across field boundaries. A dialogue to which we hope that other researchers and writers will contribute as a means to generate further understanding of this phenomenon called *Water-Based Tourism, Sport, Leisure, and Recreation Experiences*.

Subsequently, one of the challenges of writing about water-based tourism, sport, leisure, and recreation is the degree of overlap between the terms themselves and the resulting sense of ambiguity that arises from such overlap. Of course, definitions abound in regard to qualifying what each term means; however, as would be expected, these tend to be bounded by space, time, societal, cultural, religious, and political influences. In addition, economic and environmental influences and disciplinary perspectives can also influence definition construction and reconstruction. Further, in preparing a book on water-based tourism, sport, leisure, and recreation experiences, the nature, amount, and availability of empirical materials and sources of data can prove challenging, especially in newly-evolving markets, as a result of changes in fashion, methods of measurement, and standards of measurement. Moreover, in some of the water-based tourism, sport, leisure, and recreation experiences presented, there are no formal requirements for reporting or established informal reporting mechanisms. Consequently, empirical materials and data sources utilized ranged from case-specific to more generic source bases.

A majority of the contributors to *Water-Based Tourism, Sport, Leisure, and Recreation Experiences* are also participants in the water-based experiences about which they have written. Additionally, some have or still participate in more than one of the water-based experiences, while others had a keen interest and/or conducted research in the related water-based experience. All of the chapter writers, based on their various backgrounds, were informed contributors and able to present insider, that is, emic, and/or outsider, that is, etic, perspectives.

The contributors who agreed to participate in this project include, in alphabetical order, Paul Beedie, De Montfort University, United Kingdom; Kay Dimmock, Southern Cross University, Australia; Gary Easthope, University of Tasmania, Australia; Simon Hudson, University of Calgary, Canada; Gayle Jennings, Griffith University, Australia; Lilian Jonas, Jonas Consulting, United States of America; Les Killion, Central Queensland University, Australia; Gianna Moscardo, James Cook University, Australia; Harold Richins, Sierra Nevada College, United States of America; and Chris Ryan, The University of Waikato, New Zealand.

The project, *Water-Based Tourism, Sport, Leisure, and Recreation Experiences,* associated with this book is now completed. We hope it is a catalyst for others to engage in related works, research, writings, and projects as well as possible participation in water-based experiences.

Gayle Jennings

Acknowledgments

Thank you to the people who participated in the research studies that have been reported in this volume of work. As always, without such participation, our research could not be undertaken and our knowledge of the world would be subsequently diminished.

Appreciation is also extended to the owners of copyrighted materials, particularly, for permission to reproduce their works in *Water-Based Tourism, Sport, Leisure, and Recreation Experiences*.

To the institutions, families, friends, and colleagues of all the contributors, a huge thank you for your continued support of our endeavors.

Sincere thanks to the staff at Elsevier for their contributions to this project: Sally North and Jane MacDonald, for their support and commitment to the book; Dennis McGonagle, Anne McGee, Brandy Lilly, Jay Donahue, Christine Brandt, and Jack Pitts for their assistance in the manuscript preparation and production processes, as well as other staff at Elsevier who have been variously involved in the publication of *Water-Based Tourism, Sport, Leisure, and Recreation Experiences*.

Special thanks to Helen Lobegeier for her continuous and committed assistance in the preparation of the final manuscript.

Finally, to the contributing authors, thank you for your research and the timeliness of your writings. More particularly, your patience is greatly appreciated, especially when the project became delayed due to several contributors being unable to continue participation in the project.

Contributors

Paul Beedie, De Montfort University, United Kingdom

Paul Beedie, Ph.D., contributes his teaching and research in the School of Physical Education and Sport Sciences at De Montfort University, Bedford, United Kingdom. A social scientist by training, Paul started his career as a teacher of adventure education in a variety of UK-based locations. The focus of Paul's academic and practical work is an understanding of adventure in society. Two notable areas of this work are adventure education and adventure tourism; recent publications can be found in the *Annals of Tourism Research*, *Leisure Studies*, the *Journal of Risk Research,* and the *Journal of Travel & Tourism Marketing*. Sailing and paddling canoes and kayaks have been formative in a career where water based adventures, such as open sea crossings and multi-day journeys around coasts and down rivers, have formed the applied theoretical ideas emerging from his research.

Kay Dimmock, Southern Cross University, Australia

Kay Dimmock, M.Ed. Grad Dip., FET. B.Bus., Tourism (Hons), has been lecturing and researching in the School of Tourism and Hospitality Management, Southern Cross University for 8 years. Her academic and research experiences include management, managing tourism operations, tourism education, international tourism trends, and marine tourism. Like all people with a keen interest in all things marine, she enjoys recreating on, but preferably in, the ocean. While she dabbles in snorkeling and freediving, she is fanatical about recreational scuba diving, which has provided immense enjoyment and discovery, particularly along the New South Wales coastline, Australia. Kay is currently studying for her Ph.D.

Gary Easthope, University of Tasmania, Australia

Gary Easthope, Ph.D., is a reader in Sociology at the University of Tasmania. He has taught in the United Kingdom, Canada, and United States. He has published widely on research methods, health, youth, and drug use. His recent work has focused on complementary medicine. He is currently writing, with a colleague, a book on medical perceptions of lifestyle for Routledge. For the past 5 years, he has been a voluntary crew member on the sail training vessel the *Lady Nelson* and hopes to make senior crew one day!

Simon Hudson, University of Calgary, Canada

Simon Hudson, Ph.D., is an Associate Professor in the Haskayne School of Business at the University of Calgary. Prior to working in academia, he spent several years working for United Kingdom tour operators and now lectures and consults on the marketing of tourism. His research is focused on sport tourism, and he has published numerous journal articles and book chapters from his work. He also has three books to his name: *Snow Business, Sport & Adventure Tourism,* and *Tourism and Hospitality Marketing: A Canadian Perspective.* He is known worldwide for his work on the ski industry and has been invited as a keynote speaker to many international conferences. He is on the editorial board for the *International Journal of Tourism Research*, the *Journal of Teaching in Travel & Tourism,* and the *Journal of Travel Research.*

Gayle Jennings, Griffith University, Australia

Gayle Jennings, Ph.D., is an Associate Professor of Tourism Management, Department of Tourism, Leisure, Hotel and Sport Management, Griffith University, Gold Coast Campus. Part of her research agenda focuses on quality tourism experiences in water-based environments as well as the use of qualitative methodologies. Gayle has also worked for a national marine park agency. In the course of her life experiences, Gayle has been a keen participant in a number of water-based experiences. She has been a qualified/certified SCUBA diver since 1983 and has held a motor boat license since 1989. Prior to going long-term ocean cruising in the early 1990s, she enjoyed windsurfing and recreational sailing. She has also engaged in jetboating, whitewater rafting, and one-day boating adventures. She continues to sail on weekends and during vacations on her yacht.

Lilian Jonas, Jonas Consulting, United States of America

Lilian Jonas received a B.S in Biology in 1987 and a M.A. in Applied Sociology in 1990 from Northern Arizona University and a Ph.D. in Sociology in 1997 from the University of Denver. Her "research" interest has been on the qualitative nature of extended river trips (a few days to several weeks) in the western United States, including river trips on the Colorado River through the Grand Canyon. Her dissertation involved hundreds of days on various rivers examining how river guides were able to take on leadership roles during an extended recreational experience in a wilderness setting. She has also "worked" on the river as a river guide, fisheries biologist, and consultant. Lilian currently lives in southwestern Oregon (near a few good rivers) and runs her own business as an environmental and outdoor recreation consultant and occasionally gets to do more river "work."

Les Killion, Central Queensland University, Australia

Les Killion, Ph.D., is currently an Associate Professor in Tourism at Central Queensland University. Originally training as a geographer, Les developed Tourism courses at what were at that time Mitchell College of Advanced Education (MCAE) and Canberra CAE before commencing the Tourism program at Central Queensland University. Les is also trained as a sociologist and has research interests in social impacts assessment and qualitative research methodologies and their application to tourism. During his time in Central Queensland, Les has traveled through the Whitsunday Islands and the Keppel Islands of the Great Barrier Reef and has an amateur interest in fishing for all species—when the tides and weather are right!

Gianna Moscardo, James Cook University, Australia

Gianna Moscardo, Ph.D., is an Associate Professor in the Tourism program at James Cook University in Townsville. Before joining the Tourism program as an academic 4 years ago, she worked as Project Coordinator with the CRC Reef Research managing a series of research and extension activities aimed at enhancing the sustainability of marine and water based tourism activities in Northern Australia. Her qualifications in applied psychology and sociology support her research interests in understanding how tourists make decisions and evaluate their travel experiences and how communities and organizations perceive, plan for, and manage tourism and tourists. She has been an author or coauthor of more than 90 academic publications and was recently elected to the World Tourism Organization's International Academy for the Study of Tourism Scholars.

Harold Richins, Sierra Nevada College, United States America

Harold Richins, Ph.D., is Professor and Chair of the Ski Business and Resort Management program in the Department of Management at Sierra Nevada College. He has held teaching positions and directed programs at colleges and universities in Australia and New Zealand in the areas of recreation, resort management, entrepreneurship, tourism, and hospitality. Harold's industry background includes coaching at the high school and college level, volunteering with disabled skiing tours, and organizing ski and special interest tours in both the United States and Australia. He has also worked in the charter yacht industry. Harold has been active with community groups, working with sustainable resort development, environmental protection, and education.

Chris Ryan, The University of Waikato, New Zealand

Chris Ryan is a Professor of Tourism at Waikato University and a silver and bronze medalist for windsurfing at the New Zealand Master's Games. He sails a New Zealand designed 2.93 meter wide race board for recreational purposes these days, having previously raced in the United Kingdom, Greece, and Turkey. His CV includes a period as a windsurfing instructor in Greece. He also happens to be editor of Tourism Management and has written about 80 refereed journal articles on issues pertaining to tourism.

1

Water-Based Tourism, Sport, Leisure, and Recreation Experiences

Gayle Jennings

At the commencement of the twenty-first century, a wide range of niche tourism, sport, leisure, and recreation experiences provide tourists, sportspersons, people at leisure, and recreationalists with substantial choices for how to spend their non-work time. Such niches include adventure tourism, sport tourism, recreational tourism, event tourism, marine tourism, national park tourism, and "sun, sea, and sand" tourism. Additionally, choices in sports range from easy to extreme, low to high impact, individual to team pursuits, casual to committed participation, modest to sophisticated equipment usage, and from relatively inexpensive to expensive setup and participation costs. Likewise, leisure and recreation experiences provide a range of choices. To add to this diversity, tourism, sport, leisure, and recreation can be undertaken in various environments, such as subterranean, terrestrial, water-based, aerial, "outer space," and virtual environments as well as combinations of these. Diversity is also a constant in regard to the various roles for engaging in these experiences. People can be participants, spectators, umpires, referees, coaches, support and service providers, organization/association officials, or volunteers. Moreover, participation can be described as active, passive, or vicarious.

   In contemporary times, the nature of participation in niche tourism, sport, leisure, and recreation is influenced by a number of factors, such as time, finances, family life cycle, and participants' perceptions of skill, risk, novelty, adventure, and challenge. Previously, in the first half of the twentieth century, gender, ability, ethnicity, socio-economic, and cultural background were substantive limiting factors along with social, religious, and political influences. Prior to that period in industrialized nations, socio-economic class, gender and religion were strong differentiating factors. Contemporaneously, the influence of these last two sets of factors has been reduced or removed, albeit some continue to exist as will be evidenced in the following chapters.

Why a Focus on Water-Based Tourism, Sport, Leisure, and Recreation Experiences?

Various books have been written about sport, leisure, adventure and tourism (see for example, Turco, Riley, and Swart 2002; Hudson 2003; Swarbrooke, Beard, Leckie, and Pomfret 2003; Weed and Bull 2004; Higham 2005) as well as tourism, recreation, and leisure (see for example, Veal 2002; McCool and Moisey 2001; Gartner and Lime 2000). In addition, a number of books have focussed on marine tourism (such as Orams 1999; Garrod and Wilson 2003), and several have highlighted cruise tourism (Cartwright and Baird 1999; Dowling 2006). Few, however, have focused specifically on water-oriented experiences across the broad fields of study of tourism, sport, leisure, and recreation. Furthermore, few, if any, have substantively addressed a variety of water-based experiences associated with a "stable," albeit moving and movable, platform. As a consequence, this book turns the spotlight onto water-based experiences associated with some form of platform. Specifically, the book considers the water-based experiences of sailing, motor boating, motorized sports, surfing and windsurfing, sport and big game fishing, white-water rafting, kayaking, one-day boating adventures, sail training adventures, as well as scuba diving, free diving, and snorkelling, albeit that these latter three do not necessarily always associate with a platform. However, since boats are usually used to access a large number of dive and snorkelling sites and scuba divers may use underwater scooters and submersibles to access dive sites, scuba diving along with free diving and snorkelling are included in this volume. Additionally, given the extensive literature that has amassed in regard to cruise tourism, it is not included in this book.

Finally, some readers may wonder why the term marine was not used. Several authors have addressed marine tourism. Elsewhere, references have been made to water tourism (Kedrow 1987; Ministere de l'Industrie, des Postes et Telecommunications, et du Tourisme 1987), river/canal tourism (Panne 1990; Holloway and Plant 1993), nautical tourism (Laca 1996), marina-based tourism (Smith and Jenner 1995), and, more recently, lake tourism (Hall and Harkonen 2006). Apart from water tourism, the remaining terms tend to categorize by location rather than by overall resource base and related experiences. As a consequence, drawing on the term water tourism, for the intent of this book, the phrase "water-based tourism, sport, leisure, and recreation experiences" has been coined. In doing this, recognition is given to the overlap among tourism, sport, recreation, and leisure as well as to the diversity in water resources that may be used for the former. Such water resources include salt, estuarine, fresh, and frozen water in their various formations.

Background

Within Western nations, water has long been associated with restorative qualities and medicinal benefits to balance the ardor of work, life in the city, or the pollution inherent in industrial/urban areas. This association is evidenced in past practices of picnicking beside creeks, rivers, and lakes; short excursions to lake areas, thermal springs, and the seaside; the taking of seaside holidays and vacations; second-home ownership by lakes, or at the seaside; and bathing and spa therapy as well as taking in the waters and fresh or sea air.

Historically, early European engagement with water-based activities and experiences can be linked to earlier Roman habits. For example, the attraction of the seaside and seaside second-home ownership can be proffered to have its roots in early Roman practices. Ryan (2003) suggests that during the summers, upper-class Romans would relocate to their homes by the sea to escape the heat and the city. Similarly, the practice of "taking the waters"—aesthetically, physically, and spiritually—is also linked to Roman practices, particularly the Roman baths (Knappett 2003). With the onset of the industrial revolution and subsequent developments in working conditions, such as shorter working days and public holidays, discretionary income, along with the concurrent development of transportation technology, the lower-middle and working classes were able to experience to differing degrees the recreational and leisure pursuits that had previously been the purview of the upper-middle and upper-class ranks. For example, toward the end of the eighteenth century in England, spa towns, previously the realm of the upper class, were inundated with lower-middle class populaces. Subsequently, the popularity of spa towns for the upper class waned by the turn of the nineteenth century and was replaced by an attraction for seaside resorts—the preferred location used by royalty—particularly Brighton (Jeans 1990). The attraction of the seaside was also sponsored by the medical profession, which promoted the benefits of seawater. Again, the upper-class exclusivity of seaside locations changed with the development of railways, which served to make the seaside accessible to the working classes. However, until around 1920 in England, trips to the seaside were primarily just that—trips *to* the seaside—being beside the sea rather than in it (Jeans 1990). For some, this earlier trend was still the case in England in 1984 when only 25% of visitors entered the waters (Ashworth 1984).

While not a popular activity in England, "sea-bathing" was a favorite activity in early New South Wales, as Australia was then called. However, due to religious censure, sea-bathing was banned in 1833 and again in 1838 to protect social and moral values (Jeans 1990; Craik 1991). Subsequently, people were limited to using the seaside for "promenading, picnicking and paddling" (Art Gallery of New South Wales 1982, p. 4). Australian seaside resort practices exhibited a strong similarity to English seaside practices. Later in Australia, in the states of Victoria and South Australia, "bathing machines" were established to enable morally acceptable sea-bathing practices (Jeans 1990). Bathing machines enabled people, for a cost, to change from their everyday clothes into bathing clothes and also to discreetly enter the sea. Such machines were also used in England.

Traditionally, in England, seaside resorts and activities were used as a break from normal routine, whereas in Australia, due to settlement trends, particularly along the eastern seaboard, seaside resorts were integrated into urban centers. Consequently for Australians, beaches have been a way of life (Wells 1982). "For most Australians, the beach has been close, cheap, and easy to get to" (Craik 1991, p. 45), and able to be experienced by all social strata.

That being said, in Australia, proximity to the seaside was not always enough to satisfy water-based sporting, recreational, leisure, and tourism needs. People began to quest for different and less populated settings as well as different experiences. As a result, seaside resort experiences close to urban precincts began to be complemented by more expansive "sun, sea, and sand" experiences undertaken in remote locations. In addition, fishing was added to the traditional seaside recreation experience mix of going to the beach and swimming/bathing (Fabbri 1990, p. 263).

An illustration of this can be drawn from the Great Barrier Reef. As early as 1889, Green Island, located in the northern section of the Great Barrier Reef, Australia, had accommodation facilities established on it for the use of nonindigenous "fishing and hunting parties" (Tourism Review Steering Committee [TRSC] 1997, Part 2, p. 23). In addition to fishing and hunting, other seaside experience mixes, or sun, sea, and sand experiences, emerged. Organized pleasure cruises began in 1890. Then, in 1932, the first "resort" was established in the southern section of the Great Barrier Reef on Heron Island. Some five years later, the world's first glass-bottomed boat, developed for coral viewing, was introduced at Green Island. Shortly after that, in 1938, the second resort in the Great Barrier Reef was built at Green Island (TRSC 1997, Part 2, p. 23). A decade later, the central section of the Great Barrier Reef, the Whitsundays—a key hub of water-based tourism, sport, leisure, and recreation experiences offering island resorts, camping, and a multitude of water-based activities—was beginning to develop its profile. At that time, the area received 5,000 visitors. In the space of just over 30 years, visitation rates grew substantially to 182,000 p.a. (Claringbould, Deakin, and Foster 1985). From that basis, the Whitsundays has developed into a key tourism and Australian bareboat and charter boat location. In 2004, visitation numbers were 639,153, composed of 65% domestic tourists and 35% international tourists (Tourism Queensland 2004). In total, the Whitsundays region draws approximately one-third of annual tourism visitation to the Great Barrier Reef with numbers in excess of 1.8 million (Great Barrier Reef Marine Park Authority [GBRMPA] 2005).

To this point, the focus has been on England and Australia. In the United States, water-based tourism, sport, leisure, and recreation experiences have also grown due to broad societal changes resulting from industrialization, especially changes in working conditions, as already mentioned. It is also a consequence of a related demand for open space such as parks, recreational piers, and spaces within a 100-mile radius of urban precincts (West 1990) in which people could recreate in non-work times. Additionally, for the United States and other industrialized nations, socio-demographic and economic changes have also facilitated growth in water-based experiences. In particular, the growth is associated with higher income levels coupled with higher discretionary income levels, an aging population due to the baby boomer generation's influence on Western demographics, opportunities for early retirement, and a desire for active retirement, plus growth in second-home ownership, timeshare arrangements, caravan parks, and coastal hotels and motels (West 1990).

Similar parallels exist between the development of water-based tourism, sport, leisure, and recreation in Europe and what took place historically in England. However, the uptake has been somewhat slower in Asia. As a result of various changes to working conditions; perspectives and values regarding work and leisure; income; standards of living; increases in leisure time; and for some nations, moves into the capitalist market economy, participation rates in water-based experiences are starting to burgeon. For example, boating became popular in Japan in the latter part of the twentieth century (Kotani 1991), and scuba diving in Asia has grown since the 1970s (Hamdi 1995). For other nations in Asia and elsewhere in the world, social, economic, political, cultural, and religious influences have variously served to limit participation in water-based tourism, sport, leisure, and recreation. In some cases, the more affluent or privileged members of a society have been able to participate while the vast majority have not.

A Brief History of Some Water-Based Tourism, Sport, Leisure, and Recreation Experiences

As a result of European colonization of various countries of the world, European sporting, leisure, and recreation practices were transferred and adapted by the colonizers into the colonial settlements they established, and over time were taken up in varying degrees by the indigenous peoples of and other migrants to those countries. However, it must be noted that water-based activities of indigenous peoples were also taken up by colonizers and contemporary populations—for example, the sports of surfing, kayaking, and rafting. These three activities continue to be popular at the start of the 2000s. The purpose of this section is to provide a brief history behind the water-based experiences presented in this book. A more detailed exploration of specific origins and developments of each may be found in the related chapters.

Of the water-based experiences represented in *Water-Based Tourism, Sport, Leisure, and Recreation Experiences,* sailing, fishing, and surfing are probably the oldest. The activity of sailing dates back to Egyptian times (4000 BCE). History also indicates numerous types of sailing vessels used by various peoples for exploration, trade, transportation, or warfare, such as Chinese junks, Polynesian canoe-based multi-hulls, Arab trading dhows in the Indian Ocean, and Mediterranean sea feluccas (Cox 1999). As a recreational activity, sailing has its origins in the 1800s, when it was primarily a racing sport (Cox 1999). It was initially the preserve of wealthy men (Brasch 1995; Cox 1999). The 1900s saw intense growth of sailing as a recreational and leisure experience as a result of social, economic, and technological change in Western and industrialized nations. Technology, in particular, generated improvements in construction materials and equipment. The introduction of class boats, especially dinghies, made sailing affordable because the dinghy class was cheaper (Cox 1999); see Chapter 2 of this volume for details. However, despite such technological developments, strong interest in maritime history, reenactments, restoration, and replica building has seen the development of sail training vessels based on earlier counterparts such as the tall ships, including square-riggers and schooners (see Chapter 11). Interest in sail training experiences escalated in the last decades of the twentieth century as a result of a series of reenactments of exploratory voyages and related processes of colonization, with interest in tall ship races stemming from the 1950s. In addition to class boats, racing, and sail training adventures, another option for sailing is ocean voyaging. The pioneer of this activity is reported to be Joshua Slocum who completed a circumnavigation of the world between 1895 and 1898 (Cox 1999; see Chapter 2 of this volume).

Motor boating was a product of the nineteenth century. As would be expected, its roots merge with that of sailing due to the history of boat usage and design. However, the development of motors; their adaptation to numerous transportation technologies; and mass adoption, production, and in particular their use in recreational and leisure time pursuits make motor boating primarily a product of the second half of the 1900s (see Chapter 3). The development of technology in boat design, materials, and equipment, especially marine motors, facilitated the growth in commercial vessels able to provide one-day tours (refer to Chapter 10 for examples). Relatedly, motorized water sports became popular in the late twentieth and early twenty-first century. The most popular modes have been speedboats, jet boats, and jet skis—also known as aqua bikes, wet bikes, water scooters, water motorcycles, and water bobs (Schemel 2001; see Chapter 4 of this volume). Sport fishing and big game fishing had their beginnings in fishing for survival (see Chapter 6). As a tourism, sport, leisure, and recreation experience, they followed the development of motorized boats and became a fashionable activity in the 1950s and 1960s through the exploits of the wealthy and celebrities, and through their use and portrayal in shows and films.

The nascence of surfing occurred in the Pacific cultures (Orams 1999). In particular, the history of surfing has records of Polynesians using "bellyboards" circa 300 ACE (San Diego State University 2004), and surfing is purported to have originated in the tenth century (Brasch 1995). The sport entered a golden age in the 1950s (see Chapter 5), and as a recreational or leisure pursuit, surfing took off in Western nations in the late 1960s (Orams 1999). Another board-related water-based pursuit is windsurfing. Windsurfing is reported to have been "invented" in the 1970s (Orams 1999). Surfing, windsurfing, and long-term ocean voyaging share one commonality: they can be a sport, leisure, tourism, or recreation experience, as well as a lifestyle (see discussions by Pearson 1979; Macbeth 1985; Orams 1999; Jennings 1999). See Chapter 5 for details on surfing and windsurfing.

Kayaking has a longer history than windsurfing, with its beginnings as a traditional Inuit mode of travel in Arctic and Greenland waters (Effeney 1999). Appropriation of indigenous design was initiated by John Macgregor in the 1800s (see Chapter 9). Whitewater rafting, similarly, has a history founded in indigenous peoples' means of transportation, for example, Inca rafts (Paine 1997). In the United States, whitewater rafting was used by nonindigenous people for hunting and trading as well as exploration in the late nineteenth century. Its founding as a sport or recreation experience is associated with running various sections of the Green and Colorado rivers (see Chapter 8).

Finally, the start of scuba diving is associated with Jacques Cousteau and Emily Gagnan (see Chapter 7), who are primarily responsible for the development of the Self-Contained Underwater Breathing Appartus, SCUBA. This apparatus was originally developed for scientific and government use. However, the media of television and films helped to popularize it as a recreation activity, and as an established recreation experience, it is almost 50 years old (West 1990). See Chapter 7 for a discussion of scuba, free diving, and snorkeling.

Participation Overview

In the last half of the twentieth century and the early years of the twenty-first century, particularly in Western and industrial nations, there has been a significant growth in the pursuit of water-based experiences as forms of sport, leisure, recreation, and tourism (Miller 1993; Orams 1999; Jennings 2003). This section provides a brief overview of participation across the water-based tourism, sport, leisure, and recreation experiences presented in this book. Additional details may be found in the respective chapters.

Boating

In the late twentieth century, private boat ownership was estimated to be in excess of 20 million ("Pleasure Boating to Grow with Increase" 1987). The majority of owners were situated in the United States, where boating registrations have continued to increase from 10.9 million in 1990, to more than 12.5 million in 1999 (Fedler 2000). Elsewhere, participation numbers have also demonstrated growth (Brodersen 1994; Leyrat 1994; Smith and Jenner 1995; Driml 1996).

As an experience, and as a market, boating can be differentiated by the key energy source for propulsion, that is, whether it is sail driven or motor driven (Jennings 2003). Both forms continue to be popular in the twenty-first century. Boating, however, is not a singularly focused experience. It usually occurs in association with other water-related activities. This is particularly the case for motorized boating. Generally, self-contained underwater breathing apparatuses, scuba diving, and fishing are the biggest market segments linked to boat-associated activities (West 1990).

Scuba Diving

Scuba diving and the related activity of snorkeling continue to be popular water-based experiences (Dignam 1990; Tabata 1992; Hamdi 1995; Davis, Banks, and Davey 1996). Free diving is less extensive. In the early 1980s, the sport of scuba diving was projected to grow at a rate of 240,000 per annum (Matheusic and Mills 1983, cited in West 1990). Within the United States, in the 1990s, it was estimated that there were 4 to 5 million participants in scuba as recreation (West 1990). At the start of the twenty-first century, PADI (2005) estimates that there are between 5 and 7 million active divers in the world. Concurrently, the number of certified divers worldwide is in excess of 5 million (PADI 2005).

Sport Fishing and Big Game Fishing

Sport fishing and big game fishing, popular sports of the 1950s and 1960s for those who could afford it, continue to attract a core number of participants, though still only for those who can afford it. Like most forms of scuba diving (apart from, for example, beach entry dives), sport and big game fishing are reliant on motorized vessels to access key activity sites. Another popular motor-dependent activity is motorized watersports.

Motorized Watersports

Motorized watersports, such as jet skiing, wakeboarding, personal hydrofoils, and parasailing, have seen participation numbers rise sharply and then plateau in the twenty-first century as a result of fuel price increases, water resource management controls, and restrictions due to user conflicts associated with perceived losses of amenity and safety issues related to multiple use of sites.

One-Day Tours

Day tripper numbers in water-related areas—lakes, rivers, canals, coastal zones, and seas—are also growing; for example, on the Great Barrier Reef, approximately 1.5 million visitors take day cruises to access the special features of the reef and the recreation and tourism opportunities available there (Driml and Common 1996). Motorized watercraft are key elements of commercial water-based experiences and enable large numbers of people to experience a wide range of water-based environments in a variety of ways. In the Great Barrier Reef, commercial vessels carry from 20 to 400 passengers. Permitted operators have a variety of sites and numbers of days for their operations. Among the approximately 820 commercial recreational operators, there are over 1500 vessels and aircraft, with the majority of these being boat-related (GBRMPA 2005). There are, of course, other activities that are less or not at all dependent on motorized vessels.

Sail Training Experiences

Sail training experiences enable short-term, medium-length, or long-term participation. Participation may be as a passenger, active participant, or crew member. Passage offerings range from port-to-port or complete voyage (potentially incorporating multiple ports of call). Sail training is popular with maritime enthusiasts, personal youth development program organizers and participants, business personnel engaged in personal development and team-building exercises, and individuals who have a love of sailing or the sea, or seek challenge and adventure.

Surfing, Windsurfing, Kayaking, and Whitewater Rafting

Surfing and windsurfing continue to attract large numbers of participants; the same is true, to a lesser degree, for the associated sports of parasurfing and kite surfing. Additionally, kayaking has grown in popularity as an independent as well as a tourism industry component of water-based experiences. Similarly, whitewater rafting demonstrated phenomenal growth in the last four decades of the twentieth century. At the same time, however, both whitewater rafting and kayaking participation patterns are constrained by a number of limitations on water resource access (see Chapters 8 and 9).

Determination of Participation Rates in Water-Based Experiences

Determination of participation rates in water-based experiences is problematic. This is essentially the case because

- Some activities are not required to report participation.
- Some activities are independent in nature and there is no need for reporting.
- Equipment purchases are not a sound basis for prediction, as some equipment may be lent, cooperatively shared, rented, or resold.

- Equipment purchase numbers fail to identify persons who may own multiple sets of equipment, thus possibly resulting in multiple counting.
- Equipment purchase does not always indicate actual participation.
- Legislation does not require all activities to be registered.
- Not all participants comply with legislative requirements such as registration.
- Club membership only reflects those who are affiliated.
- Certification of activities does not allow capture of non-certified participants.
- Participation in one activity may mask participation in other activities, depending on which is used for reporting purposes.
- Data sets and empirical materials are dependent on researcher interests and sustained interest in building longitudinal information sets.
- Data sets may be incomplete due to changes in focus of management agencies and niche market focusing.
- Changes occur in standards for measurement and methodologies.
- Measurement may be based on adult population only.
- Ambiguity exists in definitions of tourism, sport, leisure, and recreation as well as what is a pursuit, activity, or experience.
- Inconsistency exists in definitions for use in counting and comparison.

(See Miller 1993; Wilks and Atherton 1994; Fedler 2000; Jennings 2003)

Overview of Definitions and Terms

Just as participation rates are difficult to determine, standardized definitions of tourism, sport, leisure, and recreation are similarly problematic. Over time, social, cultural, political, and religious expectations, values, and mores change, and these influence the construction and interpretation of these terms from a local to an international level. Impacts of globalization and internationalization are similarly influential. In addition, given the individualization of markets (see Weaver and Lawton 2005), definitions related to these terms may be better constructed/interpreted from the participants' point of view "in order to gain an insider's (emic) perspective" (Jennings 1999; Weber 2001; Jennings and Weiler 2005). In this section, definitions of tourism, water-based tourism, marine tourism, travel experience, touristic activity, and travel behavior are provided. Also, several definitions of recreation, leisure, serious leisure, and sport are presented to demonstrate the multiple meanings associated with these terms. Several reflexive comments are made, and a number of declarations of human rights statements in regard to leisure and sport are included.

Tourism

The World Tourism Organization (WTO 2005) defines tourism as "the activities of a person traveling outside his or her usual environment for a specified period of time and whose main purpose of travel is other than exercise of an activity remunerated from the place visited."

In another definition, Fabbri (1990) writes, "Tourism was—and essentially still is—recreational traveling" (p. xiii).

Water-Based Tourism

Water-based tourism relates to any touristic activity (see definition below) undertaken in or in relation to water resources, such as lakes, dams, canals, creeks, streams, rivers, canals, waterways, marine coastal zones, seas, oceans, and ice-associated areas.

Marine Tourism

"Marine tourism includes those recreational activities that involve travel away from one's place of residence and which have as their host or focus the marine environment (where the marine environment is defined as those waters which are saline and tide-affected)" (Orams 1999, p. 9).

Travel Experience

The travel experience involves planning, travel to, onsite, return travel, and recollection phases, which follow a circular pathway (Killion 1992, after Clawson 1963).

A travel experience is "the inner state of the individual, brought about by something which is personally encountered, undergone or lived through" (Cohen 2000, p. 216).

Touristic Activity

This refers to any activity, that is, any pursuit, sport, hobby, endeavor, pastime, game, exercise, or experience undertaken when a person is "outside his or her usual environment for a specified period of time and whose main purpose of travel is other than exercise of an activity remunerated from the place visited" (WTO 2005).

Travel Patterns

These are the "trip and visit purpose, distance traveled, duration, number of destinations, and use of particular facilities" (Leiper 2004, p.78).

Recreation

"Any action that refreshes the mental attitude of an individual is recreation. Recreation is a wholesome activity that is engaged in for pleasure; therefore, it is play" (Douglass, 1982, p. 6).

"Recreation may take various routes, but the results are the same. Recreation revitalizes the spirit. It restores a person's vitality, initiative, and perspective of life, thereby preparing the individual to return to his [sic] toil" (Douglass 1982, p. 6).

"[Recreation] embraces a wide variety of activities which are undertaken during leisure" (Mathieson and Wall 1982, p. 7).

"[A]ny activity of leisure time undertaken by choice and for pleasure would constitute recreation" (Phelps 1988, p. 34).

As a concluding comment to the definitions for recreation, the following is noted: People expect recreation to be "part of their life" (Douglass 1982, pp. 6–7). This is also reflected in the leisure subsection and is articulated as a human right in the declaration of human rights and leisure.

Recreation Experience

Clawson's (1963) concept of recreation experience was presented as a linear episode involving planning, travel to, onsite, return travel, and recollection stages.

Leisure

Article 24 of the 1948 Universal Declaration of Human Rights and Leisure states: "Everyone has the right to rest and leisure, including reasonable limitation of working hours and periodic holidays with pay" (www.un.org/rights).

Within academic literature, leisure tends to be defined based on a duality of work and non-work time, particularly non-work time that is free from obligations (Neulinger 1974; Goodale and Godbey 1988; Seabrook 1988; Godbey 1994; Bennett, Emmison, and Frow 1999; Iso-Ahola 1999). A temporal overview of leisure definitions yields a variety of interpretations.

In 1960, Kaplan described leisure as constituting:

(a) an antithesis to "work" as an economic function; (b) a pleasant expectation and recollection; (c) a minimum of involuntary social-role obligations; (d) a psychological perception of freedom; (e) a close relation to values of the culture; (f) an inclusion of an entire range from inconsequence and insignificance to weightiness and importance; and (g) often, but not necessarily, an activity characterized by the element of play. (pp. 22–25)

Several decades later, Godbey (1994) noted that four concepts applied to defining leisure: "time, activities, state of existence, or state of mind" (p. 3). The following definition was later proffered by Leiper (2004): "Leisure is a category of human experiences found in recreational and creative behavior pursued with a relative sense of freedom from obligations, and regarded as personally pleasurable" (p. 92).

The conceptual divide discourse between leisure and work has provided additional commentary. For example, Rojek (1989) has commented that work is "rewarded" by leisure (p. 9). Further, in some related literature, work and leisure begin to switch roles in regard to authenticity of self, self-identity, and the living of life. For instance, Frith (1983) comments that "[l]eisure has become the only setting for the experience of self, for the exploration of one's own skills and capabilities, for the development of creative relations with other people" (p. 262). Perhaps this is more poignantly phrased by Rojek (1995): "[f]or many, real life only occurs *outside* the workplace" (p. 127).

Vacation Experience

The vacation experience involves anticipatory, experiential, and reflective phases (Craig-Smith and French 1994).

Visitor Experience

Measurement of visitor experiences involves a number of approaches: satisfaction, benefits-based, experience-based, and meanings-based (Borrie and Birzell 2001). This results in inconsistency in empirical materials and their comparative analysis. Currently, measurement of visitor experiences is reported to be evolving (Andereck, Bricker, Kerstetter, and Nickerson 2005).

Sport

Article 1 of the 1978 UNESCO International Charter of Physical Education and Sport states, "The practice of physical education and sport is a fundamental right for all" (UNESCO 1982).

Article 1 of the Olympic Charter states, "The practice of sport is a human right. Every individual must have the possibility of practicing sport in accordance with his or her needs" (International Olympic Committee 1995; see www.olympic.org).

The core elements of sport have been defined as the following:

- They must involve a symbolic test of physical or psycho-motor skills
- There must be a competitive framework, which requires:
  - Specified, codified rules which constitute the activity
- There must be continuity over time—a tradition of past practices

(Haywood et al. 1995, p. 43).

Tourism, Sport, Leisure, and Recreation: Blurred Boundaries

To reiterate an earlier comment, definitions associated with tourism, sport, leisure, and recreation are problematic. They vary depending on their temporal nature, as well as the perspective and background of the author penning the terms. This makes it difficult to provide definitive descriptions of the terms and their meanings. (For further discussions, see also Godbey 1994; Kaplan 1975, 1991; Butler 1989; Arnold 1991; and Haywood et al. 1995.) The purpose of this section was to emphasize the difficulties associated with achieving standardized definitions as well as to make "clear" the "blurring" or "fuzziness" of boundaries between tourism, sport, leisure, and recreation. However, that being said, two working definitions will be variously applied in this book. "Water-based tourism, sport, leisure, and recreation" will be taken to mean touristic, sport, leisure, and recreation experiences in and on salt, estuarine, and fresh water or on and under frozen water. The more generic term, "water-based experience," will be used in order to acknowledge the potential for overlap among the concepts of tourism, sport, leisure, and recreation. Such overlap is further exemplified in the following vignette. "A *vignette* is a focused description of a series of events taken to be representative, typical, or emblematic" (Miles and Huberman 1994, p. 81).

Water-Based Experiences Vignette

For summer holidays, a family in the western United States decides to visit friends located in another state. During the visit, the friends take the family on a weekend sailing excursion. For the hosts, the activity may be classified as a leisure-time pursuit since it uses non-work time. On the other hand, it might be considered as recreation—the time to "re-create" themselves after a week's work, or of course it may be considered as both. The visiting family includes a daughter who races small boats each week at the local club. She sees the sailing excursion as sport, as she will be able to apply her skills and knowledge to improve the sailing performance of the boat. The rest of the family sees the excursion as just that—an activity that is part of their overall holiday/vacation. From a tourism industry perspective, the family would be counted as part of the "visiting friends and relatives" sector and the activity would be viewed as one of the onsite activities.

What does this vignette tell us? A lot and in a sense not much. A lot because the vignette indicates that there are multiple interpretations that can be made of the one experience by outside observers and insider participants. It also tells us that the one experience can be simultaneously labeled as sport, leisure, recreation, and tourism. It depends on the characteristics of the participants and their personal perspective. Therefore, as noted before, to understand what water-based tourism, sport, leisure, and recreation are requires us to ask the participants themselves—that is, the insiders—for their constructions and interpretations of the meanings associated with those terms.

Overview of Theoretical Concepts

As the introduction to each section in this book will indicate, there are a variety of theoretical concepts applied in *Water-Based Tourism, Sport, Leisure, and Recreation Experiences*. There are also a number of key themes that will resound throughout Chapters 2 to 11. These are self-actualization and flow experiences; serious leisure; tourism, sport, leisure, and recreation impacts, especially issues associated with carrying capacity, conflict between user groups, management strategies, and sustainability issues. Of these, only self-actualization and flow, and serious leisure will be given an overview in this chapter, as the other themes will be discussed in the concluding chapter, Chapter 12.

Self-Actualization and Flow

Several contributors to this volume refer to intrinsic motivation and, in particular, the use or application of Csikszentmihalyi's "flow" or "optimal arousal" concept to understand participant motivations. A number of these discuss the quest for flow experiences as well as issues associated with the need to match skills appropriately with challenges and adventure. In summary, the need for challenge and adventure can be deconstructed as a need for self-actualization (Goldstein 1939; Maslow 1970; Csikszentmihalyi 1974, 1975; Iso-Ahola 1980). The challenge is a result of personal goal setting, or engaging in a water-based experience with or without varying degrees of technological support. Adventure is associated with pushing beyond a personal comfort zone, with testing personal ability and not finding oneself wanting. Adventure is also associated with experiencing new people in new places. "As Goffman notes, adventures are not to be found within but beyond common routines" (Csikszentmihalyi 1988, p. 45). The outcomes of challenges and adventures expressed by water-based experience seekers are feelings of accomplishment and self-satisfaction. In reality, they tend to pursue their water-based experiences for their "intrinsic reward," that is, an "[experience] engaged in for its own sake" (Iso-Ahola 1980, p. 231).

Flow

Csikszentmihalyi's (1974, 1975, 1988, 1990, 1997) optimal experience or "flow" theory developed from the work of Maslow, specifically the notion of "process and product" outcomes of behavior. Csikszentmihalyi was particularly interested in understanding the nature of "intrinsic motivation," especially activities that elicit "peak experiences" (Maslow 1965, 1968). Csikszentmihalyi (1988) makes the following comment regarding Maslow's work:

Maslow ascribed the motivation to a desire for "self actualization," a need to discover one's potentialities and limitations through intense activity and experience. . . . Maslow's explanation was compelling, but it left many questions unanswered. . . . Maslow's pioneering work, primarily idiographic and reflective in nature, did not explore very far the empirical implications of these ideas. (p. 5)

In extending the work of Maslow and the nature of peak or self-actualizing experiences, Csikszentmihalyi (1974) developed his theory of optimal experience, which he calls a flow experience. What is a flow experience? In his own words,

Flow refers to the holistic sensation present when we act with total involvement. It is a kind of feeling after which one nostalgically says: "that was fun," or "that was enjoyable." It is the state in which action follows upon action according to an internal logic, which seems to need no conscious intervention on our part. We experience it as a unified flowing from one moment to the next in which we are in control of our actions, and in which there is little distinction between self and environment; between stimulus and response; or between past, present, and future. (Csikszentmihalyi 1974, p. 58)

In his research, Csikszentmihalyi (1988, p. 365) identified several dimensions of flow: intense involvement, deep concentration, clarity of goals and feedback, loss of a sense of time, lack of self consciousness and transcendence of a sense of self, leading to an autotelic, that is, intrinsically rewarding experience." According to Massimini, Csikszentmihalyi, and Delle Fave (1988), flow occurs

when a good fit results from the interaction between two lists of instructions: those contained in the rules of a cultural "game" . . . and the list of intrasomatic instructions—based on biological predispositions—which constitute the actor's skills. . . . A person in flow wishes to do what he or she is doing for the sake of the activity itself, independently of external consequences. (pp. 65–66)

Serious Leisure

Serious leisure, a term coined by Robert Stebbins, appears in several chapters in this book. He identifies "three types of serious leisure—amateurism, hobbyist pursuits, and volunteering" (Stebbins 1992, p. 5). Six qualities distinguish serious leisure from casual leisure (Stebbins 1992, pp. 6–7):

- "A need to *persevere*"
- "*Careers* in endeavors"
- "Significant personal *effort*" to acquire "*knowledge, training, skill,*" or all of these
- Lasting "*benefits,*" including "self-actualization, self-enrichment, self-expression, recreation or renewal of self, feelings of accomplishment, enhancement of self-image, social interaction and belongingness, and lasting physical products of the activity," as well as "[s]elf-gratification or pure fun," which also has overlap with casual leisure
- A "unique ethos"
- Identification with the pursuit.

Echoing Frith's viewpoint expressed earlier in this chapter, Stebbins (1992) also comments that "Serious leisure, with its interweaving of skills, knowledge, and talent, is most rewarding when the participant has been able to develop these three to an admirable degree" (p. 129).

Overview of *Water-Based Tourism, Sport, Leisure, and Recreation Experiences*

Having identified some of the resonating themes, the book's organization and structure will now be considered. To provide some comparability of structural content, each chapter discusses details about the market profile, the advantages and disadvantages, the impacts, and future directions in regard to each of the water-based experiences presented. Each chapter also includes a case study to highlight one particular element of the overall discussion provided in that chapter.

Water-Based Tourism, Sport, Leisure, and Recreation Experiences is organized into four sections:

- Sailing and Boating
- Sport or Extreme Sport
- Adventure
- Sustainability.

Boating is the organizing theme of the first section. In Chapters 2 and 3, respectively, Gayle Jennings examines sailing and motor boating. The second section investigates water-based experiences that have traditionally been derived from sport and present a challenge to participants as well as offer fun. In Chapter 4, Harold Richens considers motorized sports such as jet boating and jet skiing. In Chapter 5, Chris Ryan studies surfing and windsurfing, while in Chapter 6, Les Killion reports on sport fishing and big game fishing. In the final chapter in this section, Chapter 7, Kay Dimmock reflects on scuba diving, free diving, and snorkeling. In the third section, a key theme in the water-based experiences discussed is adventure. Lilian Jonas comments on whitewater rafting in Chapter 8; Simon Hudson and Paul Beedie focus on kayaking in Chapter 9; and in Chapter 10, Gianna Moscardo examines one-day boating adventures. The last chapter in this section is Chapter 11, in which Gary Easthope addresses sail training adventures. The final section draws on the writings of all the contributors as well as related literature to frame a consideration of the sustainability of tourism, sport, leisure, and recreation in water-based environments as well as a conclusion regarding the future directions for water-based experiences.

To reiterate, the purpose of this book is to present in one volume an overview of a number of water-based experiences that may be pursued as tourism, sport, leisure, or recreation within a variety of water-based environments.

References

Andereck, K., Bricker, K.S., Kerstetter, D., and N.P. Nickerkson. (2005). Connecting experiences to quality: understanding meanings behind visitors' experiences. In G. Jennings and N. Nickerson (Eds.), *Quality tourism experiences*. (pp. 81–98). Burlington, MA: Elsevier.

Arnold, S. (1991). The dilemma of meaning. In T.L. Goodale and P.A. Witt (Eds.), *Recreation and leisure: issues in an era of change*. (3rd ed.). State College, PA: Venture Publishing.

Art Gallery of New South Wales. (1982). *On the beach*. Sydney, Australia: Art Gallery of New South Wales.

Ashworth, G.S. (1984). *Recreation and tourism*. London: Bell and Hyman.

Bennett, T., Emmison, M., and J. Frow. (1999). *Accounting for tastes: Australian everyday cultures*. Cambridge, UK: Cambridge University Press.

Borrie, W.T., and R. Birzell. (2001). Approaches to measuring quality of the wilderness experience. In W.A. Freimund and D.N. Cole (Eds.), *Visitor use density and wilderness experience: proceedings*. (pp. 29–38). Ogden, UT: U.S. Department of Agriculture, Forest Service, Rocky Mountain Research Station.

Brasch, R. (1995). *How did sports begin?* Sydney, Australia: HarperCollins.

Brodersen, J. (1994). Nature conservation and water sports. The legal position of boat standings on banks and coasts in Schleswig-Holstein. *Naturschutz-und-Landschaftsplanung*, **26** (3), 102–105.

Butler, R.W. (1989). Tourism and tourism research. In E.L. Jackson and T.L. Burton (Eds.), *Understanding leisure and recreation: mapping the past, charting the future*. (pp. 567–595). State College, PA: Venture Publishing.

Cartwright, R., and C. Baird. (1999). *The development and growth of the cruise industry*. Oxford, UK: Butterworth-Heinemann.

Claringbould, R., Deakin, J., and P. Foster. (1984). *Data review of reef related tourism, 1946–1980*. Report on behalf of the Australian Travel Industry Association (Queensland Board). Townsville, Queensland, Australia: Great Barrier Reef Marine Park Authority.

Clawson, M. (1963). *Land and water for recreation: opportunities, problems, and policies*. Chicago: Rand McNally.

Cohen, E. (2000). Behaviour. In J. Jafari (Ed.), *Encyclopaedia of Tourism*. London: Routledge.

Cox, D. (1999). *The sailing handbook*. London: New Holland.

Craig-Smith, S., and C. French. (1994). *Learning to live with tourism*. Melbourne, Australia: Pitman.

Craik, J. (1991). *Resorting to tourism: cultural policies for tourist development in Australia*. North Sydney, Australia: Allen and Unwin.

Csikszentmihalyi, M. (1974). *Flow: studies of enjoyment*. Chicago: University of Chicago Press.

Csikszentmihalyi, M. (1975). *Beyond boredom and anxiety*. San Francisco: Jossey-Bass.

Csikszentmihalyi, M. (1988). The future of flow. In M. Csikszentmihalyi and I.S. Csikszentmihalyi (Eds.), *Optimal experience: psychological studies of flow in consciousness.* (pp. 365–383). Cambridge, UK: Cambridge University Press.

Csikszentmihalyi, M. (1990). *Flow: the psychology of optimal experience.* New York: Harper & Row.

Csikszentmihalyi, M. (1997). *Living well, the psychology of everyday life.* London: Phoenix.

Davis, D., Banks, S.A., and G. Davey. (1996). Aspects of recreational scuba diving in Australia. In G. Prosser (Ed.), *Tourism and hospitality research: Australian and international perspectives.* (pp. 455–465). Proceedings from the Australian Tourism and Hospitality Research Conference, 1996. Canberra, Australia: Bureau of Tourism Research.

Dignam, D. (1990, March 26). Scuba diving among mainstream travelers. *Tourism and Travel News.*

Douglass, R.W. (1982). *Forest recreation.* (3rd ed.). New York: Pergamon Press.

Dowling, R.K. (2006). *Cruise tourism: issues, impacts, and cases.* Wallingford, UK: CABI Publishing.

Driml, S. (1996). Coastal and marine tourism in Australia: review and policy issues. In L. Zann (Ed.), *The state of the marine environment report for Australia: Technical Report.* (pp. 159–165). Townsville, Queensland, Australia: Great Barrier Reef Marine Park Authority.

Driml, S., and M. Common. (1996). Ecological economics criteria for sustainable tourism: application to the Great Barrier Reef and the wet tropics World Heritage Areas, Australia. *Journal of Sustainable Tourism,* **4**, 3–16.

Effeney, G. (1999). *An introduction to sea-kayaking in Queensland.* Ashgrove West, Australia: Gerard Effeney.

Fabbri, P. (1990). *Recreational uses of coastal areas.* Dordrecht, Netherlands: Kluwer Academic.

Fedler, A.J. (2000). *Participation in boating and fishing: a literature review.* Report to Recreational Boating and Fishing Foundation, Alexandria, VA. Prepared by Human Dimensions Consulting, Gainesville, FL.

Frith, S. (1983). *Sound effects: youth, leisure and the politics of rock 'n' roll.* London: Constable.

Garrod, B., and J.C. Wilson. (Eds.). (2003). *Marine ecotourism: issues and experiences.* Clevedon, UK: Channel View.

Gartner, W.C., and D.W. Lime. (2000). *Trends in outdoor recreation, leisure, and tourism.* Wallingford, UK: CABI Publishing.

Godbey, G. (1994). *Leisure in your life: an exploration.* State College, PA: Venture Publishing.

Goldstein, K. (1939). *The organism: a holistic approach to biology derived from pathological data in man.* New York: American Book Company.

Goodale, T., and G. Godbey. (1988). *The evolution of leisure.* State College, PA: Venture Publishing.

Great Barrier Reef Marine Park Authority. (2005). *Tourism on the Great Barrier Reef.* Townsville, Queensland, Australia: Great Barrier Reef Marine Park Authority. Accessed October 15, 2005, from http://www.gbrmpa.gov.au/corp_site/key_issues/tourism/tourism_on_gbr.html

Hall, C.M., and T. Harkonen. (2006). *Lake tourism: an integrated approach to lacustrine tourism systems.* Clevedon: Channel View.

Hamdi, H. (1995, July). Take the plunge! *PATA travel news:* Asia/Pacific edition (pp. 6–8).

Haywood, L., Kew, F., Bramham, P., Spink, J., Capenerhurst, J., and I. Henry. (1995). *Understanding leisure.* (2nd ed.). Cheltenham, UK: Stanley Thornes.

Higham, J. (Ed.). (2005). *Sport tourism destinations: issues, opportunities, and analysis.* Oxford, UK: Butterworth-Heinemann.

Holloway, J.C., and R.V. Plant. (1993). *Marketing for tourism.* London: Pitman.

Hudson, S. (Ed.). *Sport and adventure tourism.* New York: Haworth Hospitality Press.

International Olympic Committee. (1995). *The Olympic charter.* Lausanne, Switzerland: International Olympic Committee.

Iso-Ahola, S. (1980). *The social psychology of leisure and recreation.* Dubuque, IA: Wm. C. Brown.

Iso-Ahola, S. (1999). Motivational foundations of leisure. In E.L. Jackson and T.L. Burton (Eds.), *Leisure studies: Prospects for the twenty-first century.* State College, PA: Venture Publishing.

Jeans, D.N. (1990). Beach resort morphology in England and Australia. In P. Fabbri (Ed.), *Recreational uses of coastal areas.* (pp. 277–285). Dordrecht, Netherlands: Kluwer Academic.

Jennings, G. (1999). *Voyages from the centre to the margins: an ethnography of long-term ocean cruisers.* Unpublished doctoral thesis, Murdoch University, Perth, Australia.

Jennings, G. (2003). Marine tourism. In S. Hudson (Ed.), *Sport and adventure tourism* (pp. 125–164). New York: Haworth Hospitality Press.

Jennings, G., and B. Weiler. (2005). Mediating meaning: perspective on brokering quality tourist experiences. In G. Jennings and N. Nickerson (Eds.), *Quality tourism experiences.* (pp. 57–78). Burlington, MA: Elsevier.

Kaplan, M. (1960). *Leisure in America.* New York: Wiley.

Kaplan, M. (1975). *Leisure: theory and policy.* New York: Wiley.

Kaplan, M. (1991). *Essays on leisure.* Cranbury, NJ: Associated University Presses.

Kedrow, L. (1987). Under 30 and younger. *Sport in the USSR,* (293), 8–11.

Killion, G.L. (1992). *Understanding tourism.* Study guide. Rockhampton, Australia: Central Queensland University.

Knappett, G. (2003). *The little book of Bath.* Andover, Hampshire, UK: Jarrold.

Kotani, K. (1991). Promoting the use of pleasure boats in Japan. *Japan 21st,* **36** (11), 123–125.

Laca, B. (1996). Marinas, ports, and small ports in the function of nautical tourist offer of Zadar region. *Turizam,* **44** (5–6), 127–131.

Leiper, N. (2004). *Tourism management.* Sydney, Australia: Pearson Education.

Leyrat, F. (1994). Navigation de plaisance: grand frais sur l'espace nautique European. *Espaces-Paris,* (130), 9–12.

Macbeth, J. (1985). *Ocean cruising: a study of affirmative deviance.* Unpublished doctoral thesis, Murdoch University, Perth, Australia.

Maslow, A.H. (1965). *The psychology of science.* New York: Harper & Row.

Maslow, A.H. (1968). *Motivation and personality.* New York: Harper & Row.

Maslow, A.H. (1970). *Motivation and personality.* (2nd ed.). New York: Harper & Row.

Massimini, F., Csikszentmihalyi, M., and A. Delle Fave. (1988). Flow and biocultural evolution. In M. Csikszentmihalyi and I.S. Csikszentmihalyi (Eds.), *Optimal experience: psychological studies of flow in consciousness.* (pp. 61–81). New York: Cambridge University Press.

Mathieson, A., and G. Wall. (1982). *Tourism: economic, physical, and social impacts*. New York: Longman.

McCool, S.F., and R.N. Moisey. (Eds.). (2001). *Tourism, recreation, and sustainability*. Wallingford, UK: CABI Publishing.

Miles, M., and M.A. Huberman. (1994). *Qualitative analysis: an expanded sourcebook*. (2nd ed.). Thousand Oaks, CA: Sage.

Miller, M.L. (1993). The rise of coastal and marine tourism. *Ocean and Coastal Management*, **20** (3), 181–199.

Ministere de l'Industrie, des Postes et Telecommunications et du Tourisme. (1987). *Le tourisme fluvial (Bibliographie analytique)*. Paris: Ministere de I'Industrie, des Postes et Telecommunications et du Tourisme.

Neulinger, J. (1974). *The psychology of leisure: research approaches to the study of leisure*. Springfield, Ill: Thomas.

Orams, M. (1999). *Marine tourism: development, impacts, and management*. London: Routledge.

PADI. (2005). *PADI diver statistics*. Accessed October 15, 2005, from http://www.padi.com/english/common/padi/statistics/7.asp

Paine, L.P. (1997). *Ships of the world: an historical encyclopedia*. Boston: Houghton Mifflin. Accessed October 15, 2005, from http://college.hmco.com/history/reader-scomp/ships/html/sh_052900_kontiki.htm

Panne, G. (1990). Burgundy: waterways are growing in popularity. *Espaces-Paris*, (106), 43–48.

Pearson, K. (1979). *Surfing subcultures of Australia and New Zealand*. St. Lucia, Brisbane, Australia: University of Queensland Press.

Phelps, A. (1988). Seasonality in tourism and recreation. *Leisure Studies*, **vii** (1), 34.

Pleasure boating to grow with increase in leisure time. (1987). *Business Japan*, **32** (11–12), 63–64.

Rojek, C. (1989). *Leisure for leisure: critical essays*. London: Macmillan.

Rojek, C. (1995). *Decentring leisure: rethinking leisure theory*. London: Sage.

Ryan, C. (2003). *Recreational tourism: demand and impacts*. Clevedon, UK: Channel View Press.

San Diego State University. (2004). *The History of Surfing: a Timeline from 300 A.D. to 1900*. Accessed October, 14, 2005, from http://infodome.sdsu.edu/about/depts/spcollections/exhibits/1202/timeline.shtml

Schemel, H.J. (2001). *Sport and the environment: conflicts and solutions—a manual*. Oxford, UK: Meyer and Meyer Sport.

Seabrook, J. (1988). *The leisure society*. Oxford, UK: Basil Blackwell.

Smith, C., and P. Jenner. (1995). Marinas in Europe. *Travel and Tourism Analyst*, (6), 56–72.

Stebbins, R.A. (1992). *Amateurs, professionals, and serious leisure*. Montreal, Quebec, Canada: McGill-Queens University Press.

Swarbrooke, J., Beard, C., Leckie, S., and G. Pomfret. (2003). *Adventure tourism: the new frontier*. Oxford, UK: Butterworth-Heinemann.

Tabata, R. (1992). Case study. Scuba dive holidays. In B. Weiler and C. M. Hall (Eds.), *Special interest tourism*. (pp. 171–184). London: Belhaven Press.

Tourism Queensland. (2004). *Whitsundays regional update*. Research Department, Tourism, Queensland, Australia. Accessed October, 14, 2005, from http://www. http://www.tq.com.au/tq_com/dms/A81938CB9E9EC95D99350689B313FD93.pdf

Tourism Review Steering Committee. (1997). *Review of the marine tourism industry in the Great Barrier Reef World Heritage Area*, Parts 1 and 2. Prepared by the Tourism Review Steering Committee with assistance from the Great Barrier Reef Marine Park Authority and the Office of National Tourism.

Turco, D.M., Riley, R.S., and K. Swart. (2002). *Sport tourism*. Morgantown: WV: Fitness Information Technology.

United Nations. (1948). *Universal Declaration of Human Rights and Leisure*. Accessed October 19, 2005, from www.un.org/rights

United Nations Educational and Scientific Committee. (1982). UNESCO International Charter of Physical Education and Sport. *International Social Science Journal*, (34), 303–306.

Veal, A. J. (2002). *Leisure and tourism policy and planning.* (2nd ed.). Wallingford, UK: CABI Publishing.

Weaver, D., and L. Lawton. (2005). *Tourism management.* (3rd ed.). Brisbane, Australia: Wiley.

Weber, K. (2001). Outdoor adventure tourism: a review of research approaches. *Annals of Tourism*, **28** (2), 360–377.

Weed, M., and C. Bull. (2004). *Sports tourism: participants, policy and providers.* Oxford, UK: Elsevier.

Wells, L. (1982). *Sunny memories. Australians at the seaside.* Richmond, Victoria, Australia: Greenhouse.

West, N. (1990). *Marine recreation in North America.* In P. Fabbri (Ed.), *Recreational uses of coastal areas.* (pp. 257–275). Dordrecht, Netherlands: Kluwer Academic.

Wilks, J. and T. Atherton. (1994). Fitness to participate in adventure activities: medical and legal considerations arising from recreational scuba diving. *South Pacific Underwater Medicine Society Journal*, **24** (3), 137.

World Tourism Organization. (2005). *Historical perspective of world tourism.* Accessed October 14, 2005, from http://www.world-tourism.org/facts/menu.html

I

Sailing and Boating

One of the traditional forms of water-based experiences is boating. Historically, the use of boats for transportation, exploration, trade, and warfare predates boating as a recognized tourism, sport, leisure, and recreation experience. Over time, however, societal, cultural, political, and economic changes as well as technological developments have provided both the opportunity and impetus for the development of a wide variety of water-based experiences associated with boats. These experiences range from sailboating to motorboating in all their various forms. In addition, there has been growth in a number of boating-related experiences. For example, the second half of the twentieth century saw the burgeoning of motorized sports such as jet boating, one-day boating adventures, sail training adventures, and kayaking. In addition, the pursuit of scuba diving, free diving, and snorkeling as well as sport and big game fishing have been variously facilitated by or connected to boats for access and experience support.

In this first section of *Water-Based Tourism, Sport, Leisure, and Recreation Experiences,* the focus is exclusively on sailing and boating. Motorized water sports, scuba diving, snorkeling, and free diving as well as sport and big game fishing are considered in Section II, *Sport or Extreme Sport?* Kayaking, one-day boating adventures, and sail training adventures are discussed in Section III, *Adventure.* In Chapter 2, *Sailing/Cruising,* Gayle Jennings emphasizes the multiplicity of sailing-related tourism, sport, leisure, and recreation experiences in which tourists, sports persons, people at leisure, and recreationists may engage. She outlines the historical background of sailing as an activity, sport, recreation, and leisure form, and reflects on sailing as serious leisure and as a touristic experience. Additionally, Chapter 2 focuses on long-term ocean cruisers who engage in long-distance sailing voyages as a lifestyle. In taking this specific focus, she illuminates corresponding social factors that influence leisure, recreation, and lifestyle choices. As a group, cruisers, in their quest for authentic experiences, shirk the alienating and anomic worlds of work and non-work at the center of Western industrialized societies, opting instead for self-actualization and an "empowered connectivity" in the margins of mainstream life distributed across the globe and accessed by water. In the case study presented in Chapter 2, Jennings highlights the patriarchal hegemony of sailing as well as cruising and the ways such hegemony serves to influence the overall quality of travel experiences and the gendered nature of the roles and responsibilities assumed aboard cruising vessels. (See Chapters 3, 5, and 6 for further commentary regarding the gendered nature of water-based experiences. Lifestyle issues noted in Chapter 2 are again addressed in Chapters 5, 7, and 11.)

In Chapter 3, *Motorboating,* Gayle Jennings describes the array of choices associated with motorboating. The beginnings of a number of motorboating experiences are presented. Commentary regarding the various markets notes the gendered nature of the activity as well as socioeconomic and cultural constraints to participation. The advantages of motorboating over other water-based experiences include speed of the boats, if using them as forms of transport to other connected water-based experiences such as scuba diving and fishing as well as visiting islands, cays, and reefs. The disadvantages include increasing costs of fuel, storage issues, and weather dependency for usage. Impacts mirror issues alluded to in Chapter 1 regarding management strategies and sustainability issues; specifically these include pollution, user conflicts, registration, and legislation issues. The case study focuses on the linked activities of motorboating and recreational fishing in the United States. Readers might refer to Chapter 6, *Sport Fishing and Big Game Fishing,* for a comparison between recreational fishing and sport fishing.

Key themes permeating Chapters 2 and 3 are serious leisure, gender influences on participation, challenge, adventure, and management issues and strategies.

2

Sailing/Cruising

Gayle Jennings

Overview

Sailing as an activity may be undertaken in a variety of physical locations; over varying time periods; for different reasons; with differing participant skill levels; by various numbers of participants; via formal or informal organizational structures; and using differing vessel designs or constructions, and materials drawn from a wide array of technology and corresponding levels of expenditure. As a consequence of this multiplicity of options, the boundaries between sailing as sport, recreation, and leisure—including serious leisure, touristic experience, or lifestyle pursuit—tend to be somewhat fuzzy. The purpose of this chapter is to provide background to the nature of sailing itself, some historical contexts associated with sailing, and a discussion of the various sailing experiences listed above. To focus the discussion, one style of sailing in particular will be portrayed—long-term ocean cruising—which incorporates elements of sailing as a sport, recreation, leisure, touristic experience, and lifestyle. Finally, given the gendered history of sailing, the research case study used in this chapter will highlight the lived experiences of cruising women in regard to power, politics, and decision making associated with the enterprise of long-term ocean cruising.

Background

Essentially, sailing may occur on inland waters and waterways, rivers, seas, and oceans as well as on land and ice, and in virtual spaces. However, due to the theme of this book, the latter three will not be considered in this chapter. As already noted, sailing can be experienced over varying periods of duration. For example, the experience may be as short as one hour or as long as five years or more. It can be competitive or noncompetitive and may involve pairs, groups, or teams, or be an individual experience. Additionally, management of participation in sailing can involve formal structures and organizations such as sailing, cruising, or sporting clubs, and local, national, or international associations. These organizations may teach sailing skills and etiquette and organize competitive or fun races as well as opportunities for social engagement and functions for like-minded sailing participants, their families, and friends. Government agencies may also be involved in management of sailing via regulations of recreational boating spaces, boat registration, safety equipment requirements, and boat licenses—depending on size of boat and auxiliary engine power. Semi-formal, grant-funded "intermediate organizations," such as youth organizations, support groups, and volunteer associations, can play similar roles to the formal organizations noted previously. Alternately, sailing can be organized by individuals outside of formal organizational structures, although there still may be some government regulations involved, such as the aforementioned licenses and registrations, as well as international rules of the sea. The diversity of choice in regard to sailing locations, the nature of participation, and the organization of sailing is also reflected in the technology required for the activity.

The designs of sailing vessels may vary depending on size, overall length, number of hulls, hull shape and depth, and number of masts and their locations, as well as sail configurations and construction material. There are also variations in the types of equipment and materials used, for example, note the following:

- Material for hull construction, originally timber and natural fiber bases, now includes other material choices such as fiberglass, steel, aluminum, ferro-cement, and composite materials such as composite panels.
- Sail cloth ranges from traditional canvas made from cotton or flax; to nylon, polyester, and present-day state-of-the-art fibers such as Kevlar and three-dimensional laminates; to the recent development of Cuban fiber.
- Ropes, which differ in thickness, strengths, and material, have altered substantially from the traditional hemp to various synthetic fibers.
- Masts/spars can be built from, for example, timber—the traditional material—or aluminum, polycarbon fiber.
- Sail winches can be standard or self-tailing. Sail winches can also be manual or electric, as can anchor winches.

Depending on the nature of the sailing experience, there are additional technologies such as solar panels, desalinators, life rafts, EPIRBs—emergency position-indicating radio beacons—sextants, and of course, there is a wide range of electronic equipment such as that used for navigation: geographic positioning satellite (GPS) technology, radar, chart plotters, as well as self-steering equipment. In all, as previously stated, there is a multiplicity of possible sailing experiences, vessels, and degrees of sophistication regarding sailing equipment from which a sailor may choose. There is a correspondingly wide range in cost, which extends beyond club membership fees to cover everything from equipment usage and training or initial individual setup costs to possible tuition and coaching, maintenance, equipment failure and repair, travel and transportation, and regulation and licensing, in addition to potential search-and-rescue costs.

History

Sailing has a long history. Originally, it was used as a means for survival in the search for food and safety. It also came to be used for transportation, exploration, migration, and subsequently warfare. Later uses include colonization, communication, trade, and slavery. Modern uses include sailing for sport, recreation/leisure, touristic experiences, and as a lifestyle in a quest for freedom, adventure, as well as fun and relaxation. To varying degrees, these purposes still stand in the early stages of the twenty-first century. However, as the focus of this chapter is sailing and its associated pursuits as a sport, recreation, leisure, touristic experience, or lifestyle, the other uses will not be described in further detail here. In the subsequent subsections, each of the aforementioned uses will be discussed briefly.

Sailing as a Sport

In this chapter, sport will be defined as "[i]ndividual or group recreational activities, usually physical, which involve interpersonal or intergroup competition, contests with nature (e.g., hunting), or the more general exercise of physical skills" (Jary and Jary 2000, pp. 598–599). As a sport, sailing is recorded as emerging in the seventeenth century with its origins being drawn from the Netherlands (Columbia Encyclopedia 2005a). It was introduced to England after King Charles II spent a period of exile in the Netherlands. The term "yacht" is said to be derived from the Dutch word "jaght" or "jaght schip" (International Olympic Committee 2005a). It was a sport associated primarily with the wealthy in which the key participants were men.

Racing Sailing: Individual Contests With Nature Individual contests with nature associated with the sport of sailing are exemplified by achievements such as the following:

- Joshua Slocum is recorded as completing the first solo circumnavigation of the world, in 1895–1898. His voyage involved three stopovers and some 46,000 miles of sailing.
- Sir Frances Chichester in 1966–1967 completed a solo circumnavigation of the world with one stopover, in nine months and one day.
- Dame Naomi James became the first woman to complete a single-handed circumnavigation of the world, in 1978.
- Kay Cottee became the first woman to complete a solo (single-handed) nonstop circumnavigation of the world, in 1988 (Wikipedia 2005a, 2005b, 2005c).

Racing Sailing Competitions In general, there are three generic categories of sailing races (Columbia Encyclopedia 2005b). First, there are one-design classes, which involve boats of similar design. Second, there are handicap classes, in which boats of different designs race against each other with starting times based on a handicap related to each boat's design, sail efficiency, and speed. Third, there are rating classes, which use formulas to equalize differences between different yacht designs and equipment.

In racing, one-design boats are commonly used because of their cost. This is especially important at the local club level to maximize participation rates. Popular one-design boats at the club level are Etchells, Snipes, Starr, Thistle, Lightning, Laser, and J/24. However, it must be noted that some of the larger one-design boats used at national and international levels, such as maxi yachts, are more expensive, and this reduces participation rates unless financial resources are unlimited or sponsorship and grants are available. An additional reason for use of the one-design boat in racing is the ability to differentiate winning boats from other boats based purely on skill, because all the boats are required to meet the one-design requirement. Thus, the only difference that influences results is the skill of the sailor(s).

International Sailing Competitions   In 1851, members of the New York Yacht Club (NYYC) raced the 101-foot schooner *America* against English counterparts around the Isle of Wight and won the Hundred Guineas Cup. The race was subsequently renamed the America's Cup after the winning yacht (Columbia Encyclopedia 2005a; International Olympic Committee 2005a). Since then, the majority of the series races have been won by the United States (see Table 2-1). The series still continues at the time of publication of this book.

Other international races include the Transpacific Race (from Los Angeles to Honolulu); the Volvo Ocean Race, previously known as the Whitbread Round the World Race (in 2005–2006 comprising offshore and in-port racing); and the Golden Globe Race (solo nonstop round-the-world race). The latter's counterpart is the Global Challenge ocean race. This race adopts a standard cutter-rigged sloop of 12 meters in length, designed by Robert Humphries, to test nonprofessional sailors in their ability to sail around the world taking a backward route against prevailing winds and currents. The race was instigated by Sir Chay Blyth, who in 1971 became the first person to sail solo round the world taking a westward path.

The governing body of international yacht racing is the International Sailing Federation (ISAF), previously known as the International Yacht Racing Union, and is recognized by the International Olympic Committee (IOC) (Doolin n.d.). The ISAF provides a universal set of rules and measurement standards and lists some 73 yacht classes, from the Optimist Dinghy, the smallest boat, to the Maxi One-Design, the largest (Doolin n.d.).

Table 2-1   The America's Cup, Summary of Year of Series and Winning Nation

Year of Series	Winning Nation
1851, then at various times up to and including the 1980 series	United States
1983	Australia
1988, 1992	United States
1995, 2000	New Zealand
2003	Switzerland
2007	

Source: AC-clopedia (2005).

As an Olympic sport, sailing commenced as an event in the Paris 1900 Olympics (IOC 2005b). According to the International Olympic Committee (2005a), in the early games, sailing crews of 10 to 12 people were involved. Over time, the crew numbers became smaller, with the Sydney 2000 Olympics having six events involving solo sailors and only one with a three-person crew, using the Soling class keelboat for triple handing. This continues to be a trend, right up to the 2004 Athens Games. There have been several other changes related to sailing as an Olympic sport. Historically, men and women were able to compete together in Olympic sailing events until 1984 when separate events were introduced. At the Sydney 2000 Olympics, mixed events were introduced, as well as a terminology change from "Yachting" to "Sailing" (IOC 2005a).

Motivations for the Sport of Racing Sailing   Drawing on Csikszentmihalyi's (1974) "8 Reasons ranking questionnaire," Macbeth (1985, p. 128) reported the following rank for ocean racers' participation in sailing:

1. The nature of the activity itself and the life experiences it provides
2. The pleasure of the activity and the application of associated skills
3. The competition and its ability to enable one to measure oneself against others
4. The opportunity for friendship and companionship
5. The opportunity for personal skills development
6. The ability to compare oneself with personal standards
7. The extrinsic rewards the activity generates, such as prestige and respect
8. The emotional liberation associated with the activity.

In contrast, with respect to Soling class racers, Macbeth found the following ranking:

1. The competition and its ability to enable one to measure oneself against others
2. The pleasure of the activity and the application of associated skills
3. The opportunity for personal skills development
4. The nature of the activity itself and the life experiences it provides
5. The opportunity for friendship and companionship
6. The emotional liberation associated with the activity
7. The ability to compare oneself with personal standards
8. The extrinsic rewards the activity generates, such as prestige and respect.

In both cases, the nature of the competition afforded through sailing racing was a primary determinant for participation in the respective activities. There are parallels between Macbeth's findings and Stebbins's (n.d.) amateur subtype, "the player." The player participates continuously and systematically because of competitive opportunities, team or group connectivity, personal growth, knowledge and skill development and testing, as well as testing one's limits (see discussion of serious leisure later in this chapter).

Sailing as a Recreation and Leisure Experience

For the purpose of this chapter and as associated with Western society, the following definition is given: " 'recreation' has been generally understood as an opportunity for the 're-creation' of the positive aspects of the human psyche—i.e., it is time spent in a search for psychological health to correct the stresses caused by current stressful work practices" (Ryan 1997a, p. 6).

In addition, in regard to leisure, the following definition is pertinent, as will become evident later in the chapter:

The concept of leisure is generally defined by its opposition to, and indeed its sheer difference from, the world of work: it is the 'absence' of work (Seabrook 1988: 2), or the "reward" for work (Rojek 1989: 9); leisure time, rather than the empty inauthentic time of work, is where our lives 'really' or most 'authentically take place.' (Bennett, Emmison, and Frow 1999, p. 87)

Sailing is reported to have developed as a formalized recreational experience in the eighteenth century, when the first sailing club was formed in Cork, Ireland, in 1720 (Columbia Encyclopedia 2005a). In the past, as with racing, recreational and leisure-time sailing has been thought of as a sport of the wealthy. Today, modern technology and standards of living as well as Western societal values and changes have introduced the sport of sailing to potentially all socioeconomic sectors, both genders, and any and all physical ability levels of participants. Sailing club "Open Days," boat shows, training courses, public sailing programs such as Community Boating (see http://www.community-boating.org/history.html), and contacts with friends or associates already engaged in sailing provide avenues for those interested in pursuing sailing for recreation or leisure. Such engagements enable those interested to become familiar with the sport, as well as to gain information and experience. Essentially, sailing as a recreation and leisure experience is a "ludic" activity, that is, it is a "play-sport sport" (Pearson 1979, p. 159) (Figure 2-1).

Figure 2-1   Catamaran enthusiasts launching from a beach, Yeppoon, Australia. Photographer: Ross Rynehart.

Sailing as Serious Leisure

The notion of serious leisure is associated with the "systematic pursuit of an amateur, hobbyist, or volunteer activity sufficiently substantial and interesting for the participant to find a career there in the acquisition and expression of a combination of its special skills, knowledge, and experience" (Stebbins 1992, p. 23).

According to Stebbins (n.d., 1992), there are six qualities associated with serious leisure:

1. Perseverance with adverse experiences
2. Progression in the selected leisure activity akin to career progression
3. Substantive individual effort related to the development of a leisure career via knowledge, skills, and/or training
4. Lasting gains related to self-actualization, social interaction and belongingness, lasting physical products of the activity, and self-gratification or pure fun. The latter is also experienced by those engaged in unserious leisure.
5. Development of a specific ethos or subcultural attributes
6. Identification with and advocating the leisure pursuit.

The differences between amateurs, hobbyists, and volunteers are presented in Table 2-2.

Based on participant observation over a 20-year period, sailing as a serious leisure pursuit does accommodate the various ideal types of amateur, hobbyist, and volunteer, as identified by Stebbins.

Table 2-2   Summary of Serious Leisure Ideal Types

Serious Leisure Ideal Types	Characteristics
Amateur	Selected leisure activity has strong drawing power
	Motivations for participation are linked to sincerity and dedication
	Disciplined participation via rota and preparatory activities and processes
	Part of the "professional-amateur-public" (P-A-P) system of functionally interdependent relationships
Hobbyist	Committed to the leisure activity due to long-lasting benefits
	Periodic participation
	Four types:
	Collectors
	Makers and tinkers
	Activity participant
	Player (sports and games)
	Outside the P-A-P system
Volunteer	Motivated by altruism and self-interest
	Perform assigned tasks and roles
	Input to society through "helping"
	Engage with "clients" related to the P-A-P system

Source: Stebbins (n.d., 1992).

Sailing as a Touristic Experience

Tourism has been defined by the World Tourism Organization (WTO)/United Nations Recommendations on Tourism Statistics (2005) as the "activities of persons traveling to and staying in places outside their usual environment for not more than one consecutive year for leisure, business, and other purposes."

Given the previous discussion regarding serious leisure and the above definition, sailing and tourism can obviously be linked. Once sailing amateurs, hobbyists, and volunteers move outside of their usual environments for periods of less than one year to engage in the chosen leisure experience of sailing, they simultaneously become tourists. In particular, sporting, leisure, and recreational sailing experiences such as training camps; boat shows; regattas; competitions; regional, state, national, and international titles; and sailing events will provide significant "drawing power" (Mill and Morrison 2002) for these athletes, recreationists, and serious leisure pursuers to become tourists. Consequently, these serious leisure participants become concurrently overlaid as participants on special event and sport tourism continua. (See Weed and Bull 2004, pp. 15–37, for a detailed discussion of the sports–tourism link, and Getz 1997 and 2003 for discussions of sports as special events.) Additionally, professional athletes engaged in sailing or yachting, their support teams, and spectators also will become tourists, based on the WTO definition, once they travel outside their usual environment for periods not extending beyond one year.

Recreationists and people at leisure who tow sailing boats to locations away from owners' and users' usual environments, also blur the boundaries between the leisure and recreational experience of sailing and tourism, by merging the definitions provided in this chapter.

As a specific tourism experience, sailing has long been connected with the sand, sea, and sun theme and associated menus of activities at resorts. Currently, businesses and providers offer half-day, one-day, two-day, or extended sailing adventures, cruises, and expeditions. Other options related to sailing as an onsite activity offering include crewing on yachts passing through the area, as well as chartering—specifically, bareboat, skippered, or crewed yacht charters and flotilla sailing (Richens 1992; Jennings 2003).

Sailing as a Lifestyle

A lifestyle is defined as "the manner in which an individual or group lives" (Jary and Jary 2000, p. 345). Associated with the term lifestyle is the concept of subculture. "A subculture has its own mores, language, values, and avenues for access" (Jennings 1999, p. 64). As a lifestyle pursuit, sailing becomes labeled as "cruising" and at the same time as a subculture (Macbeth 1985, 1986, 1992, 1993; Jennings 1999), which incorporates sport, recreation, leisure, and "work." Within the cruising subculture, there are different categories of participation. Cruisers may be classified by time as well as by cruising route and waters:

1. The fly-cruise segment—those who fly in and out to a destination and cruise for a period of time in their vessel in the surrounding waters

2. The extended cruise segment—those who cruise for an extended period of time within a specific geographic area. This type of cruise segment has two subcategories

   a. Those who depart and return to the same port of call
   b. Those who depart from one port and conclude the cruise at another port. There are a number of options for this type of cruise:
      i. Over time and successive extended cruises, to complete a circuit that will eventually return the vessel to its home port
      ii. Over time and successive extended cruises in which the cruise route may never return to the home port.

3. The circumnavigation segment, which involves extended and long-term periods of cruising:

   a. Global circumnavigations
   b. Geographic circumnavigations, such as Circle the Pacific, Pacific Islands, South America, Africa, Australia, Antarctica.

Additionally, Macbeth (1985) uses a somewhat different three-type classification system, based on time and work obligations:

1. Day sailors—sail near to home, restricted by time and work obligations. This category is more akin to the participants who engage in sailing as a sport, recreation, leisure, or serious leisure pursuit.
2. Short-term cruisers—cruise further afield than day sailors, cruise durations of six months to a year, set ambitious schedules and routes, intend to return to work at the completion of the cruise. This category has similarities with the fly-cruise and the extended cruise, as well as the circumnavigation segment noted above.
3. Cruisers (or voyagers)—intention of cruising indefinitely, long term. Includes circumnavigations and resembles the circumnavigation segment above. No immediate intention of returning to formal work environments.

Based on the two classification systems, elements of serious leisure are found in the fly-cruise and the extended cruise segment, and Macbeth's day-sailor and short-term cruiser categories. The circumnavigators and the cruisers (or voyagers), that is, the long-term ocean cruisers, are somewhat more problematic due to the inherent nature of cruising as the pursuit of a lifestyle. Thus, long-term ocean cruising does not primarily exhibit elements of serious leisure until long-term ocean cruisers choose to engage in organized "cruising races" such as the Sydney to Noumea Yacht Race, the Darwin to Ambon Yacht Race, and the Atlantic Rally for Cruisers.

In such cases, the serious leisure roles may become recognizable due to the roles and tasks associated with the organizing and running of the cruising race. There may also be opportunities for non-cruising serious leisure amateur and hobbyist sailors to become additional crew members for the duration of the race, and there may be roles for volunteers as well. However, outside of this type of event, long-term ocean cruisers are not engaged in serious leisure, since they generally do not have to deal with the traditional work/leisure divide and do not self-define cruising as an "activity" but rather as a lifestyle. Neither do they see that they are either at work or at leisure, although aspects of work as well as leisure pursuits may permeate their lifestyle. Essentially, they are living.

Remaining Chapter Purpose

The purpose of the remainder of this chapter is to explore cruising as a lifestyle in more detail. Sailing as a short-term, sustained activity involving several hours or days will not be examined. Focusing on long-term ocean cruisers provides the opportunity to study one of the sailing modes in greater depth. Additionally, this focus will highlight the societal consequences of such a lifestyle choice. Thus, the remainder of the chapter adds to knowledge about the "linkages between changes in society, tourist motivation and the translation of motive and expectation into holiday experiences" (Ryan 1979b, p. 97). It also addresses the postindustrial issues raised by Stebbins (n.d., 1997, 2001), Kreps and Spengler (1973), Bryan (1973), and Jenkins and Sherman (1979) related to a future that encompasses:

- A reduction in the number of jobs available
- A diminishing number of hours associated with employment
- A growth in work experiences generating worker alienation and feelings of anomie
- A quest for self-fulfillment outside of work environments
- A growth in time available for leisure
- A subsequent need for personally fulfilling leisure pursuits
- A need for effective use of leisure time to enable people to "re-create" and live fulfilling lives.

Additionally, the nature of work over a person's lifetime in a postindustrial world is forecast to include:

- Multiple work careers and breaks between careers
- Increases in part-time work and holding of multiple part-time jobs
- Casualization of work and outsourcing
- Increased numbers of people working from home.

All of the above generate the need for people to effectively pursue leisure and recreation that will ensure their personal health and well-being in a holistic way and achieve a balance between work and non-work periods.

Long-Term Ocean Cruising and Cruisers

Since the late twentieth century, the number of individuals who sail and live aboard their own yachts/vessels—that is, who go cruising—has been increasing (Jennings 2003). This has been effectively due to

- Improvements in yacht design, especially sailing efficiency and live-aboard comfort;
- The increased affordability of navigation equipment due to innovation costs being carried by earlier adopters of technological advances;
- Developments in telecommunications equipment, particularly wider ranging satellite coverage, which provides greater contact with home bases and linkages to search-and-rescue facilities;
- Improvements in port and marina facilities;
- Greater freedom and finances to travel resulting from early retirement packages, investments, and improved income bases of the middle class, especially in the late 1980s and early 1990s;

- A change in values regarding work and leisure relationships and the notion of active retirements and early retirements (Jennings 1999; Cornell 2002).

However, economic, social, and political circumstances in the early twenty-first century may temporarily decrease cruising numbers or limit the waters that are cruised or the duration of cruises.

This chapter has already noted a variety of ways sailing may be experienced and how types of cruising may be differentiated. These have included:

- Boat design
- Duration of involvement in a cruise
- Geographic locations of cruise
- Influences of the obligation to return to work.

There is a fifth means of differentiation, that is, by the number of people aboard the vessel:

- Solo or single handed
- Double handed—two people
- Crewed—more than one person aboard.

Market Profile of Cruisers

Long-term ocean cruisers or cruising "yachties" are self-defined as people who have adopted a cruising lifestyle, who live aboard their own yachts, have independent means, are self sufficient, and have been away from their port of departure for an extended period of time.

Research by Jennings (1999, 2005a) and Macbeth (1985) found that the socio-economic background of the cruising yachties, their ages, educational backgrounds, work experiences, and life experiences in Western societies also facilitated their ability to afford and enter a cruising lifestyle. In the study by Jennings (1999, 2005a), the women's ages ranged from early twenties to late sixties, while the men interviewed ranged from their early twenties to late seventies. Most of the women and men were aged between 40 and 59 years, with the mode for both genders being 50 to 59 years. In regard to family life cycle, very few cruisers were traveling with young family; most were retired people traveling without children. The majority of both genders had completed tertiary education, with women being employed primarily as lower-level professionals and the men as employers and managers, lower-level professionals, or skilled manual workers. The cruisers were primarily Australian, American, New Zealand, and British citizens, with some citizens from other European countries.

Generally, most cruisers did not need to "work" to sustain their cruising lifestyle. Cruisers had taken early retirement packages, used superannuation funds or pensions, or had real estate or other investments. Some hoped to find work opportunities along the way.

The outlay by cruisers to obtain their vessels represented a substantial investment. For example, in the early 1990s, vessel prices ranged from AUS$30,000 (US$22,000) to AUS$600,000 (US$439,000) with the majority of boats costing between AUS$50,000 (US$37,000) and AUS$100,000 (US$73,000). In addition, cruising budgets varied between AUS$4,000 (US$3,000) and AUS$73,000

33

(US$53,000) per year. The average annual budget for two people on a boat was AUS$19,500 (US$14,000). (All of the above figures are raw data from 1993 and 1994 and have not been indexed to take into account changes in the value of the dollar.) In the early twenty-first century, vessel prices may range from under AUS$50,000 (US$35,000) to over AUS$2.5 million (US$1.75 million) and cruising budgets from AUS$25,000 (US$17,500) to over AUS$100,000 (US$73,000).

Primarily, cruisers' ages, educational backgrounds, family life cycle stages, former work experiences, and life experiences in Western societies, as well as their income bases, ensure that cruisers have the financial and social propensity to adopt a cruising lifestyle. The majority of cruisers have been socialized in Western environments in which travel until recently was considered an appropriate use of non-work time; at the commencement of the twenty-first century, issues of safety and security impact on that sentiment. However, that being said, some cruisers have commented that their choice to travel by yacht was considered socially unacceptable by some of their family and friends.

Cruising Motivations

Cruisers were motivated to adopt a sailing lifestyle because of one or more of the following:

- A pursuit of freedom and a need to escape "alienation" (Marx 1963/1972) and feelings of "anomie" (Durkheim 1952/1972) in postindustrial societies
- A dream—goal seeking (Allport 1950; Dreikurs 1962), a love of sailing, and a "career" progression in sailing from an "amateur" or "hobbyist" (Stebbins n.d.) to a "lifestyle" (Adler 1935; Dreikurs 1953; Balson 1992)
- Challenge and adventure, need for fulfillment, and "self-actualization" (Goldstein 1939; Maslow 1970; Csikszentmihalyi 1974; Iso-Ahola 1980)
- Relationships with partners, spouses, family members, and friends, and associated gender relations (from radical feminist, Marxist and socialist feminist, liberal feminist, and postmodern feminist perspectives)
- A desire to travel associated with quasi-(socio)-psychological theories (see Ross 1994), psychographic profiles (for example, Plog 1974), intrinsic motivation theories (Maslow 1943, 1954; Csikszentmihalyi 1974; Iso-Ahola 1980), and sociodemographic and economic profiles (for example, Cohen 1972; Graburn 1983; Yiannakis and Gibson 1988, 1992; Nash and Smith 1991).

Self-reports by cruisers motivated to adopt a cruising lifestyle because of travel reasons mentioned a desire to see natural things and environments rather than "simulacra" (Baudrillard 1981)—they do not want to go to zoos or aquariums, or Walt Disney representations of the natural world—cruisers want to see the natural world "in situ" (Figure 2-2). In adopting a cruising lifestyle, cruisers believe they experience greater authenticity than they had previously experienced as "institutionalized" tourists (Cohen 1972), due to flexibility in their time schedules, independence, use of a boat for travel and accommodation, and access to non-touristic settings in peripheral zones, as well as the ability to seize upon the opportunistic moments that arise in their lifestyle. Further, a significant number of cruisers preferred to be away from the masses and to explore places privately in the margins. Basically, cruisers exercise choice and control in their

Figure 2-2   Yacht at anchor with a view of the "natural world," Great Keppel Island, Australia. Photographer: Ross Rynehart.

travel experiences. Cruisers seek a cruising lifestyle in order to be in control of their own life, to make their own choices, and have the freedom to do what they want when they want. Most want to do something meaningful with their life, to face a challenge, to be in control of their own destiny and their survival. Most considered work meaningful but in the sense that it provided the means to an end: the achievement and maintenance of the cruising lifestyle. A cruising lifestyle provides a challenge—a quest in both Boorstin (1964) and MacCannell's (1973, 1976) sense but more specifically to MacCannell's: cruisers determined that they were seeking authentic experiences with the world and its people in natural surroundings; they were questing for backstage interactions with both nature and people. They were also questing for fun and enjoyment through their pursuit of a ludic activity—cruising.

Advantages and Disadvantages

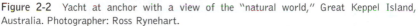

Regarding the advantages and disadvantages of cruising, cruisers were keen to comment that the advantages had been a significant influence in the decision-making process to adopt the lifestyle and that the disadvantages discussed below have been labeled that way more as a result of the interview framework—for the cruisers did not see these as disadvantages. They were part of the lifestyle. Determining a series of disadvantages was achieved by focusing on what a non-cruiser or a person who did not want to go cruising might perceive as disadvantages.

Advantages of cruising are related to:

- Achieving access to the "back regions" of societies and cultures
- Greater interaction between hosts and guests
- Traveling with your "home"
- Ease of traveling between locations in regard to transportation of personal effects
- Safety in regard to hygiene, food, and water supplies
- Control of choice and decision making unmediated by formal tourism broker
- Unmediated travel experiences.

Disadvantages of cruising are related to:

- Cruising as a mode of travel and sometimes limited flexibility to change plans due to planning logistics and access permissions
- Predominant access to the edges of "destinations" due to coastal cruising routes
- Potential for limited interactions with "locals" when in ports and at mass touristic locations
- Boat safety issues when engaging in shore excursions
- Refocusing of the tourist gaze to resident gaze; that is, cruisers become the "gazed upon" phenomenon
- Breaking the sanctity of environmental bubbles
- Seasickness
- Resident reactions.

Impacts

Cruising impacts tend to organize around socio-cultural, economic, environmental, and political orientations (Jennings 2003). Social impacts of cruising are associated with the following:

- Positive
  - Increased understanding between peoples
  - Extension of friendship networks
  - Engagements in cultural exchange

- Negative
  - Occurrences and development of social pathologies (petty theft, robbery, physical abuse, murder, rape)
  - Demonstration effects resulting from differing cultures' and societies' experiences
  - Cultural commodification
  - Varying standards of medical care and related costs.

Economic impacts of cruising comprise the following:

- Positive
  - Barter exchanges
  - Avenue for local producers to sell arts and crafts without a mediator
  - Increased income generation in host communities
  - Income and employment multiplier effects (Figure 2-3)

Figure 2-3 The boat, *Mirrabooka,* on hard stand undergoing regular maintenance, Richmond River, Australia. Photographer: Ross Rynehart.

- Negative
  - Leakages, goods and products purchased elsewhere and imported, especially in regard to substantive items of sailing equipment and technologies.

Environmental impacts of cruising include the following:

- Positive
  - Leaving only footprints
  - Appreciation of sustainable use of marine/aquatic environments
- Negative
  - Potential overcrowding of anchorages, port mooring basins, marina facilities
  - Pollution from fuel leaks and spills, waste materials
  - Coral damage from tramping, dragging boats, snorkeling, and scuba activities
  - Anchor damage on coral areas
  - Souveniring of shells and coral
  - Conflict between various user groups, for example, between sailing and motorized vessels and their activities.

Political impacts of cruising are the following:

- Positive
  - Following entry and exit procedures, permit requirements, rules and regulations, thus presenting cruisers in a positive light, paving the way for positive experiences for other cruisers who may follow
  - Visiting nations recovering from unexpected events and turmoil and engendering positive cross-nation perspectives
  - Short-term participation in aid and human resource support in adverse times
  - Being unofficial ambassadors for the nation from which cruisers come

- Negative
  - Changes to political agendas without previous knowledge and subsequent impact on cruising
  - Getting inadvertently caught in political tussles.

Future Directions

The future for sailing as tourism, sport, recreation, leisure, serious leisure, and a lifestyle is one of growth. Such growth is related to:

- Technological and design innovations and improvements
- The wider spread of market-based economies and subsequent growth of middle classes and related opportunities for leisure pursuits
- Forecast reduction in working hours and greater time available for leisure
- Multiple careers in a working life with periods of non-work time between
- Changes in postindustrial societal values and policies, which enable previously marginalized groups such as lower socioeconomic groups, women, and people with disabilities to participate in sailing
- The nature of the globalized world and the increased connectivity such a world creates enables greater contact and promotion of the various forms of sailing and subsequent adoption
- Spread of clubs, associations, and affiliations and their permit to encourage and increase participation
- The role of the media in broadcasting sailing events and thereby generating interest
- The use of sailing by advertising to portray a means of escape from a less-than-satisfying workaday world—an escape to a world that provides relaxation, challenge, and fun
- An increase in lifestyle, leisure, sport, and travel programs, which can generate interest
- Incorporation of sailing into educational programs.

However, with increased numbers participating in sailing, there will be resultant issues of crowding, of potential conflict between user groups in shared zones. In response, at the local, regional, state, and national level, there may be increased regulation, increased use and spread of user pay charges, and development of management strategies and policies to sustain tourism, sporting, recreation, and leisure resources and "quality of experiences." At an international level, all the preceding are pertinent, and there may also be a lessening of use of some areas due to global safety and security issues emanating from social, political, economic, and environmental circumstances.

Purpose of Case Study

The case study selected for this chapter contributes to sport, recreation, leisure, and tourism literature by providing an excerpt from a "fifth moment"—a postmodern period study (Denzin and Lincoln 2005). In particular, the study explores the constructed landscape of cruising, issues of power, and the construction of cruising women's (and men's) identities. It does this by focusing on the lived world of travel experiences—in this case, the lived experiences of long-term ocean cruisers. It also adopts a gendered perspective to "inspect who is making/re-making/de-making the imagined world of social/mythic experiences" (Hollinshead 2004, p. 97) associated with cruising as a lifestyle. Such investigations provide an in-depth understanding of lived experiences and how they influence the overall quality of travel experiences (Jennings 2005b).

Additionally, studies of the lived experiences of women involved in sailing are few in number and tend to focus on sailing as a sport—racing (see, for example, Crawley 1998; Bricknell 1999). Jennings (1999, 2005a) appears to be the primary researcher in the area of women who sail as a lifestyle—cruising. This case study serves to add to literature derived from standpoint research and focuses particularly on "taken-for-granted assumptions," "knowledge construction," and "ways of knowing" (see Humberstone 2004).

Case Study: Long-Term Ocean Cruisers—Roles and Responsibilities

This case study, drawn from a wider ethnographic study conducted between 1992 and 1999 and between 2000 and 2003, focuses on the experiences of cruising women involved in heterosexual relationships who have accepted a cruising lifestyle because of a choice to do so or because their partner was intent on doing so, and the women would be left behind if they did not go. In particular, it addresses the roles and responsibilities associated with women while they are cruising. In this case study, it will become obvious that Morse's (1987/1988) claim that "[s]port plays an important role in gender maintenance; indeed, sport is the last major social institution segregated by gender, and its hierarchy of value, male performances are favored" (p. 22) is highly pertinent to sailing as a lifestyle—cruising. In this case study, gender relations are examined from cruising women's and men's viewpoints. In addition, as a result of grounded theory analysis, a radical feminist theoretical lens is included. See Jennings (1999) for socialist/Marxist, liberal, and post-modern feminist informed discussions related to cruising as a lifestyle.

From a radical feminist perspective, society is viewed as patriarchal. Men occupy the ruling class positions and women the subject class positions. The key institution through which the ruling/subject class divisions are reified is the family. It is also in the family that women are most exploited through their provision of free labor in the domestic domain such as home and child care (see, for example, Rosaldo 1974). Firestone (1970, 1972) coined the term "sex class" to describe the inequalities of power and the division of labor based on biological differences between women and men.

A radical feminist and biologically based discourse resonates in cruisers' explanations of the allocation of roles and responsibilities.

I'll probably hurt a few feelings, like this, but I think the males are the hunters and gatherers. Let's face it. It's innate in most animals and we're animals. A lot of feminists would say that's a load of crap. But we're still animals and I think it's still innate in us, the hunting and gathering, going out there and venturing where the female of the species is the homebody, looking after the kids. (Cruising man 606)

I think women are totally, to use a word of a friend of mine often uses, is that women are much more broody than men, they want to nest and they want to be with their families and particularly if they are grandparents. . . . I'm sure when I have grandchildren if we do then I'll probably be broody too. (Cruising woman 323)

Moreover, the allocation of roles and responsibilities due to biological difference amongst the majority of cruisers was accepted as a "taken-for-granted" explanation. For example,

Females seem to be much better in the galley department and especially in maintaining the household, if you like to call it down below, and so forth and the guys usually handle the physical work. The sails, the anchor, etc. (Cruising man 356).

Well, [tasks are assigned] in fairly traditional roles. Females doing the domestic buying and maintaining the whole organizational skills, whereas the men tended to take on the maintenance and the navigation and that side of it, but fairly traditional sides [and roles]. (Cruising woman 801)

Sometimes physiological strength was added to the argument for the domestic/non-domestic division of cruising activities and tasks:

Well, it's probably not too popular in the current environment, but just physically I just don't think the female is as equipped to do it as the male. That's a big part of it and probably some cultural, most women aren't prepared by training for cruising. (Cruising man 406)

Yeah, to be a mechanic, and a plumber, and an electrician and all the things that you need to know about, operation of the boat. (Cruising woman 405)

I've been talking to other girls about this. Other sailing, other sailor girls, and then I think it is this way, a lot of men like have to be strong and have the power to do these things. (Cruising woman 377)

While cruisers may accept the taken-for-granted assumptions that some roles are "natural" and that physiological strength is required to sail boats, such arguments are spurious. Women given the knowledge and skills can and do sail boats independently of men as evidenced in the examples of the two women circumnavigators noted earlier. Further, as noted by one cruising woman, boats can be fitted and rigged to account for the different strengths of all cruisers aboard. In some relationships, this "natural" discourse regarding roles and responsibilities masks the underlying silence of unstated power relationships aboard some boats. Aboard these boats, the cruising man is the "boss" and maintains this position through reifying "naturally and culturally" (that is, patriarchally) ascribed roles and responsibilities. Such men deliberately withhold knowledge or "teach" in inappropriate ways, which further marginalizes cruising women from the overall enterprise of cruising. Moreover, rather than divesting knowledge in optimum learning conditions, it was given in high-stress conditions where the learner's skills and knowledge were way below that which was required by the challenge of the moment (see Jennings 1999, 2001, 2005a). In such non-conducive learning environments, the learning experience results in anxiety, fear, or low esteem as well as generates conflicts or disharmony in relationships. Such moments and environments are obviously not self-actualizing or "flow" moments for cruising women (see Csiksentmihalyi 1974 for a discussion of relationships between skills and challenges).

In the main, the older cruising men tended to reify patriarchally assigned roles and responsibilities. Within their discourses, there was strong accord with Millett's (1970) reasons for patriarchy:

- Superior male strength (biology)
- Socialization (dominance of men)
- The institution of the family (maintaining and socializing patriarchy)

- Class and subordination (women exist in a caste-like status)
- Education
- Myth and religion
- Psychology (internalization of patriarchy)
- Physical force (violence) (see Millett 1970 for further discussion).

Earlier in this research case study, a cruiser made reference to "cultural" influences. In contrast to the previous discussion regarding biological differences, Ortner (1974) argues that women's oppression is not directly associated with such processes; instead, it is due to the way that each culture defines and evaluates female biological processes through three institutional forms:

- Cultural ideology
- Symbolic devices
- Social structural arrangements (Ortner 1974).

These three forms reify the perception that women are closer to nature because of the reproductive processes associated with their bodies, and this serves to further reify their subordination. Men, on the other hand, are associated with cultural processes including the three forms just noted. As cultural processes are valued more highly than biological processes, this allows men to assume a superior social role. Thus, gender and gender roles are a result of "social and cultural processes" (Ortner and Whitehead 1981, p. 1), which reify the devalued nature of biological processes associated with women. In the interviews with cruisers, social/cultural processes were also argued as a reason for gender roles, particularly women in regard to "home and hearth" and men with external environments to the home. For example,

Well, I think that most women are brought up [to do] cooking and cleaning and the house, the home, you know. . . . Whereas a man, I think they grew up much more that way, you know [to go adventuring] . . . to rough it in a boat. It's just culturally, I don't think it's . . . you're brought up [in a particular way]. (Cruising woman 379)

Women aren't expected . . . they're not brought up to be adventurous and go out there and plus the skills to maintain and build a boat, aren't encouraged or taught. That's one thing that really annoys me—that I don't have the same skills to do that. (Cruising woman 801)

That being said, cruising women acknowledge that social and cultural processes had changed over time and gave women the potential for equality in a cruising relationship. This was due to changing attitudes, legislation, and opportunities for participation of women in men's sports—a condition for which liberal feminists have advocated.

[Sailing and by association cruising] hasn't been a woman's sport, I mean, you know, in the next 10 to 20 years, it'll definitely, we'll see more women 'cause women are involved in sports more. (Cruising woman 379)

Subsequently, the adequacy of a radical feminist explanation of "genderization" and gender roles among cruising women and men is beginning to diminish as women's participation rates in men's domains increase. This greater participation is partially a result of feminist efforts for equality and subsequent changes in socialization and cultural and educational processes. No longer is there an acceptance of a universal determinism of "natural" roles attributed to women and men. Women do not need to rely on men to go cruising and can participate skillfully, knowingly, and fully in the cruising lifestyle.

References

AC-clopedia. (2005). *32nd America's Cup milestones*. Accessed October 6, 2005, from http://www.americascup.com/en/acclopedia/since1851/phase01.php

Allport, G.W. (1950). *The nature of personality; selected papers*. Cambridge, MA: Addison-Wesley Press.

Bailey, C. (1997). Making waves and drawing lines: The politics of defining the vicissitudes of feminism. *Hypatia*, Summer, **12** (3), 17ff. Accessed April 2, 2004, from http://gateway.proquest.com

Balson, M. (1992). *Understanding classroom behaviour*, Hawthorn, Victoria, Australia: Australian Council of Educational Research.

Baudrillard, J. (1981). *For a Critique of the Political Economy*. Translation and introduction by Levin, Charles. St. Louis: Telos Press.

Bennett, T., Emmison, M., and J. Frow. (1999). *Accounting for tastes: Australian everyday cultures*. Cambridge, UK: Cambridge University Press.

Boorstin, D. (1964). *The image: A guide to pseudo events in America*. New York: Harper & Row.

Bricknell, L. (1999). The trouble with feelings: gender, sexualities, and power in a gender regime of competitive sailing. *Journal of Sport and Social Issues*, **23** (4), 421.

Bryan H. (1973). In R.A. Stebbins (n.d.), *Serious leisure: a conceptual statement*. University of Calgary. Accessed October 6, 2005, from http://playlab.uconn.edu/stebbins2.htm

Cohen, E. (1972). Toward a sociology of international tourism. *Social Research*, **39**, 164–182.

Columbia Encyclopedia. (2005a). *Sailing: history of sport sailing*. Accessed October 6, 2005, from http://www.encyclopedia.com/html/section/sailing_HistoryofSport Sailing.asp

Columbia Encyclopedia. (2005b). *Sailing: racing classes*. Accessed October 6, 2005, from http://www.encyclopedia.com/html/section/sailing_RacingClasses.asp

Community Boating Incorporated. (n.d.). *Community Boating Inc: History*. Accessed October 8, 2005, from http://www.community-boating.org/history.html

Cornell, J. (2002). *World cruising survey*. London: Adlard Coles.

Crawley, S. (1998). Gender, class, and the construction of masculinity in professional sailing: A case study of the American women's team. *International Review for the Sociology of Sport*, **33** (1), 33–42.

Csikszentmihalyi, M. (1974). *Flow: studies in enjoyment*. Chicago: University of Chicago Press.

Denzin, N.K., and Y.S. Lincoln. (2005). Introduction: The discipline and practice of qualitative research. In N.K. Denzin and Y.S. Lincoln (Eds.), *The Sage Handbook of qualitative research*. (3rd ed., pp. 1–32). Thousand Oaks, CA: Sage.

Doolin, R. (n.d.). History of ISAF. *SailNet*. Accessed October 6, 2005, from http://www.sailnet.com/collections/articles/index.cfm?articleid=doolin0014

Dreikurs, R. (1953). *Fundamentals of Adlerian psychology*. Chicago: Alfred Adler Institute.

Durkheim, E. (1952/1972). Anomy. In Ada W. Finifter (Ed.), *Alienation and the social system*. (pp. 18–23). New York: John Wiley and Sons.

Firestone, S. (1970). *The dialectic of sex, the case for feminist revolution*. London: Jonathan Cape.

Firestone, S. (1972). *The dialectic of sex*. London: Paladin.

Getz, D. (1997). *Event management and event tourism*. New York: Cognizant Communication Corporation.

Getz, D. (2003). Sport Event Tourism: Planning, Development and Marketing. In S. Hudson (Ed.), *Sport and adventure tourism*. (pp. 49–88). New York: Haworth Hospitality Press.

Goldstein, K. (1939). *The organism; a holistic approach to biology derived from pathological data in man*. New York: American Book Company.

Graburn, N.H.H. (1983). The anthropology of tourism. *Annals of Tourism Research*, **10**, 9–33.

Hollinshead, K. (2004). Ontological craft in tourism studies: the productive mapping of identity and image in tourism settings. In J. Phillimore and L. Goodson (Eds.), *Qualitative research in tourism: ontologies, epistemologies, and methodologies*. (pp. 83–101). London: Routledge.

Humberstone, B. (2004). Standpoint research: multiple versions of reality in tourism theorising and research. In J. Phillimore and L. Goodson (Eds.), *Qualitative research in tourism: ontologies, epistemologies, and methodologies*. (pp. 119–136). London: Routledge.

International Olympic Committee. (2005a). *Sailing history*. Accessed October 6, 2005, from http://www.olympic.org/uk/sports/programme/history_uk.asp?DiscCode=SA&sport Code=SA

International Olympic Committee. (2005b). *Sailing: Olympic sport since 1900*. Accessed October 6, 2005, from http://www.olympic.org/uk/sports/programme/history_uk.asp?DiscCode=SA&sportCode=SA

Iso-Ahola, S. (1980). *The social psychology of leisure and recreation*. Dubuque, IO: Wm C. Brown.

Jary, D., and J. Jary. (2000). *Collins dictionary of sociology*. (3rd ed.). Glasgow, Scotland: HarperCollins.

Jenkins and Sherman. (1979). In R.A. Stebbins. *Serious leisure: a conceptual statement*. University of Calgary. Accessed October 6, 2005, from http://playlab.uconn.edu/stebbins2.htm

Jennings, G.R. (1999). *Voyages from the centre to the margins: an ethnography of long-term ocean cruisers*. Unpublished doctoral thesis, Perth, Australia: Murdoch University.

Jennings, G.R. (2001, June 10–13). *Flow: Having the right skills for the challenge*. Proceedings from 2001: A Tourism Odyssey, Fort Meyers, FL: TTRA 32nd Annual Conference.

Jennings, G. (2003). Marine tourism. In S. Hudson (Ed.), *Sport and adventure tourism*. (pp. 125–164). New York: Haworth Hospitality Press.

Jennings, G.R. (2005a). Caught in the irons: one of the lived experiences of cruising women. *Tourism Research International*, **9** (2), 177–193.

Jennings, G.R. (2005b). Perspective on quality tourism experiences: an introduction. In G. Jennings and N. Nickerson (Eds.), *Quality tourism experiences*. (pp. 1–21). Burlington, MA: Elsevier.

Kreps, J.M., and J.J. Spengler. (1973). In R.A. Stebbins (n.d.), *Serious leisure: a conceptual statement*. University of Calgary. Accessed October 6, 2005, from http://playlab.uconn.edu/stebbins2.htm

Macbeth, J. (1985). *Ocean cruising: a study of affirmative deviance*. Unpublished doctoral thesis, Murdoch University, Perth, Australia.

Macbeth, J. (1986, July). *The study of ocean cruising*. Paper presented to the Sociological Association of Australia and New Zealand Conference 1986, University of New England, Armidale, NSW, Australia.

Macbeth, J. (1988). Ocean cruising. In M. Csikszentmihalyi and S.I. Csikszentmihalyi (Eds.), *Optimal experience: psychological studies of flow in consciousness*. (pp. 214–231). Cambridge, UK: Cambridge University Press.

Macbeth, J. (1992). Ocean cruising: a sailing subculture. *The Sociological Review*, 320–343.

Macbeth, J. (1993, April 14–16). *But we are not tourists, and this is life, not leisure*. Paper presented at the Inaugural Conference of the Australian and New Zealand Association of Leisure Studies, Griffith University, Brisbane, Australia.

MacCannell, D. (1973). Staged authenticity: arrangements of social space in tourist settings. *American Journal of Sociology*, **79** (3), 589–603.

MacCannell, D. (1976). *The tourist: a new theory of the leisure class*. New York: Schocken Books.

Marx, K. (1963/1972). Alienated labour. In Ada W. Finifter (Ed.), *Alienation and the social system*. (pp. 12–18). New York: John Wiley and Sons.

Maslow, A.H. (1970). *Motivation and personality*. (2nd edition). New York: Harper and Row.

Mill, R.C., and A.M. Morrison. (2002). *The tourism system*. (4th ed.). Dubuque, IA: Kendall/Hunt.

Millett, K. (1970). *Sexual politics*. New York: Doubleday.

Morse, M. (1987/1998). Artemis aging: exercise and the female body on video. *Discourse*, **10** (1) 20–53.

Nash, D., and V.L. Smith. (1991). Anthropology and tourism. *Annals of Tourism Research*, **18**, 12–25.

Ortner, S.B. (1974). Is female to male as nature is to culture? In M.Z. Rosaldo and L. Lamphere (Eds.), *Woman, culture, and society*. Stanford, CA: Stanford University Press.

Ortner, S.B., and H. Whitehead. (1981). Introduction: accounting for sexual meanings. In S.B. Ortner, and H. Whitehead, *Sexual meanings: the cultural construction of gender and sexuality*. Cambridge, UK: Cambridge University Press.

Pearson, K. (1979). *Surfing subcultures of Australia and New Zealand*. St Lucia, Brisbane, Australia: University of Queensland Press.

Plog, S.C. (1974). Why destination areas rise and fall in popularity. *The Cornell Hotel and Restaurant Administration Quarterly*, **14** (4), 55–58.

Richens, H. (1992). Case study. Yachting holidays: an experience with island adventures. In B. Weiler and C.M. Hall (Eds.), *Special interest tourism*. (pp. 185–197). London: Belhaven.

Rosaldo, M.Z. (1974). Woman, culture, and society: a theoretical overview. In M.Z. Rosaldo, and L. Lamphere (Eds.). *Woman, culture, and society*. Stanford, CA: Stanford University Press.

Ross, Glen F. (1994). *The psychology of tourism*. Melbourne: Hospitality Press.

Ryan, C. (1979a). The chase of a dream, the end of a play. In C. Ryan (Ed.), *The tourist experience, a new introduction. Studies in tourism series*. (pp. 1–24). London: Cassell.

Ryan, C. (1979b). Similar motivations—diverse behaviours. In C. Ryan (Ed.), *The tourist experience, a new introduction. Studies in tourism series.* (pp. 25–47). London: Cassell.

Stebbins, R.A. (n.d.). *Serious leisure: a conceptual statement.* University of Calgary. Accessed October 6, 2005, from http://playlab.uconn.edu/stebbins2.htm

Stebbins, R.A. (1992). *Amateurs, professionals, and serious leisure.* Montreal, Quebec, Canada: McGill-Queen's University Press.

Stebbins, R.A. (1997). Serious leisure and well-being. In J. T. Haworth (Ed.), *Work, leisure, and well-being.* (pp. 117–130). New York, Routledge.

Stebbins, R.A. (2001). Serious leisure. *Society,* May/June, **38** (4), 53–57.

Weed, M., and C. Bull. (2004). *Sports tourism: participants, policy, and providers.* Oxford, UK: Elsevier.

Wikipedia (2005a). *Notable global maritime circumnavigations.* Accessed October 6, 2005, from http://en.wikipedia.org/wiki/Circumnavigation

Wikipedia (2005b). *Joshua Slocum.* Accessed October 6, 2005, from http://en.wikipedia. org/wiki/Joshua_Slocum

Wikipedia (2005c). *Francis Chichester.* Accessed October 6, 2005, from http://en. wikipedia.org/wiki/Francis_Chichester

World Tourism Organization/United Nations Recommendations on Tourism Statistics. (2005). *Facts and figures: methodological notes: concepts and definitions.* Accessed October 8, 2005, from http://www.world-tourism.org/facts/menu.html

Yiannakis, A., and H. Gibson. (1992). Roles tourists play. *Annals of Tourism Research,* **19,** 287–303.

Websites

Sailing and Boating: Virtual Library of Sport—Sailing: http://sportsvl.com/water/sailing.htm

Glossary of Sailing Terms: http://boatsafe.com/nauticalknowhow/glossary.htm

Sailing Areas
Asian Yachting: http://asianyachting.com

Sailing Sites
International Soling Class: http://www.soling.com/indexmore.asp?IdArticle=1&Seccion=General%20Information&Lengua=English

Etchells Class: http://www.etchells.org/aboutus.php

Racing Sites
Global Challenge: http://www.challengebusiness.com/global/history.html

Americas Cup: http://www.americascup.com/en/acclopaedia/since1851/phase01.php

International Sailing—Related Sites
International Sailing Federation (ISAF): http://sailing.org

International Olympic Committee (IOC): Olympic Sailing History: http://www.olympic.org/uk/sports/programme/history_uk.asp?DiscCode=SA&sportCode=SA

Cruising Sites
Cruising Association: http://www.cruising.org.uk

Seven Seas Cruising Association: http://www.ssca.org

3

Motorboating

Gayle Jennings

Overview

Despite the passage of time, boating continues to maintain its popularity as a sport, leisure, and recreational experience across a number of countries such as the United Kingdom, France, the Netherlands, Germany, the United States, Australia, New Zealand, and Canada (see Frigden and Wood 1985; Roy Morgan Research Centre 1985; Foster 1986; Nederlands Research Instituut voor Recreatie en Toerisme 1986; Prokopy, Crandall, Baker, Godsman, and Tighe 1988; Brodersen 1994; Leyrat 1994; Driml 1996; Fedler 2000a,b). Globally, boat ownership is particularly concentrated in the United States and Canada ("Pleasure Boating to Grow" 1987). Within the European context, Germany, Norway, and France have tended to lead other European nations with respect to pleasure boat ownership (Leyrat 1994). In Asia, recreational boat ownership is a more recent phenomenon. For instance, boating in Japan only became an emerging market during the late twentieth century (Kotani 1991).

In addition to sport, leisure, and recreation, boating has also become a key part of the varied suite of touristic experiences offered at destinations associated with water resources (see, for example, Fairweather and Swaffield 2001). In fact, rejuvenation of some ports, harbors, and waterfronts has been associated with a refocusing on recreational boating and related business enterprises, such as marina developments (Figure 3-1). This type of rejuvenation has occurred, for example, in the United States, Portugal, Spain, Gibraltar, St Katherine's Haven, and London (Frigden and Wood 1985; Otis 1988; Smith and Jenner 1995). Recreational boating has also been included as part of a number of rural tourism enterprises, such as the Lightwater Valley in North Yorkshire, UK (Ward 1986). Further, river systems previously used for freight have been transformed to provide leisure, recreation, and tourism experiences as exemplified by the River Severn as well as the Gloucester and Sharpness Canal, UK. Traditionally used waterways have also become sites for increased touristic boating activity, as evidenced in the Burgundy

Figure 3-1   Waterfront development in Queenstown, New Zealand. Photographer: Ross Rynehart.

region, France (Panne 1990). Moreover, specific targeting of boating for rural tourism development at suitable locations has occurred in Bulgaria, Hungary, Poland, Romania, and the Czech Republic (Lazareck 1984).

While the societal, cultural, and political changes as discussed in Chapter 1 can influence participation in boating, seasonality, weather, and quality of facilities also influence participation as well as the selection of sites for boating experiences. In general, boating participation usually peaks in summer months (Roy Morgan Research Centre 1985). The popularity of boating is due to the diversity of possible experiences. Additionally, the product life cycle of boating has been buoyed by technological changes, which have resulted in a wide array of boating designs, sizes, materials, equipment, capabilities, experiences, and costs. Concomitantly, consumer demand has also changed, and this has had positive influences on boating participation. People have become more sophisticated in their tastes (see Weiler and Hall 1992). They seek active and adventuresome experiences, they value quality, and they relate this to price (see related discussions by Fay, McCure, and Begin 1987; Martin and Mason 1987; Schwaninger 1989; Ott 1990; Oelrichs 1994; Berno, Moore, Simmons, and Hart 1996; Lipscombe 1996; and Chapters 10 and 12 of this volume). Moreover, the increased attention given to providing services, infrastructure, and facilities to support boating participation has assisted in positively affecting participation rates. (See related discussion by Gjesdal et al. 2002.) Such provisions include online chandleries; conveniently situated and mobile boat maintenance providers; haul-out facilities; storage facilities; marinas and mooring buoys; fuel jetties; sewerage pump-out stations; and access to showers, laundries, toilets, and fresh water for filling water tanks for onboard consumption.

The remainder of this chapter will provide some historical and contemporary background to the development of motorboating in its various forms. It will also consider the market profile of motorboaters. Advantages and disadvantages of motorboating as a water-based tourism, sport, leisure, and recreation experience will be listed, after which an examination of impacts of motorboating will be presented. The future for motorboating will be considered before concluding with a case study, drawing on work by Fedler (2000a,b), which focuses on U.S. boating participation rates and influences, as well as marketing strategies to increase participation across identified market segments.

Background

The introduction to this chapter established the popularity of boating as a generic water-based experience. Some of the aforementioned commentary is as applicable to sail powered vessels as it is to motor powered vessels. However, the intent of this chapter is not to duplicate the discussions presented in Chapter 2, *Sailing/Cruising,* Chapter 4, *Motorized Watersports*, Chapter Six, *Sport Fishing and Big-Game Fishing*, Chapter 8, *Whitewater Rafting*, Chapter Nine, *Kayaking*, Chapter 10, *One-Day Boating Adventures,* or Chapter 11, *Sail Training Adventures*. So it needs to be emphasized here that, due to the nature of the water-based experiences presented in each of those chapters, there will be commonalities between their texts and this chapter. Therefore, the chapters should be read as complementary to each other. The focus of *this* chapter is the various forms of motorboating.

Motorboating is boating that uses a motor as the key or only means of propulsion. Motors may be outboard or inboard (Schemel 2001). Outboard motors are usually attached to the transom (back side) of boats, and the propeller is directly linked to the engine/motor. Inboard motors are positioned inside the boat, and a propeller shaft connects the motor/engine to the externally located propeller. While some sailboats have auxiliary motors, as mentioned in Chapter 2, these will not be considered in this chapter. Additionally, the chapter will not focus on hovercrafts, airboats, or everglade boats. Furthermore, since the art of "paddling" is taken up in Chapter 8 and is a major theme of Chapter 9, boating associated with paddling, rowing, and punting will also not be discussed in this chapter.

History of Motorboating

The history of motorboating is tied to the history of sailing. Both of their origins are derived from the development of boat technology from earlier propulsion using poling, paddling, and rowing. (Readers may wish to review the history of sailing reported in Chapter 2 and read about kayaking in Chapter 9 for comparative background.) Along the way to the development of motorboats, there were other related boating developments, such as steam-powered boats, paddlewheel-driven and electric-driven motors, as well as oil-, diesel-, and gasoline-fueled motors. Significant technological developments for motorboating include electric batteries and engines, floating charging stations, oil-fueled engines, use of aircraft engines in speedboats, hydroplane and displacement hull developments, and development of flying boats.

In 1882, the United Kingdom's Electrical Power Storage Company began manufacturing electric river launches designed by Reckenzaun, as commercial enterprises.

As early adopters of the technology, the upper class, nobility, and royalty acquired personal electric launches as a means of transportation between their Thames riverside homes and social events. Later, around 1898, William Sargeant began building electric boats as well as floating stations for recharging motors along the river Thames. The *Mary Gordon,* a 70-foot luxury electric launch, and similar launches plied Britain's Lake District. These electric launches were to be exported internationally and, in order to meet demand and extend markets, a shipyard was established in the United States to produce the launches. By the time of the First World War, however, electric engines had been replaced by oil-fueled engines (Hobden n.d.).

In the 1920s and 1930s, the American Gar Wood made significant contributions to the development of speedboats, especially motor and hull designs. According to Baulch and Shermever (n.d.), Wood introduced airplane engines into speedboats and developed displacement hulls, which were to be adopted by the U.S. Navy as the basis of the PT boats used in World War Two. In addition to achievements in boat design and mechanics, Wood repeatedly won the motorboat equivalent of the America's Cup, the Harmsworth Trophy races in England. The first win was in 1920, in a speedboat called *Miss America I.* In 1931, in *Miss America IX,* he reached speeds in excess of 100 mph, again with an aircraft engine. As a result, he became the first man to achieve the feat of traveling at 100 mph in a boat. Later, he achieved a speed of 124 mph in *Miss America X.* Glenn Curtiss, another American, allegedly developed and flew the first flying boat in 1912 (Wikipedia 2005).

Contemporary Motorboating Experiences

At the start of the twenty-first century, people interested in experiencing boating have a plethora of choices. As was discussed in Chapter 2, design, construction materials, and patterns of usage serve to differentiate boats. Motorboating experiences may be classified in relation to the vessels themselves. Boats may be:

- Monohulls (one hull) or twin hulled (two hulls)
- Hydroplanes or displacement hulls
- Open (no cabin and full exposure to the elements), half cabin (a mix between open and half a cabin, which provides some shelter from the elements and possibly half or full berths in the bow of the boat), or full cabin (a fully enclosed vessel providing full shelter from the elements and varying degrees of live-aboard comfort)
- Inboard or outboard (Schemel 2001).

The boating experience may also be classified by participant characteristics:

- Recreational and leisure-time users or "liveaboards" (the boat is equivalent to a person's home). Liveaboards may be permanent at a site or transient
- Locals, quasi-locals (that is, second home-owners), or tourists (see related discussion by Meyer 1999)
- Day boaters, overnight boaters, and racers (Donnelly, Vaske, and Graefe 1986)
- Inexperienced or experienced (see Manfredo 1989)
- Low, medium, and high specialists (Wellman, Roggenbuck, and Smith 1982; Kaufman and Graefe 1984; Williams and Huffman 1986; Fedler 2000a)
- Passive and active users (West 1990)
- Casual and serious leisure participants (see Stebbins 1992).

Based on a literature review regarding recreation specialization by Kerstetter, Confer, and Graefe (2001), further differences between boaters may be associated with:

- Motivations
- Management preferences
- Resource dependency
- Trip satisfaction
- Amount of mediated interaction
- Perception of quality of experience
- Environmental preferences.

Market Profile of Boaters

Since the mid-twentieth century in Western nations, the sport, leisure, recreation, and touristic experiences of boating and fishing have generally maintained or increased participation levels, although there have been instances of declining participation (see Fedler 2000a). Of noteworthiness is the fact that boating and fishing tend to occur together (Kenchington 1993; Dovers 1994; Jennings 1998; Fedler 2000a, 2000b). Moreover, as West (1990) comments in regard to marine environments, "[f]ew boaters are single-use consumers of the marine environment but engage in several different activities while on the water" (p. 267). So while boating and fishing may co-occur, it must be recognized that other activities can be involved, such as relaxation, sightseeing, and experiencing the wilderness or communing with nature (see discussions by Johnson and Orbach 1986; Jackson 1986; Fedler and Ditton 1994; Jennings 1998; Fedler 2000b). Boating, like other water-based experiences in this book, has a history of being gendered in nature (see, for instance, Ministry of Tourism and Recreation, Tourism Research Section 1985; Struna, Mangan, and Parke 1987; Jennings 1998; Fedler 2000b). Socioeconomic, cultural, as well as ethnic backgrounds may also serve to influence and constrain participation (see discussion in Fedler 2000a and 2000b).

The major market for boating is men. Age ranges are variously reported as:

- Between 36 and 50 and highly educated when linked to boating guide usage (Ministry of Tourism and Recreation, Tourism Research Section 1985); or
- Between 45 and 49 years of age, employed as skilled workers, service industry employees, or professionals (Jennings 1998); or
- Post–young adulthood with participation beginning to taper off at 45 years (Fedler 2000b).

Additionally, the market may be segmented by the previously noted characteristics of boaters, repeated below:

- Recreational and leisure-time users or liveaboards
- Locals, quasi-locals, and tourists
- Day boaters, overnight boaters, and racers
- Inexperienced or experienced
- Low, medium, and high specialists
- Passive and active users.

Due to the overlap that occurs between boating and other forms of water-based experiences, market segmentation needs to consider the complementarity of other related market segments. It should also consider further research that attempts to gain a deeper insight into the various participants and their motives, as well as expectations and satisfaction levels, the multiplicity of activities that are associated with boating, and what makes a quality boating experience.

Advantages and Disadvantages

As previously mentioned in this chapter, over time, social, cultural, and political changes; technological developments; and increases in boating-related support services, facilities, and infrastructure have served to increase participation in boating. As a result, a number of advantages and disadvantages can simultaneously occur in regard to this water-based experience. A number of these are presented in the two subsections that follow.

Advantages

One of the advantages of boating as a tourism, sport, leisure, and recreation experience is the fact that it can be conducted as a group activity with family and friends (see Jennings 1998 and Fedler 2000b). It can also be pursued as an individual activity. Further, boating enables access to wilderness sites (Jennings 1998). The advantages of motorboating over other water-based experiences include speed of boats, especially when using boats as a form of transport to reach or participate in other connected water-based experiences such as scuba diving; fishing; photography; or visiting islands, cays, reefs, and popular locations. Other advantages are related to:

- Access to suitable facilities to support boating experiences (see Reed-Andersen et al. 2000)
- Various water and boating rules and regulations (see Wang 2000; Gabe and Hite 2003)
- Presence of rangers, police, and other related agencies to ensure compliance with safety, rules and regulations, codes of conduct, information, and education services
- Opportunities to recreate and engage in touristic experiences across a range of recreational and tourism experiences (Stankey and Wood 1982; Driver 1989, as cited in Watson 1989; Butler and Waldbrook 1991)
- Travel to compete in races outside home environs
- Being able to participate in sport, recreation, and leisure activities with similarly minded people via club affiliations and networks.

Disadvantages

In overview, the disadvantages include increasing costs of fuel, storage issues, weather dependency for usage, safety issues and accidents, and conflict between users. The latter has long been an issue in outdoor recreation and leisure experiences.

As Jaakson (1989, p. 96) has commented, "[f]reedom is a central tenet in recreation. The sharing of an area with other users, however, often detracts from the freedom that users may perceive to be important for their recreation satisfaction." (p. 96). Relatedly, Gartside (1986), Kenchington (1993), and Dovers (1994) have discussed conflicts between user interests; wherein "conflict is defined as goal interference attributed to another's behavior" (Jacob and Schreyer 1980, p. 369). Such interference can impact on satisfaction levels. Essentially, among boaters, there is the potential for conflict at water resource sites between various user groups, such as motorboaters, sail-powered boaters, motorized water-sport participants, recreational and commercial fishers, and commercially operated boating, as well as scuba divers. Elsewhere, in relation to recreational fishing, Graefe and Fedler (1986) have indicated that satisfaction associated with recreational fishing experiences can be affected by crowding and congestion. Such is the case with boaters. In fact, the mixing of various water-based users at popular locations can cause a sense of crowding and subsequent loss of satisfaction (see Jennings 1998). This is particularly exacerbated when the location is viewed as a "wilderness" one.

Additional disadvantages of boating relate to:

- Storage facilities (Fedler 2000b). Depending on the size of boat, home facilities, and local regulations, boats may have to be stored elsewhere. Associated disadvantages of storage relate to cost (see Lipton and Hicks 1999), degree of ease of access, and distance between home and storage site
- Time taken up in travel between storage and the intended water resource site, as well as time taken to travel between home and the storage site
- Difficulties in sustaining participation in boating when family members lose interest in boating (Fedler 2000b)
- Difficulties with participation when local and easily accessible areas are limited or nonexistent (Fedler 2000b)
- Limitations of time and/or budget availability (Fedler 2000b)
- Maintenance and repair costs (Fedler 2000b), related time out from "actually boating," as well as time needed to make repairs if personally maintaining or repairing the boat
- Quality and nature of facilities (Ministry of Tourism and Recreation, Tourism Research Section 1985), such as boat ramps, launching sites, showers, fuel, LPG (gas), water, showers, toilets, laundries, wash down areas, haul-out areas, waste disposal
- Number of marinas not matching boat ownership (Smith and Jenner 1995)
- Potential carbon monoxide poisoning (see Silver and Hampson 1996)
- Potential fire and explosions related to fuel and gas (LPG) leakages and spills
- Alcohol consumption and related accidents (see McKnight, Lange, and McKnight 1998; Logan, Sacks, Branche, Ryan, and Bender 1999)
- Popular sites and facilities leading to perceptions of crowding and congestion
- Perceptions of overregulation
- Introduction of regulations and legislation without necessary infrastructure or facilities to enact them, such as sewerage discharge regulations introduced into Sydney Harbor and elsewhere in Australia in association with an initial lack of sufficient pump-out facilities to support the regulations.

As would be apparent to readers, some of the advantages and disadvantages of boating as a water-based experience are linked to positive and negative *impacts* of boating. These are considered in the next section.

Impacts

Impacts of motorboating mirror those noted in Chapter 2, such as pollution, user conflicts, loss of amenity, registration, legislation, and conservation and preservation issues. In the following subsections, some of the socio-cultural, environmental, and economic impacts will each be considered in turn.

Socio-Cultural Impacts

At the broader societal level in industrialized nations, the key potential socio-cultural impacts on boating include:

- Continuing changes in the developed world's leisure patterns, for example, increased opportunities for leisure, recreation, and travel
- In Western nations, an aging baby boomer demographic desiring active and rewarding experiences (see also Chapter 10)
- Western nations' baby boomer generation with an extended life due to improvements in standards of living, health, and medical care and support
- Potential rising unemployment and greater amounts of non-work time (see Chapter 2)
- Time between contract work (see Chapter 2)
- Lower socioeconomic groups not being able to participate in self-funded boating endeavors and experiences (see case study in this chapter and in Fedler 2000b).

Obviously, some of these impacts are pluses and some are minuses for boating.

At the more localized level of participation, user conflicts, perceptions of congestion and crowding, and loss of amenity will impact on a mismatch between expectations and participation and satisfaction levels, and consequently the quality of participants' boating experiences. Boating can also influence pride in place and community as a result of boating technological developments and associated accolades as well as in relation to sporting competitions, special events, and personal feats. It can also act to sponsor disadvantaged people to have "extraordinary" experiences through benefactor and public programs.

Finally, boating can have a significant impact on quality of life of participants by providing them with opportunities to "re-create" themselves, spend time with family and friends, meet new friends, relax, experience challenge and adventure, appreciate nature, engage and interact with others outside their usual milieu, as well as develop skills and knowledge regarding boating as a tourism, sport, leisure, or recreation experience.

Environmental Impacts

As already noted, aspects of sailing covered in Chapter 2 have relevance to discussions in this chapter. This is particularly true of environmental impacts, so these will only be briefly reiterated here. They will also be readdressed in Chapter 12. The primary impacts relate to:

- Disturbance to ecosystems (see discussions by Mabie, Johnson, Thompson, Barron, and Taylor 1989; West and Church 1991; Pickering 1995; Galicia and Baldassarre

1997), such as negative impacts to bird colonies as a result of motorized activities occurring in their habitats (see Chapter 4 for a detailed discussion of these impacts)

- Jetty, marina, or pontoon constructions change "traditional" marine, estuary, or riverine, wetland ecosystems. (See Widmer, Underwood, and Chapman 2002 for insight into one study of resident perceptions regarding environmental impacts of boating. Refer also to Chapter 4.)
- Boat standings causing ecological problems (Brodersen 1994)
- Boat maintenance materials impacting on the environment. For example, lead-based antifouling has been banned in a number of nations due to the toxicity of leaching.
- Onboard waste management (see Vander-Stoep 1997)
- Boating groundings and impacts
- Dealing with no-longer-relevant boating materials from a waste management perspective.

Economic Impacts

Boating can generate private, public, and nonprofit ventures; small business entrepreneurship; and employment (British Waterways Board 1986). Boaters can also contribute significantly to local communities as a result of their daily expenditure patterns as evidenced in research associated with British waterways usage (British Waterways 1990). Expenditures on boating trips include boat and car fuel, provisions and en-route snacks, restaurant meals, and entertainment (Lee 2001). The magnitude of boat trip expenditure is exemplified by a study in Michigan in 1998, where it was found that US$635 million was spent as a result of 18.4 million individual boating days linked to 652,000 registered boats (Lee 2002). See also Smith (1987) for further discussion of "relative local magnitude of tourism" measurements related to boating and cottaging.

Additionally, marina developments (Figure 3-2), while possibly considered a negative environmental impact, can also be positive due to related income, investment, and employment generation as well as associated multiplier effects (see Agricultural Experiment Station, Michigan State University 2000). In the past, however, coastal locations in the Mediterranean have experienced some economic difficulties following the boom years of the 1980s. In the subsequent recession, older established marinas were seen to have a competitive edge over newer ones that struggled to succeed (Smith and Jenner 1995). Further, negative marina impacts are linked to marina occupancies being related to water levels, and low water levels reduce occupancy rates (Agricultural Experiment Station, Michigan State University 2000). On the other hand, waterfront developments associated with boating can positively impact on economies, since boats tend to be part of the "waterscape" attraction either for passive or active consumption.

To conclude this subsection, a comment regarding the weather, an integral ingredient in the quality of boating experiences, will be made. In the early 2000s, economic impacts of boating have been severely impacted in coastal zones following catastrophic natural events, such as the 2005 Hurricane Katrina and Hurricane Wilma events and the Tsunami in Asia. After such events, there are major rebuilding and reestablishment issues as well as the need to win back consumer confidence in accessing such areas for boating experiences. Initially after

Figure 3-2 Motor and sailing boats, Keppel Bay Marina, Australia. Photographer: Ross Rynehart.

such times, expenditure on sport, leisure, recreation, and tourism takes a back seat while key basic services, goods, infrastructure, superstructure, and facilities are reintroduced into the affected areas. That is not to say sport, leisure, recreation, and tourism are not valued. They are relevant; it is just that other core needs are usually addressed first.

As with most water-based experiences, boating is associated with both positive and negative socio-cultural, environmental, and economic impacts. So what is the future for boating, and will it prove to be a "sustainable" water-based experience? The next section reflects on this question.

Future Directions

Boating looks likely to continue as a popular water-based experience, if only because it is affiliated with other water-based experiences. In addition, when nations such as the United States, where the majority of the world's boat ownership is concentrated, embark on a national strategy to increase participation in boating as well as fishing (see this chapter's case study), then the future of boating looks assured in the short to medium term. However, the key to the positioning of boating as one of the industrialized world's most popular water-based activities lies in the diversity of boating opportunities, linkage with other related water-based experiences, continued technological development, improved standards of living, socialization practices that esteem and value boating for a variety of reasons, influence of the demonstration effect, marketing strategies and endeavors by companies, industry sectors (and government agencies), education of users and potential users, infrastructure and facility development, and diligent and careful resource management strategies.

In regard to the latter, implications for resource managers appear to indicate a need for ongoing and further research concerning boating participation (see Fedler 2000b, for example), boating patterns, and interpretations of quality boating experiences. With such scientific data and empirically based information, informed dialogue can occur to develop strategies founded upon consultation with stakeholders so as to ensure the quality and "sustainability" of boating and other water-based experiences.

Therefore, to ensure quality of boating experiences and sustainability of water resources, management agencies and stakeholder groups might consider the following range of tools already used by the Great Barrier Reef Marine Park Authority as well as other agencies:

• Resource inventories
• The precautionary principle
• Research
• Public participation
• Tourism and recreational opportunity spectra
• Zoning maps
• Representative areas plans
• Management plans
• Permits
• Education
• Best practice codes
• Enforcement strategies (see Jennings 1998 for an extended discussion, as well as Chapter 12 in this volume).

Further, it is anticipated that consideration of global warming in regard to water resources, jetties, marinas, boating storage, and boating access points will become an issue (see Wall and Clair 1998). So too, the influence of El Niño and La Niña and resultant weather turmoil such as Hurricanes Katrina and Wilma and their impacts on coastal zones, boating-related infrastructure, and facilities and response strategies will continue to be issues in the future.

Case Study: Recreational Boating and Fishing Foundation

This study focuses on the nonprofit Recreational Boating and Fishing Foundation (RBFF) in the United States. The foundation was established in 1998 in order to develop a "national strategic plan" for the National Outreach and Communication Program as a result of US$36 million in funding associated with the Sportfishing and Boating Safety Act (RBFF 2005). The Act was amended in 2005 (for amendments, see http://www.theorator.com/bills109/s421.html). The mission of the foundation is "to increase participation in recreational angling and boating and thereby increase public awareness and appreciation of the need for protecting, conserving, and restoring this nation's aquatic natural resources" (RBFF 2005). According to the RBFF, although fishing and boating participation involves over 50 million

Americans, growth in fishing and boating has not matched population increases or reflected positive consequences from improved economic growth. In fact, the RBFF reports a decline in participation numbers in some states. Essentially the RBFF is concerned with:

- "Aquatic resources stewardship
- Quality of life
- The economy" (RBFF 2005).

After a process of consensus building among key stakeholders such as state and federal fisheries, natural resources and tourism agencies, conservation groups, and boaters and fishers (RBFF 2005), the National Outreach and Communication Program identified five objectives. The first was related to increasing participation; the second, user education; the third, specific market targeting; the fourth, stakeholder education; and the fifth, ensuring ease and simplicity in access and availability of boating and fishing sites (Fedler 2000b).

In addressing the third objective, Fedler (2000b) conducted a literature review for the RBFF to determine the current status of participation, factors influencing participation, and marketing strategies to increase participation. As a result, Fedler (2000a) made the following background comments regarding the United States:

- There is a slowing in growth in the population.
- Population in 2000 was estimated at 275 million.
- In 2000, population was estimated to be constituted of whites 82%, Blacks 13%, others 5%.
- By 2020, an estimated 37% of population growth would be associated with minority groups, primarily African Americans and Asian minorities.
- By 2020, those of Hispanic ethnic origin will comprise 47% of growth.
- By 2020, Anglo Americans were estimated to continue to represent the majority of the population and therefore also the most of the growth.

Fedler (2000b) made the following key comments regarding boating participation:

- There are an estimated 22 to 24 million adult (16 years and over) boaters.
- Annually, 37 to 46 million people go boating.
- Women represent approximately 50% of the population; 16% of women go boating.
- Approximately 47% of the population has gone boating a minimum of once in their lives.
- Boating registrations increased over the period 1990–1998.
- 60–70% of boaters engage in fishing.
- A majority of boaters live in urban or near urban precincts.
- Age, gender, and ethnicity influence participation in boating.
- Participation in boating declines markedly around age16; this is particularly apparent in young women.
- Significant decline in young women's participation can be attributed to socialization toward what are deemed as "feminine" activities.
- A second decline in boating participation occurs around age 45.
- Participation by women in boating is affected by other social role expectations, their gender assignation as women, safety and security issues, as well as limited boating knowledge and skill bases.
- Participation by Blacks, Hispanics, and Asians is substantially low.

In relation to marketing strategies, Fedler (2000b) recommends the following priority markets:

(a) Men in order to
  - Hold constant and/or increase participation rates and frequency
  - Mentor children
  - Socialize spouses and friends.

  Marketing emphasis—"challenge, relaxation, and family."

(b) Women in order to
  - Increase participation.

  Focus on
  - Those over 45, the aging market;
  - Education regarding affordability of boating.

  Marketing emphasis—outdoors, independence, agency.

(c) "Dropouts" (from boating participation) in order to
  - Reconnect with boating, especially women

  Focus on
  - Those over 45, the aging market.

  Marketing emphasis—outdoors, family activity, challenge, escape, relaxation.

(d) Youth in order to
  - Maintain participation.

  Focus on research to determine reasons for "dropping out" in order to develop marketing emphasis.

(e) Minority groups in order to
  - Increase and/or maintain participation.

Focus on research to determine reasons for participation and nonparticipation as well as participation rates in order to develop appropriate marketing strategies. Focus on state rather than federal marketing strategies due to the diversity in distribution of minority groups all across the United States.

In conclusion, Fedler (2000a) comments that "[o]verall, the literature review identifies a clear need for focused research, particularly for boating" (p. 9). It is hoped that this research will be taken up by interested readers, in order to increase our knowledge about this particular form of water-based experience.

References

Agricultural Experiment Station, Michigan State University. (2000). The benefits of boating. *Futures*, **4** (1–2), 24–26.

Baulch, V., and P. Shermever. (n.d.). Gar Wood, speed-boat king. *The Detroit News*. Accessed October 28, 2005, from http://info.detnews.com/history/story/index.cfm?id=126&category=sports

Berno, T., Moore, K., Simmons, D., and V. Hart. (1996). The nature of the adventure tourism experience in Queenstown, New Zealand. *Australian Leisure,* **7** (2) 21–25.

British Waterways. (1990). *Seven waterways: 1990 boating survey.* Planning and Research Paper. Ricksmansworth, Hertfordshire, UK: British Waterways.

British Waterways Board. (1986). *The British waterways system. Leisure and tourism on inland waterways.* Leisure Research Paper No. 23. Watford, Hertfordshire, UK. British Waterways Board.

Brodersen, J. (1994). Nature conservation and water sports. The legal position of boat standings on banks and coasts in Schleswig-Holstein. *Naturschutz-und-Landschaftsplanung,* **26** (3), 102–105.

Butler, R.W. (1989). Tourism and tourism research. In E.L. Jackson and T.L. Burton (Eds.), *Understanding leisure and recreation: mapping the past, charting the future.* (pp. 567–595). State College, PA: Venture Publishing.

Butler, R.W., and L.A. Waldbrook. (1991). A new planning tool: the Tourism Opportunity Spectrum. *Journal of Tourism Studies,* **2** (1) May, 2–14.

Ditton, R., Loomis, D., and S. Choi. (1992). Recreation specialization: re-conceptualization from a social worlds perspective. *Journal of Leisure Research,* **24** (1), 33–51.

Donnelly, M.P., Vaske, J.J., and A.R. Graefe. (1986). Degree and range of recreation specialization: toward a typology of boating related activities. *Journal of Leisure Research,* **18** (2), 81–95.

Dovers, S. (1994). Recreational fishing in Australia: review and policy issues. *Australian Geographical Studies,* **32** (1), 102–114.

Driml, S. (1996). Coastal and marine tourism and recreation. In L. Zann (Ed.), *The state of the marine environment report for Australia: technical report.* Townsville, Great Barrier Reef Marine Park Authority for Ocean Rescue 2000 Program, Department of Environment, Sport and Territories, Canberra, Australia.

Driver, B. (1989). In M. Watson, *Recreation planning: a seminar summary and discussion of the ROS and LAC models.* Report submitted to the Great Barrier Reef Marine Park Authority, Townsville, Queensland, Australia.

Fairweather, J.R., and S.R. Swaffield. (2001). Visitor experiences of Kaikoura, New Zealand: an interpretative study using photographs of landscapes and Q method. *Tourism Management,* **22** (3), 219–228.

Fay, C.H., McCure, J.T. and J.P. Begin. (1987). The setting for continuing education in the year 2000. *New Directions for Continuing Education,* **36** (Winter), 15–27.

Fedler, A.J. (2000a). *Participation in boating and fishing: a literature review: Executive Summary.* Report to Recreational Boating and Fishing Foundation, Alexandria, Virginia. Prepared by Human Dimensions Consulting, Gainesville, FL.

Fedler, A.J. (2000b). *Participation in boating and fishing: a literature review.* Report to Recreational Boating and Fishing Foundation, Alexandria, Virginia. Prepared by Human Dimensions Consulting, Gainesville, FL.

Fedler, A.J., and R.B. Ditton. (1994). Understanding angler motivations in fisheries management. *Fisheries,* **19** (4), 6–13.

Foster, S.E. (1986). Public rights of navigation on inland waterways. *Journal of Planning and Environment,* May, 336–339.

Frigden, J.D., and J.D. Wood Jr. (1985). Recreation and tourism in the coastal zone. In *Proceedings of the 1985 National Outdoor Recreation Trends Symposium II,* concurrent sessions, **II,** 6–20. Held at Myrtle Beach, SC, February, 24–27. Atlanta, GA: Science Publications Office, National Parks Service, U.S. Department of the Interior.

Gabe, T.M., and D. Hite. (2003). The effects of boating safety regulations. *Coastal Management,* July/August, **31** (3), 247–254.

Galicia, E., and G.A. Baldassarre. (1997). Effects of motorized tourboats on the behavior of nonbreeding American flamingos in Yucatan, Mexico. *Conservation Biology*, **11** (5), 1159–1165.

Gartside, D.F. (1986). Recreational fishing, Paper presented to National Coastal Management Conference, Coffs Harbour, Australia in *Safish*, **11** (2), March/April, 15–17.

Geen, G., and P. Lal. (1991). *Charging users of the Great Barrier Reef Marine Park*. Report to the Great Barrier Reef Marine Park Authority, Australian Bureau of Agricultural and Resource Economics, Canberra.

Gjesdal, O., Sulebak, J.R., Borge, M., Woer, K., Frew, A.J. and M. Hitz. (2002). Market research in the boat tourism segment. *Information and communication technologies in tourism 2002: Proceedings of the International Conference in Innsbruck, Austria, 2002*. Wien, Austria: Springer-Verlag.

Graefe, A.R., and A.J. Fedler. (1986). Situational and subjective determinants of satisfaction in marine recreational fishing. *Leisure Sciences*, **8** (3), 275–295.

Graefe, A., Donnelly, M., and J. Vaske. (1986). Crowding and specialization: a re-examination of the crowding model. In *Proceedings of the National Wilderness Research Conference: Current Research*. (General Technical Report INT-212, pp. 333–338; R. Lucas, Ed.). Denver, CO: U.S. Department of Agriculture, Forest Service Intermountain Research Station.

Hobden, H. (n.d.). *Mary Gordon Electric Boat history and restoration. Origins of the Mary Gordon Electric Launch, the source of the electric power*. Accessed October 28, 2005, from http://www.marygordon.org.uk/batteries.htm

Jaakson, R. (1989). Recreation boating and spatial patterns: theory and management. *Leisure Sciences*, **11**, 85–98.

Jackson, E.L. (1986). Outdoor recreation participation and attitudes to the environment. *Leisure Studies*, **5**, 1–23.

Jacob, G.R., and R. Schreyer. (1980). Conflict in outdoor recreation: a theoretical perspective. *Journal of Leisure Research*, **12**, 368–380.

Jennings, G. (1998). *Recreational usage patterns of Shoalwater Bay and adjacent waters*. (Research publication No. 50). Townsville, Queensland, Australia: Great Barrier Reef Marine Park Authority.

Johns, N., and V. Clarke. (2001). Mythological analysis of boating tourism. *Annals of Tourism Research*, **28** (2), 334–359.

Johnson, J.C., and M.K. Orbach. (1986). The role of cultural context in the development of low-capital ocean leisure activities. *Leisure Sciences*, **8** (3), 319–339.

Kaufman, R., and A. Graefe. (1984). Canoeing specialization, expected rewards, and resource related attitudes. In J. Popodic, D. Butterfield, D. Anderson, and M. Popodic (Eds.), *Proceedings of the National River Recreation Symposium*. (pp. 629–641). Baton Rouge: Louisiana State University.

Kenchington, R. (1993). Tourism in coastal and marine environments—a recreational perspective. *Ocean and Coastal Management*, **19**, 1–16.

Kerstetter, D.L., Confer, J.J., and A.R. Graefe. (2001). An exploration of the specialization concept within the context of heritage tourism. *Journal of Tourism Research*, **39**, 267–274.

Kotani, K. (1991). Promoting the use of pleasure boats in Japan. *Japan 21st*, November, **36** (11), 123–125.

Lazareck, R. (1984, October 19–20). Cooperative tourism and rural organization in Bulgaria, Hungary, Poland, Romania, Czechoslovakia. *Proceedings of Le Tourisme en Milieu Rural.* (pp. 115–117). Madrid, Spain: Congres de Madrid.

Lee, H.C. (2001). Determinants of recreational boater expenditures on trips. *Tourism Management*, **22** (6), 659–667.

Lee, H.C. (2002). Regional flows of recreational boater expenditures on trips in Michigan. *Journal of Travel Research*, **41** (1), 77–84.

Leyrat, F. (1994). Navigation de plaisance: grand frais sur l'espace nautique european. *Espaces-Paris*, No. 130, 9–12.

Lipscombe, N. (1996). The aged and adventure: a perfect match. *Australian Leisure*, **7** (3), 38–41.

Lipton, D. W., and R. Hicks. (1999). Boat location choice: The role of boating quality and excise taxes. *Coastal Management*, **27** (1), 81–89.

Logan, P., Sacks, J.J., Branche, C.M., Ryan, G.W., and P. Bender. (1999). Alcohol-influenced recreational boating operation in the United States: a study of recreational boats, boaters, and accidents in the United States. *American Journal of Preventative Medicine*, **16** (4), 278–282.

Mabie, D.W., Johnson, L.A., Thompson, B.C., Barron, J.C., and R.B. Taylor. (1989). Responses of wintering whooping cranes to airboat and hunting activities on the Texas coast. *Wildlife Society Bulletin*, **17** (3), 249–253.

Manfredo, M.J. (1989). An investigation of the basis for external information search in recreation and tourism. *Leisure Sciences*, **11** (1), 29–45.

Martin, W.H., and S. Mason. (1987). Social trends and tourism futures. *Tourism Management*, **8** (2), 112–114.

McCool, S. F. (1989). Limits of acceptable change: some principles. In R. Graham and R. Lawrence (Eds.), *Towards serving visitors and managing our resources.* (pp. 195–200). Proceedings of workshop on visitor management, University of Waterloo, Ontario, Canada.

McKnight, A.J., Lange, J.E., and A.S. McKnight. (1998). *Accident Analysis and Prevention*, **31** (1), 147–152.

Meyer, R. (1999). Activity involvement, equipment, and geographic connection to recreation area: the case of boaters in southeastern Norway. *Norsk Geografisk Tidsskrift*, **53** (1), 17–27.

Ministry of Tourism and Recreation, Tourism Research Section. (1985). *1984 Ontario/Canada boating guide survey.* Toronto, Ontario, Canada: Ministry of Tourism and Recreation, Tourism Research Section.

Nederlands Research Instituut voor Recreatie en Toerisme. (1986). *Tourism Trends 1986.* Breda, Netherlands; Nederlands Research Instituut voor Recreatie en Tourisme.

Nielsen, J., Shelby, B., and J.E. Haas. (1977). Sociological carrying capacity and the last settler syndrome. *Pacific Sociological Review*, **20** (4), October, 568–581.

Oelrichs, I. (1994, April). Values tourism and endemic tourism planning: sustainable tourism with a community focus. *Tourism ecodollars.* Conference proceedings, Mackay, North Queensland, Australia.

Orams, M. (1999). *Marine tourism: development, impacts, and management.* London: Routledge.

Otis, S.H. (1988). It's high time for tourists at rejuvenated marinas. *Parks and Recreation*, **23** (4), 32–37.

Ott. (1990). Situation and potential for Bavarian tourism. *Idegenforgalmi*, (2), 36–37.

Panne, G. (1990). Burgundy: waterways are growing in popularity. *Espaces-Paris*, (106), 43–48.

Pickering, H.J. (1995). Conserving the threatened coastal resource against all odds. *Natural Areas Journal*, **15** (1), 50–60.

Pleasure boating to grow with increase in leisure time. (1987). *Business Japan*, **32**(11–12), November/December, 63–64.

Prokopy, J., Crandall, D.A., Baker, P.R., Godsman, J., and A.J. Tighe. (1988). Outlook for rail travel; recreation: the use of the National Park Service, the cruise industry; and arts and tourism. In *1988 Outlook for travel and tourism*. Proceedings of the U.S. Travel Center's Thirteenth Annual Travel Outlook Forum, October 27, 1987, Reno, NV, pp. 233–252. Washington, DC: U.S. Travel Data Center.

Reed-Andersen, T., Bennett, E.M., Jorgensen, B.S., Lauster, G., Lewis, D.B., and Nowacek, D., Riera, J.L., Sanderson, B.L. and R. Stedman. (2000). Distribution of recreational boating across lakes: do landscape variables affect recreational use? *Freshwater Biology*, **43** (3), 439–448.

Recreational Boating and Fishing Foundation. (n.d.). *What is RBFF?* Accessed October, 14, 2005, from http://www.rbff.org/about/index.cfm?exp=yes

Roy Morgan Research Centre. (1985). *Australians' physical activity, July 1984; January–February, 1985*. A report for the Department of Sport, Recreation and Tourism. Melbourne, Australia: Roy Morgan Research Centre.

Schemel, H.-J. (2001). *Sports and the environment: conflicts and solutions—a manual*. Translated by Arne A. Jaaska in consultation with Wolfgang Strasdas. 3rd rev. ed. Oxford: Meyer and Meyer Sport.

Schwaninger, M. (1989). Trends in leisure and tourism for 2000–2010: Scenario with consequences for planners. In S.F. Witt and L. Mouton (Eds.), *Tourism marketing and management handbook*. New York: Prentice Hall.

Silver, S.M., and N.B. Hampson. (1996). Carbon monoxide poisoning among recreational boaters. *Journal of Safety Research*, **27** (4), 273.

Smith, C., and P. Jenner. (1995). Marinas in Europe. *Travel and Tourism Analyst*, (6), 56–72.

Smith, S.L.J. (1987). Regional analysis of tourism resources. *Annals of tourism research*, **14** (2), 254–273.

Sportfishing and Recreational Boating Safety Act of 2005. Accessed October 29, 2005, from http://www.theorator.com/bills109/s421.html

Stankey, G.H., McCool, S.F., and G.L. Stokes. (1984). Limits of acceptable change: a new framework for managing the Bob Marshall Wilderness Complex. *Western Midlands*, Fall, 3–7.

Stankey, G.H., and J. Wood. (1982). The recreation opportunity spectrum: an introduction. *Australian Parks and Recreation*, February, 6–14.

Stebbins, R.A. (1992). *Amateurs, professionals, and serious leisure*. Montreal, Quebec, Canada: McGill-Queen's University Press.

Struna, N.L., Mangan, J.A., and R.J. Park. (1987). "Good wives" and "gardeners," spinners and "fearless riders": middle and upper rank women in the early American sporting culture. In J.A. Mangan (Ed.), *From "fair sex" to feminism: sport and the socialization of women in the industrial and post-industrial era*. (pp. 235–255). London: Frank Cass.

Swedburg, R.B., and L. Ostiguy. (1994). Welcome to the ice age. *Parks and Recreation*, **29** (1), 56–61.

U. S. Department of the Interior, Bureau of Land Management. (1990). *Issues and alternatives for management of the lower Deschutes River.* Prineville, OR: U. S. Department of the Interior, Bureau of Land Management.

Vander-Stoep, G.A. (1997). *Michigan recreational boater compliance with the Clean Vessel Act in use of pumpout and dump stations: relationships between attitudes, knowledge, socio-demographic factors, and behavior.* General Technical Report. Radnor, PA: USDA Forest Service, Northeastern Forest Experiment Station.

Wall, G., and T.A. Clair. (1998). Implications of global climate change for tourism and recreation in wetland areas. Canadian freshwater, wetlands, and climate change. *Climate-change,* **40** (2), 371–389.

Wang, W. (2000). The effects of state regulations on boating accidents and fatalities. *Applied Economics Letters,* **7** (6), 373–378.

Ward, D. (1986). Lightwater Valley: farm, quarry, and leisure. *Estates Gazette,* **280**, (6306), 351–354.

Watson, M. (1989). *Recreation planning: a seminar summary and discussion of the ROS and LAC models.* Report submitted to the Great Barrier Reef Marine Park Authority, Townsville, Queensland, Australia.

Weiler, B., and C.M. Hall. (1992). *Special interest tourism.* London: Belhaven Press.

Wellman, J., Roggenbuck, J., and A. Smith. (1982). Recreation specialization and norms of depreciative behavior. *Journal of Leisure Research,* **14**, 323–340.

West, C., and S. Church. (1991). The Basingstoke canal: a wildlife survival strategy. *Ecos,* **12** (1), 40–43.

West, N. (1990). *Marine recreation in North America.* In P. Fabbri (Ed.), *Recreational uses of coastal areas.* (pp. 257–275). Dordrecht, Netherlands: Kluwer Academic.

Widmer, W., Underwood, A., and M. Chapman. (2002). Recreational boating on Sydney Harbor: public perception of potential environmental impacts. *Natural Resource Management,* **5** (1), 22–27.

Wikipedia. (2005). *Glenn Curtiss.* Accessed October 28, 2005, from http://en. wikipedia.org/wiki/Glenn_Curtiss

Williams, D., and M. Huffman. (1986). Recreation specialization as a factor in back-country trail choice. In R. Lucas (Ed.), *Proceedings of the National Wilderness Research Conference: current research.* (pp. 339–344) (USDA Forest Service, General Technical Report, No. INT-212). Ogden, UT: Intermountain Research Station.

Wu, T.C., Mahoney, E.M., and D.J. Stynes. (1997). Segmentation as a method for improving model generated estimates of recreational boating use. *Visions in Leisure and Business,* **15** (4), 9–19.

Wu, T.C., Mahoney, E.M., and D.J. Stynes. (2000). Segmentation as a method for improving model generated estimates of recreational boating use. *Visions in Leisure and Business,* **18** (3), 15–25.

Zann, L. (Ed.). (1996). *The state of the marine environment report for Australia: technical report.* Townsville, Great Barrier Reef Marine Park Authority for Ocean Rescue 2000 Program. Canberra, Queensland, Australia: Department of Environment, Sport and Territories.

Websites

British Waterways: http://www.britishwaterways.co.uk
Great Barrier Reef Marine Park Authority: http://www.gbrmpa.gov.au
Recreational Boating and Fishing Foundation: http://www.rbff.org

II

Sport or Extreme Sport?

The water-based experiences discussed in this section include motorized water sports; surfing and
windsurfing; sport and big game fishing; and scuba
diving, snorkeling, and free diving. As readers are
aware, all of the water-based experiences presented
in this book have their origins in sport, leisure,
and/or recreation. With that being said, the four
chapters that constitute Section II, due to the discourses that surround them, have been categorized
as sport-based experiences and in some instances
may be described as extreme sport experiences.
Harold Richens introduces the notion of extreme
sports in Chapter 4, and Chris Ryan discusses it in

Chapter 5. Variously, the water-based experiences in this section of the book may be engaged in along a continuum from easy to extreme, depending on the presence and degree of mediation, for example, by providers, coaches, instructors, and guides, as well as the nature of match or mismatch between participant skills and challenge(s) of the particular activity.

In Chapter 4, Harold Richins reviews various classifications of motorized sports to offer a global perspective of what constitutes motorized water sports. He compares market share patterns of boating in general with motorized water sports and notes differing trends between the two water-based experiences during the 1990s. Various organizations that promote motorized water sports or participate in impact management are also discussed. Relatedly, Richins provides an intensive coverage of the impacts of motorized water sports, such as physical stress on aquatic life, pollution, loss of amenity, conflict of user interests, and associated management issues, before presenting two case studies respectively drawn from Barbados and Australia. The Barbados example tracks issues related to the establishment of a marine area and subsequent related multi-use issues and strategies used by management to support multiple use of the area. The Australian case study considers a river system, the associated issues of motorized water sports in the system, and the development of a relevant management plan.

Chris Ryan in Chapter 5 presents an extensive background relating to the development of surfing and windsurfing as well as the impact of technology changes on both. Ryan also makes a brief commentary about snowboarding. The consequences of product life cycle and product diffusion are considered. Additionally, Ryan purports that surfing and windsurfing may be labeled as both sports and "cult lifestyle." Motivations related to surfing and windsurfing include a union with nature, as well as self-actualization and "flow" (Csikszentmihalyi 1975, 1990). He identifies a decline in participation from the 1980s to 2000 and suggests that the perception of surfing and windsurfing as established adventure sports served to reduce the number of new participants. Moreover, it is Ryan's opinion that a potential market share among the aging population was not being effectively leveraged. He also notes the historically gendered nature of the sports and discusses the sports' various impacts, especially in lobbying in regard to water quality. The case study, in particular, located in southwest England, reiterates the environmental lobbying function of surfers.

Sport fishing and big game fishing are the focus of Chapter 6. In this chapter, Les Killion focuses on commercial operations related to these types of fishing, in particular charter operations and international big game fishing competitions. He identifies the key locations for pursuit of these water-based experiences and intimates that sport and big game fishing are expensive segments when it comes to participation costs. Killion also acknowledges the role of esteem and ego-enhancement, as well as self-actualization, especially "flow," in relation to motivations for sport and big game fishing participation. In the chapter, he identifies the issues of seasonality as affecting this water-based experience, as well as codes of conduct/ethics, certification, and resource management legislation. He further notes that due to the expensive nature of participation, possible social distance issues between hosts and guests may arise, and this may be especially exacerbated in developing nation–hosted sites. The case study presented in Chapter 6 is situated in Mexico and highlights issues related to codes of conduct or ethics.

In Chapter 7, Kay Dimmock presents an historical overview of the development of scuba diving, snorkeling, and free diving. She reflects on differentiations among tourism, sport, leisure, and recreation experiences and iterates an earlier comment in this book regarding ambiguity and overlap between the terms and their related experiences. Dimmock considers the global dive tourism market and the additional influence on the market of dive sites situated in tropical locations. In considering the market, Dimmock utilizes a special interest typology to assist in market segment differentiation. She also focuses on management issues from three perspectives: education, equipment, and experiences. Additionally, she addresses issues related to small business operations in regard to dive tourism; in particular, Dimmock applies the competing values framework (Quinn, Faerman, Thompson, and McGrath 2003). The chapter identifies preservation, demonstration effects, and loss of amenity as some of the impacts associated with scuba diving, snorkeling, and free diving. The case study focuses on Julian Rocks, an extremely popular dive site adjacent to Byron Bay, Australia, and associated diver behaviors and carrying capacity issues.

In this section of *Water-Based Tourism, Sport, Leisure, and Recreation Experiences,* there are some thematic trends across the four chapters. The themes include extreme sports (Chapters 4 and 5), adventure (Chapters 4, 5, 6, and 7), product life cycles (Chapters 4 and 5), the gendered nature of some water-based experiences (Chapters 5 and 6), subcultural traits (Chapters 5 and 7), as well as management issues and options, which pervade all four chapters and which will be reconsidered in Chapter 12.

4

Motorized Water Sports

Harold Richins

Overview

The popularity of and high participation in marine tourism has been recently acknowledged (Hall 2000) and this has led to challenges, particularly in areas where diverse uses come into contact. Some water- and beach-based activities involve slow-paced, low-impact behavior, while other activities in the same area may involve fast-paced activities with high-impact or safety and noise issues (Fiedler 1996; Vandeman 1998).

Mixing these diverse activities can lead to conflict between the various user groups who are often motivated by divergent or polarized interests (Rockwell 2002). Motorized water sport user groups generally fall into one of the following categories: (1) *leisure,* or those motivated by leisure interests; (2) *active,* or those motivated by activity interests; and (3) *competitive,* or those motivated by competition interests (Queensland Government 1998, 2002). *Leisure* includes sightseeing, looking, learning, unwinding, escaping, relaxing, and experiencing peace and quiet. The desires of this user group are often in direct conflict with those of the *active* group, which includes fitness, skills improvement, using test equipment, challenge, conquering nature, as well as the *competitive* group, which includes motivational dimensions such as maximum distance, minimum time, fastest, most accurate, and most difficult. This diversity and conflict has created emotive and polarized views on the use of motorized water sports.

Various organizations and authors have attempted to define motorized water sports. Some have focused on the motor aspect, while others have focused on the extreme or fast-paced nature of these sports. An organization that focuses on adventure, action, and extreme activities, Rednut Sports (2004), has created a list of extreme sports under its water category, some of which are wind or surf related and some of which are motorized. These include the following:

- Body boards
- Kite surfing

- Drag boats
- Skim boarding
- Surfing
- Wakeboarding
- Freestyle jet skiing
- Wake skating
- Waterskiing
- Hydrofoil
- Whitewater rafting
- Windsurfing
- Powerboat racing.

Of the various organizations that have attempted to define motorized water sports, some have focused on the personal nature of the activity or the propulsion mechanism or speed of the craft. Examples can be found in the United Kingdom, the United States, and Australia. In the UK, the government identified three key areas under their category of Motorized Water Sports. These include powerboating, waterskiing, and jet skiing. Powerboating was defined in terms of offshore ocean activity, with the exception of larger inland bodies of water ("The Effectiveness of Planning Policy Guidance" 1998). The Wales Tourism Board (WTB) identified motorized water sports under their heading of Adventure Tourism (WTB 2002). Motorized water sports included jet skiing, waterskiing, ribbing, and wakeboarding. Additional personal motorized watercraft include names such as Wave Runner, Aqua Jet, Wave Jammer, Wet Jet, Sky Ski, Air Chair, personal hydrofoils and hovercraft, parasailing, barefooting, jet boat, sea cycle, Water Bike, Surf Jet, miniature speedboats, and air boats (National Park Service 1998; Pearce 2000; Aquaskier 2006). The South Carolina government has used the phrase "jet-ski watercraft" and referred to "watercraft that has an inboard motor that uses an internal combustion engine powering a water jet pump as its primary source of motor propulsion" (Regulation of Motorcycle and Jet-Powered Watercraft 1998). The Great Barrier Reef Marine Park Authority (GBRMPA), Australia, has also defined motorized water sports as "activities such as jet skiing, water skiing and parasailing . . . along with any other activities that involve a high-speed vessel if towing a person on the water or in the air and any other activities involving irregular driving of a motorized [water-based] vessel" (GBRMPA 2003). Finally, the Environmental News Service (Lazaroff 2002) has defined powered water craft (PWC) as small vessels that use an inboard motor powering a water jet pump as their primary source of power, and are operated by persons sitting, standing, or kneeling on the vessel.

The terms *personal watercraft* or *personal motorized watercraft* are often used to identify primarily jet ski, water bikes, or "see-doo" type activities (Shank 2002). This category normally includes aquatic craft that are propelled by a water jet drive that enables them to operate in shallow water and be highly maneuverable and capable of high relative speed and acceleration. These watercraft are normally less than three meters in length, are capable of exceeding 15 knots, and have a capacity of one or two people (Monterey Bay National Marine Sanctuary 2001; Bluewater Network 2002).

Throughout the literature, motorized water sports have been classified as more active than other water sports activities and sometimes competitive (Hall 1992), as active non-holiday and holiday activities (Standeven and De Knop 1999), as residing within the adventure tourism form of physical activity and the activity-based tourism category, and occurring on the continuum between less adventurous and more adventurous (Swarbrooke, Beard, Lecki, and Pomfret 2003). Motorized water sports have also been classified as soft adventure rather than hard adventure (Hill 1995; Lipscombe 1995), and part of tourism that includes sport content or sports participation (Weed and Bull 2004).

Standeven and De Knop (1999) developed a typology that merges the nature of the tourist experience (natural or man-made) and the sports experience (environmental and interpersonal). This typology suggests that motorized water sports activities are within the context of the artificial-environmental-natural-coastal experience. Another classification system places adventure on a matrix based on the degree of challenge and independence and includes the following four quadrants: leisure, recreation, adventure competition, and high adventure (Swarbrooke et al. 2003). Motorized water sports may be assigned to the leisure-recreation quadrants in this matrix due to the limited specialist skills required and the independent nature of the experience.

A number of special interest tourism directories have classified water sports activities. Of the approximately 230 special interest tourism categories listed in the Speciality Travel Index (2006), a large number utilize motor methods for some aspects of their primary activity. The identified water sports activities include the following:

- ATV/watercraft rental
- Barge/canal cruising
- Canoeing/kayaking
- Cruise shore excursions
- Cruise expeditions
- Cruises/sailing
- Dolphin research/swim
- Extreme sports/stunts
- Fly-in hiking/rafting
- Houseboating
- Jet boat expeditions
- Jet skiing
- River cruises/expeditions
- River/whitewater rafting
- Sailing
- Scuba/snorkeling
- Sea kayaking
- Seaplane services
- Surfing
- Waterskiing
- Whale watching
- Windjamming
- Windsurfing
- Yacht charter, bareboat
- Yacht charter, crewed
- Yacht charter, power.

Travel-Quest Specialist Travel Directory (2004), a UK-based enterprise, has listed 19 water sports in their index. These include the following:

- Canal/barge cruises
- Canoeing/kayaking
- Cruises (ocean)
- Cruises (river/lake)
- Diving/snorkeling
- Jet skiing
- Kite surfing
- Powered boating
- Sailing (catamaran)
- Sailing (large boat/sail ship)
- Sailing (small boat/yacht)
- Sea canoeing/sea kayaking
- Surfing
- Swimming
- Theme cruises
- Wakeboarding
- Waterskiing
- Whitewater rafting
- Windsurfing.

Similar water sports remain in the company's directory in 2006 (Travel-Quest 2006).

In reviewing the definitions for motorized water sports above, the primary similarities include a focus on the motor aspect, as well as the extreme or fast-paced and maneuverable nature of these sports, many of which are conducted by one individual or by two people. The next section will discuss the market profile of these specialized water activities.

Market Profile

Boating use grew rapidly in many countries for a number of decades during the second half of the twentieth century (Talhelm and Vrana 1995); however, some reports suggest that recent international boat ownership has had a sharp decrease. Though leisure spending has dramatically increased, the share of boating purchases as a portion of total leisure purchases decreased by half over a 10-year period in the late 1990s (Standeven and De Knop 1999). The reasons for this decline are uncertain, but it may be due to an aging population or a shift to other forms of leisure activities. Further research is needed to examine this trend in more detail.

Although there has been a period where the share of boating purchases has decreased or slowed internationally, there has been an increase in motorized water activities in general in the U.S. market. Between 1983 and 1995, motorboat ownership based in the United States grew at a much higher rate (40%) than the rate of increase in the U.S. population (15%). Waterskiing, on the other hand, grew at almost the same rate (13%) as the rate of increase in the U.S. population (Cordell 1999).

Segments of the Australian market have a similarly strong involvement in motorized water activities. The Australian Bureau of Statistics (2000) conducted a study of Australian participation in outdoor recreational activities in 1999–2000. Of the 9,000 people surveyed, just over 2% of the total indicated involvement in waterskiing and powerboating. In Queensland, Australia, however, a South East Queensland Recreation Demand Study conducted in 1997 found that 25% of people over 15 years of age had ridden on a motorized watercraft (Queensland Government 1998). This is significantly higher than those indicating participation in non-motorized watercraft activities (17% of respondents). In addition, 32% of nonparticipants expressed their interest in future participation in motorized water sports. Reasons cited by nonparticipants for their lack of involvement included "no time," "too busy," "no equipment," and "can't afford it." A similar study conducted in Central Queensland, Australia, supported the high involvement of Queenslanders in motorized water sports, finding that 31% of respondents indicated having ridden on motorized watercraft while just under 18% indicated involvement in non-motorized watercraft activities (Queensland Government 2000). Table 4-1 compares the results from the more recently published 2002 Outdoor Recreation Activities in Queensland study and the Central Queensland study in 2000.

A variety of demographic segments are represented in motorized water sports. Though there is participation across a broad range of age groups, it is particularly high with younger people (under 20) and lower with those 65 or older, as one would anticipate. The "under 20" segment participates in motorized water sports an average of just over three times per year (3.3) compared with non-motorized watercraft at 2.5 times per year (Queensland Government 2000). Results of the 1998 South East Queensland Recreation Demand Study showed women to be significantly less likely to participate in motorized watercraft (21%) compared to males (30%).

Finally, in examining the market profile of jet ski use only, the jet ski market reached a plateau in 1995 and has steadily decreased in units sold (Figure 4-1). Reasons for this reduced demand have included the stage in the product life cycle,

Table 4-1   Outdoor Recreation Activities in Queensland

	South East Queensland (2001)	Central Queensland (2000)
Picnicking	67%	62%
Walking or nature study	49%	54%
Swimming (not in built pools)	–	47%
Driving 2WD on unsealed roads	24%	46%
Driving 4WD on tracks/unsealed roads	23%	37%
Camping	33%	36%
Riding on motorized watercraft	27%	31%
Bicycle riding	26%	20%
Riding on non-motorized watercraft	19%	18%
Driving other vehicles	7%	13%
Horse riding	7%	11%
Abseiling or rock climbing	6%	6%

Sources: Kiewa, Brown, and Hibbins. (2002). South East Queensland Outdoor Recreation Demand Study for (September–November 2002) for Queensland Government and Central Queensland Study, Queensland Government (2000).

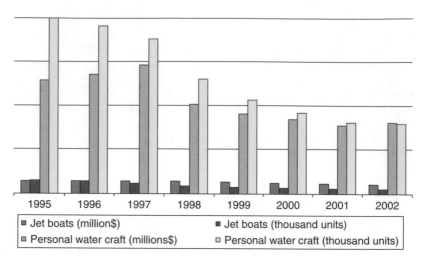

Figure 4-1 Number of personal watercraft sales 1995–2002 in the United States (total units sold and total sales including jet skis). Source: National Marine Manufacturing Association (1998; 2003).

and even though numerous new models have been introduced, the total sales have continued to decline. Another reason for this reduction in the jet ski market is the image problem arising from negative publicity due to environmental or water pollution and safety issues (Shank 2002).

Advantages

The advantages of motorized water sports have some similarity to those of other forms of special interest tourism. Economic benefits for the local community, extending the range of offerings for a local area (value adding to the base leisure product), and the sense of adventure and enjoyment in participating in these outdoor water sports and activities for the consumer are the key advantages (Figure 4-2).

As with most tourist offerings, there can be substantial economic benefit to the local and regional community. A study of yearly expenditure on outdoor recreational activity in South East Queensland found that respondents spent an average of AU$1,277 (US$968) on activities related to motorized watercraft (Australian Bureau of Statistics 1998). This is close to four times the money spent on non-motorized watercraft and equates to the second-highest total yearly expenditure among recreational activity (just below motorized sports, which includes four-wheel driving).

A number of advantages of using personal motorized watercraft have been suggested. These have primarily focused on affordability, ease of use, handling and maneuverability, exhilaration, and excitement (Fontaine 2002; Williams, C. 2003). Monita Fontaine, Executive Director of the Personal Watercraft Industry Association, believes it is the "perfect vessel. It is the boat of the future, and it is

Figure 4-2 Jet boat shuttle bus, Shotover River, Queenstown, New Zealand. Photographer: Gayle Jennings.

here today. It can be tailored. It has high performance standards. It is convenient. It is something that anybody can handle with the appropriate education. And it is something that is going to appeal to the busy family that wants to take time to take their children out on the water. You don't have to be wealthy to have one. You don't have to have a huge SUV [Sport Utility Vehicle] to tow it. It makes sense from an environmental point of view. I can't think of a more affordable, better boat for the family than this" (Fontaine 2002, p. 24).

Though a number of types of motorized water sports have many of the characteristics of adventure tourism, they are seldom included in academic definitions or in the adventure tourism literature. Motivations for involvement in motorized water sports, particularly personal motorized watercraft, would be similar to that for special interest tourism and would include a deliberate risk component (Weiler and Hall 1992), high level of participation, challenge, physical exertion, and activity (Iso-Ahola 1980; Kearsely 1990), and involvement in recreation that is fun and exciting in a natural setting (Weaver 2001). Figure 4-3 shows an example of the latter.

Impacts

The advent of specialized water sports as an increasing tourism activity has presented both opportunities as well as threats for the local community, creating particular concern for those committed to sustainable management practices. This section begins with an overview of those organizations that have attempted to control and minimize the impacts of motorized water sports and then provides a more in-depth discussion of these impacts.

Numerous organizations at the regional, national, and international levels have attempted to control and minimize the impacts of motorized water sports in natural areas. Table 4-2 is a list of some of those organizations.

In addition, there are a number of organizations that advocate or promote various forms of motorized water sports. Some of these are listed in Table 4-3.

Figure 4-3   Shotorver jet boat, Shotover River near Queenstown, New Zealand. Photographer: Gayle Jennings.

A variety of impacts have been identified regarding use of motorized watercraft (Sports Council 1993; Standeven and De Knop 1999). Two key concerns were found to be wildlife disturbance and habitat erosion (UK Ceed 1993; Ward and Andrews 1993; Warrington 1999). As these concerns were further explored, the

Table 4-2   Organizations Focused on Minimizing and Controlling Personal Motorized Water Sports

Organization	Focus on Issues Related to Personal Motorized Watercraft (PMW)
Australian Marine Conservation Society	Marine conservation in Australia
Bluewater Network	Minimizing jet ski use in natural areas
British Columbia Marine Awareness Society	Awareness of marine issues and related motorized watercraft issues
Center for Marine Conservation	Marine conservation
Fly Rod and Reel	Minimizing PMW near fishing areas
Health Watcher	Safety of PMW
National Parks and Conservation Association	Conservation of national parks
Natural Trails and Waters Coalition	Various, land, snow, and water impacts
Ontario Environmental Network	Focus on environmental issues in Ontario
Swan River Trust	Control of PMW usage in Swan River, Perth, Australia
Port Hacking Protection Society	Control of PMW usage in Port Hacking, New South Wales, Australia
Black Hills Audubon Society	Concerned with effects of PMW on bird life
Noise Pollution Clearinghouse	Various forms of noise issues and their impact on human disturbance

Table 4-3   Organizations Focused on Advocating and Promoting Personal Motorized Water Sports

Organization	Focus on Issues Related to Personal Motorized Watercraft (PMW)
American Water Ski Association	Promotion and development of water ski sports
Americans for Responsible Recreational Access	Advocating use of public lands and waterways for recreational use
British Water Ski Association	Promotion and development of water ski sports
I. R. Iran Canoe/Kayak and Water Ski Federation	Multiple water sports development and promotion
International Jet Sports Boating Association	Promotion and development of waterskiing, internationally
International Water Ski Federation	Promotion and development of jet sports, internationally
Personal Watercraft Industry Association	Advocating the free use of PMW
Singapore Water Ski and Wakeboard Federation	Promotion and development of waterskiing and wakeboarding
Turkish Underwater Sports, Life-Saving, Water Ski, and Fin Swimming Federation	Multiple water sports development and promotion
Australian Water Ski Federation	Promotion and development of water ski sports
International Council of Marine Industry Associations	Development and advocacy of various water sports associations

following impact categories were identified: (1) direct physical stresses on aquatic organisms, (2) negative impacts on the physical environment, and (3) biological effects of pollutants (Stolpe 1992; Standeven and De Knop 1999; Stokowski 2000).

Another framework was developed for categorizing the impacts of a specific motorized watercraft, towed water sports. Various impacts from towed water sports were identified in a handout published by the International Water Ski Federation and included the following categories: Noise—engine and human; Pollution—chemicals, gases, solid wastes, and biological contamination; Geomorphology; Hydrology—shoreline and flora degradation and turbidity; and Birds and Wildlife—disturbance and dislocation (International Water Ski Federation n.d.).

There have been particular concerns regarding the effects of marine motors on fish life (Tjarnllund, Ericson, Lindesjoo, Petterson, and Balk 1993; Tjarnllund 1996), on bird life (Burger 1998; Rogers and Smith 1995), and on other aspects of aquatic ecosystems (Jeffries and Mills 1990). In addition, waterfowl have been found to be particularly affected by fast-moving, water-based motorcraft. Further, fisheries have the potential to be significantly jeopardized by watercraft usage, as the majority of fisheries are dependent on estuaries for their livelihood.

The UK Marine SACs (Special Areas of Conservation) Project (2001) identified the following areas of impact for waterskiing in coastal regions:

1. Launching from access points that involves trampling and scouring of the feature
2. Launching from informal access points that may result in compaction and erosion of features and vegetation damage
3. Noise disturbance that may have an impact on marine mammals and has an amenity impact on humans

4. Disturbance to wildlife is normally localized; however, wildlife may be disturbed where concentration occurs.
5. Where depth of water is more than two meters, studies have shown minimal disturbance to features.

References are also made to engine emissions; however, it is noted that water-ski craft often use propane fuel, which has lower hydrocarbon emissions.

Further negative impacts of motorized watercraft activities are listed in Figure 4-4, with a fourth impact category added, related to human interaction.

The impacts of motorized water activities are discussed in more detail below using the four primary categories identified in Figure 4-4: (1) direct physical stresses on aquatic organisms, (2) biological effects of pollutants, (3) negative impacts on the physical environment, and (4) impact on the human leisure experience.

1. Direct Physical Stresses on Aquatic Organisms

a. Impacts by Propeller Leading Edges

This can have a significant impact on various water life including large marine mammals and fish. The speed of certain motorized watercraft makes it virtually impossible for many marine mammals to respond. Waterfowl are normally not as

Direct physical stresses on aquatic organisms	Negative impacts on the physical environment
Impacts by propeller leading edges	Hydrocarbon increase
Impacts of hull parts	Boat engine emissions
Propeller- or jet-generated turbulence and shear force	Leaching of toxics
Propeller bottom scouring	Spills during fuelling operations
Hull-generated rotational forces	Bank vegetation damage
Animal disturbance	Erosion of riverbanks
Noise pollution	Carrying capacity on environmental effects
Biological effects of pollutants	**Impact on human leisure experience**
Thermal loading	Noise disturbance
Increased turbidity	Crowding
Disruption of stratification of water	Fumes
	Safety
	Conflict of fast versus slow moving watercraft
	Conflicts with other leisure interests

Figure 4-4 Impacts of motorized watercraft. Adapted from Bluewater Network (2002); Fiedler (1996); Milius (1998); Natural Trails and Waters Coalition (2004); Nelson (1998); Pearl and Smith (1997); Rockwell (2002); Standevan and De Knop (1999); Stokowski (2000) Stolpe (1992); and UK Marine Sacs (2000).

affected due to their ability to react quickly to threatening situations and respond in a manner to avoid harm (Holland and Sylevester 1983; Stolpe 1992).

b. Impacts of Hull Parts and Bottom Scouring

When hulls come in contact with sand banks, river bottoms, and other marine structures, it can have a negative impact on marine life and potentially other wildlife. This is also relevant to further disturbances described next (Pearson, Killgore, Payne, and Miller 1989).

c. Propeller- or Jet-Generated Turbulence and Shear Force

Studies have shown fish eggs and larvae to be substantially affected by water turbulence (Morgan, Ulanowicz, Raisin, Noe, and Gray 1976; Holland and Sylevester 1983; Killgore and Conley 1987; Pearson et al. 1989).

d. Hull-Generated Rotational Forces

High maneuverability and speed of watercraft have been found to generate potentially high rotational forces, which move water at great speed. This may have a disturbing effect on the biology of a marine environment, especially in shallower waters (Stolpe 1992).

e. Animal Disturbance

In addition to noise disturbance, the high-speed movement of personal motorized watercraft has been shown to have a disturbing influence on a variety of wildlife species (Paton, Ziembicki, Owen, and Heddle 2000).

f. Noise Pollution

The high levels of noise created by most motorized watercraft have been found to be of potentially high disturbance to wildlife, especially waterfowl and other bird life. This can result in major negative effects on feeding, nesting, and breeding patterns (Milius 1998; Burger and Leonard 2000).

2. Biological Effects of Pollutants

a. Thermal Loading

Though the degree to which increased temperatures due to motorized watercraft usage may be debated, it is known that thermal increases can have a significant impact on marine wildlife (Stolpe 1992).

b. Increased Turbidity

Prolonged use of motorized watercraft in shallow waters may result in increased turbidity (Hilton and Philips 1982; Asplund 1997). Increased turbidity has been found to affect breeding volumes in various fisheries (Breitburg 1988; Newcombe and MacDonald 1991).

c. Disruption of Stratification of Water

Few studies have been conducted to show potential negative effects of water stratification disturbance due to increased movements of water.

d. Disturbance of Sediment

In environments where sediment has covered previously placed toxic substances, extensive movement of sediment due to powerful motorcraft may disturb sediment, and therefore some toxic substances might be released into the water system (Stolpe 1992). A study conducted by Yousef in 1974 showed substantial re-suspending of bottom sediments by motorized watercraft. Personal motorized watercraft, due primarily to the use of water jets, are capable of traveling at very high speeds through shallow water. Therefore, the potential disturbance of water and sediment may be greatly exacerbated (Stolpe and Moore 1997).

e. Bottom Vegetation Survival

A number of studies have shown that increased turbidity due to motorized watercraft may result in decrease in the diversity and extent of water-bottom vegetation (Garrad and Hey 1987; Liddle and Scorgie 1980).

3. Negative Impacts on the Physical Environment

a. Boat Engine Emissions and Spills

With motorized personal watercraft, a certain percentage of fuel enters water systems (Van Moumerik and Hagemann 1999). Though this has been gradually reduced to less than 1% of the total fuel, this still amounts to a substantial amount of fuel leaking into a concentrated area. For example, in one bay in New Jersey, the use of an estimated 25,000 tons per year of recreational fuel would amount to close to 250 tons of fuel released into the bay from motorized watercraft. This is certainly not caused solely by personal motorized watercraft; however, it does show a substantial potential impact on a marine environment. Leaked fuel generally floats for a substantial period of time on the surface of water, and this can also have an impact on waterfowl as well as marine life (Stolpe 1992). Though emission quantities may be relatively low, studies have found that surface micro layers may be significantly affected by these emissions and potential fuel spills, which occur most often in near-shore waters and estuaries, thus resulting in developmental and survival issues for various marine life (Von Westerhagen et al. 1987).

In addition to the above damage to wildlife, the additional fuel use and leakage adds to the worldwide problem of increased hydrocarbons being released into the environment.

b. Leaching of Toxic Substances

Toxic substances from watercraft usage may leach into the water habitat and, after potential buildup, may result in genetic changes to plants and animals and may ultimately affect biodiversity and long-term environmental sustainability (Stolpe 1992).

c. Erosion of Riverbanks and Vegetation

High speeds of watercraft can often create high water wakes that can quickly reach riverbanks and lakes (Lethlean 2003). Over time, this can cause significant erosion and can have detrimental effects on the biology of the local environment. This can then result in substantial sensitive vegetation loss, which may in turn have further effects on wildlife habitat.

d. Carrying Capacity for Environmental Effects

Carrying capacity is generally considered to be the level of visitation beyond which unacceptable ecological impacts will occur (Inskeep 1991). This capacity to withstand the increased use has been looked at for various motorized water sports. Both speedboating and waterskiing had among the lowest carrying capacity of visitors per day per hectare. Only 5 to 10 visitors per day per hectare would meet the environmental carrying capacity after which unacceptable ecological impacts would occur (Urban Research and Development Corporation 1977). Presumably jet skiing would be within a similar carrying capacity.

4. Impact on Human Leisure Experience

There have been substantial concerns expressed about the use of personal watercraft and its effect on the human leisure experience (Fiedler 1996; Pearl and Smith 1997; Natural Trails and Waters Coalition 2004; Milius 1998; Nelson 1998; Bluewater Network 2002; Rockwell 2002). A study conducted in 2001 found that 67% of respondents oppose the use of off-road vehicles such as jet skis, dirt bikes, and snowmobiles in America's National Parks (Fetto 2001). Pigram and Jenkins (1999) discuss "incompatible recreation activities, amongst which power boating and water skiing probably arouse most opposition from less aggressive forms of recreation such as swimming and fishing" (p. 174).

Some very emotive words have been used to describe jet skis in particular, such as "locusts of the sea," "the final motorized insult," "nuisance activities," "users find they just cannot co-exist with the jet skis," "they're noisy, they're intrusive, they're obnoxious," "a menace," "a floating chainsaw," "it's like having a dang mosquito crawling in your ear," and "dirt bikes of the ocean" (Sidaway 1991; Rolland 1997; Fraser 1998; Rockwell 2001, 2002; "Pollution Claim in Jetski Debate" 2004).

a. Noise Disturbance to Leisure Experiences

In terms of the negative impacts of motorized water activities, noise pollution, or problems with the noise caused by motorized craft have been identified as the key areas of conflict with people desiring leisure experiences in water environments (Komanoff and Shaw 2000). A study of people affected by personal motorized watercraft was conducted in the United States. Respondents in beach settings were asked to comment on what they would pay to rid the waterways of jet ski noise, assuming there was an organization that would take their money and be able to eliminate the noise. Keeping in mind these are hypothetical amounts, the average jet ski represented US$47 of noise pollution on beachgoers per year (US$0.39 to US$7.02 average per jet ski encounter depending on location, secluded lake to popular ocean setting). Based on an average usage of jet skis of 15 days per year, this equates to about US$700 in noise pollution costs. The study suggested a figure of US$908 million in noise costs per year overall.

Noise problems, particularly with regard to jet skis, are based on the high decibels (15 dBA higher than other motorized watercraft) of the exhaust/motor system, the magnifying and revving effect of jet skis continually leaving the water, the variable nature of the pitch and volume of water creating variable noise, and the smacking "whomp" sound of the jet ski re-entering the water either over waves or when traveling at high speeds (Komanoff and Shaw 2000).

b. Crowding

Crowding relates to the perceived tolerance when motorized sports come into contact with other people and activities. Due to the noise, visual effect, motion, maneuverability, and speed of most motorized water sports, the potential to have a perceived sense of crowding can be accentuated (Pigram and Jenkins 1999).

c. Fumes

Due to the two-stroke nature of most personal motorized watercraft, unpleasant odors can be another issue for those in relatively close contact with the craft (Howe and Cole 1999).

d. Safety

Safety has been identified as a serious issue due to the incompatibility of fast-moving and maneuverable watercraft in close proximity to other watercraft and people in marine environments (Vandeman 1998). There have been numerous studies of safety issues, particularly with regard to personal watercraft (Branche 1997; Martin 1999). In 1998, personal watercraft accounted for the second-highest fatality rate per million hours of operation. Canoes, surprisingly, were the most dangerous personal watercraft with 42 fatalities per million hours of operation, and personalized water craft or PWCs (which are normally motorized) accounted for the next highest (24). This was almost twice the number of fatalities for open motorboats (14) and far greater than for cabin motorboats, which were found to have only 1 fatality per million hours of operation (Dickinson 2000). Though fatalities by recreational boating have been progressively falling since 1973 in spite of the strong increase in motorboat usage, personal watercraft accounted for close to 34% of accidents (33.9%) in 1999, even though their usage has been estimated at only 10% ("Fatalities Hit Record Low" 2001).

In California in 2000, personal watercraft owners made up 19% of boat owners but were accountable for 45% of injuries (Rockwell 2001). Personal watercraft accidents, injuries, and deaths have steadily increased from 376 accidents, 156 injuries, and 5 deaths in 1987, to 4070 accidents, 1812 injuries, and 84 deaths in 1997 (U.S. Department of Transportation 1998). Injury rates have been found to be over eight times higher than rates for other forms of motorboats (Branche 1997).

Other aspects related to the safety of personal motorized watercraft, particularly jet skis, include hours of operation, continuous nature of power, rudderless nature, lack of braking, rental nature, and exposure (Mecozzi 1997). Personal motorized watercraft are often used for more hours per day and more days per season than other forms of motorized watercraft. In addition, they are under almost constant power as compared to other watercraft, cannot turn when people let go of the steering, and lack braking mechanisms (Rockwell 2001). A large percentage (close to 60%) of accidents occur with rented personal motorized watercraft. Moreover, personal motorized watercraft are used out in the open, exposed to elements with little barrier between the driver and anything with which the watercraft might come into contact (Mecozzi 1997).

e. Conflict of Fast- Versus Slow-Moving Watercraft

There have been numerous examples of conflicts due to the relative speed of watercraft. Normally, non-motorized watercraft travel at much slower speeds, yet often operate in similar environments to personal motorized watercraft, unless controlled. Issues of perceived crowding, difficulty in reacting to fast-paced craft, wave motion, and disturbance can all add to this continual conflict of various water-based experiences (Pigram and Jenkins 1999).

A new area of conflict is arising between jet ski users and surfers along the coast of California. Some surfers are utilizing jet skis to tow them out further in search of larger waves. This approach has resulted in division among Northern California's surfing community where both surfers and environmental groups have argued for banning jet skis due to the noise and water pollution, which threatens both the pristine experience and the wildlife habitat (Enge 2003; see also Chapter 5 of this volume regarding surfing and windsurfing user conflicts and water quality issues).

f. Conflicts with Other Leisure Interests

Conflict of interest also arises with people interested in relatively pristine water environments who seek relaxation, peace, serenity, or environmental or educational experiences. This is often in direct conflict with high-speed, high-volume watercraft. The growing number of ecotourists and wildlife-related tourists may account for up to US$1 trillion a year (Hvenegaard 1994). Therefore, this is an issue requiring immediate attention and more extensive research.

Guidelines and Regulations

In order to address the significant impacts previously identified, there have been numerous guidelines and recommendations developed for personal watercraft, waterskiing, and other forms of motorized water sport use (Sports Council 1992; Elson 1994; Royal Yachting Association 1997; Commonwealth of Australia 2000; UK CEED 2000; UK Marine SACs 2000; Conservation Action Network 2003; Wellington Regional Council [WRC] 2004). Throughout the world, there are examples of specific guidelines for waterski and jet ski use. In Wellington Harbor, New Zealand, special lanes were set up to accommodate recreational multi-use, allowing waterski and jet ski access lanes identified with marker poles, speed limits, direction of travel, and various use guidelines (WRC 2004). Additional categories of guidelines included common sense, courtesy, give way approaches, buffer zones of other water users, noise reduction, education, training, and preparation.

A marina group located in Colwyn Bay in North Wales introduced a number of regulations for motorized watercraft in their region. This was in response to eye-witness accounts of full-body hitting of a swan at full speed within the Conway Marina complex. Regulations aimed at safety, include compulsory education and qualifications for jet skiers and powerboat users and the construction of a purpose-built jet ski berth (Williams M. 2002). Another example is the Northern Territory Government of Australia, which developed small craft regulations with categories related to reckless navigation, warning methods, restricted areas, speed limits and corridors, observation for water-skiers, and automatic engine cutouts for personal watercraft (Northern Territory Government 2004).

Numerous government legislatures have proposed or passed regulatory bills that empower and allow towns, villages, and cities the authority to regulate or prohibit personal watercraft (DiNapoli and Marcellino 2000). For example, a bill proposed by the Massachusetts legislature is intended to allow individual towns the right to decide whether to ban jet skis from their diverse waterways (Conservation Action Network 2003).

Throughout the 1990s there were many initiatives to further regulate or ban personal watercraft on various waterways (Gordon 1998; Hughes 1998; Pearce 1998; Stienstra 1998; Wood 1998; McCabe, 1999; "Public Opposition Prompts Restrictions" 1999). A major example of these initiatives includes the U.S. National Park Service, which in 2000 adopted regulations in parks that allowed motorized watercraft. This included the banning of personal motorized watercraft in approximately 75% of parks under their jurisdiction. A ban would also be imposed for the rest of the parks if strict rules were not developed by the regional district areas (Bluewater Network 2000).

Strategies have been suggested for reducing the noise impacts of jet skis (Komanoff and Shaw 2000). These include the need to develop much quieter jet skis, to establish requirements to operate much further from shore, and to restrict the areas and bodies of water in which they are allowed to be operated. These strategies would be very difficult to achieve, if the goal was, for example, a 75% reduction in noise pollution in countries such as the United States. This would require a ban on 90% of current jet ski numbers from 90% of all lakes, bays, rivers, and oceans. Alternatively, restrictions on use and strict regulation on distance from population would be a possible solution.

Another issue is the definition of personal watercraft used in some jurisdictions. Though a number of marine zones have restricted the use of motorized personal watercraft since the early 1990s, normally with boundary zones identified for use, in response to this a number of manufacturers have developed larger watercraft that can be used by more people and that do not fall under the motorized personal watercraft definition (Monterey Bay National Marine Sanctuary 2001).

A number of organizations, some of which are involved in the promotion of personal motorized watercraft, as well as those involved in the control and management of personal motorized watercraft, have united to develop codes of conduct regarding personal motorized watercraft. In addition, many personal motorized watercraft have been donated to public agencies to teach safer and better operation practice (Mecozzi 1997). Some organizations in favor of personal motorized watercraft have worked directly with other organizations to develop safety programs for users. For example, the following are key items that have been put forward to include in a Code of Conduct for water-skiers and watercraft drivers (International Water Ski Federation n.d.).

1. Comply with all the club's bylaws at all times.
2. Respect speed limits on the water at all times.
3. Take care not to disturb wildlife and waterfowl, particularly during nesting and molting and in sensitive areas.
4. Use unleaded fuel or propane gas instead of leaded fuel.
5. Do not idle engines unnecessarily.
6. Drive the watercraft in a manner that produces the least fuel emissions.
7. Reduce wash as much as possible.
8. Stay out of shallow water and well away from shorelines.
9. Meet requirements for boat registration.
10. Meet requirements for insurance.
11. Respect club policy on noise emissions and display noise emission certificate on watercraft.
12. Follow accepted standards of watercraft etiquette including acting with due consideration for swimmers, fishermen, and all other water or shoreside users.
13. Abide by regulation that specifies the distance from shore that waterskiing is permitted.
14. Abide by regulation that specifies hours of operation permitted for waterskiing and motorized watercraft.
15. Respect all restrictions placed on sensitive areas and areas that are seasonally constrained.
16. Only refuel away from any sensitive wildlife areas.
17. Follow club policy and state law that no person shall drive a vessel, observe in a vessel, or water-ski behind a vessel while under the influence of alcohol.
18. Follow the club safety code and carry a copy of the code at all time.

A bill introduced to the U.S. House of Representatives in 1999 (Personal Watercraft Responsible Use Act of 1999) acknowledged the growing popularity of personal motorized watercraft and the issue of competing for limited space in waterways. The bill took into consideration that the thrill craft nature of personal motorized watercraft is associated with maneuverability at high speeds in shallow areas, which is significantly different from other uses, and that the potential for irresponsible operation of personal motorized watercraft poses numerous risks regarding safety and environmental impacts. The bill attempted to ensure safe and responsible use in America's waterways, protect sensitive shallow-water habitat, reduce conflict among leisure boaters, introduce collaborative management approaches, and increase the ability to enforce boating laws and regulations.

It is unclear what long-term effect these guidelines and regulations will have on the personal motorized water sports industry and the various stakeholders on each side of the polarized debate regarding usage on public waterways.

Having considered the overall nature of personalized water sports, the market impacts, and guidelines, two case studies are considered to contextualize the previous discussion. The first focuses on Folkestone Marine Park and Reserve, Barbados. The second focuses on the Noose River Plan, Australia.

Case Studies

Folkestone Marine Park and Reserve, Barbados

A marine reserve was established in 1981 along the West Coast of Barbados (Cumberbatch 2001). A study was funded in the late 1990s to explore the feasibility of enhancing the 2.2 km reserve for multi-use as a recreational and marine reserve. Various stakeholders were identified to be involved in the process of understanding issues and determining ways to deal with them. These interested parties included residents, businesses, water sports operators, fishing participants, government agencies, and beach users.

In evaluating the potential for recreational and marine reserve use, a number of issues were identified. These included (1) the size of the reserve relative to its usage (only one-eighth was used for scientific purposes); (2) the impacts from external factors such as motorized water sports activities, contaminated domestic waste, and agricultural and golf course chemicals; (3) lack of information provided on restrictive use of resources including reef walking and use of motorized water sports; (4) limitations on funding for effective reserve management; (5) inconsistencies on enforcement of regulations on activities that do not comply; and (6) conflict among user groups, a main source of which has involved the use of jet skis. There have been numerous complaints from others regarding violation of speed restrictions, weekly near misses with other watercraft, accidents, and lack of skills of riders. Other conflicts have involved visitor crowding, divers destroying reef assets, and beach vendors impacting other visitor experiences.

In order to address some of these issues, particularly with regard to personal motorized watercraft, four areas were set up with strict designations for use. These included (1) a scientific zone to be used for marine research, which specified that no motorized watercraft were to have access except for research and then at only 5 knots; (2) two separate zones designated for use by fast-moving motorized watercraft, but with restrictions on speed near the shore. In these zones, jet skis are allowed at higher speeds when over 200 meters from shore; (3) a recreational zone in which there are no restrictions on types of watercraft; however, there are strict speed limitations in order to allow people to be involved in such activities as swimming and snorkeling.

Noosa River Plan, Australia

The Noosa River lies within a region along the coast of Eastern Australia, two hours north of Brisbane in Queensland. The river, which is fed by springs draining through major sand deposits in the Cooloola National Park, is one of the few Queensland rivers that has virtually a continuous, year-round freshwater flow. Being primarily surrounded by national park also enables the river to maintain high-quality ratings compared to other estuaries in Queensland. The river system includes four lakes and waterways between these lakes that ultimately reach the ocean and Laguna Bay near Noosa Heads, the most popular tourism location for visitors to Noosa, a significant coastal tourism resort destination in South East Queensland.

A number of values are considered inherent in the Noosa River system. These include a river and numerous lakes, the perceived natural aspect of the river, attractive settings that range from near-wilderness to urban, relatively small tidal ranges, relative safety of most of the waterways, easy access to the river, easy access to services and facilities, and the diverse ranges of available activities (Noosa Council 2003).

In 1997 and again in a 2003 update, a Noosa River Plan was developed and updated to deal with the many issues existing within the multi-use setting. The one major overriding issue that has existed in the area relates to the inadequacy of not being able to deliver a coordinated management regulatory framework. This has resulted in conflicts in decision making, disagreements on the appropriate use of the river for recreational and other purposes, and major limitations and constraints on effective management of the river and its estuaries.

Issues identified included the following: bed and bank habitat and ecosystem health, water quality, visual amenity, public safety, cultural heritage, noise levels and congestion on the river, motorized water sports and transportation conflicts (particularly personal motorized water sports), jetty condition and placement, boat ramps, mooring and marine service developments, and other commercial operations on the river and issues with living on board vessels.

Regarding personal motorized water sports, three key issues were identified. These included issues of noise and amenity disturbances and safety stemming from aggressive riding and excessive speed. There was also a perceived incompatibility between personal motorized water sports, particularly jet skis, and other activities. This was primarily due to the focus of Noosa River activities on "the Noosa recreation experience, that is, the enjoyment of the area's scenic qualities and its tranquil natural environment" (Noosa Council 2003, p. 22). Finally, a third issue was the concern expressed about the effect of jet skis on fish and the impacts on fish stocks in the Noosa River. In the Noosa case, however, there are already numerous regulations and management approaches to dealing with key issues of motorized watercraft, especially personalized craft on the Noosa River. There is already a 20-knot speed limit, and personal motorized watercraft are already in quite small numbers on the river. In addition, there are regulations on watercraft including restrictions on noise and time of operation and on the use of personalized watercraft for freestyling, surfing, and wave jumping.

In order to address these issues, the five following dimensions of change were considered and corresponding recommendations were put forward: natural environment, water quality, visual amenity, public safety, and quality of experiences. Key recommendations were to develop a coordinated management structure of the river by all relevant agencies including specific desired outcomes for river uses and activities to secure long-term sustainability, action plans for management agencies to effectively implement, monitoring of river uses and activities, and a need for legislative reform to deal with a number of important issues.

A vision for the future of the Noosa River system was developed that sought to have it (1) recognized internationally for the natural, recreational, scenic, cultural, and economic values flowing from the river's rich biodiversity and habitat; (2) managed within an effective coordinated framework that strives for sustainability and best practice in nature-based recreation and ecotourism; and (3) valued by government, industry, and a community that takes an active role in maintenance and enhancement (Noosa Council 2003, p. 8).

The plan addresses various issues with motorized water sports and transportation. First, motorized water sports and transportation are to be conducted in a manner that minimizes adverse impact on the natural and cultural values of the river system; considers the amenity and safety of other water users and surrounding land uses, including maintaining low ambient noise levels; and conforms with the low-key recreation character of the Noosa River system. Second, the plan also indicated that high-noise craft such as hovercraft, airboats, seaplanes, helicopters, and other such intrusive uses are not permitted.

Third, the plan also suggests that there would be a minimization and ultimately prohibition of high-speed motorized watercraft, especially personal motorized watercraft, which would be formally restricted to just one section of the river at the community of Noosaville. In addition, the plan requires personal motorized watercraft to meet strict marine safety requirements. There are also speed, location, and time restrictions and guidelines on waterskiing, with only specific areas where waterskiing is allowed. The plan indicated the need for monitoring closely the management and operation of personal watercraft to ensure issues of noise, safety, and amenity are under control. Finally, the plan provides a framework for management of conflicting uses of waterways in a potentially sustainable way. Though strong actions are put forward in the plan, the vision creates a basis for compatible use of motorized water sports in pristine natural areas.

Concluding Discussion

This chapter has provided a background in understanding personal motorized water sports, included discussion of the types of motorized water sports and craft, and categorization frameworks that have been developed. Also provided was a brief overview of the market, popularity, and advantages of personal motorized water sports. In addition, organizations were identified that have focused on either promoting these activities or have been concerned with minimizing and controlling their impacts. Impacts of personal motorized water sports and issues surrounding their use received specific attention. Four impact areas were identified including (1) direct physical stresses on aquatic organisms, (2) negative impacts on the physical environment, (3) biological effects of pollutants, and (4) the impact on the human leisure experience. Specific issues within these categories were discussed. A number of guidelines and regulations were also described that have been initiated to deal with the many issues and the negative impacts of personal motorized water sports. Finally, two case studies were reviewed to highlight the issues and identify approaches that have been taken by two regions to address the challenges involved in the area of personal motorized water sports activities.

Future Directions

There are still substantial challenges ahead in order to achieve best practice use of our waterways. The goal is to optimize the opportunity for enjoyment for the majority of people within the community without compromising the sustainability of one of our most valuable resources—our waterways. Approaches to address the numerous concerns that have polarized various sections of the community and special interest groups need to be developed. User groups seeking activities centered on speed, noise, and exhilaration are in direct conflict with those seeking a sense of peace, personal serenity, and environmental conservation. Within the next 10 years, a number of changes in technology, changes in tastes, and implementation of various regulations and planning schemes will most likely lead to solutions of a number of these issues, with some stakeholders' needs being more closely met than others'. There are no easy win–win solutions; however, with extensive community consultation and education, a diversity of wants and needs may be accommodated, including those of local planners, operators, participants, and other stakeholders.

References

Aquaskier. (2006). *Water sports resources.* Accessed 17 August 2006, from http://www.aquaskier.com

Asplund, T. (1997). *Investigations of motor boat impacts on Wisconsin's lakes.* Madison: Wisconsin Department of Natural Resources.

Australian Bureau of Statistics. (1998). *Participation in sport and physical activities 1996–97.* Canberra: Australian Government Publishing Service.

Australian Bureau of Statistics. (2000). *Participation in sport and physical activities 1999–2000.* Canberra: Australian Government Publishing Service.

Bluewater Network. (2000, December 20). *Bluewater Network and National Park Service reach agreement over jet ski lawsuit.* Publicity release.

Bluewater Network. (2002). *Jet skis position paper.* San Francisco: Earth Island Institute.

Branche, C. (1997). Personal watercraft-related injuries: a growing public health concern. *Journal of the American Medical Association,* **278** (8), 664.

Breitburg, D. (1988). Effects of turbidity on prey consumption by striped bass larvae. *Transactions of American Fisheries Society,* **117**, 72–77.

Burger, J. (1998). Effects of motorboats and personal watercraft on flight behavior over a colony of common terns. *Condor,* **100** (3), 72–77.

Burger, J., and J. Leonard. (2000). Conflict resolution in coastal waters: the case of personal watercraft. *Marine Policy,* **24** (1), 61–67.

Coleman, R. (1999). *Outdoor recreation in American life: a national assessment of demand and supply trends*. Champaign, IL: Sagamore.

Commonwealth of Australia. (2000). *Australian national guidelines for cetacean observation*. Canberra: Environment Australia.

Conservation Action Network. (2003). *Jet ski pollution and hazards*. Newsletter of Conservation Action Network. Plainville, MA: Appalachian Mountain Club.

Cordell, H.K. (1999). *Outdoor recreation in American life: a national assessment of demand and supply trends*. Champaign, IL: Sagamore Publishing.

Cumberbatch, J. (2001). *Case study of the Folkestone Marine Park and Reserve*. Barbados: Caribbean Natural Resources Institute (CANARI).

Dickinson, E. (2000, November 21). Boating Safety Exposed. *Boat/US Magazine*.

DiNapoli, T., and C. Marcellino. (2000). Creation of Personal Watercraft Regulation Zones. New York: New York Assembly.

Douglas, N., Douglas, N. and R. Derritt. (2001). *Special Interest Tourism*. Brisbane: Wiley.

The effectiveness of planning policy guidance on sport and recreation. (1998). Available online at http://www.odpm.gov.uk/stellent/groups/odpm_planning/documents/page_plan_6061

Elson, M. (1994). *Planning and provision for motorized water sports*. London: The Sports Council.

Enge, M. (2003, June 25). Surfboard towing creates controversy. *Mercury News*.

Fatalities hit record low. (2001, November). *Boat/US Magazine*.

Fetto, J. (2001). Off-road vehicle support. *American Demographics*, **23** (8).

Fiedler, T. (1996, July 23). A personal watercraft boom makes waves; noise and safety among the concerns. *Star Tribune*.

Fontaine, M. (2002, June). Fontaine of youth. *Watercraft*, p. 24.

Fraser, D. (1998, July 19). Noisy? Dangerous? Or fun? Watercraft debate gets personal. Accessed 17 August 2006. http://www.vsv.cope.com/~harharb/news/jetski.html

Garrad, P., and R. Hey. (1987). Boat traffic, sediment resuspension and turbidity in a broadland river. *Journal of Hydrology*, **95**, 289–297.

Gordon, R. (1998, August 14). City plans shoreline ban on jet skis. *San Francisco Examiner*, p. A-1.

Great Barrier Reef Marine Park Authority. (2003). Motorized water sports. Australian government. Available online at http://www.gbrmpa.gov.au/corp_site/key_issues/tourism/motorised_water sports

Hall, C.M. (1992). Adventure, sport, and health. In C. Hall and B. Weiler (Eds.), *Special interest tourism*. London: Belhaven.

Hall, C.M. (2000). Tourism and the environment: problems, institutional arrangements, and approaches. In C.M. Hall and S. Pae (Eds.) *Tourism in South and Southeast Asia: issues and cases*. Oxford: Butterworth-Heinemann.

Hill, B. (1995). A guide to adventure travel. *Parks and Recreation*, **30** (9), 56–65.

Hilton, J., and G. Philips. (1982). The effect of boat activity on turbidity in a shallow broadland river. *The Journal of Applied Ecology*, **19**, 143–150.

Holland, I., and J. Sylevester. (1983). Distribution of larval fishes related to potential navigation impacts on the upper Mississippi River. *Transactions of the American Fisheries Society*, 112.

Howe, P., and C. Cole. (1999, May 29). Group says jet skis cause great harm to air, waterways. *Associated Press*.

Hughes, J. (1998, September 3). Ban sought on jet ski in national parks. *Augusta Chronicle*.

Hvenegaard, G. (1994). Ecotourism: a status report and conceptual framework. *Journal of Tourism Studies, 5* (2), 24–34.

Inskeep, E. (1991). *Tourism planning*. New York: Van Nostrand Reinhold.

International Water Ski Federation. (n.d.). *Environmental handbook for towed water sports*. Unteraegeri, Switzerland: International Water Ski Federation.

Iso-Ahola, S. (1980). *The social psychology of leisure and recreation*. Dubuque, IA: Brown.

Jeffries, M., and D. Mills. (1990). *Freshwater ecology*. London: Belhaven.

Kearsely, G. (1990). Tourism development and users' perception of wilderness in Southern New Zealand. *Australian Geographer, 21* (2), 127–140.

Kiewa, J., T.J. Brown, and R. Hibbins. (2002). South East Queensland outdoor recreation demand study: Septembere-November 2001. Milton, Australia: Quuensland Outdoor Recreation Federation.

Killgore, K., and K. Conley. (1987). Effects of turbulence on yolk sac larvae of paddlefish. *Transactions of the American Fisheries Society, 116*, 670–673.

Komanoff, C., and H. Shaw. (2000). *Drowning in noise: noise costs of jet skis in America*. Report for the Noise Pollution Clearinghouse. Montpellier, VT: Noise Pollution Clearinghouse.

Lazaroff, C. (2002). National Park Service bans jet skis in five parks. *Environmental News Service.*

Lethlean, C. (2003). *River Murray sustainable recreation. site planning, and implementation guide, Sustainable Recreation Steering Committee*. Adelaide, Australia: River Murray Catchment Water Management Board.

Liddle, M., and H. Scorgie. (1980). The effects of recreation on freshwater plants and animals: a re-view. *Biological Conservation, 17*, 183–206.

Lipscombe, N. (1995). Appropriate adventure: participation for the aged. *Australian Parks and Recreation, 31* (2), 41–45.

Martin, L. (1999). *Caught in the wake: the environmental and human health impacts of personal watercraft*. Gaithersburg, MD: Izaak Walton League of America.

McCabe, M. (1999, March 17). Watercraft restrictions added at 3 reservoirs. *The San Francisco Chronicle.*

Mecozzi, M. (1997, June/July). *The buzz over water bikes*. Madison: Wisconsin Natural Resources.

Milius, S. (1998). Oh, not those jet-ski things again! *Science News, 154* (7), 107.

Monterey Bay National Marine Sanctuary. (2001). *What is a motorized personal watercraft?* Available online at http://www.montereybay.noaa.gov/visitor/craft

Morgan, R., Ulanowicz, R., Raisin, V., Noe, L., and G. Gray. (1976). Effects of shear on eggs and larvae of striped bass and white perch. *Transactions of the American Fisheries Society, 106.*

National Marine Manufacturing Association. (1998). *US recreational boating domestic shipment statistics*. Chicago: National Marine Manufacturing Association.

National Marine Manufacturing Association. (2003). *The boating market*. Chicago: National Marine Manufacturing Association.

National Park Service, Department of the Interior. (1998, June 24). *Proposed rule: personal watercraft use within the NPS system*. Washington, DC: National Park Service, Department of the Interior.

Natural Trails and Waters Coalition. (2004). *Impacts on public health and safety*. Available online at www.naturaltrails.org

Nelson, C. (1998, June/July). Jet skis suck, making waves. San Clemente, CA: Surfrider Foundation.

Newcombe, C., and D. MacDonald. (1991). Effects of suspended sediments on aquatic ecosystems. *The American Journal of Fisheries Management*, **11**, 72–81.

Noosa Council. (2003). *Noosa River Plan 2003 draft*. Noosa, Queensland, Australia: NSC.

Northern Territory Government. (2004). *Amendments to regulations*. Darwin, Australia: Department of Infrastructure, Planning and Environment, Marine Branch.

Paton, D., Ziembicki, M., Owen, P., and D. Heddle. (2000). *Disturbance distances for water birds and the management of human recreation with special reference to the Coorong Region of South Australia*. Adelaide, Australia: National Wetlands Program.

Pearce, A. (2000). Water adventure for 2000 and beyond. *Insider*.

Pearce, J. (1998, July 17). Jet skis targeted as polluters of Michigan's great lakes. *The Detroit News*, p. A-1.

Pearl, P., and S. Smith. (1997, April 30). *Wildlife impacts of personal watercraft. Preliminary briefing materials and resources on personal watercraft and their use in the national park system*. Available online at http:// www.nps.gov/noca /PWCComplete. htm

Pearson, D., Killgore, K., Payne, B., and A. Miller. (1989). *Environmental effects of navigation traffic: studies on fish eggs and larvae*. Department of the Army Environmental Impact Research Program Technical Report. Vickburg, MS: Army Engineer Waterways Station.

Personal Watercraft Responsible Use Act of 1999, HR 3141, 106th Congress. (1999).

Pigram, J., and J. Jenkins. (1999). *Outdoor recreation management*. London: Routledge.

Pollution claim in jetski debate. (2004, January 16). *Noosa News*, p. 3.

Public opposition prompts restrictions against jet-powered personal watercraft. (1999, February 12). *USA Today*, p. 4d.

Queensland Government. (1998). *The South East Queensland outdoor recreation demand study*. Brisbane, Australia: Department of Energy Services.

Queensland Government. (2000). *The Central Queensland outdoor recreation demand study*. Brisbane, Australia: Department of Communication and Information, Local Government, Planning and Sport, and the Department of Natural Resources.

Rednut Sports. (2004). *Adventure, action, extreme sports categories*. Available online at http://www.rednutssports.com/forums/index

Regulation of Motorcycle and Jet-Powered Watercraft Manufacturers, Distributors, Dealers, and Wholesalers, Bill 323, South Carolina General Assembly, 112th session. (1998).

Rockwell, P. (2001, August 16). Why jet skis kill. *Inmotion*. San Diego, CA: NPC Production.

Rockwell, P. (2002, January 27). Jet ski frenzy: Must Californians leave the wilderness in search of peace and quiet? *Inmotion*. San Diego, CA: NPC Production.

Rogers, J., and H. Smith. (1995). Set-back distances to protect nest bird colonies from human disturbances in Florida. *Conservation Biology*, **9**, 89–99.

Rolland, D. (1997, May 29). Tomales Bay advisors urge jet skis limits. *Point Reyes Light*. Available online at http://www.ptreyeslight.com/stories/may29/jetski.html

Royal Yachting Association. (1997). *Tidelines 1997*. Codes of practice for water skiing. Available from the Royal Yachting Association, http://www.rya.org.uk

Shank, M. (2002). *Sports marketing—a strategic perspective* (2nd ed.). Upper Saddle River, NJ: Prentice Hall.

Sidaway, R. (1991). *Good conservation practice for sport and recreation*. London: Sports Council.

Speciality Travel Index. (2006). Available online at http://www.specialtytravel. com/activities/frames.html

Sports Council. (1992). *Planning and provision for motorized water sports*. London: Sports Council.

Sports Council. (1993). *Water skiing and the environment*. London: Sports Council.

Standeven, J. and P. De Knop. (1999). *Sport tourism*. Champaign, IL: Human Kinetics.

Stienstra, T. (1998, July 8). Park Service to ban personal watercraft. *Examiner Outdoors*.

Stokowski, P. (2000). Assessing social impacts of resource-based recreation and tourism. In W. Gartner and D. Lime (Eds.), *Trends in outdoor recreation, leisure, and tourism*. New York: CABI.

Stolpe, N. (1992, July 29). A survey of potential impacts of boating activity on estuarine productivity. *New Jersey Fishing*. Available online at http://www.fishing.nj/artobm1.htm

Stolpe, N., and M. Moore. (1997, March). Boating workshop raises tough questions. *New Jersey Fishing*. Available online at http://www.fishing.nj/artobm2.htm

Swarbrooke, J., Beard, C., Leckie, S., and G. Pomfret. (2003). *Adventure tourism—the new frontier*. Oxford, UK: Butterworth-Heinemann.

Talhelm, D., and K. Vrana. (1995). *Status and potential of Michigan natural resources*. East Lansing: Michigan State University, Center for Maritime and Underwater Resource Management.

Tjarnllund, U. (1996). Further studies of the effects of exhaust from two-stroke outboard motors and fish. *Marine Environmental Research*, **42**, 267–271.

Tjarnllund, U., Ericson, G., Lindesjoo, E., Petterson, I., and L. Balk. (1993). *Investigation of the biological effects of 2-cycle outboard engines' exhaust on fish*. Stockholm, Sweden: Institute of Applied Research, University of Stockholm.

Travel-Quest. (2006). Travel-Quest Specialist Travel Directory. Available online at http://www.travel-quest.co.uk

UK Ceed. (1993). *Waterskiing and the environment*. London: Sports Council.

UK Ceed. (2000). *A review of the effects of recreational interactions within UK European marine sites*. Maes-y-Ffynnon, Penrhosgarnedd, Bangor, Gwynedd: Countryside Council for Wales.

UK Marine SACs Project. (2001). *Guidelines for water skiing*. London: UK Marine SACs Project.

UK Marine SACs Project. (2000). *Summary of environmental impacts*. London: UK Marine SACs Project.

Urban Research and Development Corporation. (1977). *Guidelines for understanding and determining optimum recreation carrying capacity*. Pittsburgh, PA: Urban Research and Development Corporation.

U.S. Department of Transportation. (1998). *Boating statistics 1997*. Washington, DC: U.S. Coast Guard.

Vanderan, M. (1998, June 14). Jet skis in our national parks. *Newsletter of Earth Island Institute*.

Van Moumerik, M., and M. Hagemann. (1999). *Water Quality Concerns Related to Personal Watercraft Usage*. Fort Colins: Water Resources Division. National Park Service.

Von Westerhagen, H., Landolt, M., Kocan, R., Furstenberg, G., Janssen, D., and K. Kremling. (1987). Toxicity of sea surface microlayer: Effects on herring and turbot embryos. *Marine Environment Research* (pp. 1136–1141).

Wales Tourist Board. (2002). *Time for action—an adventure tourism strategy for Wales.* Cardiff: Wales Tourist Board.

Ward, D., and J. Andrews. (1993). Waterfowl and recreational disturbance on inland waters. *British Wildlife*, **4** (4), 221–229.

Warrington, P. (1999). *Impacts of recreational boating on the aquatic environment.* Vancouver, BC, Canada: BC Government.

Weaver, D. (2001). *Ecotourism.* Milton, Queensland, Australia: Wiley.

Weed, M., and C. Bull. (2004). *Sports tourism: participants, policy, and providers.* Amsterdam: Elsevier.

Weiler, B., and C. Hall. (1992). *Special interest tourism.* New York: Belhaven.

Wellington Regional Council. (2004). *Environment management—Wellington Harbour.* Wellington, Australia: Wellington Regional Council.

Williams, C. (2003, May 21). Personal watercraft loved, hated. *Atlanta Journal-Constitution.*

Williams, M. (2002, March 2). Marina makes waves with jet skis rulings. *North Wales Weekly News.*

Wood, D. (1998, September 21). National park ban is latest buzz for watercraft. *The Christian Science Monitor,* p. 3.

Wood, M., and C. Bull. (2004). *Sports tourism—participants, policy, and providers.* Oxford, UK: Elsevier.

Yousef, Y. A. (1974). *Assessing effects on water quality by boating activity.* EPA technical survey. Cincinnati, OH: National Environmental Research Center.

5

Surfing and Windsurfing

Chris Ryan

Overview

This chapter describes a history of both surfing and windsurfing, highlighting the linkages with commercial sponsorship from the early 1900s and the adoption of the sports' images by media and commerce, even while both sports engage their participants in activities of personal fulfillment and potential membership in an alternative subculture. However, market changes have meant sporting organizations have had to respond to an emergent graying market, as both surfing and windsurfing might be said to represent "early" adventure sports that have subsequently been supplanted within youth culture by more extreme sports such as skateboarding that are located in an urban milieu.

Background and Market Profiles

Becoming Established

The history of surfing prior to the arrival of Europeans in Hawaii is uncertain, but would appear to be of some antiquity. For example, "the Christian missionary William Ellis (1794–1872) recalls that Kaumualii, the great mo'i (king) from the island of Kauai, was renowned as an accomplished surfer. Ellis also recalls seeing the elderly Big Island chiefs Karaimoku and Kakioena… both between fifty and sixty years of age, and large corpulent men, balancing themselves on their long and narrow boards, or splashing about in the foam, with as much satisfaction as youths of sixteen" (http://surfart.com/surf_history/Kings.html).

Similarly, John Papa Li (1800–1870) notes in his Hawaiian chronicles that Kamehameha the Great (1753–1819) and Kaahumanu (1768–1832), his favorite wife, the Queen Regent, were keen surfers (http://surfart.com/surf_history/ Kamehameha.htm). Yet indirectly, it was the actions of Kamehameha that brought about a decline in surfing when in 1819 he declared the end of the *Kapu* system of law and religious festivals as the influence of Christian missionaries and European-based legal systems, including that of land ownership, began to dominate previous social systems. Surfing, with its role in religious and sporting festivals, suffered as did other aspects of traditional Hawaiian life. Hence, by the late 1870s, surfing had seemingly gone into some decline, only to be revitalized on the world stage when, in the early 1900s, an American real estate developer, Henry E. Huntingdon, invited George Freeth to visit California in a marketing blitz "about the man who could walk on water" (http://surfart.com/surf_ culture/lifeguard/lifegd5.htm). Freeth attracted literally thousands to Redondo Beach where Huntingdon was engaged in property development. Although Freeth died in 1919 as a result of respiratory problems contracted while lifesaving, he had caught the public imagination of California. His legacy is not simply the popularity of surfing but also the institution of the Californian lifeguards, and perhaps more indirectly, both windsurfing and the more recent television phenomenon of *Baywatch*!

From these beginnings, surfing began to establish itself as a world phenomenon. In 1912, the New South Wales Swimming Association invited Duke Kahanamoku to Australia, and while there he not only broke his own 100-yard world swim record, but he also introduced the sport of surfing to Australia. By the 1920s, surfing had become an established sport and a technological revolution accompanied its growth. Foremost among the board shapers of the 1920s was Tom Blake, who in 1930 patented his Hawaiian Hallow Surfboard, and went on to produce it commercially. The sport also attracted leading personalities from Hollywood, and thus was perceived as glamorous and exciting. Surf clubs prospered, and a growing ownership of automobiles meant that the sport's participants became mobile in the search of the "perfect wave," thereby extending their presence upon different beaches in California, Hawaii, Australia, and elsewhere (Figure 5-1).

After a hiatus during the Second World War, the sport entered into a golden age in the 1950s, with board construction based upon fiberglass and resin. Surfers and shapers were young—the emergence of the "teenager" market and the postwar economic boom generated an excitement, while a surfing media existed to create household names, at least among the cognoscenti, so that Hap Jacobs, Mike Doyle, and others became as heroes to the younger generation. Credence to the new lifestyle was subsequently provided by the long-term success of the Beach Boys (suitably dressed in Aloha shirts), who provided a musical soundtrack to days of surf, sea, and sand with their 1960s anthems to the lifestyle.

By comparison, windsurfing is a comparatively young sport in that it has a history of little more than four decades. It also serves to illustrate the role that chance can play in the development of individual companies, for rarely in any sport or business would the activities of a 12-year-old boy with tent material and curtain rings play such a pivotal role in company fortunes, or an article in *Playboy* magazine have

Figure 5-1 Surfers and mini-bus, Selangan, Bali, Indonesia. In the early 2000s, surfers still use motor vehicles to access sites. Photographer: Danny O' Brien.

a dramatic effect on company diversification strategies. The development of the sport is thus a history of chance, technological development, the enthusiasm of individuals, and the role of company marketing plans. To describe the development of the sport throughout the world would be difficult. Therefore, this chapter seeks to primarily outline the development of windsurfing in the United Kingdom and the United States, but many of the principles are applicable to other areas of the world. Additionally, the sport in the UK has always been subject to outside influences. For example, throughout most of this period, imported boards have accounted for over three-quarters of the total sold in Britain. In terms of sailing skills, the influence of the Hawaiian sailors has been historically strong in serving as a model for the development of not only board shapes but also styles of sailing.

The early history of windsurfing grew from the activities of the surfers of Hawaii and California in the late 1960s. One theory is that it evolved from the California surfboards of that decade. As portrayed in John Milius's film, *Big Wednesday*, the surfboards of the 1960s were much longer and wider than those in contemporary general use until about the late 1990s, when longboard surfing made a comeback. In part, this was associated with a graying market and a wish to take advantage of more normal wave conditions. At some time in the 1960s, someone had the idea of fixing a mast and a sail to one of these longboards to enjoy waveless days or to ease the trip back out over the waves. One documented history was that in 1965, the American Newman Darby invented what he termed a "sailboard" with a diamond-shape sail, a single straight boom on one side of the sail, and a mast held to the board by a cord, thus forming a crude "universal joint." The sailor thus steered by moving the rig. The design was published in the August 1965 edition of *Popular Science*. However, the "invention" was stillborn, and the modern sailboard began when in 1967, Jim Drake and Hoyle Schweitzer produced the "Windsurfer" and took out a patent for their invention.

The following year, *Playboy* magazine sponsored a "one-of-a-kind regatta" where Hoyle Schweitzer demonstrated his Windsurfer. This attracted the attention of a Dutch company, Ten Cate. They brought a few of Schweitzer's boards to Europe with the intention of both selling them and using them as an advertising medium. Following the initial success of sales, Ten Cate became the official European importers for the Windsurfer. In 1977, Ten Cate began to produce boards in Europe under license from Schweitzer. In 1979, they began sales of their own designs, the TC 36 and TC 39, which they sold alongside Schweitzer's new board, the Windsurfer Rocket.

The early history of British windsurfing began when the British subsidiary of Ten Cate Textiles brought a Windsurfer to the UK to be displayed at a rally organized by the magazine *Yachting World*. Ten Cate used the Windsurfers to help advertise their sail cloth, and demonstrations of the boards were given throughout Britain in 1972. One of the first enthusiasts to take up windsurfing was Clive Colenso, then working at *Yachting World*. By 1973, Colenso began importing the Windsurfer boards into Britain and displayed one at the Southampton Boat Show. He also began to organize races.

Initially, windsurfing was slow to take off in Britain, unlike in France and Germany. At the island of Sylt, Germany, in 1976, the first European championships took place at a time when there were but a few hundred windsurfers in Britain. That same year, a company in Poole, England, purchased 100 "Surfsailers" from a Spanish supplier and rapidly sold them, but then withdrew them when faced with legal action from Hoyle Schweitzer's company, Windsurfing International, for selling unlicensed boards.

British windsurfing from 1976 to 1984 was characterized by a number of key features:

1. Implications of the Peter Chilvers case (see below), with subsequent abandonment of the Schweitzer license arrangements in Britain
2. Emergence of British manufacturers
3. Development of the sport's official structure
4. Emergence of new technologies.

The increasing popularity of the sport in Britain in the late 1970s attracted into the industry both British manufacturers and companies importing boards from France and Germany. Not all of these companies paid royalties to Windsurfing International. The reluctance to pay these royalties stemmed from essentially two factors. The first was the high cost of the license, amounting to as much as 15% of the price of the board. With many companies having small production runs and thus no economies of scale, this represented a significant proportion of revenue. The second factor was that with the growth of popularity of the sport, the initial article describing the work of Newman Darby became well known within the sport, and thus there was a strong feeling that Schweitzer's work did not constitute an original concept as required by patent legislation. Nonetheless, Schweitzer took out his patent in 1967, renewed it in 1982, and also took out patents in Holland, Britain, Australia, and Japan in addition to his original United States patent. Schweitzer was to vigorously enforce his patents. In 1982, Hayling Windsurfing had to withdraw the French "Jet" range of boards from the British market, while Surf Sails had to simultaneously withdraw the "Sainval," both companies agreeing to out-of-court penalty payments. Until 1982, any British company falling foul of the license arrangements either agreed to pay a license fee or settled out of court for the simple reason that none had the financial resources to fight an action that they knew would go to the Appeals Court if they should happen to win the case initially. One alternative was to devise new rigs or other designs that might not be seen as compatible with the original design. Thus, the Sea Panther had a peculiar shaped "quad" boom, while in France the Skail, produced in Le Havre, required that the sailor hold the sail aloft him- or herself without a mast. Generally, these and other alternatives had less-than-satisfactory performance.

In 1982, both in Britain and in Europe, due to manufacturers overestimating the rate of growth in the market, there was excess capacity, and the German "Wind Glider" company founded by Fred Osterman was taken over by Baron Bic's "Dufour" company. Schweitzer duly announced that the agreement between him and Osterman was terminated, and he proceeded to take action in the UK against the British importer of Dufour boards for the sale of unlicensed Windsurfers. In this case, however, Dufour (one of a consortium of companies operating in the UK that had set up a fighting fund for such a contingency, and further supported by the financial resources of the Bic company) decided to take the action to court. The main defense was that the windsurfer had been invented in 1958 by Peter Chilvers, who at that time had been a boy of 12 years of age. In the June 1984 issue of *On Board* magazine, Chilvers is quoted as describing this board as follows:

(I) used sheets of plywood around a wooden framework for the hull, which was 8 feet by about 2 feet 6 inches. The dagger board went straight up and down. The mast was a wooden pole, the canvas sail was tacked around the mast and the boom was two rods lashed at either end. The uphaul was a length of rope attached about 18 inches above the boom and the "universal joint" was two hooks closed around each other, one screwed to the mast, the other to the board itself. Many people ask me why I made the rig a freestyle system. I did it out of sheer necessity—the board was too narrow to support a conventional rig. I began with a foot-operated tiller, fell in a lot and didn't get anywhere. Then I yanked the rig out of the board one day—it bore off and I actually sailed for two or three hundred yards. Realizing that I could steer the board by moving the rig, I shortened the tiller arm, screwed it to the deck and the rudder became a skeg in effect. It was all pretty obvious stuff in the circumstances. The man who really deserves the credit is Jim Drake. He actually sat down with a piece of paper and engineered the concept—which is quite incredible.

His mother gave evidence (including a photograph) of having witnessed how, in 1958, Chilvers had built and sailed this craft, and the court subsequently decided that this did constitute "prior art" and in consequence, Schweitzer's patent was not valid within the UK. Schweitzer duly appealed, and in 1984 the case reached the Appeals Court. There again the judges upheld the Dufour case, stating, "Mr. Chilvers knew perfectly well what he was doing and he was doing it to achieve exactly the same results as the patent in suit" (see also Windsurfing International Inc. v. Tabur Marine (GB) Ltd [1985] RPC 59).

The implications of the Chilvers case were that British companies did not have to pay royalties on boards produced, and hence it was predicted that there might be an emergence of new British board manufacturers. This emergence was not as great as expected due to primarily two considerations:

1. By 1982, and certainly by 1984, there was already fierce competition for the production of longboards. Any new company would have difficulty gaining the market share that would permit production runs to generate economies of scale and thus lower prices.

2. The market was changing, and thus the opportunities for new boards lay with the short boards. These new opportunities were primarily exploited by Cornish and West Country-based small surfboard shapers who could expand their activities without the need to pay license fees.

In the spring of 1980, the first windsurfing exhibition in the UK took place at the Royal Horticultural Halls in Westminster, and the show attracted 3000 in spite of an underground (subway) strike on that Saturday. Of the manufacturers then present, only Dufour (as Bic) continues as a board manufacturer in 2006.

Technological Change

Both surfing and windsurfing have become highly technologically driven sports. Indeed, in the 1980s, a convergence between the two occurred with the advent of the shortboard and sinkers in windsurfing. A number of claims exist for the honor of being the first to sail a shortboard in windsurfing. Ken Way of Tiga, UK (personal communcation), remembers Derk Thys appearing at the 1975 Speed Week with a normal sail attached to a surfboard. The combination in the prevailing conditions was uncontrollable and British windsurfers were of the general consensus that the shortboard had no future. At this time, many of the shortboards that did appear were essentially Windsurfer boards cut down in size. They thus had a high amount of volume, wide tails, and a poor distribution of volume throughout the board that made them difficult to sail, especially when connected to the early rigs. The credit for the emergence of the modern shortboard is usually given to Jürgen Honscheid and John Hall. In 1978, the Australian John Hall was working as a board shaper in the West Country (UK) at Braunton, when Jürgen Honscheid purchased some Tiki boards for his shop in Sylt. He subsequently attached a rig to these boards, was pleased with the result, and returned in 1980 to commission specially designed boards from John Hall. Honscheid put the new boards to good use when, in October 1981, he appeared at the Weymouth Speed Trials to sail a "sinker" to a world record of 24.75 knots. Peter Hart later recalled, "this display amazed and excited British Windsurfers who viewed this display with glazed eyes and open mouth—not appreciating that it was actually easier to sail a board of that type in the prevailing conditions than the 'logs' they were used to" (1984, p. 41).

The following year, British sailors returned from Hawaii with ideas for new designs. Existing board shapers such as Tad Ciastula, who had been in business at Vitamin Sea since 1979; Jimmy Lewis (formed in 1965); and Phil Jenkins at New Waves (formed in 1980) were among the generation of existing shapers who were soon to be followed by a number of new companies in the period of the early 1980s such as K-Bay (1982), Lightwave (1983), MK Windsurfing (1981), and Valhalla Custom (1984). These companies primarily produced custom boards with small production runs or shaped to the individual preference of the sailor. They were, however, vulnerable to downturns in the market as evidenced by the liquidation of Limited Edition in 1987 and Lightwave in 1990. The nature of the vulnerability is basically twofold. First, like the industry as a whole, these companies were sensitive to general economic conditions, but possibly of more importance is that serious shortboard sailors are not loyal to brands, but to performance. Hence, they will switch to what are perceived as better boards, or even make their own.

The performance of both a surfboard and a sailboard is a function of a number of factors. First, there is the issue of the shape, which includes its length, the design of the edges of the board known as the "rails," the shape of the tail (stern) and underside, and the angle of the nose of the board (the "rocker"). The construction of the board is also important in terms of its stiffness, volume ("floatability"), and weight. In addition, the overall performance in windsurfing will be heavily influenced by the shape of the rig—that is, the sail. Finally, of course, the sailor's level of skill is very important. In addition, a number of marginal factors have some importance such as the shape of the fins (or skeg).

Initially, the boards were long—about 3.7 meters—heavy (often well in excess of claimed weights of 20 kilograms), had various arrangements of skegs, and, for windsurfers, a wooden dagger board that had a fixed position, or was otherwise slung around the sailor's shoulder with a rope. For windsurfers, the sail was a simple regatta triangular design, taken from dinghies, with a traveling center of effort. The result was a board that was difficult to sail, had a tendency to veer from a straight line due to the small skegs, and became a real handful in wind forces of over Force 4 on the Beaufort Scale.

In addition, the boards were of varying stiffness and quality. Quality control was a problem, but by 1981, consistency in production was better with companies utilizing new molding machines to ensure uniform thickness, as well as quality inspections. Also by 1981, for windsurfers, the concept of the "swivel" dagger board was becoming more common. That is, the sailor was able to change the angle of the dagger board while sailing by using his or her feet. Nonetheless, in an *On Board* magazine list of all the boards available in March 1981, none had a fully retractable dagger board—that is, one that retracted into the board to alleviate "spin out" that occurs from a buildup of pressure on the dagger at high speed and tips the board on its side. By 1984, this "retractability" was almost a standard feature. Indeed, by about 1982 to 1984 (if not sooner) many of the aspects of the modern board were apparent, including foot straps and sliding mast tracks.

In 1989, a new generation of boards like the Mistral Imco, the Equipe, and the Bic Bamba appeared, representing a return to high-volume boards, but with pronounced hard rails, while carbon fiber also began to be used. Similarly, boards appeared that were designed for specific functions. The epitome of this was the "gun board." Short and narrow, it almost resembled a ski, and was designed for speed. Its effectiveness was amply shown in 1989 when Britons Nick Luget and Eric Beale both broke the 40-knots barrier, with Beale establishing a new speed record for sailed craft.

As boards have become more sophisticated, so too have sails. As already mentioned, sails were initially similar to those of dinghies, being flat, triangular in shape, and often without battens. However, there are significant differences between dinghy sailing and windsurfing, notably the ability of the windsurfer to lean the sail into the wind due to the mastfoot's universal joint, while in a dinghy the mast remains at right angles to the boat. Originally, the thinking was dominated by sail theory borrowed from dinghies. In one of the first articles on windsurfing design, Roger Tushingham (*On Board* 1981) wrote about the importance of the luff curve, and how this was affected by the tension caused by the tightness placed upon the outhaul and downhaul by the sailor when rigging the sail. Such pressure altered the shape of the sail by affecting the bend of the mast and the leech shape. By June 1982, Tushingham was advertising a range of sails including a low-cut race sail with leech battens, that is, having a greater proportion of the sail below the boom than formerly. By February 1983, sails were appearing to fit the shorter booms, thereby permitting the sailor to have greater control, and, combined with a higher clew (lower corner of sail—foot—not directly connected to the mast), the sails also began to have greater degrees of stability due to a more fixed center of effort. Nevertheless, the sails still tended to have a triangular shape and be made of conventional sail materials such as Dacron. However, by the summer of 1983, the boardsailing magazines were introducing their readers to the new "wonder" material of Mylar, a polystyrene film made by Du Pont and ICI. Mylar has the advantages of being lighter than Dacron and nonabsorbent, so that water simply ran off the surface of the material. Initially seen as too expensive and for use only by advanced sailors, it was quickly to become the standard material for sails. By the end of 1983, high-aspect sails (high length-to-width ratios) were also becoming standard. By 1984, sails featured full-length battens, thus giving them a stiffness and rigidity that made control in higher winds much more possible and reducing the significance of the Force 4 barrier. Most of these advances were made possible by experience from the Hawaiian sailors, who in high wind and large waves were requiring equipment that made control possible in "radical" conditions. One of their requirements was a short boom and high-cut sail to stop the end of the boom and the bottom of the sail from catching on the surf as they turned away from the bottom of waves, and from these beginnings the slalom sail was developed. In addition, the world championship was a cause of technical advancement for both boards and sails, as was the growing popularity of speed sailing. In part it was the latter that was responsible for the increased stiffness of the sail and the introduction of the rotational and camber-induced sail. These were introduced sequentially, and both were attempts to create a smooth airflow on both sides of the sail. By 1985 the sail designers were utilizing computer technology and experience from gliders and aircraft to assess the amount of "lift" that could be generated. Fully rotational sails were introduced in 1983 and were pioneered by Barry Spanier and Geoffrey Bourne of Maui Sails, and by 1984, Neil Pryde had launched its RAF (Rotational Asymmetrical Foil) System sails as a mass-market product. The same year had also seen at the Weymouth Speed Trials an experimental sail by Gordon Fenn that was built around a standard mast but with a large luff that was foam-filled to form a wing-shaped leading edge. This could be considered one of the predecessors of the camber-induced sail in that the objective was the same, that is, to form a smooth shape on each side of the luff. However, the practicalities for mass production were limited, and there was also the weight disadvantage, especially if the rig were dropped in the water. The answer was to utilize plastic inserts that were placed on the luff end of the batten. These inserts had "arms" that went around the mast, and as the sail was tensioned, they pulled the luff sleeve into shape. By the time of the Dusseldorf show in 1985, both Gaastra and F2 were showing the camber-induced sail.

The 1990s saw further radical changes in design, of which the short but wide high-volume board as initially epitomized by the Starboard Go and the Bic Tecno were probably the most far-reaching in windsurfing. Combined with skegs (fins) of 200 cm plus in length, these boards offered planning abilities in light winds, greater manageability in high winds, and an ability to carry larger sails than before. Such was the success of these boards that the race board ceased to be manufactured with the exception of the Mistral Imco board, which was primarily retained because it was the board used for the Olympic Games until 2004. In the 1990s, sail designs moved away from cambers as new technologies provided greater sail stability without the disadvantage of large luff sleeves that hindered water starting, and by the start of the twenty-first century, windsurfing equipment was lighter, more novice friendly, and more stable, while still providing hard-core experiences.

Surfboards tended to show less technical advances, but two crossovers from windsurfing have occurred, albeit with mixed success. The first was the introduction of footstraps in the late 1990s, used by the more radical Hawaii-based surfers who introduced somersaults into their routines, which were being adapted from the sports of windsurfing and skateboarding, but overall this innovation has not been widely adopted. The second and still very radical advance was demonstrated by Laird Hamilton in initial shots for a 2002 James Bond movie, which was the adaptation of the skeg or fin to form a hydrofoil that gave such impressive speed off the waves that the film producers decided not to use the sequences because it was thought to stretch the credibility of the audience too far!

This is not to say that these technological developments always followed in a logical sequence without designers sometimes turning into cul de sacs. In October 1984, Fred Heywood appeared at Weymouth with not only an asymmetric P-shaped boom, but also a sail tensioned with wires, some of which were attached to the sailor. On the other hand, valid ideas appeared, but were not always capitalized upon due to either deficiencies in other aspects of the equipment, or perverse weather, leading people to draw the wrong conclusions. For example, Austin Farrar provided Gordon and Ken Way with a fully battened sail that featured a solid wing shape built up around the mast for the Speed Trials of 1976. However, with a size of 7.8 square meters, neither of the brothers could successfully handle the sail in high winds, and the ideas effectively (from a commercial viewpoint) were laid to rest for another five or more years.

Organizationally, both sports have benefited from the emergence of satellite television as sports enthusiasts offered a niche audience prepared to spend money in pursuit of a lifestyle while providing exciting and glamorous images beloved by the media. However, both sports also suffered from being weather dependent, and in an attempt to ensure some television coverage, "freestyle" requiring little wind came back into the windsurfing world championship circuit. Of the two sports, windsurfing has the greater number of organizations. This might be explained in part by a connection to dinghy sailing, its acceptance as an Olympic sport, a history of connections with major manufacturers with interests other than the sport (notably Bic), and a club structure that was partly based upon inland waters in the case of Europe and North America. Surfing, on the other hand, has tended to remain more independent and true to its roots of simply groups of enthusiasts turning up at the beach, although the advent of Web cams and cell phones has created high degrees of informal networks whereby, given good conditions, a beach can quickly fill with surfers.

Arguably, both sports can be said to conform to marketing theories of the product life cycle and product diffusion (Jennings 2003). In 1981, there were 21 importers/manufacturers in the British market offering 58 different types of boards (as listed in *On Board* magazine, April 1981). By 1984, there were 49 different companies manufacturing or importing 178 different boards. This figure rapidly fell to 20 companies in 1986. Since then, this figure has continued to slowly decline, although separate brand names continue when companies have merged. One notable example was the effective takeover of Tiga by Bic.

The market has been affected by a number of factors, including those of demographics, social change, and cost structures. Briefly, it might be argued that both surfing and windsurfing were among the first of the new extreme sports that were characterized by an appeal to youth, especially males; a free-wheeling alternative culture (especially true in the United States, but also true elsewhere); a high degree of individualism; a patronage by media seeking such imagery; and a technical and colloquial language that created "insiders" and "outsiders," associated with what might be described as cult lifestyles. In a sense, these sports appealed to those motivated by a wish to excel at sports requiring skill and dedication, providing a strong sense of achievement, adrenalin rush, and "flow" as described by Csikszentmihalyi (1975, 1990), and initially costs were low. However, if these reasons are valid, they are also the reasons that account for the comparative decline of these sports. First, as has been described above, the two sports, and in particular windsurfing, became more technologically complex and hence more expensive, meaning that in order to achieve peak performance, higher incomes or corporate sponsorship was needed. At the highest levels, the sports created world championships, but as the prize money compared with other sports is modest, the perpetuation of the desired lifestyle is made possible only by the interest of various corporations who wish to employ the imagery created by the sports, such as companies producing caffeine-based soft drinks. This adoption of the sport by corporate entities reduced its appeal for some as an alternative lifestyle, and encouraged the emergence of other sports that possess simplicity and accessibility through low cost and urban usage. The first of these was mountain biking, and by the early 1990s, many windsurfing retail outlets in the UK and elsewhere also sold mountain bikes. Crossover sports such as ski boarding and later skateboarding, BMX biking, rollerblading, and then kitesurfing emerged to offer a wide range of alternative lifestyle sports to the same age groups. Some of these sports, notably skateboarding, were less weather dependent and more urban based, which was the milieu of many adherents who also crossed over into the urban-based rap scene. Thus, between 1980 and 2000, both surfing and windsurfing began to lose a dominant position among those seeking adventure sports and began to occupy a position akin to skiing—that is, they were well-established sports no longer at the cutting edge of "radical," "awesome," and "wicked," to use street parlance of the early 1990s. Early adopters, as described by Rogers (1995), were no longer being drawn to these sports. Nonetheless, Humphreys (1997) concluded that in the case of snowboarding, the market-driven popularity actually helped create social space to "retain unique philosophies of alternative youth, such as cooperation, fun, and freedom," and that links are maintained with other non-mainstream youth activities and subcultures including surfing (p. 147). By extension, it can be argued that surfing and windsurfing still permit social space for subcultures to flourish that, like all such cultures, pose by their very existence norms and perspectives as alternatives to mainstream society. One such norm is the embracing of risk through its generation of experiences of enjoyable excitement (Midol 1993).

A second factor that accounted for the comparative decline of surfing and windsurfing was that as the sports began to lose the age group that normally took them up, it became even more important for manufacturers and sporting organizations to retain its aging adherents. Like jogging, which commenced as a mass movement in the 1980s, only to see its ranks become dominated by those over 40 in the late 1990s, both surfing and windsurfing manufacturers began to market their product to an increasingly skilled but aging and arguably more affluent age group. Noting these trends, national associations began to establish schemes designed to attract younger people into the sport, and targeted in particular the children of these older enthusiasts, thereby hoping to acquire new adherents before they reached the teenage years. Thus, particularly in Europe as exemplified by initiatives of the Royal Yachting Association (RYA), special classes designed for those under 15 years of age were established to both bring in "new blood" and to copy the schemes of excellence being adopted by other sports in a more professional age of sporting development and achievement—motivated in part by a wish to achieve success in the Olympics and various world championships. These attempts, at least in Europe, are beginning to show signs of success as the regattas organized for these age groups are attracting larger numbers of entrants of both genders.

Admittedly, both sports also suffered from an image of being dominated by males who adopted attitudes and lifestyles perceived as unwelcoming to females, particularly younger females. This is somewhat ironic, as in part the popularity of surfing was due to films like *Gidget Goes Hawaiian* and *Ride the Wild Surf* in which Linda Benson, Pacific Coast Women's Champion in 1959, 1960, and 1961, did most of the action shots. A revival of the genre in 2002 with *Blue Crush*, a film adapted from the magazine article "Surf Girls From Maui," by Susan Orlean, has also created a new interest in surfing by females at a time when young women are feeling increasingly empowered in a number of sports, as is evidenced by the professional football (soccer) league in the United Kingdom. Within the sport's magazines and videos, there has been a continued tension: on the one hand, there are the "beach bunnies" and shots of bikini-clad females, but on the other, there has been a grudging acceptance by males of the skill of professional female competitors, a recognition that females require different sports equipment (such as different harnesses for windsurfing), and the fact that a growing and significant proportion of participants are female. Thus, in 2002 and 2003, *Boards* magazine ran a regular column series by Bronwen Johnston called "The Board Housewife," in which the author described the trials and tribulations of being mother, wife, and windsurfer. The column attracted much favorable comment, and the response to its demise in late 2003 as Johnston moved on to other things showed that the column had hit a chord among readers of both genders. Certainly, studies such as those of Wheaton and Tomlinson (1998) demonstrate that many females feel empowered by their participation in surfing and windsurfing and derive self-confidence and control over their bodies while enjoying many of the same facets of the sport as their male counterparts. Nonetheless, the fact that the sport of surfing has a history of chauvinism is described in a number of studies. For example, Jaggard (2001) describes how women in Australia were excluded from the national saving body until 1980, while Law (2001) goes further in identifying "surfies" as part of a culture of irresponsibility where (male) youths sought unemployment to sustain a lifestyle.

Advantages and Disadvantages

One of the major appeals of both surfing and windsurfing is the potential that each sport provides for a sense of union with the forces of nature. For many of its participants, it is this fact that causes them to regard power-based water activities like jet skiing as "lesser sports," being noisy, polluting, and intrusive on the essential quietness of nature. The adrenalin high of "surfing the big one" or sailing in high winds is for many enthusiasts a quintessential fulfillment of the concept of "flow." Csikszentimihalyi (1975) defined the "flow" experience as "one of complete involvement of the actor with his activity" (p. 36) and identified the following seven indicators of its frequency and occurrence:

1. The perception that personal skills and challenges posed by an activity are in balance
2. The centering of attention
3. The loss of self-consciousness
4. An unambiguous feedback to a person's actions
5. Feelings of control over actions and environment
6. A momentary loss of anxiety and constraint
7. Feelings of enjoyment or pleasure.

(Csikszentimihalyi 1975, pp. 38–48)

However, for the flow experience to be felt, there are four prerequisites:

a) Participation is voluntary.
b) The benefits of participation are perceived to derive from factors intrinsic to participation in the activity.
c) A facilitative level of arousal is experienced during participation in the activity.
d) There is a psychological commitment to the activity.

The specifics of both surfing and windsurfing are the search for a constant balance (almost literally) between competency and challenge, where the challenge of enhancing competency is rewarded by new senses of achievement within a context of feeling even closer to forces of waves and wind, and a testing of self. Both sports require a "go for it" attitude, where hesitation means loss of momentum, and where success creates feelings of significant achievement and "one-ness" with movement, body, and conditions. Kelly Slater, former world surfing champion, has referred to surfing as a dance with nature. More academically, Jackson, Thomas, Marsh, and Smethurst (2001) have found clear associations between surfing, "flow," and positive self-concept, while Stranger (1999) writes that "the surfing aesthetic involves a postmodern incarnation of the sublime that distorts rational risk assessment" (p. 265). Farmer (1992) concludes that surfing creates a dizzy-like "high" and differs from many other sports in that the main motive is not competition against others, but the achievement of a sense of self-transcendence. He argues that surfing is not, however, a culture but rather a "scene" where conformity is enforced through peer pressure and charismatic figures exert "authority" through endorsement of performance by their peers. Intuitively it would be expected that such sports engage participants in long-term involvement, and evidence of this is provided by Havitz and Howard (1995), who distinguish between situation-specific and a more general sports involvement and argue that a positive relationship exists between activity involvement scores and participation.

It has been noted that both surfing and windsurfing create images that manufacturers, television producers, and tourism companies seek to utilize for purposes of promotion, while within the subcultures, many of the same images are consumed through the purchase of videos and magazines. This commodification of image is also consumed by surfers and windsurfers themselves to feed back into self-image. Ryan and Trauer (2003) have argued that adventure tourism needs to be located within a nexus of not only demand and supply of product and place, but also image and media consumption, while Preston-Whyte (2002) argues that surfers construct social space from images of normative wave environments—the perfect wave is as much a social as it is a physical construction. Stranger (1999) claims that the imagery of surfing is a construction and reinforcement of the sublime within a wider society. Like much human activity, the norms of the sport are derived from the activity itself but in part are interpreted with reference to a wider nexus of need, social frameworks, and commercial pressures (Figure 5-2).

Impacts

It is perhaps for these reasons that the two sports have emerged in the vanguard of movements concerned about the quality of the environment, and in particular the quality of water. This is epitomized by the UK-based movement, Surfers Against Sewage (SAS). Their mission statement reads, "Surfers Against Sewage campaign for clean, safe recreational waters, free from sewage effluents, toxic chemicals and nuclear waste" (http://www.sas.org.uk). Using a solution-based argument of viable and sustainable alternatives, SAS highlight the inherent flaws in current practices, attitudes, and legislation, challenging industry, legislators, and politicians to end their "pump and dump" policies (www.sas.org.uk, November 28, 2003). The case study in this chapter draws on this organization for its subject matter. That their concerns about potential harm for those engaged in water immersion sports at beaches and lakes is merited is well evidenced in the academic literature, for example, in Ellis (1991) and Bradley and Hancock (2003).

Figure 5-2 Surfers in a boat with their boards en route to Grupuk Bay, Lombok, Indonesia. Photographer: Troy Lister.

The influence of the surfing and windsurfing phenomenon is not restricted to environmental matters alone, but, as evidenced above, has had significant social impacts through the portrayal of lifestyles that have struck a chord in urban-based communities. Aspects of the sport of surfing such as its ability, like other sports, to create senses of flow, but this time in an intimate relationship between an individual and natural forces, present images and lifestyles that run counter to the norm of the contemporary workday. The sales achieved by the Beach Boys records are not simply accounted for by the numbers who actually surf. It is also not without significance that one of the fastest growing activities of the early twenty-first century is "surfing the Web"—the use of the term "surfing" is deliberately chosen to identify the unstructured, free-wheeling nature of the activity. Yet, like surfing on waves, an acquisition of skill in terms of formulating search terms will produce better results. In addition, surfing and windsurfing have both had an impact on leisure wear—from Aloha shirts to the Mambo-style shorts, the "shades" (sunglasses), the use of neoprene as a material, and the use of body-hugging fashion for sun suits. There is rarely a holiday brochure that does not feature a windsurfer—the activity evokes images of summer by reason of the activity itself and the bright colors of the sails.

A combination of the activity and its associated lifestyle, language, and dedicated technologies supported by a specialist media are, for a commentator like Butts (2001), the characteristics of a subculture that offer specific individualistic benefits and, like many adventure sports, provide an important escape mechanism in a society that arguably is becoming more risk averse (Ryan 2003), an observation used in the 1991 film *Point Break*.

Future Directions

In terms of conventional product life-cycle theory, there are signs that surfing and windsurfing are in a rejuvenation phase as they begin to attract younger people again. The paradox is that for a sport initiated on a premise of a rejection of organization and authority, it is the sporting organizations like the RYA and commercial interests that are spearheading various initiatives to develop participation rates. The reasons are generally self-evident. National sporting organizations assess success by criteria such as membership, participation rates, and achievement in international sporting events, which requires increasing degrees of professionalism commencing at younger ages and grounded securely in grassroots organizations, as evidenced by the Australian experience with its Institute of Sport. Commercial organizations are motivated by a need to profitably sell their product. Hence, windsurfing in particular not only retains at its heart the dance with waves and wind, but also copes with a changing role in the portfolio of sports available today. Today, both surfing and windsurfing are often seen as "mature sports" and occupy a niche akin to skiing, as mentioned earlier. More youth-oriented sports have emerged such as skateboarding and kitesurfing, yet in this loss of extreme status, both surfing and windsurfing are still capable of offering an experience of "flow" to those who are older and wish to regain that experience. The new high-volume, wide windsurf boards offer the capability of high-speed sailing in less challenging wind conditions, and the resurgence of longboarding offers surfing fun without a need to surf with the famous *Jaws*. With an aging but younger-feeling and fitter cohort that is increasingly a common feature of the demographics of advanced economies (Ryan and Trauer 2004), the ease of access to an adventure sport offers opportunities for sports and tourism organizations. Additionally, the emergent female market also provides opportunities that to a large extent have been spurned by past practices. It is thought unlikely that these sports will enjoy the rapid growth that they achieved in the 1980s when, for example, in the Netherlands in a little over a decade, windsurfing was said to possess a participation rate of 6% of the population (Smit 1988). However, having weathered the downturn of interest from the end of the 1980s to the mid-1990s, the sports have emerged in a positive state with technological gains still being made and new adherents finding the pleasures of "dancing with nature."

Case Study: Surfers Against Sewage

Formed in 1990 in the southwest region of England because of fears of the quality of sea waters at favorite surfing beaches, Surfers Against Sewage (SAS) has become both national and high-profile through a combination of media-catching images, argument based upon commissioned and published research, and a willingness to take water and sewage-treatment companies to court. As early as 1993, it achieved a major victory as a pressure group when Welsh Water became the first company to adopt a policy of full treatment for all coastal and estuarine sewage discharges. SAS publicly supported this policy and encouraged the Welsh Tourist Board to promote Welsh beaches with clean water as a significant advantage. From early on, the group included other water users and not simply surfers, while in 1999 it built upon previous European networks to present views on the European Bathing Waters Directive. That their concerns about water quality are real was made evident by the death of Heather Breen and the illnesses contracted by children swimming in the seas at Dawlish, in southwest England, in 1999 from inhaling $E.\ coli$ 0157 that had survived in a spill of raw sewage into the sea—a case that achieved more national media coverage than articles in medical journals that had long indicated possible dangers resulting from practices of pumping untreated sewage out to sea.

The organization believes in utilizing publicity and is known for its "inflatable turds" that help represent its case, such as when it lobbied the European Parliament prior to the vote on the Bathing Water Quality Directive in October 2003. However, the strength of the organization comes from many sources besides the commitment of its executive. These assets include well-researched arguments based upon medical evidence, and careful sampling of waters and obtaining of data about water company practices. Second, there is wide support for the organization in the surfing and windsurfing community, and SAS appeals to the anti-authoritarianism norms of many of the sports' practitioners. Its irreverent approach through the use of turds, broken bottles, and detritus in its demonstrations has shown that demonstrating is not simply serious, it can be fun. The water sports community is quick to report untoward incidents to the organization in the knowledge that while water companies and local authorities might be tempted to hide issues, SAS will campaign to improve water conditions. Given that many health professionals also surf and windsurf, SAS has been able to use professional help from committed sports people. While its concern is about the quality of lake and sea water for recreational use, SAS has recognized that its interests are not incompatible with those of marine conservation groups, and particularly in the United Kingdom, SAS has worked with such groups throughout the 1980s and 1990s to expose deficiencies in clean beach campaigns.

The organization is funded through membership fees, sponsorship, merchandising, and fund-raising activities, and its accounts show an income of about £400,000 (US$748,213), making it one of the least financially endowed pressure groups. This has not stopped the organization from a series of initiatives that include the development of educational packets for use within school curricula. After 13 years of existence, increasing demands on the group leaders' time come from those it formerly campaigned against. In addition, politicians at the local and national level as well as water board officials seek to obtain the organization's views as an authoritative source representing recreational water users. Details about SAS can be obtained at www.sas.org.uk.

References

Bradley, G., and C. Hancock. (2003). Increased risk of non-seasonal and body immersion recreational marine bathers contacting indicator microorganisms of sewage pollution. *Marine Pollution Bulletin*, **46** (6), 791–794.

Butts, S.L. (2001). Good to the last drop: understanding surfers' motivations. *Sociology of Sport Online—SOSOL*, **4** (1), 1–7.

Csikszentmihalyi, M. (1975). *Beyond boredom and anxiety.* San Francisco: Jossey-Bass.

Csikszentmihalyi, M. (1990). *Flow: the psychology of optimal experience.* New York: Harper & Row.

Ellis, J.B. (1991). Bacterial water quality and public health risks associated with the recreational use of urban waters. *Environmental Health*, **99** (9), 233–236.

Farmer, R.J. (1992). Surfing: motivations, values, and culture. *Journal of Sport Behavior*, **15** (3), 241–257.

Havitz, M.E., and D.R. Howard. (1995). How enduring is enduring involvement in the context of tourist motivation? *Journal of Travel & Tourism Marketing*, **4** (3), 95–99.

Humphreys, D. (1997). Shredheads go mainstream? Snowboarding and alternative youth. *International Review for the Sociology of Sport*, **32** (2), 147–160.

Jackson, S.A., Thomas, P.R., Marsh, H.W., and C.J. Smethurst. (2001). Relationships between flow, self-concept, psychological skills, and performance. *Journal of Applied Sport Psychology*, **13** (2), 129–153.

Jaggard, E. (2001). Tempering the testosterone: masculinity, women and Australian surf lifesaving. *International Journal of the History of Sport*, **18** (4), 16–36.

Jennings, G. (2003). Marine tourism. In S. Hudson (Ed.), *Sport and adventure tourism.* (pp. 125–164). New York: Haworth Hospitality Press.

Law, A. (2001). Surfing the safety net: "dole bludging," "surfies," and governmentality in Australia. *International Review for the Sociology of Sport*, **36** (1), 25–40.

Midol, N. (1993). Cultural dissents and technical innovations in the "whiz" sports. *International Review for the Sociology of Sport*, **28** (1), 23–32.

Preston-Whyte, R. (2002). Constructions of surfing space at Durban, South Africa. *Tourism Geographies*, **4** (3), 307–328.

Rogers, E.M. (1995). *Diffusion of innovations.* (4th ed.). New York: The Free Press.

Ryan, C. (2003). Risk acceptance in adventure tourism: paradox and context. In J. Wilks and S.J. Page (Eds.), *Managing tourist health and safety in the new millennium.* (pp. 55–66). Oxford, UK: Pergamon.

Ryan, C., and B. Trauer. (2003). Involvement in adventure tourism: toward implementing a fuzzy set. *Tourism Review International,* 7 (3–4), 143–152.

Ryan, C., and B. Trauer. (2004). Ageing populations: trends and the emergence of the nomad tourist. In W. Theobald (Ed.), *Global tourism.* (3rd ed). Oxford, UK: Butterworth-Heinemann.

Smit, L.J. (1988). Windsurfing along the right lanes: harmonization between windsurfing and other forms of water sports (Plankzeilen in goede banen: over de onderlinge afstemming van plankzeilen en andere vormen van waterrecreatie). *Recreatie Reeks,* 1, 1–50.

Stranger, M. (1999). The aesthetics of risk. A study of surfing. *International Review for the Sociology of Sport,* 34 (3), 265–276.

Wheaton, B., and A. Tomlinson. (1998). The changing gender order in sport? The case of windsurfing subcultures. *Journal of Sport and Social Issues,* 22 (3), 252–274.

Websites

Surfers Against Sewage: http://www.sas.org.uk
http://www.surfart.com

6

Sport Fishing and Big Game Fishing

Les Killion

Overview

Fishing in its various guises has long been a favored form of water-based recreation and, for some, a necessary means of subsistence. As with many "survival" activities, fishing has become a popular sport motivated by the challenges of competition, whether against others or against the self. Differentiated from early subsistence fishing only by contemporary technology and inevitable regulatory requirements aimed at sustainability, sport fishing and particularly the pursuit of big game fish remain primary pull factors drawing visitors to destinations in both developed and developing locations. The principal focus of this chapter is on big game fishing in the context of charter operations and what have become international competitive tournaments. Big game fishing is considered a subset of the wider category of sport fishing, other forms of which may occur from smaller vessels, off rocky headlands, from beaches, and in river locations.

While largely avoiding a species-specific approach, the chapter explores some of the locations where big game fishing has become popularized. Inevitably, some reference to fish species occurs since particular locations are renowned for the species (and hence the type of activity) available. Consideration is also given to the nature of big game and sport fishing markets. A generalized profile is provided of those seeking to satisfy their recreational needs by pursuing large game fish in various watercraft using sophisticated sounding and fishing apparatus, and at destinations that brand and position themselves by association with big game fish. The rising popularity of the activities associated with big game fishing demands a further focus on the regulatory frameworks devised by government and other authorities to minimize detrimental impacts and promote sustainability.

Background

In the pursuit of big game fish and other forms of sport fishing, much has changed since the time when Izaak Walton penned *The Compleat Angler* (1653/2002) in which he remarks, "if I might be the judge, God never did make a more calm, quiet, innocent recreation than angling," although doubtless significant numbers of recreationists still follow Walton's suggestion contained in the words "I have laid aside business, and gone fishing." Walton's description of the idylls of trout fishing in rustic, preindustrial England stands in dramatic contrast to the scenario on board a big game fishing charter boat when the billfish first takes the hook and the fight is on to tag, if not land, the catch. The recreational dimensions of sport fishing that are explored in this chapter are depicted largely in the context of big game fishing, although it is acknowledged that sport fishing may take on several alternate forms, including fishing in rivers and streams for trout! Of course, included among the forms of sport fishing are those that take place off beaches and shores, as well as forms that distinguish inner reef and outer reef locations from the open sea. Much difference also surrounds the type of tackle and other equipment used. The sporting dimension of these forms of angling also makes for difference. To reiterate, the focus throughout the chapter is on competition among big game anglers through international angling tournaments. It is acknowledged that as a form of water-based recreation, fishing of a noncompetitive, even nonsporting kind represents a further dimension in this aquatic activity.

Despite an image of widespread popularity as a recreational activity, fishing does not figure prominently in the leisure preferences of a number of Western nations. For example, according to one study in Australia, even allowing for the generic nature of some categories, fishing did not rate in the list of leisure pursuits of Australians the vast majority of whom, regardless of gender differences, prefer to spend their time television viewing, entertaining, shopping for pleasure, or visiting with friends and relatives (Australian Bureau of Statistics [ABS] data, cited in Lynch and Veal 1996). When listing activities in which they participated in the week prior to being surveyed, 5.2 % of males and 1.6 % of females indicated fishing as a recreation pursuit among the top 57 activities listed. Fishing was also more likely to be undertaken by people who were full-time employed in skilled manual and supervisory occupations (Lynch and Veal 1996). Some of the characteristics of those who go fishing as a preferred form of recreation will be considered further in discussing attributes of the market for big game fishing. For now, the differences in participation between men and women in fishing are noteworthy and reflect a wider picture presented by McKay (1991), Dovers (1994), and Rowe and Lawrence (1998) of male hegemony in Australian sport.

Sport fishing in general and big game fishing in particular are species and, therefore, location specific, although seasonal fish movements make choice of destination more flexible. Reef or bottom fishing (also referred to as "bottom bouncing") is centered on such species as red emperor, coral trout, and nannygai. Heavy hand lines (60–100 lb) are used, and in some cases rod and reel. Light-tackle bluewater sport fishing generally targets such species as Spanish mackerel, northern bluefin tuna, dogtooth tuna, mahi mahi, giant trevally, Pacific sailfish, and juvenile black marlin, depending upon the month. In the Cairns and Port Douglas area around Cape Bowling Green, and around Lizard Island and

Cooktown, Australia (Figure 6-1), for example, Spanish mackerel and juvenile black marlin are more numerous during the winter months from May to September, while black marlin and sailfish are more abundant in the warmer months from October to March. The pursuit of these and other pelagic species is typically undertaken on luxury "live-aboard" charters vessels or "mother-ship combined charters." Light tackle and fly-fishing add to the experience. In addition to offshore fishing for bluewater species, fly-fishing is also a favored form of sport fishing in estuarine areas and in freshwater streams, pursuing species such as barramundi. The latter, a prime target species in Australia, has become itself the focal point of competitive fishing, and in the Rockhampton area of Queensland the so-called Barra Bounty has become a significant event on the annual fishing calendar.

Big game fishing, whether for competitive tournaments or noncompetitive sport, is centered on the larger pelagic (that is, found in the open sea) sport fish commonly known as "billfish." As Davie (cited in Vallon n.d.) comments, all billfishes belong to the family *Xiphiidae* or *Istiophorida*. The latter comprises three genera: the sailfishes (*Istiophorus*), the spearfishes and striped and white marlin (*Tetrapturus*), and the blue and black marlins (*Makaira*). The billfishes inhabit tropical and temperate oceanic zones, and Table 6-1 outlines some details of species distributions.

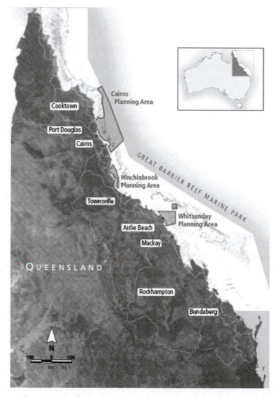

Figure 6-1   Great Barrier Reef Marine Park, Australia. Source: Cooperative Research Center (CRC) Reef Research Center (2003). Map courtesy of the Spatial Data Centre, Great Barrier Reef Marine Park Authority.

Table 6-1   Distribution of Billfishes

Common Name	Distribution
White marlin	Atlantic Ocean
Striped marlin	Indo-Pacific Ocean
Atlantic blue marlin	Atlantic Ocean
Indo-Pacific blue marlin	Indo-Pacific Ocean
Black marlin	Indo-Pacific Ocean
Broadbill swordfish	Worldwide
Indo-Pacific sailfish	Indo-Pacific Ocean
Atlantic sailfish	Atlantic Ocean
Short-bill spearfish	Indo-Pacific Ocean
Mediterranean spearfish	Mediterranean Sea
Long-bill spearfish	Atlantic Ocean
Round-scale spearfish	Mediterranean Sea and adjacent Atlantic Ocean

Source: Vallon (n.d.).

As noted earlier, the distribution patterns of billfishes reflect aspects of habitat, patterns of predation spawning behaviors, and seasonal water temperatures. These variables also create the basis for seasonality in big game fishing as a recreational activity, reflected in the seasonal rotations of competitive tournaments as well as the seasonal travels of noncompetitive big game angler tourists. As Davic (cited in Vallon n.d.) comments with regard to the black, blue, and striped marlins, "[t]heir size, speed, and athletic ability make marlin spectacular sporting fishes, sought after by recreational fishermen and women who often target marlins and their billfish relatives in special billfish tournaments." Such fish have also been the targets of commercial fishing operations, an aspect that will be considered later in the context of resource use conflict and the need for management strategies.

The billfish recreational industry has had a long history in the waters of the Pacific Ocean. In New Zealand, for example, big game fishing enjoyed enormous popularity in the 1920s following the fishing exploits of Zane Grey, who recorded his catches on film for global distribution and later wrote of his experiences in *Tales of the Angler's Eldorado* (Primetime Charters and Game Fishing n.d.). In Australia, Cairns became the sport fishing capital of the world in September 1966 when an American (Richard C. Obach) landed a world-record 1064-pound black marlin on 80-pound test line. As noted by Australian Fishing Expeditions (n.d.),

[n]ot only was this the first Grander Black Marlin caught in Cairns but also the first Thousand Pound Marlin of any kind caught on 80# test line anywhere in the world. This made international sports fishing history for Cairns and Australia's Great Barrier Reef region. Big game fishermen from all over the world flocked to Cairns in subsequent years, with hundreds succeeding in capturing their dream billfish.

Billfishing at other global locations in the Atlantic and Pacific oceans has a similar history of development giving rise to an international network of competition. The Pacific Ocean remains a primary focus with locations such as Australia, Hawaii, and New Zealand being joined more recently by tournaments in countries such as Vanuatu and Papua New Guinea. The Pacific is also the location for conflicting resource use between commercial fishing interests and recreational big game fishing. Davie (cited

115

in Vallon n.d.), for example, observes that around 90% of the marlin catch in the Pacific Ocean is taken by longline fishing vessels that primarily target tuna species, with billfish comprising about 18% of the total tuna longline catch. In his view, the recreational and subsistence billfish catches are comparatively "small, but not insignificant." Within the Atlantic Ocean, as Davie further reports, following the decline in recreational and commercial swordfish fisheries off the coast of Florida, management strategies were put in place in order to maintain recreational billfish fisheries. The Atlantic Ocean has been the focus of big game fishing contests based in Florida, Mexico, and more recently in such countries as Puerto Rico, Venezuela, and Jamaica. In the Indian Ocean, there has been notable development of big game fishing off the coast of Western Australia and such countries as Thailand and the Maldives. In all of these instances, as will be discussed later, the conflict between commercial and recreational fishing has necessitated the intervention of government agencies seeking sustainable development in the interests of all parties.

Market Profile

Relatively little in the way of specific data exists to depict the characteristics of the big game fishing market. Some speculative conclusions can, however, be drawn from the central features of this form of water-based recreation. For example, at a cost exceeding AU$1,000 (US$759) for an eight-hour deep sea fishing charter and AU$550 (US$417) for a half-day reef fishing charter (Seahunter Charters n.d.), it can be concluded that it is upper-income socioeconomic groups who find such activities affordable. Further, even a random search of big game fishing websites, especially those featuring tournament results, indicates the predominance of men who pursue this activity. For example, in the listing of winners at the June 2005 Emerald Coast Blue Marlin Classic, Sandestin, Florida, of 11 prize-winning anglers, only 2 were women (Sandestin Golf and Beach Resort n.d.). A similar conclusion is reached from a cursory glance at the photographs of winning anglers on the numerous websites featuring such global contests.

A somewhat more accurate profile of the big game fishing market was captured in the research of Ditton and Gillis (1996) in 1995 at the three tournaments conducted from Cabo San Lucas. This research followed earlier studies completed in the late 1980s (Falk, Graefe, and Ditton 1989). The findings from the mail survey of participants not unexpectedly revealed that the majority (94%) were male and over 65% were in the age range of 36 to 54, average age of participants being 46 years. Respondents were predominantly white (98%), had a median education level of three years of college, and a median household income of US$130,000–US$150,000 (Ditton and Gillis 1996). In terms of psychographics (Plog 1991, 1994), the profile presented through these surveys indicates a largely "midcentric" market, seeking a particular experience resembling that of more adventurous "allocentric" tourists, but from the relative safety of a fully crewed and equipped charter boat (Figure 6-2).

On average, respondents reported 12.6 years of billfish fishing, and an average of 23.6 years of saltwater fishing experience, and most (54%) indicated that fishing was their most important outdoor activity. While most reported participating in only one tournament in the previous year, a number had participated in two or more tournaments. In terms of the role played by angling organizations as pressure

Figure 6-2   Midcentric big game fish anglers. Source: Seahunter Charters. Available online at http://www.websight.net.au/seahunter/

groups responding to government controls and regulations, it is significant that almost 30% of respondents were members of the International Game Fishing Association (Vallon n.d.). In relation to the earlier surmise concerning socioeconomic status, respondents to the Ditton and Gillis survey reported an average total expenditure of US$4,949 for their last trip to Mexico for a fishing tournament, more than half of which was expended on tournament fees and charter costs. Blue, black, and striped marlin were reported (in that order) as the fish angler respondents were most interested in catching. Importantly in light of the impacts of commercial fishing targeting these species, and the related regulation of commercial trawling, which will be discussed later in this chapter, almost a quarter of these respondents indicated that commercial fishing activity posed the greatest threat to the continuation of the activity, and that they would travel to other locations (the Pacific Coast of Costa Rica, Hawaii, Venezuela, Panama, and the Caribbean) to satisfy their quest for big game fishing (Vallon n.d.).

Such alternate locations provide some indication of the global significance of the big game fishing market, particularly when it comes to tournament competition. Such contests also now take place all across the developing world, wherever billfish are to be found. Throughout the Pacific Rim, countries such as Papua New Guinea offer this form of sport fishing. In Vanuatu in May 2005, the marlin-specific tag-and-release Vanuatu Marlin Classic tournament proved so popular among local and international anglers that organizers were forced to reprogram the event to "allow more participation [so] that each boat available for entry into the competition will be eligible to fish with two teams" (Vanuatu Marlin Classic 2005).

This tournament that takes place over six days was "purposely designed to promote the sport of game fishing as well as fisheries conservation" and carries total prize monies of AU$50,000 (US$38,000) (Vanuatu Marlin Classic 2005).

There is opportunity for further research into the socioeconomic impacts of such events when these are conducted at exotic destinations in the developing world where it would seem local populations serve as little more than deckhands and gaff holders for visitors who, in addition to possessing cultural differences, also come from a strikingly different socioeconomic segment with contrasting motivations.

Fishing for sport is clearly not motivated by the necessity of satisfying Maslow's (1970) basic needs for food and sustenance, although it may well be the case for those who fish for commercial gain and subsistence as will be seen in the case study presented later. However, in keeping with any form of sporting prowess, participation in game fishing tournaments is often motivated by the need for esteem and ego enhancement, and for some, the attainment of more intrinsic self-actualization. Equally apparent in such contexts is support for Iso-Ahola's (1980) contention that leisure behaviors are motivated by the search for optimal arousal. Csikszentmihayli's (1990) concept of "flow" that seeks to link the notions of intrinsic motivation and optimal arousal provides a further insight into the motivations of big game fish anglers. The extent to which engagement in such pursuits is characterized by feelings of timelessness and intense satisfaction is founded, at least from the perspective of the flow concept, by the equilibrium created between opportunities for action and the skills and abilities of the individual—a balance between potential anxiety and possible boredom. Again, the case study that appears later provides some insight into this state of balance for the big game angler.

The forces that motivate anglers to pursue big game fishing provide one view of the market for this form of water-based recreation. Viewed in somewhat different marketing terms, fishing for big game fish is now used as a significant factor in destination branding. As noted by Morrison (2002), the association between destination branding and available tourism product has a positive impact in positioning the destination in the minds of visitors. Nowhere is this more apparent than in Cairns, Queensland, Australia. Here the coastal zone is popularly referred to as the Marlin Coast, the marina affording access to the Great Barrier Reef bears the name "Cairns Marlin Marina," accommodation in the city frequently carries such names as "Black Marlin Motel," and, as if to reinforce the image and position even more strongly, the local soccer team is known as the Marlin Coast Club (Cairns Port Authority n.d.).

Advantages and Disadvantages

Ultimately, sport fishing and particularly big game fishing are special interest forms of tourism attractive to quite specific niche markets. The nature of these recreational activities and their market profiles set them apart from the wider ambit of mass tourism. As such, sport fishing has much in common with other forms of special interest tourism when it comes to disadvantages. In particular, as discussed in wider terms by Douglas, Douglas, and Derrett (2001), all forms of special interest tourism development carry potential for destination development, at least for as long as the interests of specific niche markets remain viable. However, it can also be argued that a dominant focus on the products and attractions of given forms of special interest tourism can serve to alienate other alternative sources of visitor demand. That is, in achieving strength of positioning in the minds of would-be tourists, destinations may become so closely associated with the particular form of special interest tourism that visitors seeking different experiences and recreational activities turn to other locations seen to offer a more generic destination mix. Hence, destinations such as Queensland's Marlin Coast, while well known for the attractions that such a descriptor signifies, may in the final analysis be losing market interest from other segments. The saving grace in this situation is that such destinations usually have an underlying wider appeal to visitors seeking the more general products and attractions associated with marine tourism.

What remains of further concern is that the activities at the base of sport fishing are invariably seasonal in nature. That is, whether a targeted fish species is abundant is determined by seasonal currents and associated spawning behaviors. Thus, those whose principal livelihoods rely on big game fishing are forced to seek alternate opportunities in the off season, while still maintaining high-cost capital resources in the form of charter boats, equipment, and related staff resources. Of course, where fishing is also aligned with tournament competitions, the effects of seasonality are even more pronounced. Again, the synergies inherent in all forms of marine and coastal activities and attractions may offer a reasonable fallback position when the competition, like the season, has come to an end.

Conversely, it can be argued that the nature of international competition and the associated organization and professionalization of sport fishing, and especially big game fishing, offers notable advantages. These activities, in marked contrast to some other forms of special interest tourism, have a long and well-established history of organizational development on an international scale. Prime among the international organizations relevant to these activities is the International Game Fishing Association (IGFA). The IGFA was established in 1939 to

encourage the study of game fishes for the sake of whatever pleasure, information, or benefit it may provide; to keep the sport of game fishing ethical, and to make its rules acceptable to the majority of anglers; to encourage this sport both as recreation and as a potential source of scientific data; to place such data at the disposal of as many human beings as possible; and to keep an attested and up-to-date chart of world record catches. (IGFA n.d.)

Since that time, the association has grown to include 325 representatives and members in around 120 countries and territories and, in line with its original charter, continues its activities in scientific research and collaboration with government authorities regarding legislation aimed at promoting game fish conservation. As the organization website states, "The anglers and scientists who first envisaged this organization had . . . broader purposes in view than the mere maintenance of world record information" (IGFA n.d.). As important as its scientific research and policy advisory roles, the IGFA operates a system of accrediting operators as "certified captains" and thereby enforces adherence to a code of ethical practice. More recently, the association has instituted a system of "certified observers" able to travel with charter groups and to officially witness record-breaking catches prior to the release of the fish. In both respects, such mechanisms contribute directly to the objectives of sustainable resource management and conservation.

At a more localized, but no less significant level, professional associations and organizations contribute to resource management strategies and policy advice. Typical of these is the Cairns Professional Game Fishing Association (CPGFA), which has had ongoing communications with such agencies as the Great Barrier Reef Marine Park Authority in the formulation of zonal management plans.

Impacts

In its general assessment of marine tourism on the Great Barrier Reef, the Cooperative Research Center (CRC) Reef Research Center concluded,

The level of fishing by tourists is small compared with that of other recreational and commercial fishers and accounts for approximately 3% of the estimated total catch. A small but financially significant game-fishing industry operates predominantly in waters offshore from Port Douglas. The industry probably has low environmental impact because it focuses on large oceanic species such as marlin, most of which are tagged and returned to the water. About 120 charter vessels also offer day and extended fishing charters, mostly in the southern and central Great Barrier Reef. Fishing is managed by both Commonwealth and State Governments. Where fishing is permitted, the Queensland Fisheries Service also regulates the size and number of fish taken. (CRC Reef Research Center 2003)

The general view of the CRC Reef Research Center regarding the wider category of marine tourism was that

[t]he 'footprint' of marine tourism on the Reef is considered to be small and generally localized. However, because of the size and significance of the tourism industry, careful science-based management and responsible self-regulation by the industry is needed to ensure that tourists do not damage the environment that attracts them (CRC Reef Research Center 2003).

The CRC Reef Research Center suggests that the environmental impacts of big game fishing are minimal. As will be discussed later, the tag-and-release programs implemented in locations such as the Great Barrier Reef and other billfish fisheries represent a meaningful alternative to the inevitable species endangerment associated with any recreational hunting activity if resource carrying capacity is exceeded. In other locations, commercial imperatives as well as recreational demands must be satisfied from the same finite resource base. Species impacts notwithstanding, it should also be observed that the infrastructure associated with this and other marine-based activities may create the basis for impacts of greater magnitude. The construction of marinas, pontoons, and moorings that alter the marine habitat, as well as waste discharge, littering, and anchoring may be considered environmental impacts of sport fishing to which other marine activities also contribute. There is potential here also for spatial conflict between the infrastructure and access requirements of big game fishing charter vessels and other marine-based activities, giving rise to possible health and safety issues that need to be addressed through judicious planning that allows for a mutually beneficial "mix" of activities and pursuits. (See related discussions of such conflict in Gartside 1986; Graefe and Fedler 1986; Kenchington 1993; Dovers 1994; and Jennings 1998; as well as Chapter 4 in this book.)

Compared with research into environmental impacts, relatively little specific research evidence exists regarding the social and economic impacts of marine tourism on local communities. Some indication of the economic significance of such activities can be ascertained from the following assessment:

Marine tourism has the highest commercial value of any activity in the Great Barrier Reef Marine Park with an estimated contribution of more than $1.5 billion (US$1.13 billion) per year to the Australian economy. Approximately 1.6 million visitors travel to the Great Barrier Reef Marine Park on commercial tourism operations each year. In addition, more than one million visitor nights per year are spent on island resorts. (CRC Reef Research Center 2003)

Not all of this contribution can, of course, be attributed to big game fishing alone, or even to more general sport fishing. Nonetheless, the economic returns from marine tourism are significant. What remains largely under-researched is the extent to which similar economic returns are achieved at other destinations, especially those in the developing world that have come to depend on income generated by tourism. Moreover, the extent of leakages from local economic systems remains unclear. While big game and sport fishing are high cost/high value pursuits, the extent to which monies expended on boat hire, equipment, accommodation services, and other amenities remain within local economies or flow to external industry intermediaries responsible for arranging charters needs to be assessed before any firm conclusions can be reached regarding the positive economic impacts of these activities. Certainly, for some destinations in the developing world, providing personnel for the charter may be an important source of income for those employed on the vessel, and potentially for local charter boat owners as well.

The differences in economic level between host communities at destinations from which big game fishing charters originate, and those who travel to such destinations to participate in these activities are reflected in the nature and costs of the activities themselves. In addition to the apparent economic distances that this situation exacerbates, there are also social distances of equal importance. Many of the early investigations into tourism's social impacts reported by Mathieson and Wall (1982) were, ironically, set in destinations that in the context of contemporary tourism are favored for big game fishing throughout the Caribbean and Pacific Island nations such as Fiji, Tonga, and the Cook Islands. While not exclusively related to big game fishing or to tourism alone, in the wider spectrum of tourism impacts on societies and cultures, there are many issues related to servility, neocolonialism, and a "plantation approach to tourism," with associated issues concerning the external leakage of income. Servility and social inequality between hosts and guests may be particular issues when, for instance, the local population is employed only as unskilled deckhands on charter boats, possibly on a seasonal basis, and in some areas seeking to supplement income derived from commercial fishing at other times. While this may seem to be an issue confined to developing world destinations, it is not unheard of in destinations such as Cairns for local fishermen and women to enter the charter boat market as a seasonal supplier in order to capture the additional dollars resulting from seasonal demand.

Future Directions

Questions of sustainable development ultimately surround any form of human activity, including recreational pursuits. Such questions are, however, especially pertinent when the form of recreation is closely aligned with, and dependent upon, natural resources. This issue is exacerbated when the same resource is targeted by alternate user groups whose interests, motivated by commercial gain, fall outside the recreation domain. All of this poses a series of complex challenges in contemplating the future of big game fishing.

In terms of future patterns of market demand, it can be argued that pressures on the resource base are less potent for forms of special interest tourism where niche markets are relatively small in number, and better informed with respect to resource impacts and consequences of overuse. Big game fishing reflects a picture of a relatively small, specialist market that through greater knowledge and involvement in and with professional bodies is unlikely to exceed critical threshold levels of overfishing. There is a wider awareness that the form of recreation and its dependence upon finite fish populations has, through unbridled demand, the capacity to destroy the resource base that is its primary attraction. Should big game fishing become attractive to mass tourism markets, this assessment would inevitably change. However, it would seem that among the complex set of market forces, the costs of participation serve as a filter for the growth of future demand. Perceptions of big game fishing as an elitist form of recreation, due to its high costs, act as a further social constraint on the activity being widely adopted by mass markets.

All of this notwithstanding, there is a clear need for judicious resource management strategies in order to ensure the future viability of the resource base. It is here that two approaches reach a point of intersection. First, there are both actual and potential conflicts between forms of resource use, particularly between those who target billfish for longline commercial fishing, and those who place value on these species for recreation. Attempts to resolve this level of resource conflict have required the entry of government and the enactment of legislative controls. In 1979, for example, Australia excluded longline fishing vessels from its sections of the 200-mile Exclusive Economic Zone. Similar measures were enacted in Mexico in 1983 and in New Zealand in 1987 (Davie, cited in Vallon n.d.). Such actions have had the effect of declaring marlin and other billfish species as the preserve of the recreational angler. Similar provisions formulated by the International Commission for the Conservation of Atlantic Tunas and the Atlantic Billfish Management Plan, implemented by the U.S. Department of Commerce in 1988, sought to "maintain the highest availability of billfishes for the recreational fishery" (Davie, cited in Vallon n.d.).

In 1998, following an Australian House of Representatives Inquiry (1996), the Commonwealth Fisheries Legislation Amendment Bill (No. 1) was enacted, which placed a ban on commercial fishing for blue or black marlin in the Australian Fishing Zone to replace the earlier voluntary bans. Similar bans have been sought more recently to protect the striped marlin in both Western Australia and New South Wales, where research conducted by the Saltwater Trust indicated that "the gross value of the recreational catch of striped marlin exceeded that of the commercial sector by approximately AU$52.32 million (US$39.66 million)" (Sportfish Australia n.d.).

These measures should also be viewed concurrently with the zonal resource use restrictions imposed by the Great Barrier Reef Marine Park Authority (GBRMPA), although such limitations have not always been welcomed by game fishing operators. When the GBRMPA announced its Representative Areas Program in 2003 aimed at expanding the extent of marine protected areas (or green zones), many operators felt their livelihood was threatened by unreasonable limitations, outlawing their charter fishing activities in bioregions that historically had been the best fishing spots (Cairns Professional Game Fishing Association n.d.). A similar response greeted the announcement by the Western Australian state government to impose comparable restrictions on recreational fishing around the Rowley Shoals offshore from Broome, where sailfish are the attraction for big game anglers (Day 2005).

The level of resistance against the resource management strategies of government authorities such as GBRMPA is not entirely without reasonable foundation. Armed with an internationally recognized code of ethics, professional accreditation standards, and a notable level of awareness of the need for resource protection and conservation, big game anglers and charter operators have actively supported other government initiatives that have resulted in highly successful tag-and-release programs. In New South Wales, for example, the Game Fish Tagging Program was established in the 1970s, supported by more than 170 angling clubs affiliated with the Game Fishing Association of Australia (GFAA) or the Australian Sport Fishing Association (GFAA n.d.). While such programs characterize the nature of fishing tournaments that now include a tag-only category, they are also directly linked to government-funded research programs in which anglers play a pivotal role in recording species movements and populations. Moreover, and again with the interests of sustainable resource management at the fore, increasing numbers of big game anglers utilize the technology of barbless hooks and other devices designed to ensure that once tagged, the released fish experiences minimal trauma as part of a "release them alive" ethic (GFAA n.d.). However, as will be seen in the case study that follows, the same levels of resource awareness are not necessarily found among operators in developing countries where commercial imperatives are all-powerful motivators.

Case Study: Catch and Keep or Catch and Release

The purpose of this case study is to provide a reflective account of the lived experience of big game fishing in Mexico.

Having learned on day one of an eight-day vacation in Cabo San Lucas, Mexico, that swimming, snorkeling, and diving over coral were not, after all, on the menu, I decided to devote three of my days to the other alleged specialty of the Cabo: big game fishing. Big game fishing is perhaps the last contest between man and wild beast, with the possible exception of bullfighting. I read somewhere that, pound for pound, the strongest animal on land is the Siberian tiger. In the ocean it is the marlin. Other fish may fight with all the strength they can muster, but they all tire before the fisherman [sic]. Only the marlin goes on and on, hour after hour.

Those who know sea angling will recall the chaos that occurs on an afterdeck when men [sic] lulled half to sleep by the cradle-rocking of the ocean suddenly hurl themselves all over the place. As the customer, I just threw myself into the fighting chair and yelled for the boatman to pass me the rod. And still the line roared out. Taking the bucking rod from the boatman's hands, I waited for the fish on the other end to cease its first freedom run. It finally did so and I was able to turn the handle on the reel and recover a few meters of line. This caused the line to go taut; thus it would remain for the duration of the fight. With a sinking heart I noted the fish had taken 800m of line, and each centimeter would have to be recovered with sweat and pain. Above my head on his flying bridge, Roberto was yelling "Marlin!" and far down the wake the pelagic predator roared out of the sea, glittering turquoise, aquamarine, slate and sea spray for one magical moment before plunging back under water. Then it began to fight. The angler has the technology of a carbon-fibre rod whose springiness absorbs some of the shocks of the

123

plunging fish, a brass reel with plenty of line, and that thin filament of nylon with a breaking strain of 36 kg. The key is the reel. It has a slipping clutch, set in this case at 22 kg. When the fish pulls more than this, the line unwinds against the drag and the angler can only hold on and suffer. Even as the fight started, I realized I had two disadvantages. Trying to economize I'd booked a boat with basic equipment and that included the fighting chair. When I yelled for the harness, a shrug told me there wasn't one. Not good news. The harness helps spread the strain from wrists and arms to the chest and torso. It also links the angler to the chair. A big fish has been known to jerk the angler clean into the sea. The other disadvantage was the boatman whose job is to assist the angler once a big fish is on the hook. Unfortunately I had observed mine was as thick as a plank.

Metre by metre the 800m of line came back onto the reel. Then the marlin broke away and took it back. It is a matter of serious grief to hold onto a rod with screaming muscles and see the reel being stripped back almost to the brass drum. But that is what it is all about. The marlin takes the strain; the angler takes the pain. The contest is about who will concede first: man [sic] or beast.

Within the first hour the marlin came to within 45m of the boat 10 times, and 10 times took all the line back again. Halfway into the second hour I thought the freedom runs were getting shorter and the pauses longer. Then the marlin took another 180m of line back and the contest began again. You do not get to love a marlin that is trying to pull your arms out. In fact the language gets bluer than the ocean. But you learn to respect it.

After two hours my hands were arthritic claws. . . . My watch told me later it was two hours and 40 minutes after the strike when the great fish came up under the stern and touched the boat with her javelin bill. That counts as caught. Of the boatman I could only see two trousered buttocks as he leant over the stern to the water. What he thought he was going to do with 250kg of marlin I do not know. Lift it out of the water? I noticed the hook of the flying gaff still unused in the corner, and knew that if he plunged that 25cm spike into her, the lady of the sea was dead. Roberto was coming down the ladder from the flying bridge to lend a hand. He would surely not forget the gaff. There was a bait knife sliding about in the scuppers. I leant down from the chair and cut the line. In a second she was gone, back to her cool, dark home below. Roberto made plain he was not a happy mariner. After a while I realized he would have received a premium for bringing home a dead marlin of that size, so I asked how much it would have been and made him happy with a $100 bill.

I will not fish off Mexico again, because I strongly support the tag-and-release scheme. The trouble is, the Third World spares nothing, which is why game-fishing hot spots are getting cooler and cooler. Fish are not stupid. When they sense they are taking repeated losses near a certain coast, they avoid it.

Source: Forsyth (2005)

Case Study Reflections

Within this case study, there are fairly clear signs that the motives for seeking big game fishing as a form of recreation are not vastly different from those surrounding any form of "hunting" pursuit. Reference is made to the competition between man and beast as a significant ingredient in the contest that forms a central part of the onsite experience. At a somewhat deeper level, there are also indications of motives that point to the possible "flow experience" that such pursuit may engender for some big game fisherfolk. This is a good deal different from the competitive nature of the activity, and in contrast reflects the all-absorbing nature of that stage in the pursuit of the game fish when it has taken the hook and the contest commences. Indeed, Forsyth (2005) alludes to the lapse in time as the hunt continued, only looking at his watch *after* the event and noting that more than two hours had passed. It could also be argued that such an experience is reflected in the self-actualization that drives such a challenge between man and a beast that, in the end, will be released, leaving the game fisher with a sense of satisfaction that the fish had been caught, and the feeling that that in itself was satisfaction enough.

The case study also infers several issues related to big game fishing in developing nations. There is clear evidence that the activity is frequently in the hands of poorly equipped operators, keen to earn income by taking anglers to known fishing locations. The more difficult issue centers on the local attitude toward the resource. The boatman was obviously more intent on earning an additional "premium" by taking home a dead marlin, rather than seeing the fish set free. Underlying the final comments of Forsyth, such a situation has the potential to undermine the resource base as fishing grounds are either depleted of stock, or fish seek more protective environments. The dilemma thus is between an immediate return from the resource, and an approach that favors sustainable resource management as found in other nations and locations.

References

Australian Fishing Expeditions. Accessed July 28, 2005, from http://www.australian-fishingexpeditions.com/black_marlin.htm

Australian Government House of Representatives Inquiry. (1996). *Managing commonwealth fisheries: the last frontier.* Accessed August 7, 2005, from http://www.aph.gov.au

Cairns Port Authority. (n.d.). *Marina guide.* Accessed August 6, 2005, from http://www.cairnsport.com.au/marina/default.htm

Cairns Professional Game Fishing Association. Accessed August 7, 2005, from www.cpgfa.asu.au

CRC Reef Research Center. (2003). *Marine tourism on the Great Barrier Reef.* Townsville, Queensland, Australia: Cooperative Research Center. Available: http://www.reef.crc.org.au/publications/brochures/index.html

Csikszentmihayli, M. (1990). *Flow: the psychology of optimal performance.* New York: Harper & Row.

Day, M. (2005, March 19–20). Out of the blue. *The Weekend Australian Magazine.* Surry Hills, Sydney: National News Pty.

Ditton, R.B., and K.S. Gillis. (1996). *Characteristics of billfish anglers: social and economic study of billfish tournament anglers in Cabo San Lucas.* Accessed July 30, 2005, from http://www.catchbillfish.com/marlin.htm

Ditton, R.B., Grimes, S.R., and L.D. Finkelstein. (1996). *A social and economic study of the recreational billfish fishery in the Southern Baja Area of Mexico.* Report to

International Billfish Research and Conservation Foundation, Fort Lauderdale, Florida.

Douglas, N., Douglas, N., and R. Derrett. (2001). Introduction. In N. Douglas, N. Douglas, and R. Derrett (Eds.), *Special interest tourism*. (pp. xvii–xxviii). Milton, Queensland, Australia: Wiley.

Dovers, S. (1994). Recreational fishing in Australia: review and policy issues. *Australian Geographical Studies*, **32** (1), 102–114.

Falk, J.M., Graefe, A.R., and R.B. Ditton. (1989). Patterns of participation and motivation among saltwater tournament anglers. *Fisheries* (Bethesda), **14** (4), 10–17.

Forsyth, F. (2005, March 12–13). The day of the tackle. *The Weekend Australian, Weekend Travel* (pp. 1–2). Surry Hills, Sydney, Australia: Nationwide News Pty.

Game Fishing Association of Australia. The NSW Gamefish Tagging Program. Accessed July 23, 2005, from http://www.gfaa.asn.au/html/2tag_01.htm

Gartside, D.F. (1986, March/April). Recreational fishing. Paper presented to the National Coastal Management Conference, Coffs Harbour, Australia. *Safish*, **11** (2), 15–17.

Graefe, A.R. and A.J. Fedler. (1986). Situational and subjective determinants of satisfaction in marine recreational fishing. *Leisure Sciences*, **8** (3), 275–295.

International Game Fish Association. Accessed August 7, 2005, from http://www.igfa.org/about.asp

Iso-Ahola, S. (1980). *The social psychology of leisure*. Dubuque, IA: Wm. C. Brown.

Jennings, G.R. (1998). *Recreational usage patterns of Shoalwater Bay and adjacent waters*. (Research Publication No. 50). Townsville, Queensland, Australia: GBRMPA.

Kenchington, R. (1993). Tourism in coastal and marine environments: a recreational perspective. *Ocean and Coastal Management*, **19**, 1–16.

Lynch, R., and A.J. Veal. (1996). *Australian leisure*. South Melbourne, Australia: Longman.

Maslow, A. (1970). *Motivation and personality*. (2nd ed.). New York: Harper & Row.

Mathieson, A., and G. Wall. (1982). *Tourism: economic, physical, and social impacts*. Essex, UK: Longman Scientific and Technical.

McKay, J. (1991). *No pain, no gain? Sport and Australian culture*. Sydney, Australia: Prentice Hall.

Morrison, A. (2002). *Hospitality and travel marketing*. (3rd ed.). Albany, NY: Delmar Thomson Learning.

Plog, S. (1991). *Leisure travel: making it a growth market . . . again!* Chichester, UK: Wiley.

Plog, S. (1994). Developing and using psychographics in tourism research. In J.R.B. Ritchie and C.R. Goeldner (Eds.), *Travel, tourism, and hospitality research: a handbook for managers and researchers*. (2nd ed.). Chichester, UK: Wiley.

Primetime Charters and Gamefishing. (n.d.). Accessed July 30, 2005, from http://www.primetimecharters.co.nz/marlin.htm

Rowe, D., and G. Lawrence. (Eds.). (1998). *Tourism, leisure, sport: critical perspectives*. Rydalmere, New South Wales, Australia: Hodder Education.

Sandestin Golf and Beach Resort, Florida. Accessed August 6, 2005, from http://www.fishecbc.com

Seahunter Charters, Bermagui, New South Wales. Accessed August 6, 2005, from http://www.websight.net.au/seahunter

Sportfish Australia. Accessed July 27, 2005, from http://www.sportfish.com.au

Vallon, J. (n.d.). John Vallon's (El Mackerele) Billfish Fishing Site. Accessed July 30, 2005, from http://www.catchbillfish.com/marlin.htm

Vanuatu Marlin Classic. (2005, May). Accessed July 28, 2005, from http://www.pacificholidays.com.au/vamarlin.htm

Walton, I. (2002). *The compleat angler, or the contemplative man's recreation.* (4th ed.). Transcribed by I. C. Teas, Project Canterbury, UK. (Originally published 1653).

Recommended Reading

Craik, J. (1991). *Resorting to tourism.* Sydney, Australia: Allen and Unwin.

Hall, C.M. (1997). *Tourism in the Pacific Rim.* (2nd ed.). Melbourne, Australia: Addison-Wesley Longman.

McKercher, B. (1998). *The business of nature-based tourism.* Melbourne, Australia: Hospitality Press.

Ryan, C. (1991). *Recreational tourism: a social science perspective.* London: Routledge.

Weiler, B., and C.M. Hall. (Eds.). (1992). *Special interest tourism.* London: Belhaven Press.

Websites

Australian Fishing Expeditions: http://www.australianfishingexpeditions.com/lauries.htm

Cairns Marlin Marina: http://www.cairnsport.com.au/marina/default.htm

Gulf Coast Offshore Adventures: http://www.gcoafishing.com/

7

Scuba Diving, Snorkeling, and Free Diving

Kay Dimmock

Overview

This chapter will discuss aspects of three popular water-based experiences: scuba diving, snorkeling, and free diving. An historical overview introduces the work, followed by a discussion of what each experience involves. The change in characteristics of the international market profile as a result of increasing demand is discussed, together with a number of relevant management issues. Consideration of issues related to these sports as recreational tourism activities leads into a review of a range of impacts that can result. The work concludes with case analysis of a popular Australian diving site, Julian Rocks, located within the Cape Byron Marine Park.

Historical Overview

Human involvement with the underwater environment has strong historical links. Pearling, underwater warfare, and deep salvage are some of the pursuits that have been carried out for centuries by divers who relied mainly on their ability to hold their breath (Cherry 1976) in order to earn a living. The Australian aborigine was possibly one of the first to use a snorkel. They used a hollow reed as a breathing tube (Stone 1999). However, as recreational activities, diving and snorkeling are considered relatively new. In the 1930s, sport divers in the Mediterranean swam underwater holding their breath to hunt for fish. Early equipment consisted only of goggles; fins were patented as "Lifesaving and Swimming Propelling Devices" in 1933 (Cherry 1976). Meanwhile, the first safe, reliable prototype equipment for scuba diving was provided by Jacques Cousteau and Emily Gagnan in 1943 (Stone 1999). SCUBA is the acronym for Self-Contained Underwater Breathing Apparatus and has become the generic term to describe diving with air support.

Growth of recreational activities that involve being underwater was aided by the first publication of *Skin Diver* magazine in 1951, released to nurture the industry and to promote underwater photography and travel. The 1960s saw the formation of the commercial scuba education organization, Professional Association of Dive Instructors (PADI).

What Are Scuba Diving, Snorkeling, and Free Diving?

Scuba diving, snorkeling, and free diving are three water-based experiences that access the marine environment using different approaches, equipment, and techniques. Snorkeling and free diving use less equipment, as they only require the assistance of a mask to see clearly underwater, a snorkel to breathe on the water surface, and fins to enable propulsion. Free divers might use a small amount of weight to assist descent. Snorkelers primarily swim on the water surface face down, searching and discovering the marine world below. Free diving is sometimes described as "breath-hold diving" and was traditionally called "skin diving" (Cherry 1976). It involves taking a breath before plunging below to swim immersed for a short time in the underwater realm. With practice, free divers develop the ability to remain submerged for some minutes before needing to surface for air.

Those seeking greater immersion can experience scuba diving, which is said to have evolved as a natural consequence of snorkeling and free diving (Stone 1999). To participate requires substantially more equipment including portable but limited air supply, mask, and fins, as well as weights and a wet suit. Scuba divers can regularly spend more time at depths beyond those visited by other forms of diving. Scuba requires training and practice to develop the necessary skills to become comfortable in the underwater environment in order to safely enjoy the range of situations and experiences the sport offers.

Differentiation Among Sport, Leisure, Recreation, and Tourism Activities

Reasons why an individual might pursue these activities have been shown to be linked to personal motivation and desire for ongoing involvement with the activity. This especially pertains to scuba diving and, more recently, free diving (Free Dive Vancouver n.d.; *DiversTravel.com* 2003). For example, scuba can be undertaken while on vacation as part of a one-time "resort dive" or "introduction to scuba" experience. In this situation, the diver is closely accompanied by an instructor to a water depth of approximately 12 meters after minimal training, practice, and equipment familiarization. Some people may participate in scuba, snorkeling, or free diving as an occasional recreational activity, whereas others pursue ongoing and regular involvement for the purpose of sport and leisure. Regularity of participation will often be the point that defines involvement as a recreation, leisure, sport, or tourism experience. Social clubs are often formed at dive shops that encourage regular scuba, snorkeling, or free diving. Ambiguity surrounds distinct definitions between the terms sport diving, leisure diving, recreational diving, and dive tourism. This is emphasized by views in the literature as to what constitutes the four types of experiences.

Dive tourism is recognized as travel where at least one scuba diving expedition is included (Tourism Queensland 2005). A dive tourist may be a regular sport diver or occasional leisure diver. Sport is considered something that is undertaken regularly within leisure time (Colquhoun 1993). There is an expectation that sport will constitute elements of play, freedom, and spontaneity (Huizinga, cited in Standeven and De Knop 1999). Others, however, suggest competition and institutionalized physical activity are components of sport (Luschen and Guttman, cited in Standeven and De Knop 1999). Certainly, competition is evident in free diving at the professional level (Performance Freediving 2006). However, as tourist activities, scuba diving, snorkeling, and free diving are generally recognized as noncompetitive activities that comprise elements of fun, physical activity, and freedom. Jablonski (1999) acknowledges that any form of scuba diving that is unpaid, regardless of whether it be cave, wreck diving, or reef diving, is considered recreational diving. It is likely that those with a high level of involvement and interest in scuba or free diving consider themselves to be sport divers because of their regular involvement with the activity during leisure time (Colquhoun 1993). This view is supported by publications that identify with the activities as sport and recreation and presume participants have regular involvement (see, for example, *Sport Diver, Scuba Diver, International Free Diving,* or *Spearfishing News,* and *Deeper Blue*).

Market Profile

As a rapidly growing component of global tourism, diving is undertaken in many coastal areas of the United States, Australia, and Japan (Davis, Harriott, MacNamara, Roberts, and Austin 1995); the Wider Caribbean, Pacific coast of Central America (Green and Donnelly 2003); the Pacific Islands, Papua New Guinea (*Dive Log Australasia* 2004); and Asia including Thailand and Malaysia (Musa 2003). Much growth in scuba activity has occurred in tropical environments where clear, warm waters and diverse geophysical and biological features of coral reefs provide attractive settings (Inglis, Johnson, and Ponte 1999). International diving locations include the Red Sea of Israel, Egypt, and Jordan (Hawkins and Roberts 1994), islands of the Indian Ocean including Maldives and the Seychelles, and the Philippines (*Working paper for the Cape Byron Marine Park* 2003). In fact, coral reefs in any tropical location provide a major impetus for tourism development that supports dive- and snorkel-related activities (Hawkins and Roberts 1994). This does not detract from the quality of dive and snorkel opportunities available in more temperate coastal and offshore island locations (Stone 1999). Rather, accelerated tourism development in tropical locations appears to have stimulated and aided mass appeal (Hawkins and Roberts 1992).

Demand for dive tourism by international visitors to Australia has increased dramatically to a point where state government tourism organizations have identified dive tourists as a specific market segment (Tourism Queensland 2005). In 1989, approximately 239,000 international visitors indicated they had participated in scuba diving or snorkeling while in Australia. This number increased to 436,600 by 1995 (Blamey and Hatch 1998). Exact numbers of participants are difficult to determine. However, estimates of active divers worldwide have been quoted at 5 to 7 million (Tourism Queensland 2005). PADI estimates that it is responsible for about 50% of annual basic certification, with 5 million certifications recorded in 1994 (Davis and Harriott 1996; Townsend 2003). Growth in certification numbers in Canada was predicted to increase by 20,000 per year (Labuda 1981), and there are an estimated 2.5 million divers in the USA (Tourism Queensland 2005), while 1996 Australian certification figures were recorded at approximately 100,000 per year (Davis and Harriott 1996). At Australia's Great Barrier Reef Marine Park, growth in visitor numbers has increased from 150,000 visitor days in 1980 to more than 1.5 million visitor days in 1995 (Inglis et al. 1999). Other estimates suggest that more than 1 million recreational scuba dives are undertaken annually from commercial vessels on the Great Barrier Reef (Wilks 1991), and 1.8 million visitors either dived or snorkeled (Tourism Queensland 2005) the Reef in 2002.

The proliferation in diving experiences has been encouraged by establishment of recreational scuba training facilities at many locations (Market Research.com n.d.). More than 250 operators are located in Florida alone, with a further 650 in the wider Caribbean and Pacific coast of Central America (Green and Donnelly 2003). One estimate (Davis 1996) indicated 424 recreational dive training and retail operations in Australia. More recently, the number has risen to a level where the Great Barrier Reef Marine Park alone supports 684 operators that hold a scuba permit (Tourism Queensland 2005).

The growth in global dive and snorkel activity has seen a shift in the profile of the contemporary recreational diver. The international recreational diving market was formerly the domain of experienced, rich or intrepid, predominantly male divers. However, with a growing number of people traveling for the purpose of experiencing scuba diving or to snorkel (Market Research.com n.d.), the market profile is quite dynamic. For example, Mundet and Ribera (2001) describe the average diver coming to the Spanish Costa Brava islands as an employed person in middle- to high-level professional activities, aged between 31 and 45 years. In contrast, visitors to the township of Byron Bay who travel to dive at Julian Rocks Aquatic Reserve are typically 20 to 30 years of age and predominantly male (Doyle 1996). Meanwhile, the visitor profile to the Great Barrier Reef includes 20% of visitors represented in each age group, 20–29 years, 30–39 years, and 40–49 years, with 50.8% being female (Shafer, Inglis, Johnson, and Marshall 1998). Issues such as access, language, marketing, and motivation to travel to the destination are offered to explain demand by specific markets at differing destinations. From a global perspective, however, market characteristics are heterogeneous.

Demand for these activities by a heterogeneous population suggests the move from a traditionally special interest tourism experience toward a more mainstream or general tourism experience (Brotherton and Himmetoglu 1997). In an effort to better organize the heterogeneous markets, a number of options are possible. Choice to segment or categorize markets will depend on a specific characteristic (Kotler, Chandler, Brown, and Adam 1994). For example, Rice (cited in Tabata 1992) categorized scuba divers into three groups, identified in Table 7-1, according to their level of participation with the activity, which in turn influenced their choice of destination.

The demand for recreational scuba has occurred predominantly in the "potential" and "tourist" categories that Rice (cited in Tabata 1992) identifies. This consideration acknowledges that the level of diver training and experience deemed

Table 7-1 Scuba Diver Categories

Potential	Experience scuba if it is available at destination
Tourists	Undertake scuba on vacation and select destination where scuba is available
Hard Core	Choose destination based on quality of diving conditions

Source: Adapted from Rice, cited in Tabata (1992).

safe for recreational scuba is quite different compared with more complex diving activity that is sometimes referred to as "technical" diving. Jablonski (2001) recognizes that "technical diving" resists easy description, but does suggest increased depth beyond recreational limits as well as increased task loading associated with decompression obligations and complicated environments.

To help explain the variety in participation, Brotherton and Himmetoglu (1997) developed a Special Interest Tourist (SIT) Typology that consists of four groupings with particular characteristics as explained in Table 7-2.

Participation begins with "inexperience," where emphasis is on the destination and "dabbling" in the activities available (Brotherton and Himmetoglu 1997). This parallels Rice's "potential diver." Ongoing involvement moves the participant to become an "enthusiast" or Rice's (cited in Tabata 1992) "tourist." Further involvement results in a developed interest in the activity. The "expert" stage is being reached. Here destination choice is dependent on availability of the preferred activity, which is likely to result in a more adventurous form of vacationing (Brotherton and Himmetoglu 1997). Rice's "hard core" diver is likely to be a "fanatic."

Table 7-2 Special Interest Tourist (SIT) Typology

Dabbler	Enthusiast	Expert	Fanatic
Comfortable with other inexperienced participants	Progressed from sampling to experience	Extensive knowledge and skill with activity	Extreme levels of involvement with activity
Focus on safety in involvement decisions	Social element an important component	Activity central to life and focus of lifestyle	Activity dominates travel choices
Choice depends on attitude to risk, with decision likely to be fashionable or contemporary	Activity likely to be a lifestyle enhancement, not a complete change of behavior	Activity central to self-identification with equipment and challenging environment is vital	Poses a marketing challenge with specialization beyond standard packages
Need persuasion by marketers to participate	Seeks new but not overly demanding opportunities to practice interest	Ongoing development and learning provide stimulation and challenge	Highly skilled at activity with own equipment and technical experience

Source: Adapted from Brotherton and Himmetoglu (1997).

From Brotherton and Himmetoglu's (1997) research, 61% of respondents indicated they "dabbled" in scuba diving as an activity while on vacation, 16% indicated they were "enthusiasts," and 13% said they were "experts" at the activity. These findings align with comments by Van Treeck and Schuhmacher (1998) that scuba diving has become a mass movement, although the spirit of an individual adventure sport still exists. Research further supports a view that adventurous and more challenging environments remain the domain of sport and experienced divers (Stone 1999), while leisure and recreational involvement in a more managed situation has become the mass movement that supports a contemporary dive tourism industry. From a business management perspective, a number of possibilities present.

Supply and Access

Access to the aquatic environment has been stimulated by advancements in technologies, particularly the open-system scuba unit by Cousteau and Gagnan (Market Research.com n.d.), which led to development of reliable and affordable diving equipment (Davis and Tisdell 1996). Technological advances have also produced marine craft that are able to travel greater distances in shorter times. These craft can access outlying and previously less accessible locations (Parker 2001) (Figure 7-1). In addition, the cumulative effects of global tourism have extended demand and opportunity for dive operations to be established at an increasing number of destinations (Cater and Cater 2000).

While snorkeling and free diving may be pursued independently at coastal locations, recreational scuba divers are likely to utilize the services of scuba agencies or operators. To do so, participants are required to get certification and training. There has been an explosion in the last few decades in the global scuba education industry. It has been dominated in the last 30 years by two training organizations— PADI and Scuba Schools International (SSI) (Davis and Tisdell 1994). In addition, a number of training agencies also exist, including Associated Underwater Scuba Instructors (AUSI) and the National Association of Underwater Instructors (NAUI), as well as the two organizations mentioned above (Stone 1999). Dive tourism operators will have affiliation with at least one of these scuba education agencies and provide similar standards and education products, ranging from a 1-day resort dive experience to a 14-day scuba instructor program.

Management of Diving Operations

For the dive operator, there are three main areas of output for customers: education, equipment, and experience. All are essential to industry longevity with two, education and equipment, influencing current standards. Resulting from this is the third output, experience.

1. Education: For a scuba diver to dive with a "buddy" and without assistance of an instructor requires basic training, known as "open-water" or "c-card" certification (Wilks 1991). Recreational training products available include introductory, beginning to advanced, and instructor levels.

Figure 7-1 Commercial dive operator tows divers back to the mothership. Whitsunday Islands, Australia. Photographer: Jessica Carlsson.

2. Equipment: This is needed to participate and can often be rented or purchased. Many operators offer to service equipment and accessories. The importance of equipment to the income stream will influence whether contemporary dive and snorkel gear feature as part of the retail element in the business.
3. Experience: The dive component offered by the scuba operator will include charter trips, dive travel, and local site information. The dive operator should be able to provide information on current conditions, safety, legal issues, customs, and local marine flora and fauna. Knowledge of the site and factors such as visibility, weather, and water temperature will influence management of the visitor experience.

Operators will vary in the combination and extent to which each element is provided. Factors that will influence this variation include the location of the operator, profile of main target markets, and training facilities and resources. For example, certain recreational dive tourism managers in New South Wales (NSW), Australia, do not place a high priority on providing education because facilities and staff resources are not adequate. Rather, their core business is focused on dive travel and equipment service and sales to many regular customers (Dimmock 2004).

Participating in diving is made more appealing by the existence of marine protected areas (MPA) for dive sites (Davis and Tisdell 1996). MPAs can be defined as any area of coastal zone or ocean conferred at a level of protection for the purpose of managing use of resources and ocean space, or protecting vulnerable or threatened habitats and species. Marine sanctuaries and marine parks are one of seven categories available, with marine parks able to encompass multiple use zones (Agardy 1997) that can include recreational diving and snorkeling.

Australia has 303 marine parks, which total about 5% of the country's total marine environment. However, 74% of the area is located within the Great Barrier Reef Marine Park (GBRMP) (Stone 1999). Using marine parks as the dive site will have management implications for more than one organization. The commercial operator will have specific objectives, as will those responsible for managing the marine environment, such as the NSW Department of Environment and Conservation. For the dive operator, objectives will focus on achieving business outcomes within a risk-free environment. For the department responsible for the marine park, the focus will primarily be toward ensuring conservation of natural resources and offering a level of recreational amenity (*Working paper for the Cape Byron Marine Park* 2003).

McKercher and Robbins (1998) recognize that challenges associated with running a nature-based tourism operation in Australia are similar to the generic issues associated with many small business operations. Such a perspective supports a view that issues associated with marketing and management of the operation require attention, particularly within competitive business environments. Compounding the challenge for dive tourism managers is the need to achieve business success, and provide satisfying experiences and satisfactory customer experiences while maintaining a level of responsibility toward protecting the natural site (Dimmock 2004; see also comments in Chapter 10 regarding tourism and recreation businesses).

As small business managers, dive tourism operators should remain abreast of characteristics, attitudes, and needs of their markets (Lovelock, Patterson, and Walker 1998). Visitor perception of risk involved with scuba, snorkeling, and free diving, particularly at early involvement stages, requires a high level of monitoring and attention by dive staff. Similarly, there is a need for managers to be cognizant of the type of experience being sought by divers and what is required to provide such experiences. For some participants, the dive may be a once-only occurrence, whereas others will pursue ongoing involvement through education and training. Business success for dive operations relies heavily on the quality of diver experience with the site as well as factors related to the service, information, and equipment.

What constitutes the work of a manager has been a point of focus for researchers (Mintzberg 1980; Schermerhorn 1999; Carroll, cited in Leiper 2003) in the general business literature, with consensus that variation exists and numerous skills are required to be successful. Authors of the *Competing Values Framework* (CVF) (Quinn, Thompson, Faerman, and McGrath 2003) contend that four main models of management can accommodate much of the range and variety within the manager's task. These four models recognize that

1. Staff needs and objectives can be achieved through the *Human Relations* model;
2. Organization stability and continuity is possible through the *Internal Process* model;
3. Productivity and profit can be maximized within the *Rational Goal* model;
4. Adaptability and external support are achievable through the *Open Systems* model (Quinn et al. 2003).

The thesis that underpins the Competing Values Framework acknowledges that variety is prevalent in the managerial task, with the view that success relies on competency in each of the four management models. The authors advise that most managers have strengths in particular areas and limitations in others. Mastery of management is said to exist when a balance in competency is achieved across all four management models (Quinn et al. 2003). A visual representation of the Competing Values Framework appears in Figure 7-2.

A study of NSW, Australia, dive tourism managers was conducted using theories and concepts of the Competing Values Framework that investigated management challenges. The study found that aspects related to managing external business relations were given the least attention by the sample group. Many managers within that study identified difficulties such as working with local government agencies and other user groups with interests in the dive site that were inherent to running their business. Moreover, these difficulties were often compromised because of a need to address internal business issues (Dimmock 2004).

For dive tourism managers, one stakeholder group responsible for tourist activity in public marine environments, the issue of managing external relations provides ongoing challenges in the provision of a safe, satisfying, and fun dive tourism experience. Within the Competing Values Framework, managing external relations is reflective of a manager's attention to identifying opportunities and successfully managing the organization through periods of change (Quinn et al. 2003). Indeed, dynamic characteristics of the diving market provide opportunity for managers to remain current with external changes that influence the customer base.

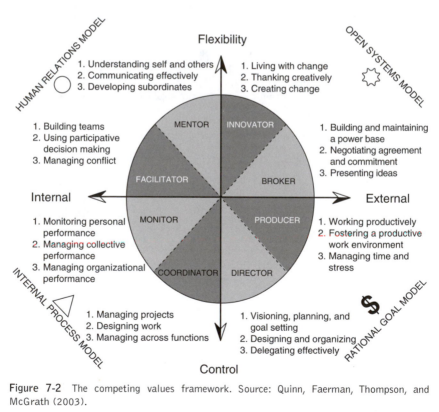

Figure 7-2 The competing values framework. Source: Quinn, Faerman, Thompson, and McGrath (2003).

Advantages and Disadvantages

Participation in scuba diving provides several advantages, including longer and deeper bottom time than is possible with snorkeling and free diving. Therefore, opportunity to be more involved with the marine location and to observe marine wildlife is possible. This fact alone has encouraged the growth of underwater photography as a popular hobby (Cherry 1976; Sylvester 1987). The experience allows divers to see, learn, and discover the marine location.

Ongoing involvement and regular scuba diving normally involves further skills training, which contributes to personal physical development and education. Basic open-water education allows divers to experience up to 18 meters of depth in a non-overhead environment. This level of training provides basic skills including finning techniques, mask clearing, and some "buddy" communication signals. Further training can extend skill and diving parameters to include rescue skills, deeper diving, night diving, and cave and wreck diving. Increased training and education will involve greater management of technical issues such as extended depth, equipment malfunction, physiological risks, understanding decompression profiles, and mixed gas diving. As the complexity of the diving task increases, the need for further diver education also increases (Jablonski 1999).

Snorkeling and free diving, on the other hand, require less equipment and mental and physical involvement. For these reasons, many prefer the freedom of snorkeling and free diving (Cherry 1976). Snorkeling is something that everyone can do, whereas scuba can restrict some participants. For example, people with asthma will not obtain medical clearance to scuba dive (personal communication). Snorkeling and free diving require less financial involvement because there is no need to service or rent large amounts of equipment. Similarly, the investment in terms of time and cost for training and education is reduced for free divers and snorkelers. However, training in basic water skills is fundamental to safety in all activities, with free divers needing to be aware of physical discomfort and risks associated with breath-hold diving (Cherry 1976). Indeed, involvement in any of these activities can have a range of impacts.

Impacts

Social and cultural impacts include changes in value systems as a result of scuba diving, snorkeling, or free diving as tourism activities (Mathieson and Wall 1982). The tourists' encounter is a major factor that influences the level of understanding about impacts.

Social stability can be fostered at a destination as a result of positive economic experiences with tourists. This can assist the local community to achieve the preservation of local heritage (Weaver and Oppermann 2000). To illustrate, certain communities are heavily reliant on dive tourism business either through employment, revenue, or development of infrastructure. Numerous developing communities in coastal locations that were previously dependent on the ocean for extractive processes have realized the benefits of preserving coral reefs and marine environments. For example, dive tourism is important to residents of Sipadan, Malaysia (Musa 2003), and Vanuatu (Howard 1999). However, the level of host community control and ownership of tourism can suggest negative outcomes for the resident population.

Negative social and cultural impacts can result from demonstration effects where particular behaviors, attitudes, or lifestyles are imposed on host communities (Leiper 2003). Dive tourism destinations in communities with social or cultural norms that are in contrast to Western lifestyles are likely to be susceptible to effects from visitor behavior that include social conduct, dress codes, and language (Dimmock and Tiyce 2001). As a corollary, Townsend (2003) reminds us that local residents should not be excluded from pursuing recreational activities at the expense of privileged outsiders. This can occur when access to marine locations is denied or restricted to local communities because of a decision to attend to tourist markets and their interests.

The popularity of a site can result in development of infrastructure to improve access through better transport facilities and pontoons with the aim to provide for a population growth. The development of tourism infrastructure in the Red Sea area of Israel and Jordan included reclaiming land to establish facilities to attract international tourists and increase visitation numbers sevenfold (Hawkins and Roberts 1994). However, outcomes can result in a loss of social amenity for those involved that includes crowding, congestion, and inconvenience (Inglis et al. 1999; Bushell 2001). Musa (2003) found that poor control of visitor numbers resulted in crowding at the destination both underwater and on land. Dive tourists considered this a major social impact on experiences in Sipadan. Experiences for visitors were further diminished by noise from a constantly running generator.

At the heart of work on social impacts, social carrying capacity has been debated in the literature dealing with natural sites. The concept has mainly been discussed in the context of terrestrial parks and wilderness areas (West 1981; Stankey and McCool 1984; Graefe, Vaske, and Kuss 1984; Manning, Lime, and Hof 1996). A body of literature, resulting from a need to consider capacity in natural locations, deals with social aspects of the visitor experience (Manning 1997). More recently, a shift in thinking has occurred that demands an understanding of desired social and biophysical conditions rather than a focus on quantifying how many people an area can sustain (McCool and Lime 2001).

Dive tourists are drawn to attractive locations because of the existence of marine flora and fauna (Davis and Harriott 1996). From information provided by dive briefs, information sessions, or other forms of interpretive material, as well as the visitor's physical experience, greater knowledge and understanding about the site can be achieved. Through education and awareness of particular habitats as a result of involvement, outcomes can achieve a desire to protect and preserve cultural elements of the site.

There are implications also for snorkeling operators. Inglis et al. (1999) sought to identify perceptions of crowding for snorkeling on the Great Barrier Reef where the activity is undertaken by approximately 70% of visitors. They utilized images of snorkeling groups above and in water to gauge perceptions of crowdedness among different user groups. Respondents with experience in marine settings were less tolerant of the presence of human-made structures (Inglis et al. 1999). Results support findings in terrestrial environments that more experienced participants seek wilderness experiences and have a sense of displacement in crowded situations, while less experienced participants are more comfortable with others nearby (West 1981).

There can also be social perceptions and stigma associated with those who undertake high-risk activities. This can either support or contrast with social representation that occurs within the sport social group. Research by Vanreusel and

Renson (1982) with scuba divers found external perceptions contrasted within group social representation. Scuba divers in that study had high levels of technical knowledge and environmental awareness complemented by commitment to training and skill development. The study also identified a low tolerance toward risky attitudes adopted by novice divers. While social stigma can be attached to and reinforced by subcultural value systems, the external stigma of risk related in only a minor way to divers in this study.

Economic impacts of marine tourism have been described as both pervasive and seductive (Orams 1999). Positive benefits can support local communities, providing improved infrastructure and social services. Direct benefits from foreign exchange earnings of international tourists spending on goods and services can result in employment for those working directly with tourists. These are the jobs created to support tourism activities (Leiper 2003). The total value of recreational diving in Australia is estimated at AU$520 million (US$395 million) annually (Davis 1996). Communities with a reliance on the income received from dive and snorkeling tourism will usually experience positive economic impacts as long as the economic leakage (Leiper 2003) is restricted or minimized. Revenue in the form of entry fees to marine parks has the potential to assist marine conservation and management. However, many marine locations are open-access environments and fee collection does not occur in a traditional terrestrial park–style manner. Instead, operators are in a position to collect fees as part of the dive tourist service fee (Townsend 2003). Nevertheless, transparency in user fees is preferred with dive experiences in order to recognize the contribution toward conservation (Davis 1996).

Meanwhile, financial challenges for dive tourism operators are compounded when higher fees are introduced. Price competition is high, and in some regions the price of offering scuba education and experiences has increased little in the last two decades. Certain New South Wales dive tourism managers indicated they are only able to provide competitive dive education because training dives are undertaken outside the marine park in more accessible locations (Dimmock 2004).

Examples that highlight negative economic impacts resulting from marine tourism present at those destinations where tourism has destroyed the attraction on which the industry has been based. Negative impacts include price inflation, which can result in reduced spending by residents, which can lead to increased negative social outcomes and economic leakage that diminishes the benefits of tourist spending within the community (Orams 1999).

Environmental impacts associated with marine tourism activities fall into two categories. One is the infrastructure built to support tourism, such as marinas, resorts, and pontoons. The other arises from activities pursued in the marine environment (Moscardo, Pearce, Green, and O'Leary 2001). Diving and snorkeling do not demand extensive facilities and infrastructure. However, when the scale of operations begins to increase and the number of snorkelers, charter divers, and student divers increases, pontoons and other on-water facilities may be developed.

Impacts caused by diving where water movement is slow, such as lakes or lagoons, result in an accumulation of pollutants from motorboats, including hydrocarbons and lead compounds. Similarly, propeller action from motors that are over 25 horsepower disrupts physical and chemical gradients by mixing water layers. Meanwhile, propeller action and anchoring will cause physical damage to underwater vegetation with motorboats generally disrupting habitats, especially during spawning (Labuda 1981; see also discussions in Chapter 4).

Because coral reef communities have become increasingly popular as sites for recreational divers, ecological impacts of scuba have been the focus of studies by numerous authors (see, for example, Hawkins and Roberts 1992; Davis and Harriott 1996; Rouphael and Inglis 1997; Zakai and Chadwick-Furman 2002). The level of knowledge about site influences on ecological impacts of marine recreation is less developed than on terrestrial locations (Rouphael and Inglis 1997). Some have gone so far as to say that diver impact on marine ecosystems has scarcely been considered (Davis, Harriott, MacNamara, Roberts, and Austin 1995).

What is known is that marine sites are impacted as a result of various types of behavior. Scuba, snorkeling, and reef walking are predicted to have the greatest impacts where fragile corals are abundant (Rouphael and Inglis 1997). Damage can result from fin and scuba tank contact, causing coral breakage and the raising of sediments (Hawkins and Roberts 1992). Coral damage includes paint scraping; crushed coral; and fabric threads when divers kick, hold, bump into, stand on, or kneel on corals (Rouphael and Inglis 1997).

Talge (1993, cited in Davis and Harriott 1996) suggested that briefly touching and finning near corals at normal levels of diver activity did not cause degradable damage to coral colonies in the Florida Keys, whereas breakage of coral caused by striking with fins, gauges, hands, or knees is of great concern (Hawkins and Roberts 1993). As a result, sites of high intensity are likely to incur greater impact. Tratalos and Austin (2001) compared low- and high-use sites and found hard coral and massive coral cover considerably lower on coral reefs in the Cayman Islands in sites where diver use was intensive.

Lack of diver awareness of the impacts caused is an important point to note. Davis et al. (1995) indicated from their work at Julian Rocks that divers were surprised to learn of the number of contacts with coral that had occurred. Similarly, divers studied in Vanuatu by Howard (1999) were unable to suggest any impacts they might cause. Implications for managing diver behavior result. Scuba agencies have been asked to provide dive briefs, which give advice on how to avoid damage to sites by improved buoyancy, gear configuration, and diving techniques, and build awareness of marine biology (Wilks 1991; Davis and Harriott 1996; Howard 1999).

Future Directions

Indications are that growth in popularity of diving and snorkeling are set to continue. The ocean's popularity as a source of recreation has transformed many quiet and once remote coastal locations. Resorts, marinas, and coastal urban development are indicators of human desire to live, work, and play in and by the sea. Better access and greater discretionary incomes, together with packaged diver education (Dimmock 2004) available at attractive locations are contemporary features of an industry that caters to heterogeneous global diving markets.

Efforts by recreational industries are anticipated to continue to reduce the perception of risk involved with these activities through the provision of appealing, affordable, and uncomplicated dive and snorkeling products. Challenging this issue is a view that the standard of diver skill has been questioned as a consequence of a process of dismantling recreational scuba education and training in order to develop and market a broader variety of products that access a broader range of interest groups (Jablonski 1999; Dimmock 2004). A counter argument is that diving and snorkeling have become more accessible to recreationalists as a result of these factors, which in turn creates further demand.

From a biophysical perspective, the environment and ecological quality of dive sites that host increasing numbers of dive tourists continues to be impacted through excess in the biological, physical, and social capacity of the site. Regular monitoring of both biophysical and social dimensions of involvement is required to manage impacts of the activities from a holistic perspective. Strategies for management agencies involved have been categorized by Orams (1999) as (1) physical, (2) regulatory, (3) economic, and (4) educational, as outlined in Table 7-3.

Access to high-quality diving and snorkeling sites is destined to become a pressing issue that will ultimately have economic implications as high demand and scarce supply of quality marine environments force costs of management and access upward (Orams 1999). For those involved in managing aspects of recreational diving and snorkeling, challenges ahead include ability to provide a

1. High level of safety
2. Low level of risk
3. Quality dive location
4. Competitive service
5. Quality experience.

In the event that environmental degradation and excessive carrying capacity result in restricted access to marine sites, an alternative to natural reef systems exists in the form of human-constructed or artificial reefs that can become the home of marine flora, thus attracting fish and other marine fauna (Van Treeck and Schuhmacher 1998).

Table 7-3   Strategic Options for Marine Management

Physical	Regulatory	Economic	Educational
Increase durability	Limit visitor numbers	Differentiated fees for various user groups	Brochures and printed information
Remove from sensitive areas	Prohibit certain activities	Fines and bonds for damage caused	Signage and interpretation
Design durable equipment	Close specific areas from all use	Reward litter collection and report poor behavior	Guided and instructional sessions
Sacrifice areas for intensive use	Separate activities geographically	Entrance fees for all user groups at site	Marine Park Visitor Center
Rehabilitate to improve quality	Restrict use to certain skill level		Radio broadcasting conditions and use impacts

Source: Orams (1999).

Technological advances in equipment will continue to provide divers with information concerning geographic and tracking aspects of sites, as well as continued improvement in the standard of devices that monitor air supply, consumption, and decompression commitments (Stone 1999).

Ultimately, the future of diving and snorkeling will be impacted by the level of harmony between competing water-based tourism user groups. The existence of marine management areas will become a central feature to the debate surrounding how to maintain the quality of such a highly prized natural resource (Agardy 1997; Orams 1999).

Conclusion

This chapter has explored scuba diving, snorkeling, and free diving as water-based tourism activities and experiences. A focus has been given to the growth in market demand for these activities, internationally and within Australia. Discussion has also been given to the supply of tourism facilities and infrastructure to support the growth in demand. Implications exist for managing those who pursue these activities and experiences, with a typology provided to organize those seeking involvement. Characteristics for each group within the typology allow for better identification of training needs and involvement with the respective activities and experiences. Advantages and disadvantages to participant involvement have been identified, together with discussion of environmental, social, cultural, and economic impacts of scuba diving, snorkeling, and free diving.

Case Study: Julian Rocks

Julian Rocks is a popular and intensively used scuba site (Davis and Harriott 1996) located within the Cape Byron Marine Park (CBMP), described as one of the best diving locations on the Australian east coast (Wright 1990, cited in Davis and Tisdell 1996). Located 2.5 kilometers northeast of the township of Byron Bay in northern New South Wales, Julian Rocks is a rocky outcrop with surrounding reef system located where tropical and temperate waters meet and mix. Such locations typically have high marine biodiversity (Hartley 2003). The site supports a number of threatened species, including turtles and grey nurse sharks; provides sanctuary to migrating whales (*Working paper for the Cape Byron Marine Park* 2003); and hosts an abundance of sea stars, colorful sponges, and hard and soft corals. In fact, at least 530 different species of fish and 33 coral species have been identified at Julian Rocks (Hartley 2003). The presence of this and other marine life provides a major attraction for an international diving and snorkeling community.

Julian Rocks Aquatic Reserve was declared in 1982 in an amendment under the Fisheries and Oyster Farms Act of 1979 and extends over an area of approximately 80 hectares. On November 1, 2002, Julian Rocks Aquatic Reserve became a part of the Cape Byron Marine Park, which extends for approximately 37 kilometers from Lennox Head to Brunswick Heads (Marine Parks Authority 2006; McGreedy 2004).

Visitors to Julian Rocks are typically accommodated at Byron Bay, which receives estimated tourist numbers in the vicinity of 1.2 to 1.7 million per annum.

They include visiting friends and relatives (VFRs), day trippers, and overnight tourists (personal communication). Tourist activities available around Byron Bay are categorized as (1) earth based, (2) air based, (3) mind and body, and (4) sea based (Byron Bay n.d.), with the main attraction considered to be the ocean and associated activities, including diving and snorkeling (Davis and Harriott 1996).

As a recreational experience, diving at Julian Rocks has reached a level where 50,000 dives were recorded in 2001 (Ashby 2001). One dive operator estimates that currently 25,000 to 30,000 divers visit Julian Rocks each year for that business alone (personal communication). A large percentage of divers are novices or beginners, with 45% of divers sampled by Ashby (2001) having logged 20 or fewer dives in total.

Julian Rocks hosts a range of dive sites that vary in depth from 5 to 30 meters. While shallower sites are used for training and snorkeling, they appeal to all divers because they are home to reef fish, juvenile species, wobbegong sharks, and turtles. Deeper sites ranging from 15 to 30 meters are where moray eels, grey nurse sharks (depending on the season), and many species of large fish can be sighted (Dive Byron Bay 2003).

Only a five-minute boat ride from the mainland, Julian Rocks is serviced by two local dive operators who provide guided scuba dives and snorkeling experiences as well as scuba education, and equipment rental and sales (Harriott and Davis 1996). The number of snorkelers who visit Julian Rocks is about 20% of the number of divers (personal communication), and no tensions exist between the two user groups. In fact, a level of camaraderie is often shared, especially on the return boat trip from Julian Rocks when humpback whales can be sighted during their annual migration. However, increased activity at Julian Rocks has contributed to negative social impacts concerning space at the access point to Julian Rocks. Tensions can arise between sunbathers, swimmers, surfers, and other boat user groups at "The Pass" when dive boats are launched while swimmers and surfers recreate in the same area (Harriott and Davis 1996).

When wind and ocean conditions prevail, all divers may visit only one site at Julian Rocks because of negative conditions elsewhere. This situation can also occur during cooler months when grey nurse sharks are present and tourists are eager for sightings. Rules governing diver behavior in critical habitat zones are mostly adhered to by divers. However, Hayward (2003) found that some divers blocked entrances to caves or gutters during shark sightings. This is possibly a result of poor diving skill, strong current, and/or the presence of other divers.

Scuba diving and snorkeling were previously considered as benign environmental activities (Davis et al. 1995). However, this view has since altered (Priskin 2003):

[Examination of diver behavior at Julian Rocks (Roberts and Harriott 1994) concluded that the carrying capacity was likely to be exceeded. Since then diver numbers have increased thereby increasing likelihood of impacts. Diver impacts on benthic communities are likely to include: physical contact with the bottom (possibly resulting in chronic levels of disturbance and physical damage to corals and benthic life), damage from bubbles in caves and over hangs and increased sedimentation and turbidity. Impacts can result from: removal of sea urchins (for fish feeding), encouraging algal growth or disturbance to feeding patterns of some fish species. Significant differences have been found in coral and algal cover between regularly dived sites and un-dived sites within Julian Rocks. (Hartley 2003)

The decline of marine conditions is acknowledged by long-term users and coincides with an increase in the recreational pressure at the site (Davis et al. 1995). Yet recent work by McGreedy (2004) found that divers continue to be satisfied

143

with diving at Julian Rocks. The presence of marine mega-fauna (turtles, sharks, rays, and large fish) provides a high level of satisfaction, and only a small percentage of divers believe the site to be environmentally degraded.

A number of possibilities exist to explain this view:

1. Divers have too limited an experience with marine flora and fauna to be aware of damage to coral and marine communities.
2. The level of diver experience could indicate little experience with other dive sites to compare the ecological quality.
3. Existence of high-quality marine biodiversity suggests divers are likely to sight marine life, which improves the quality of the experience.

To continue providing a satisfying experience as well as protecting environmental resources, there is a need for further research on diver amenity at Julian Rocks. Similarly, ongoing baseline data is needed to provide current detail on environmental impacts. The content of diver briefings should continue to inform divers of current site conditions, how to assist marine preservation, the implications of poor buoyancy, and the need to manage diver skill.

References

Agardy, T.S. (1997). *Marine protected areas and ocean conservation*. Georgetown: R. G. Landes and Academic Press.

Ashby, J. (2001). *An educational interpretive pamphlet for divers who utilize Julian Rocks Marine Reserve at Byron Bay, NSW, Australia*. Unpublished integrated project, Southern Cross University, School of Resource Science and Management, Lismore, NSW, Australia.

Blamey, R., and D. Hatch. (1998). *Profiles and motivations of nature-based tourists visiting Australia*. (Occasional Paper No. 25). Canberra, Australia: Bureau of Tourism Research.

Brotherton, B., and B. Himmetoglu. (1997). Beyond destinations—special interest tourism. *Anatolia*, **8** (3), 11–30.

Bushell, R. (2001). Practice, provision and impacts. In N. Douglas, N. Douglas, and R. Derrett (Eds.), *Special interest tourism*. (pp. 29–55). Brisbane, Australia: Wiley.

Byron Bay. (n.d.). Accessed May 24, 2004, from http://www.byron-bay.com/things/index.html

Cater, C., and E. Cater. (2000). Marine environments. In D. Weaver (Ed.), *The encyclopedia of ecotourism*. New York: CABI.

Cherry, G. (1976). *Skin diving and snorkeling*. London: Adam and Charles Black.

Colquhoun, M. (1993). *The leisure environment*. London: Pitman.

Davis, D. (1996). *The development and nature of recreational scuba diving in Australia: a study in economics, environmental management, and tourism*. Unpublished doctoral thesis, University of Queensland, Brisbane, Australia.

Davis, D., and V. J. Harriott. (1996). Sustainable tourism development or a case of loving a special place to death? In L. Harrison and W. Husbands (Eds.), *Practicing responsible tourism* (pp. 422–444). New York: Wiley.

Davis, D., Harriott, V., MacNamara, C., Roberts, L., and S. Austin. (1995, Autumn). Conflicts in a marine protected area: scuba divers, economics, ecology, and management in Julian Rocks Aquatic Reserve. *Australian Parks and Recreation,* 29–35.

Davis, D., and C. Tisdell. (1996). Economic management of recreational scuba diving and the environment. *Journal of Environmental Management,* **48**, 229–248.

Deeper Blue. Accessed April 15, 2004, from http://www.deeperblue.net

Dimmock, K. (2004). Managing recreational scuba experiences: exploring business challenges for New South Wales dive tourism managers. *Tourism Review International,* **7** (2), 67–80.

Dimmock, K., and M. Tiyce. (2001). Festivals and events: celebrating special interest tourism. In N. Douglas, N. Douglas, and R. Derrett (Eds.), *Special interest tourism.* (pp. 355–383). Brisbane, Australia: Wiley.

Dive Byron Bay. (2003). Accessed May 24, 2004, from http://www.byronbaydivecentre.com.au/dive_sites.html

Dive Log Australasia. (189). (2004, April). Guys Hill Victoria Australia: Mountain Ocean and Travel Publications Pty Ltd.

DiversTravel.com. (2003). Accessed April 15, 2004, from http://www.diverstravel.com/freedive.html

Doyle, S. (1996). *The Gold Coast recreational scuba diving industry: a management/tourism perspective.* Unpublished graduating seminar report, Southern Cross University, Center for Tourism, Lismore, NSW, Australia.

Free Dive Vancouver. (n.d.). Accessed June 5, 2004, from http://www.holdyourbreath.ca/start.htm

Graefe, A., Vaske, J., and F. Kuss. (1984). Resolved Issues and Remaining Questions about Social Carrying Capacity. *Leisure Sciences,* **6** (4), 497–507.

Green, E., and R. Donnelly. (2003). Recreational scuba diving in Caribbean marine protected areas: do the users pay? *Ambio,* **32** (2), 140–144.

Hartley, S. (2003). Environmental controls of marine benthic community structure at Julian Rocks in the Byron Bay Marine Park. Unpublished postgraduate research application, Southern Cross University, School of Environmental Science and Management, Lismore, NSW, Australia.

Hawkins, J., and C. M. Roberts. (1992). Effects of recreational SCUBA diving on fore-reef slope communities of coral reefs. *Biological Conservation,* **62**, 171–178.

Hawkins, J., and C. M. Roberts. (1993). Effects of recreational SCUBA diving: trampling on reef-flat communities. *Journal of Applied Ecology,* **30**, 25–30.

Hawkins, J., and C. M. Roberts. (1994, December). The growth of coastal tourism in the Red Sea: present and future effects on coral reefs. *Ambio,* **23** (8), 503–508.

Hayward, A. (2003). *Observations of grey nurse shark* (carcharias taurus) *and scuba diver behaviour.* Unpublished honors thesis, Southern Cross University, School of Environmental Science and Management, Lismore, NSW, Australia.

Howard, J. L. (1999). How do scuba diving operators in Vanuatu attempt to minimize their impact on the environment? *Pacific Tourism Review,* **3**, 61–69.

Inglis, G., Johnson, V., and F. Ponte. (1999). Crowding norms in marine settings: a case study of snorkeling on the Great Barrier Reef. *Environmental Management,* **24** (3), 369–381.

Jablonski, J. (1999). *Doing it right: the fundamentals of better diving.* High Springs, FL: Global Underwater Explorers.

Jablonski, J. (2001). *Getting clear on the basics: the fundamentals of technical diving.* High Springs, FL: Global Underwater Explorers.

Kotler, P., Chandler, P. C., Brown, L., and S. Adam. (1994). *Marketing: Australia and New Zealand.* (3rd ed.). New York: Prentice Hall.

Labuda, K. (1981). Activity profiles for three water-based recreational activities. Ontario, Canada: National Park Service, Interpretation and Visitor Services Division.

Leiper, N. (2003). *Tourism management.* Melbourne, Australia: Pearson.

Lovelock, C., Patterson, P., and R. Walker. (1998). *Services marketing: Australia and New Zealand.* Sydney, Australia: Prentice Hall.

Manning, R. (1997, October). Social carrying capacity of parks and outdoor recreation areas. *Parks and Recreation,* **32** (10), 32–39.

Manning, R., Lime, D., and M. Hof. (1996). Social carrying capacity of natural areas: theory and application in the U.S. national parks. *Natural Areas Journal,* **16** (2), 118–127.

Marine Parks Authority, New South Wales. (2006). *Cape Byron Marine Park.* Accessed 21 August 2006 from http://www.mpa..nws.gov.au/cbmp/cbmp.htm

Market Research.com. (n.d.). Accessed April 12, 2003, from http://www.market rsearch.com/researchindex/952684.html

Mathieson, A., and G. Wall. (1982). *Tourism: economic, physical, and social impacts.* Harlow, UK: Longman.

McCool, S.F., and D. Lime. (2001). Tourism carrying capacity: tempting fantasy or useful reality? *Journal of Sustainable Tourism,* **9** (5), 372–388.

McGreedy, T. (2004). *A pilot study investigating SCUBA diver attitudes towards the Julian Rocks Aquatic Reserve in the Cape Byron Marine Park, Northern NSW.* Unpublished honors minor study, Southern Cross University, School of Environmental Science and Management, Lismore, NSW, Australia.

McKercher, B., and B. Robbins. (1998). Business development issues affecting naturebased tourism operators in Australia. *Journal of Sustainable Tourism,* **6** (2), 173–188.

Mintzberg, H. (1980). *The nature of managerial work.* Englewood Cliffs, NJ: Prentice Hall.

Moscardo, G., Pearce, P., Green, D., and J.T. O'Leary. (2001). Understanding coastal and marine tourism demand from three European markets: implications for the future of ecotourism. *Journal of Sustainable Tourism,* **9** (3), 212–227.

Mundet, L., and L. Ribera. (2001). Characteristics of divers at a Spanish resort. *Tourism Management,* **22**, 501–510.

Musa, G. (2003). Sipadan: An over-exploited scuba-diving paradise? An analysis of tourism impact, diver satisfaction, and management priorities. In B. Garrod and J.C. Wilson (Eds.), *Marine ecotourism: issues and experiences.* (pp. 122–137). Clevedon, UK: Channel View Publications.

Orams, M. (1999). *Marine tourism: development, impacts and management.* London: Routledge.

Parker, S. (2001). Marine tourism and environmental management on the Great Barrier Reef. In V. Smith and M. Brent (Eds.), *Hosts and guests revisited: tourism issues of the 21st century* (pp. 232–241). New York: Cognizant Communication Corporation.

Performance Freediving. (2006). Accessed March 14, 2004, from http://www.performancefreediving.com/team/kirk.html

Priskin, J. (2003) Tourist perceptions of degradation caused by coastal nature-based recreation. *Environmental Management,* **32** (2), 189–204.

Quinn, R.E., Thompson, M.P., Faerman, S.R., and M.R. McGrath. (2003). *Becoming a master manager: a competency framework.* (3rd ed.). New York: Wiley.

Rouphael, A., and G. Inglis. (1997). Impacts of recreational scuba diving at sites with different reef topographies. *Biological Conservation,* **82**, 329–336.

Schermerhorn, J.R. (1999). *Management* (6th ed.). New York: Wiley.

Shafer, C.S., Inglis, G.J., Johnson, V.Y., and N.A. Marshall. (1998). *Visitor experiences and perceived conditions on day trips to the Great Barrier Reef.* (CRC Reef Research Technical Report No. 21). Townsville, Queensland, Australia: CRC Reef Research Center.

Standeven, J., and P. De Knop. (1999). *Sport tourism.* Champaign, IL: Human Kenetics.

Stankey, G., and S. McCool. (1984). Carrying capacity in recreational settings: evolution, appraisal, and application. *Leisure Sciences,* **6** (4), 453–473.

Stone, P. (1999). *Dive Australia: A handbook for scuba divers.* Yarram, Australia: Ocean Enterprises.

Sylvester, B. (1987). *The magic of Scuba: A complete introductional guide for the Australian diver.* Dingley, Australia: Wednell.

Tabata, R.S. (1992). Scuba diving holidays. In B. Weiler and C. M. Hall (Eds.), *Special interest tourism.* (pp. 171–184). New York: Wiley.

Tourism Queensland. (2005). *Special interest reports.* Accessed May 14, 2004, from http://www.tq.com.au/research

Townsend, C. (2003). Marine ecotourism through education: a case study of divers in the British Virgin Islands. In B. Garrod and J. C. Wilson (Eds.), *Marine ecotourism. issues and experiences.* (pp. 138–154). Clevedon, UK: Channel View Publications.

Tratalos, J., and T. Austin. (2001). Impacts of recreational SCUBA diving on coral communities of the Carribean island of Grand Cayman. *Biological Conservation,* **102**, 67–75.

Vanreusel, B., and R. Renson. (1982). The social stigma of high-risk sport subcultures. In A. Dunleavy, A. Miracle, and C. Rees (Eds.), *Studies in the sociology of sport.* (pp. 183–202). Fort Worth: Texas Christian University Press.

Van Treeck, P., and H. Schuhmacher. (1998). Mass diving tourism—A new dimension calls for new management approaches. *Marine Pollution Bulletin,* **37**, (8–12), 499–504.

Weaver, D., and M. Oppermann. (2000). *Tourism management.* Brisbane, Australia: Wiley.

West, P. (1981). *On-site social surveys and the determination of social carrying capacity in wildland recreation management.* (Research Note NC-264). St. Paul, MN: U.S. Department of Agriculture, Forest Service, North Central Forest Experiment Station.

Wilks, J. (1991, Winter). Beyond the C-card: continuing education among Queensland scuba divers. *ACHPER National Journal,* 10–13.

Working papers for the Cape Byron Marine Park. (2003). Sydney, Australia: New South Wales Marine Park Authority.

Zakai, D., and N. E. Chadwick-Furman. (2002). Impacts of intensive recreational diving on reef corals at Eilat, northern Red Sea. *Biological Conservation,* **105**, 179–187.

III

Adventure

As was noted in the preceding sections, adventure is part of the motivation for participating in sailing and motorboating; motorized water sports; surfing and windsurfing; sport and big game fishing; as well as scuba diving, snorkeling, and free diving. While adventure was a subtheme in Section II, it is the key organizing theme for this section albeit that a sense of challenge also infuses the chapters. However, the term "adventure" is used for this section as it continuously resonates within the various chapters and is associated with related discourses for each of the water-based experiences focused on herein: whitewater rafting, kayaking, one-day boating adventures, and sail training adventures. Both adventure and challenge are often associated with self-actualization, the latter being another strong theme in this section that has also been discussed in preceding sections.

In Chapter 8, Lilian Jonas introduces the concept of adventure as it pertains to whitewater rafting. In particular, she draws on the work of Simmel (1965) to situate the discussion as well as Goffman's (1967) concept of "fateful action." She also explores the "amateur" form of Stebbins's (1979) idea of serious leisure in relation to whitewater rafting experiences. Additionally, Jonas describes types of rafts and water ratings. She identifies two types of whitewater rafting participants—river guides and passengers—and analyzes the various roles and responsibilities of each, including how each participant role contributes to the notion of adventure associated with the whitewater rafting trip. In particular, Jonas explores the constructed notions of danger and the mediation of whitewater rafting experiences (and authenticity) to ensure satisfaction of clients. As well as a desire for adventure, other motivations for participation are escape from the everyday life (see also Chapters 2 and 11), challenge, and a desire to learn new skills. The case study focuses on whitewater rafting down the Colorado River through the Grand Canyon.

Kayaking is the focus of Chapter 9. In this chapter, Paul Beedie and Simon Hudson link sea kayaking to the continuum of "paddling" experiences and specifically that of canoeing. The range of kayaking experiences is variously considered as tourism, sport, leisure, and recreation. Technological developments as well as rules and regulations are also discussed in relation to their impacts on kayaking. The sense of going on a journey as well as the paddling environments also relate to participation trends. An overview of the kayaking market incorporates consideration of hard and soft adventure market segments; classification by the degree of facilitation of the experience; as well as, for sea kayakers, a four-segment market cluster. Beedie and Hudson remark on the commodification of whitewater to which Jonas, in Chapter 8, similarly alluded in regard to the construction of danger within whitewater rafting experiences. The authors also note a linkage between kayaking and serious leisure (Stebbins 2001). Lobbying by kayakers is discussed, as it was in Chapter 5 in regard to surfers. The Chapter 9 case study examines sea kayaking as a holiday adventure departing from Milos, the Cyclades Islands, Greece.

In Chapter 10, Gianna Moscardo examines one-day boating adventures. As was noted earlier in the book, boating usually occurs in association with other water-based experiences. This is also the case for one-day boating tours. In this chapter, drawing on Bergsma (2000), Moscardo analyzes major trends in tourism and relates them to one-day boating tours. Those trends include consumer changes, environmental changes, technological changes, and business practice changes. Additionally, using an international perspective, she outlines the different types of one-day boat tours, tour markets, and consumer satisfaction levels. Moscardo also discusses issues associated with one-day boating tours as business enterprises (see also discussion by Dimmock in Chapter 7 in regard to scuba diving businesses). She identifies several concerns associated with one-day boating tours: safety issues and environmental changes and their resultant impacts on tourism. The case study addresses participation trends in one-day boat tour operations in the Great Barrier Reef, Australia.

The last chapter in this section, Chapter 11, explores sail training adventures. In this chapter, Gary Easthope uses a first-person narrative writing style. He clearly situates himself as an insider in regard to this water-based experience and thereby provides an emically informed interpretation of sail training adventures. He introduces the reader to a variety of such adventures, exploring the differences between this type of sailing and other forms (see also Chapter 2 for a discussion of various types of sailing experiences). The main motivation for participation is explained as personal development along with associated elements of "peak experience" and "flow" (Csikszentmihalyi 1974). Easthope also reports that escape from everyday life (see Chapters 2, 5, and 8) is another motivation and links escape to "liminality" (Turner 1969). Other reasons for participation include a quest for authenticity of experience (see also Chapters 2 and 8), a sense of adventure, a desire for *communitas* (Turner and Turner 1978), as well as the subcultural nature of the activity (see also Chapters 2, 5, and 7 for further discussions of subculture). The chapter concludes with a case study that highlights a tall ship, the *Lady Nelson,* in order to study participation in a sail training adventure as a form of serious leisure.

In addition to adventure, other common themes in this section include serious leisure (Chapters 8, 9, and 11) and liminality or escape (Chapters 8 and 11).

8

Whitewater Rafting

Lilian Jonas

Overview

This chapter explores the sport of whitewater rafting. Wherever there is a stretch of un-dammed river through a canyon or other narrow area with obstructions that create rapids, there are whitewater rafters. While facing the dangers involved in rafting whitewater only occupies a fragment of time on a rafting trip, the adventure of facing such dangers is a central aspect of the whitewater rafting identity (Jonas 1999; Holyfield and Jonas 2003; Jonas, Stewart, and Larkin 2003). According to Simmel (1965), adventurers leave the security of everyday life and abandon themselves to the "powers and accidents of the world, which can delight [them], but in the same breath can also destroy [them]" (p. 193). Whitewater rafters seeking adventure thus go on whitewater trips to face fate by running the dangerous rapids, as well as surviving the uncertainty of life in the river wilderness. In this chapter, the term "wilderness" implies a remote natural setting and does not necessarily connote legislatively designated wilderness areas.

While numerous whitewater rafting opportunities are available all across the globe, with many in close proximity to cities and towns, this chapter focuses on those that are located in the rugged American West, away from civilization and deep in the wilderness. Some whitewater rafting trips can take less than an hour and cover only a few miles, while others take weeks or even months and cover hundreds of miles. In order to describe the full whitewater experience, this chapter examines the multi-day or extended rafting trip. A prime example of an ultimate whitewater rafting adventure is a trip down the Colorado River through Grand Canyon National Park, which is the longest single stretch of navigable river in the United States (277 miles from Lees Ferry to Lake Mead). This section of river offers everything that a river enthusiast could want: whitewater adventure, spectacular scenery, and a pronounced feeling of isolation. Trips through the Grand Canyon take anywhere from 5 to 30 days, easily enough time for rafters to be away from civilization and take on adventurer roles deep in the wilderness.

Whitewater rafting involves maneuvering a boat down a river through a number of rapids. Boats include rubber rafts and catarafts, wooden or metal dories, and rubber pontoon boats ("snouts," "J-rigs," and "boloney boats"). Kayaks, canoes, and inflatable kayaks or "duckies" often accompany rafting trips (see Chapter 9 for more about kayaking). Rafts, catarafts, and dories range between 12 and 18 feet in length and are typically paddle or oar powered. Pontoon boats range from 22 to 37 feet and tend to be motor powered.

Whitewater rafters are divided into two types of participants: river guides and their passengers. The river guides are the ones who maneuver (i.e., row, motor, or steer) the boat downriver. By taking charge and managing the dangers provided by the rapids, which may verge on "complete chaos," river guides engage in extreme adventure or "edgework" (Lyng 1990). Adventure, drawing upon Goffman's (1967) notion of "fateful" action, allows one the chance to maintain self-command under trying or uncertain circumstances. It is through facing such fateful action or risk and demonstrating that the person is able to manage his- or herself in the situation by standing both "correct and steady in the face of sudden pressures" (Goffman 1967, p. 217), that the person emerges with character. Risk, which separates those who have character from those who do not, often leaves the risk taker with a sense of superiority (Hughes and Coakley 1991). River guides who face the risk of whitewater rafting often emerge with perceived strong character or charisma, occasionally being imputed with the desirable identity of "river god/goddess" (Jonas 1997, 1999; Holyfield and Jonas 2003).

Facing whitewater, however, only involves a fraction of a river guide's time. River guides spend considerably more time involved with more mundane duties on the river, including boat operation during periods of flat water, camping decisions, food preparation, setting up and taking down porta-potties, and a variety of other day-to-day activities. River guides are also involved with all the pre-trip preparations, including obtaining permits/licenses, preparing gear, packing food, making shuttle arrangements, and the like.

While running western whitewater rivers requires considerable skill, background knowledge, and physical ability on the part of the river guides, little is required of the passengers who often merely show up at the "put-in" in time to pack up their personal gear and depart on the river. Depending entirely on the competence of the river guides to provide the adventure experience, and paying them for that experience, passengers become "adventure consumers" (Holyfield 1995).

The interactions between river guides and their passengers on a whitewater rafting trip are what constitute the whitewater river experience. Passengers recognize the guide's role in contributing to the river experience (Bishop, Boyle, Welsh, Baumgartner, and Rathbun 1987; Stewart, Larkin, Orland, Anderson, Manning, Cole et al. 2000). In fact, river guides are fundamental in facilitating or orchestrating that experience (see, for example, Cockrell, Bange, and Roggenbuck 1984; Arnould and Price 1993; Price, Arnould, and Tierney 1995; Holyfield 1997, 1999; Jonas 1997, 1999; Gibson 1998; Arnould, Price, and Otnes 1999), or at least exert normative influence over the evaluation of the experience (Cockrell et al. 1984).

Even the central feature of whitewater rafting, the thrills and adventure of running the rapids, is an experience negotiated through the interactions between river guides and passengers. Danger is typically defined objectively as the potential for physical injury, or even death, if the participants fail to adequately perform specific tasks (see, for example, Mitchell 1983; Brannigan and McDougall 1987; Lyng

1990; Celsi, Rose, and Leigh 1993). However, as will be made clear throughout this chapter, especially in the case study, danger is not an objective fact, but a perception constructed situationally (Douglas and Wildavsky 1982). The associated adventure felt with running whitewater is a phenomenon orchestrated by the interactions among whitewater rafters, with the river guide acting as the conductor.

Background

In the past, explorers, trappers, and traders floated rivers in the western United States in search of inland water routes, access to beavers for their pelts, or trade routes between different peoples and places. On May 24, 1869, retired Major John Wesley Powell and a small band of men launched four boats to begin what would be a 99-day expedition from Green River, Wyoming, to southern Nevada. On this 1,000-mile trip through "the great unknown" (Powell 1875), Powell was the first to face the ominous whitewater in Cataract and Grand Canyons, and he recorded sufficient observations of latitude and longitude, elevations, and estimates of distance to allow mapmakers to show the river's course. Although he had faced numerous tragedies and spills, Powell conducted a second trip in 1871. Following Powell's expeditions were a number of prospecting and trapping trips, as well as two expeditions to determine the feasibility of a railway along the river from Colorado to California.

While Powell and those directly after him experienced the adventures and spectacular wilderness settings afforded by the Grand Canyon, these experiences were not the reason for engaging in their whitewater rafting trips. In fact, it was the whitewater aspect of the trips that they dreaded, and rightfully so, as they experienced their fair share of tragedy and death. Today, with the exception of a few research and education trips, whitewater rafting is idealized as a form of adventure leisure. The primary purpose of embarking into "the great unknown" is to experience the once-dreaded whitewater:

First comes the roar of the water in the tight canyon, a sound like distant thunder, followed by the straining of the boatmen to see over the drop. The boat then seems to float out onto the tongue, a strangely quiet, slick spot where things go calm and smooth at the head of every rapid, like a lull before the storm—that first wave. Your heart pounds, your fists clench and you are in it: whitewater. (Rennicke 1988, p. 5)

Whitewater is the result of rapids, which are objective barriers in a river's main channel formed by rocks or other debris, often brought in by flooding side streams. Rapids typically occur in narrow areas of the river, such as tight canyons, where water rushes over the rocks and causes a variety of holes ("pour-overs," "keepers," "hydraulics," "stoppers") and waves ("haystacks," "V-waves," "rooster tails," "standing waves"). Many rapids are given ominous names such as Satan's Gut, Damnation Alley, Dragon's Tooth, Hell's Half Mile, Disaster Falls, Meatgrinder, and Slaughterhouse Falls, which emphasize their ferocious nature. River guides attempt to maneuver their boats around many of these to avoid "flipping" (i.e., capsizing), "wrapping" their boats around a rock, or "pinning" against a rock or cliff wall.

Rapids are rated by their degree of difficulty. The International Scale classifies rapids according to 6 different classes, while the Western Scale uses 10.

Adopted from McGinnis (1975), the rating scale listed in Table 8-1 incorporates the two.

A river, or a portion of river, is generally rated according to its most difficult typical rapids. For example, the Colorado River through the Grand Canyon is rated a Class IV+ (Cassady, Cross, and Calhoun 1994), although it includes at least one Class V rapid, Lava Falls, and other rapids are also considered Class V at various water levels. The majority of rapids, however, are Class IV or lower.

While it may seem obvious that the higher a river is rated, such as a Class IV or V, the more "dangerous" the rapids and the more adventurous the rafting trip. Further investigation, however, reveals that there is more to the perceived danger than the technical nature of the rapids. Some identically rated rapids seem more dangerous than others. Even the same rapids can appear more difficult to different rafters, or to the same rafter on a different trip. Moreover, river guides and passengers tend to perceive rapids differently. In short, there are other social-psychological processes involved than merely an "objective" rating scale in the perceived danger of a river trip.

Market Profile

In addition to the division between river guides and their passengers, rafters are also separated into two groups: commercial and private. Private rafters are those who take it upon themselves to organize the rafting trip, gather equipment and food, and run the trip, with expenses being shared equally among those on the trip. River guides on private trips do not receive monetary compensation for their work, which they consider leisure, and can thus be regarded as amateurs (Stebbins 1979). The rafting trip is also considered leisure by the passengers, although they are generally required to participate in some of the daily chores on the trip, such as cook-

Table 8-1   Rapids Rating Scale

International Scale	Technical Description of Rapids	Western Scale
	Flat water	0
I	Easy. Small waves; clear passage; no serious obstacles	1, 2
II	Medium. Rapids of moderate difficulty with passages clear	3, 4
III	Difficult. Numerous waves, high, irregular; rocks; eddies; rapids with clear passage though narrows, requiring expertise in maneuvering; scouting usually needed	5, 6
IV	Very Difficult. Long rapids; waves powerful, irregular; dangerous rocks; boiling eddies; passages difficult to scout; scouting mandatory first time; powerful and precise maneuvering required	7, 8
V	Extremely Difficult. Exceedingly difficult, long, and violent rapids, following each other almost without interruption; riverbend extremely obstructed; big drops; violent current; very steep gradient; close study essential but often difficult	9, 10
VI/U	Unrunnable	U

ing, helping the guides to load and unload gear from the boats, and generally assisting the guides.

Commercial trips (Figure 8-1) are organized by commercial outfitters with licensed, paid river guides who are in charge of on-river activities, such as boat operation, camping decisions, food preparation, and so forth. Commercial guides thus consider the river trip as work. To the passengers, commercial whitewater trips are a form of leisure akin to "guided tours" that include "all forms of tourism where the itinerary is fixed and known beforehand, and which involve some degree of planning and direct participation by agents apart from the tourists themselves" (Schmidt 1979, p. 441). Passengers on commercial trips are generally not required to participate in any on-river chores, as the guides take care of all their needs.

Demographic information regarding whitewater rafters on four different rivers or river segments in the western United States is presented in the rest of this section. All of the data were collected in 1998 by Hall and Shelby (2000) and include information pertaining to commercial passengers, commercial river guides, and private rafters (both passengers and guides) who floated down the Colorado River through the Grand Canyon. Also included are demographics data on whitewater rafters (guides, passengers, and commercial and private groups combined) collected by Reiter and Blahna (2001) on some shorter river segments that are popular whitewater rafting destinations in southeastern Utah: the upper and lower segments of the San Juan River and the Colorado River through Westwater Canyon. Compared to a Grand Canyon rafting trip that can take anywhere from five days to several weeks to complete, trips down the southeastern Utah river segments take roughly from two days to one week. The rivers in Utah can also be considered less dangerous, as they have lower difficulty ratings (Class II–IV). A comparison of these rivers is provided in Table 8-2.

Figure 8-1　Commercial rafting office sign, New Zealand. Photographer: Gayle Jennings.

Table 8-2   Comparison of Rafting Trips in the Grand Canyon and Southeastern Utah

	Grand Canyon Commercial Trip	Grand Canyon Private Trip	Upper San Juan	Lower San Juan	Westwater Canyon
Number of Rafters (1998)	19,643	3,371	5,600	5,900	14,000
Min. Segment Length (miles)	255[1]	255	26	58	17[2]
Average Trip Length (days)	10 days[3]	17 days	2 days	6 days	2 days
Rapid Classes	IV–V	IV–V	II–III	II–III	III–IV

Notes:

[1] While the Colorado through the Grand Canyon from Lees Ferry to Lake Mead is 277 miles, the first point where vehicles can drive down to the river and boats can be taken out is at Diamond Creek, mile 255. Most commercial rafters, however, do not complete a "full canyon" trip (from Lees Ferry to Diamond Creek or Lake Mead), but end or begin their trips at Phantom Ranch (river mile 88 via hiking or mule ride) or Whitmore Wash (river mile 187 via helicopter). In 1998, only 27% of commercial passengers compared to 85% of private boaters completed a full canyon trip.

[2] Many rafters include a 25-mile section upstream of Wastewater Canyon in their trip, which increases the trip length by one or two days.

[3] Since most commercial passengers do not complete a full canyon trip, they spend seven days on average on the river.

There were more men on whitewater rafting trips in the four river segments reviewed, with the exception of the upper San Juan River where women made up roughly two-thirds of all rafters in 1998 (see Table 8-3). Only one-third of all rafters on Grand Canyon private trips and Westwater trips and only 27% of all commercial guides were women. This may be the result of the perceived danger levels of the Grand Canyon and Westwater, which have the highest rapid ratings. Private trips are also considered more dangerous than their commercial counterparts due to typically smaller rafts and less experienced guides. As previous studies have shown, men pursue risk adventure and risk occupations at much higher rates than women (Metz 1981; Lyng 1990; Lois 2001). Although the rapids on the lower San Juan section are as mild as those on the upper segment, there is greater perceived adventure due to increased time spent, requiring the rafter to be self-supportive in a wilderness environment. The risk is also greater, as the entire 58 miles of the lower San Juan is inaccessible by road, complicating any potential emergency. In comparison, the upper San Juan is a relatively short stretch of river with minor rapids that are easily transversed by novice rafters, with numerous access points by road.

The average age of recreational rafters in all river segments surveyed in 1998 was roughly 43 years. Commercial guides in the Grand Canyon, however, were roughly seven years younger than their passengers or private rafters. This may reflect the fact that many commercial guides are college students who take on guiding as a summer job. Interestingly, in 1975, commercial passengers were 33 years old on average, while private rafters were 28 years old (Shelby and Nielsen 1976). The older average age of passengers today is to be expected, as commercial companies are now directing their advertising to a broader range of prospective clients, specifically older individuals, by stressing the safety, comfort, and accessibility of river rafting to all age groups.

Rafters tend to have higher education levels than the national average, with 71% to 80% of all rafters having at least a college degree, compared to the national average of only 21%. While differences occur between the rafter groups, they are less dramatic when compared to the national average (Table 8-3).

Household incomes between groups, presented in Table 8-4, varied. The most striking difference between rafters was between Grand Canyon commercial passengers and all other groups. In 1998, nearly half of the commercial passengers had household incomes of US$100,000 or above, compared to 12% of the nation as a whole, and 11% to 20% of all other rafter groups having such high family incomes.

In 1998, the average fare per person per day on a commercial raft was approximately US$215. The average commercial passenger spent seven days on the river, thus paying roughly US$1,500 for the trip. In 2006, trip costs range from US$1,300 for four days (Whitmore Wash to Diamond Creek, roughly 68 miles) to over US$4,000 for a two-week trip. Prices vary depending upon the type of boat used (paddle raft, pontoon boat, or dory) and length of trip (longer trips are cheaper by the day), but roughly average US$300 per person per day. These costs, however, do not include tips for the guides.

In comparison, private whitewater rafters pay considerably less money per day and per trip than their commercial counterparts. Since no one on the private trip is supposed to make a wage or profit, trip participants share all costs for the trip, including the cost of the permit, food, gas, and shuttle fees. A private trip can thus

Table 8-3   Gender, Age, and Education

	Grand Canyon Commercial Passengers	Grand Canyon Commercial Guides	Grand Canyon Private Rafters	Upper San Juan	Lower San Juan	Westwater Canyon	1998 National Average
Men	56%	73%	67%	35%	56%	67%	49%
Women	44%	27%	33%	65%	44%	33%	51%
Mean age	43 years	36 years	43 years	43 years	45 years	42 years	—
Some high school	4%	3%	0%	3%	3%	2%	15%
High school diploma	3%	2%	4%	5 %	5%	8%	32%
Some college	13%	23%	16%	13.2%	20.3%	17.9%	25%
College degree	41%	55%	45%	39%	32%	49%	16%
Post-graduate degree	40%	17%	35%	40%	39%	27%	5%

Table 8-4   Household Income

Average, Before-Taxes Household Income (US$)	Grand Canyon Commercial Passengers	Grand Canyon Commercial Guides	Grand Canyon Private Rafters	Upper San Juan	Lower San Juan	Westwater Canyon	1998 National Average
Under $10,000	2%	1%	2%	9%	2%	4%	6%
$10,000–39,999	11%	20%	21%	17%	39%	21%	37%
$40,000–69,999	16%	36%	37%	29%	26%	34%	30%
$70,000–99,999	19%	29%	31%	29%	14%	22%	15%
≥$100,000	47%	14%	11%	17%	19%	20%	12%

be under US$50 per person per day, although costs can be considerably higher for trips that rent river equipment and use prepackaged food. In addition, the rafting trip is often free for the guides as compensation for supplying their own gear, making trip costs for the passengers slightly higher. For the river guide, however, purchasing gear can be rather pricey, considering the average 16-foot raft and associated equipment (frame, oars, cam straps, waterproof storage containers, life-jackets, ice chests, safety equipment, etc.) when bought new costs roughly between US$8,000 and US$10,000. However, in the long run, whitewater rafting is relatively inexpensive for the river guide who owns his or her own equipment and continues to go on cheap and often free trips.

Advantages and Disadvantages

Facing rapids and experiencing adventure are just two aspects of a whitewater rafting trip. In general, river trips through the Grand Canyon, or many western rivers with long, free-flowing stretches, provide wilderness experiences. The peaceful desert environment and deep canyon walls isolate rafters from reminders of civilization. Those who venture into such wildernesses do so for a variety of reasons, including escaping routines of everyday life, seeking privacy, experiencing challenge, and learning new skills (Knopf, Peterson, and Leatherberry 1983; Driver, Brown, and Peterson 1991; Cohen and Taylor 1992; Hammitt and Rutlin 1995).

Within this wilderness setting, rafters are rewarded with spectacular scenery; access to remote side canyons, waterfalls, and secret grottos; close encounters with wildlife; visits to ancient ruins; and studies of exposed layers of geologic formations. While guiding the rafts requires skill and physical agility from the river guides, passengers on both commercial and private trips can experience the benefits of river rafting without needing to have guiding skills. The elderly and disabled, as well as children, all have access to rafting experiences. In fact, commercial outfitters provide special-access trips on which passengers with even severe mobility impairments can be accommodated.

Whitewater rafting not only allows people with various physical abilities to access remote backcountry areas, including designated wilderness areas where motorized vehicles are not permitted, it also allows such access with comfort. As opposed to backpacking or kayaking trips (see Chapter 9 for details on kayaking) where space for gear is limited, rafts provide sufficient room for seemingly luxurious items, such as tables, chairs, umbrellas, high-tech stoves, cast-iron cookware, multiple ice chests, fresh food, and numerous "toys" (frisbees, volleyball nets, horseshoes, etc.).

Whitewater rafting is typically not a solitary activity, with as many as 30 people on a single commercial rafting trip in the Grand Canyon, although many commercial trips tend to be smaller. The maximum size for a Grand Canyon private trip is 16 participants. While having such large groups of people crammed into relatively small spaces, such as on the raft or on narrow beaches, may seem contrary to the wilderness experience, the interactions among members of the group often enhance the trip. When asked, many rafters recognize the social benefits of whitewater rafting, including spending quality time with family and friends as well as making new friends and acquaintances (Hall and Shelby 2000; Stewart et al. 2000). Another social benefit is the negotiation and validation of desirable adventurer identities (Jonas et al. 2003).

What all the above factors demonstrate is that the whitewater rafting experience is a dynamic phenomenon, which emerges as a result of the interaction among the spectacular setting, the multi-day nature of the trip, and the participants involved (Nielsen and Shelby 1977). Together, they provide the makings of an "extraordinary" (Arnould and Price1993; Price et al. 1995; Arnould et al. 1999) or "optimal" (Beck 1987) experience, which is characterized by spontaneous and unique events that trigger intense, deep-felt emotions. Many rafters describe their first river trip as a "once-in-a-lifetime experience," with roughly 90% of all Grand Canyon rafters surveyed in 1998 describing their trip experience as excellent or perfect (Hall and Shelby 2000; Stewart et al. 2000).

The fact that the vast majority of rafters seem to be extremely satisfied with their rafting experience does not cancel out the fact that negative attributes can occur on a trip that can reduce satisfaction, though usually only temporarily. Adverse impacts include perceived crowding (Shelby and Herberlien 1986), especially at popular attraction sites. Some trips actually pass up the opportunity to visit a site if it is thought to be too crowded. However, not everyone is deterred by overcrowding at some popular sites, such as the mouth of Havasu Creek, 157 miles into the Grand Canyon. On busy summer days, dozens of boats can be found tied to each other in the narrow mouth of the creek, with rafters having to crawl across various boats to make it to shore.

The feeling of crowding also occurs at camp. Since the closure of Glen Canyon Dam in 1963, sand bars used as campsites downstream in Grand Canyon have noticeably decreased in number and size (Schmidt and Graf 1990; Kearsley, Schmidt, and Warren 1994; Webb 1999). The most noticeable reduction of camping beaches occurs in sections of the river where they were already limited, mainly along the narrowest sections such as the inner gorge, which mostly consists of sheer rock wall down to the water's edge.

The concept of crowding hints at what is probably the largest disadvantage of whitewater rafting, the limited miles of free-flowing rivers suitable for the sport around the globe (see related discussion in Chapter 9). Due to damming, diversions, dredging, and other river modifications, only a handful of rivers have floatable sections necessary for extended trips, which results in increased pressure by users to gain access to what remains. Due to this increased pressure, managing agencies require both commercial companies and private users to obtain river permits. Commercial companies are typically allowed a certain number of "user days" per season, while those requiring a private trip permit must obtain a separate permit for each trip. Many private permits are obtained through a lottery system where individuals send in applications around the first of the year, and drawings are held soon after. Other permits are obtained on a first come, first served basis. Many private rafters are unable to secure a permit for a specific stretch of river the year they apply for the permit, and thus need to wait.

Individuals wishing to go on a commercial trip do not need to worry about obtaining a river permit, but need only to purchase a spot on a trip. The downside to commercial trips is their expense and a perceived lack of authenticity. "Serious-action-seekers," Goffman (1967) has argued, are both contemptuous and fearful of any organization that might attempt to stifle spontaneity or "individual agency." Consequently, it is not assumed that individuals purchasing rafting trips are "true adventurers," as commercial trips provide a commodified adventure (Holyfield, Jonas, and Zajicek 2004). Commercial trips are seen as relatively safe and are structured for everyone, including the less adventuresome.

Passengers on most commercial trips in the Grand Canyon are piled on large, safe "baloney boats," and are distanced from even the drenching effects of whitewater. In this light, Mitchell (1983) describes commercial passengers as "glorified baggage":

Outdoor adventure enthusiasts on commercial white-water raft journeys . . . find that much of the significant action is prescripted by the professional staff and that they are regulated to the role of largely helpless incompetents, of glorified baggage. For example, on some Colorado River raft trips no more is required of customers than a willingness to get wet and some effort to remain in the boat. Planning, logistics, scouting, route selection, boat management, camp setup, cooking, and even fireside entertainment are provided by guide service personnel. Outings such as these are clearly fateful encounters, but the participants have little to do with the outcomes. (p. 218)

Most river guides would agree with the typification of passengers as "glorified baggage," which assists them in their own claim to a higher status as river god/goddess (Jonas 1997, p. 99; Holyfield and Jonas 2003; Jonas et al. 2003). However, passengers still engage in adventure, as the idea of adventure is a relative one that is "perhaps best revealed as people talk about their experiences as the accomplishment of a great event and the overcoming of major obstacles" (Neumann 1992, p. 185). For the many commercial passengers, the act of leaving civilization and going into the wilderness is an adventure in itself (Fine 1992). The new skills they learn, such as how to pack a rubberized dry bag, attach a life jacket and use it in case of an emergency, and, in some cases, how to manipulate a paddle, "provide tangible manifestations of the new skills and control the novice rafters gain from the first moments [of the river trip]" (Arnould and Price 1993, p. 36). As the case study demonstrates, facing danger, a central aspect to the adventure identity, is orchestrated by the river guides so that passengers, albeit those "high and dry" on baloney boats, can emerge as adventurous.

Impacts

Impacts on natural and cultural resources that result from whitewater rafting generally occur when rafters are on shore. Since many western rivers, including the Colorado River through the Grand Canyon, are located in arid locations, the riparian areas adjacent to the river are important ecosystems for plant and wildlife communities. These riparian areas are also fragile and sensitive to trampling from the mooring of boats and camping.

Rafters generally use sandbars and other barren shorelines for camping purposes. While camping in these areas has little impact on vegetation as they are naturally devoid of vegetation, such activities result in adverse impacts to soil due to compaction and erosion (National Park Service [NPS] 1989). On many western rivers whose ecosystems and sediment loads are altered due to upstream dams, campsites are only available in a limited number and thus receive a high amount of camping pressure. For example, the building of Glen Canyon Dam on the Colorado River through the Grand Canyon changed a once-muddy river to a clear-flowing stream with little sediment to replenish beach losses due to erosion. Camping is thus possible in only a limited number of locations in the Grand Canyon because the shoreline is unsuitable.

Rafters also go onshore to visit attractions such as waterfalls, side canyons, and archaeological and historical sites. These activities also tend to result in soil disturbance, accelerated erosion, and trampling of vegetation. This is especially true of popular attraction sites that are visited by numerous trips on a daily basis.

Whitewater rafting trips provide rafters access to fragile cultural resources (NPS 1989). Foot traffic and camping on cultural sites have created trails and areas of compaction that divert the natural flow of water and often become paths of severe erosion. Over time, these trails can become gullies or arroyos that wash away character-defining elements of the cultural resources. In some cases, visitors have climbed onto walls or over rubble and trod on fragile artifacts, inadvertently damaging sites. Visitors also affect sites by collecting artifacts and placing them in piles at various points on the site, and they are known to rearrange rocks in features (e.g., rebuild walls), destroying the integrity and research potential of these ancient sites, some of which had remained undisturbed for thousands of years. Much less common, but often more damaging visitor impacts include intentional destruction of site integrity through theft, graffiti, excavation, and feature destruction. Rafters also impact sites considered sacred by certain American Indian groups. For example, rafters in the Grand Canyon often hike up the mouth of the Little Colorado River to visit the "sipapu," which is the Hopi's sacred "place of emergence" from which all life sprung forth. Many other places of religious importance to several tribal groups are within reach of whitewater rafters. Just visiting these sites can be disturbing to the tribal groups.

The concentration of rafters at the limited number of campsites and attraction sites also has a social impact due to increased numbers and duration of encounters between groups. Encountering other groups of rafters is often viewed as detracting from the solitude and disrupting the tranquility of one's raft trip. Indeed, a substantial portion of outdoor recreation research has searched for negative effects of encounters, or points at which encounters with other groups decrease satisfaction, detract from the quality of recreation experiences, and lead to perceptions of crowding and conflict (Shelby and Heberlein 1986; Schneider and Hammitt 1995; Manning 1999). The adverse impacts of excessive encounters are mostly apparent when groups need to forego visiting an attraction site or popular hiking trail due to crowding. In other instances, two or more groups may compete for a campsite, actually racing each other to make it there first and inevitably leaving the "loser" to seek out another place to camp. When the competition occurs late in the evening, the group seeking a campsite risks being on the water at nightfall, often being forced to choose a less-than-desirable area (e.g., a rocky shoreline with little flat ground to pitch a tent.)

Future Directions

Whitewater rafting has experienced an explosive increase in participants since the 1960s. The first commercial rafting trip took place the summer of 1938 when Norman Nevels of Mexican Hat, Utah, took the first fare-paying passengers down the Green and Colorado Rivers. Although a number of exploratory, trapping, and prospecting trips, as well as a few "private" trips had been launched prior to Nevels's commercial venture, all together only 100 people had rafted through Grand Canyon by 1949. The 1,000th person floated the river 12 years later, in 1961 (Cole 1989). From 1960 to 1972, the annual number of rafters grew from 205 to 16,432 persons. In 1972, increasing problems with management of campfires, human waste, and trash along the river; damage to fragile soils and vegetation; unofficial trails; and destruction of prehistoric sites prompted Grand Canyon National Park to regulate river use more closely, placing a cap on use based on 1972 numbers (NPS 1979). This stabilized use during the 1970s, and it was allowed to increase during the 1980s. Since 1986, the number of people floating the Colorado River through Grand Canyon has exceeded 21,000 a year (NPS 1989). Approximately 15% of that number consists of private rafters, while the remaining 85% are commercial passengers.

Despite the increase in the number of rafters through the Grand Canyon during the 1980s, opportunities to float the river did not meet demands, especially among private rafters (Cole 1989). In 1988, there were approximately 4,000 people on the waiting list to receive a permit from the National Park Service for a private trip, with an average of six years for an applicant to reach the top of the list to obtain 1 of roughly 250 permits allocated each year. In reality, only about half of those on the waiting list actually waited the six years to obtain a permit. The other half were able to obtain a canceled permit or a launch date that was not selected by any applicant, resulting in one-quarter of the 1988 permits going to people who had been on the list for less than a year. Only those individuals who were able to organize a river trip with minimal lead time, however, could use this cancellation policy. The national park has recently modified its rules to allow people who have waited the longest to have the first chance for canceled launches, making it now almost impossible to obtain a permit the same year one applies.

In 2003, there were 8,228 individuals on the waiting list to obtain a private river permit, increasing the waiting period for new, private-permit applicants to 32 years. In contrast, anyone who desires to venture on a commercial rafting trip and is somewhat flexible on dates can most likely book a trip the same year. At the time of writing this chapter, the National Park Service was working on revising the Colorado River Management Plan and evaluating options regarding the private permit system as well as total allocation of allowable rafting use in the Grand Canyon. Since the number of available camping beaches in narrow sections of the canyon limits the carrying capacity of the river, it is unrealistic to expect that the proposed increase in allowable use will accommodate demand. The Park Service was offering additional private permits during the winter months to offset some demand, and was seeing some success. It was also experimenting with a statistical, computer-implemented model for estimating movements and interactions among river trips (Roberts and Gimblett 2000). This model can potentially be used to evenly distribute rafting trips in the Grand Canyon, which would reduce conflicts between rafters competing for limited camping sites and potentially increase carrying capacity. However, it is safe to say that demand will never be met, and those private rafters desiring to experience the adventure associated with facing the dangerous Grand Canyon whitewater will always need to wait. A "Record of Decision" for the Colorado River Management Plan occured on February 17, 2006.

Case Study: Constructing Whitewater Adventure

Even though the Colorado River through the Grand Canyon contains less than 10% whitewater, facing and enduring the whitewater is the prime focus of rafting trips. As a result, there is constant anticipation of the next rapids and the thrills they will afford. Since the actual act of running the rapids takes no more than a few minutes, anticipation both prolongs and amplifies the perceived danger, thus enhancing the adventure experience. In a leisure setting where experiencing danger is desirable because it leads to a sense of adventure, experienced recreationists frequently manage novices' level of anticipation and perceptions of danger (Holyfield 1995; Fine and Holyfield 1996). Whitewater rafting is no exception, as river guides play a primary role in facilitating passengers' view of the rapids as dangerous (Holyfield 1997, 1999; Jonas 1997, 1999; Holyfield and Jonas 2003). Only after the successful orchestration of the dangerous experience can all participants on a rafting trip emerge as adventurers (Jonas et al. 2003).

While whitewater is "real," how it is experienced is dependent upon a number of ritualistic displays and dramaturgical performances (Goffman 1959; Hochschild 1983), primarily on the part of the river guides. Such performances occur well before encountering the fretful whitewater, often in pre-departure events such as "safety talks":

If your boat goes over or you somehow manage to get thrown in the river, get out from under the boat. If the boat is on top of you and pins you against a rock, you'll know what it means to be between a rock and a hard place. You'll be squashed, and that's bad.

Anyway, if you find yourself dumped in the river in a rapid, you want to swim on your back with your feet downstream so if you hit a rock you'll hit it with your feet and bounce off safely. As soon as you decide which shore to head for, aim at it with your head at a forty-five-degree angle, upstream, and paddle with your arms. Your life jacket will help you keep your head up to watch for rocks. (Wood 1984, p. 28)

While safety talks are used to instruct passengers on how to avoid injury, especially during an emergency, they also serve another function. Passengers who hear all the possible things that might happen while running the rapids cannot help but feel anxious, which in turn intensifies their perception of potential danger.

Guides often tell passengers how they plan to run a particular set of rapids, which is usually tied into safety talks as they discuss the precautions that need to be taken to avoid injury. However, river guides also appear to discuss these things with their passengers primarily to terrify them:

Terry spent considerable time drawing lines and circles in the sand representing water, boats, holes, and rocks, and showing the passengers exactly how the boatmen planned to get through and what to do in case they screw up and they ended up getting caught in a "keeper." I asked Terry why he tried to scare the passengers so much, considering that this wasn't all that dangerous a set of rapids. He just said, "just so that they could get their money's worth." So, they paid to get terrified. (Field-notes/private trip)

The concept of "getting one's money's worth" is an important one in the construction of adventure on the river. Running the rapids is a major part of the river-running experience, and part of that experience is to be terrified; otherwise, the passengers would feel that they had been cheated. Thus, river guides do their best to meet the passengers' expectations. Probably one of the most successful performances aimed at terrifying the passengers prior to running the rapids occurs during the scouting of the rapid. Scouting entails mooring the rafts and hiking to a vantage point directly above the rapids to determine the safest route through:

The dance of danger begins at Lava's lip. The boats are beached, and in ritualistic fashion the guides climb to the sacred vantage, a basalt boulder about 50 feet above the cataract. Once there, weight shifts from heel to heel, fingers point, heads shake, and faces fall. This is high drama, and passengers eat it up. The reason people pay more money than for a three-star-hotel holiday to sleep on hard ground, eat stew mixed with sand, and go without hot running water and flush toilets is, quite simply, to get terrified in a safe, spectacular setting. Lava gives everyone his or her money's worth, and dividends. (Bangs 1989, pp. 17–18)

Most river guides tend to take their time when scouting rapids, which both prolongs and intensifies the experience for them and the passengers. In fact, as the above observation suggests, scouting often seems to be performed specifically for the benefit of the passengers, to terrify them and thus build their sense of adventure; it gives them their "money's worth."

After engaging in their specific scouting rituals, the river guides double-check their gear to see if it is securely tied, have a few last words with their passengers about safety, untie their boats, and float toward the rapids. From the passengers' standpoint, as long as they get downstream, no matter what kind of run it is, they feel as if they have been "delivered" and have a cause for celebration.

A "good run" for the river guides involves running the rapids exactly as planned (i.e., taking the exact route as decided during scouting), which usually means avoiding all major holes, waves, rocks, and other obstacles. A "bad run" means missing the planned route and "eating" major holes, waves, rocks, or other obstacles that could have been avoided. However, bad runs or "wild" rides are the ones that enhance the passengers' experience and preserve the mystique of the rapids. On a trip down the Grand Canyon, for example, one guide claimed to have "abnormally good runs" through all the major rapids, but purposely took his passengers on a wild ride at Lava:

My run was too clean [very low amount of water coming into the boat] in the upper portion of the rapids. Although I could have missed the BIG wave at the bottom, I purposely put the nose of my boat into one side of it so that the boat was engulfed in water and the passengers got their money's worth. We built up Lava so much, and I could have run it with a cup of water in my boat. But if I didn't get them wet, they'd feel as if they'd been cheated. (River guide/private trip)

Although only getting "a cup of water" in the boat while running Lava would have truly proven the river guide's skills at the oars, the mystique of Lava as dangerous rapids certainly could have been threatened if the passengers came through high and dry. Giving the passengers their money's worth by not "cheating" the rapids and having "clean" runs ratifies the perception of the rapids as dangerous and intensifies the feeling of adventure. Thus, river guides purposely run rapids in a manner that provides the passengers with the greatest thrill and delivers an adventurous experience.

References

Arnould, E., and L. Price. (1993). River magic: extraordinary experience and the extended service encounter. *Journal of Consumer Research*, **20**, 24–45.

Arnould, E., Price, L., and C. Otnes. (1999). Making consumption magic: a study of white-water river rafting. *Journal of Contemporary Ethnography*, **28** (1), 33–68.

Bangs, R. (1989). Metamorphosis. In C. O'Connor and J. Lazenby (Eds.), *First descents: in search of wild rivers* (pp. 11–20). Birmingham, AL: Menasha Ridge Press.

Beck, L. (1987). The phenomenology of optimal experiences attained by whitewater river recreationists in Canyonland National Park (Utah). Unpublished doctoral dissertation, University of Minnesota.

Bishop, R., Boyle, K., Welsh, M., Baumgartner R., and P. Rathbun. (1987). Glen Canyon Dam releases and downstream recreation: an analysis of user preferences and economic values. *Glen Canyon Environmental Studies Report*, **27/87**, 319–326.

Brannigan, A., and A. McDougall. (1987). Peril and pleasure in the maintenance of a high risk sport: a study of hang-gliding. In A. Yiannakis, T. McIntyre, M. Melnick, and D. Hart (Eds.), *Sport sociology: contemporary themes.* (pp. 284–291). Dubuque, IA: Kendall/Hunt.

Cassady, J., Cross, B., and F. Calhoun. (1994). *Western whitewater: from the Rockies to the Pacific*. Berkeley, CA: North Fork Press.

Celsi, R., Rose, R., and T. Leigh. (1993). An exploration of high-risk leisure consumption through skydiving. *Journal of Consumer Research*, **20**, 1–23.

Cockrell, D., Bange, S., and J. Roggenbuck. (1984). Persuasion and normative influence in commercial river recreation. *The Journal of Environmental Education*, **15** (4), 20–26.

Cohen, S., and L. Taylor. (1992). *Escape attempts: the theory and practice of resistance to everyday life*. London: Anchor Books.

Cole, D. (1989, Fall). The Grand Canyon of the Colorado: a challenge to float, a challenge to manage. *Western Wildlands*, 2–7.

Donnelly, P., and K. Young. (1988). The construction and confirmation of identity in sport subcultures. *Sociology of Sport Journal*, **5**, 223–240.

Douglas, M., and A. Wildavsky. (1982). *Risk and culture*. Berkeley: University of California Press.

Driver, B., Brown, P., and G. Peterson. (1991). *Benefits of leisure*. State College, PA: Venture Publishing.

Fine, C.A. (1992). Wild life: authenticity and the human experience of "natural" places. In C. Ellis and M. Flagherty (Eds.), *Investigating subjectivity.* (pp. 156–175). Newbury Park, CA: Sage.

Fine, G.A., and L. Holyfield. (1996). Secrecy, trust, and dangerous leisure: generating group cohesion in voluntary organizations. *Social Psychology Quarterly*, **59**, 22–38.

Gibson, M. (1998). *A qualitative investigation of river rafting expeditions: the guide's perspective*. Unpublished doctoral dissertation, University of Northern Colorado, Greeley.

Goffman, E. (1959). *The presentation of self in everyday life*. Garden City, CA: Doubleday.

Goffman, E. (1967). *Interaction ritual*. Garden City, CA: Doubleday.

Hall, T., and B. Shelby. (2000). *1998 Colorado River boater study, Grand Canyon National Park*. Report prepared for the Grand Canyon Association and Grand Canyon National Park.

Hammitt, W., and W. Rutlin. (1995). Use encounter standards and curves for achieved privacy in wilderness. *Leisure Sciences,* **17**, 245–262.

Holyfield, L. (1995). *Generating excitement: organizational and social psychological dynamics of adventure*. Athens, GA: University of Georgia Press.

Holyfield, L. (1997). Generating excitement: experienced emotion in commercial leisure. In R. Erickson and B. Cuthbertson-Johnson (Eds.), *Social Perspectives on Emotion*, **4**, 257–281. Greenwich, CT: JAI Press.

Holyfield, L. (1999). Manufacturing adventure: the buying and selling of emotions. *Journal of Contemporary Ethnography*, **28** (1), 3–32.

Holyfield, L., and L. Jonas. (2003). From river god to research grunt: identity, emotions, and the river guide. *Symbolic Interaction*, **26** (2), 285–306.

Holyfield, L., Jonas, L., and A. Zajicek. (2004). Adventure without risk is like Disneyland. In S. Lyng (Ed.), *Edgework: The Sociology of Risk Taking*. New York: Routledge.

Hochschild, A. (1983). *The managed heart*. Berkeley: University of California Press.

Hughes, R., and J. Coakley. (1991). Positive deviance among athletes: the implications of overconformity to the sport ethic. *Sociology of Sport Journal*, **8**, 307–325.

Jonas, L. (1997). *The making of a river guide: the construction of authority in a leisure subculture*. Unpublished doctoral dissertation, University of Denver.

Jonas, L. (1999). Making and facing danger: constructing strong character on the river. *Symbolic Interaction*, **22** (3), 247–267.

Jonas, L., Stewart, W., and K. Larkin. (2003). Encountering Heidi: wilderness encounters as audiences to the adventurer identity. *Symbolic Interaction*, **32** (4), 403–431.

Kearsley, L.L, Schmidt, J.C., and K.D. Warren. (1994). Effects of Glen Canyon Dam on Colorado River sand deposits used as campsites in Grand Canyon National Park, USA. *Regulated Rivers: Research and Management*, **9** (3), 137–149.

Knopf, R., Peterson, E., and E. Leatherberry. (1983). Motives for recreational river floating: relative consistency across rivers. *Leisure Sciences*, **5**, 231–255.

Lois, J. (2001). Peaks and valleys: the gendered emotional culture of edgework. *Gender and Society*, **15**, 381–406.

Lyng, S. (1990). Edgework: a social psychological analysis of voluntary risk taking. *American Journal of Sociology*, **95**, 851–886.

Manning, R. (1999). *Studies in outdoor recreation: search and research for satisfaction*. (2nd ed.). Corvallis: Oregon State University Press.

McGinnis, W. (1975). *Whitewater rafting*. New York: Times Books.

Metz, D. (1981). *Running hot*. Cambridge, MA: Abt Books.

Mitchell, R. (1983). *Mountain experience: the psychology and sociology of adventure*. Chicago: University of Chicago Press.

National Park Service. (1979). *Colorado River management plan*. U.S. Department of the Interior, Grand Canyon National Park, AZ.

National Park Service. (1989). *Colorado River management plan*. U.S. Department of the Interior, Grand Canyon National Park, AZ.

Neumann, M. (1992). The trail through experience: finding self in the recollection of travel. In C. Ellis and M. Flaherty (Eds.), *Investigating Subjectivity*. (pp. 176–201) Newbury Park, CA: Sage.

Neumann, M. (1999). *On the rim: looking for the Grand Canyon*. Minneapolis: University of Minnesota Press.

Nielsen, J., and B. Shelby. (1977). River-running in the Grand Canyon: how much and what kind of use. *Proceedings of the River Recreation Management and Research Symposium*, Grand Canyon National Park, Colorado River Research Series, Contribution No. 18.

Powell, J.W. (1875). *The exploration of the Colorado River*. New York: Anchor Books.

Price, L., Arnould, E., and P. Tierney. (1995). Going to extremes: managing service encounters and assessing provider performance. *Journal of Marketing*, **59**, 83–97.

Reiter, D. and D. Blahna. (2001). *Utah River study results report: recreational use, value, and experience of boaters on rivers managed by the BLM in Utah*. (volume III). Report prepared for the Bureau of Land Management, Salt Lake City, UT.

Rennicke, J. (1988). *River days: travels on western rivers*. Golden, CO: Fulcrum.

Roberts, C., and H.R. Gimblett. (2000). Computer simulation for rafting traffic on the Colorado River. *Proceedings of the 5th Biennial Conference of Research on the Colorado Plateau*. U.S. Department of the Interior, U.S. Geological Survey, Flagstaff, AZ.

Schmidt, C. (1979). The guided tour: insulated adventure. *Urban Life*, 7 (4), 441–467.

Schmidt, J.C., and J.B. Graf. (1990). Aggradation and degradation of alluvial sand deposits, 1965 to 1986, Colorado River, Grand Canyon National Park, Arizona, USA, *United States Geological Survey*, Professional Paper 1493.

Schneider, I., and W. Hammitt. (1995). Visitor response to outdoor recreation conflict: A conceptual approach. *Leisure Sciences*, **17** (3), 223–234.

Shelby, B., and T. Heberlein. (1986). *Carrying capacity in recreation settings*. Corvallis: Oregon State University.

Shelby, B., and J. Nielsen. (1976). *Private and commercial trips in Grand Canyon*. Colorado River Research Contribution No. 31, Tech. Report No. 4. Grand Canyon, AZ: Grand Canyon National Park.

Simmel, G. (1965). *Essays on sociology, philosophy, and aesthetics*. New York: Harper & Row.

Stebbins, R. (1979). *Amateurs: on the margin between work and leisure*. Beverly Hills, CA: Sage.

Stewart, W., Larkin, K., Orland, B., Anderson, D., Manning, R., Cole, D., et al. (2000). *Preferences of recreation user groups of the Colorado River in Grand Canyon*. Report submitted to the Grand Canyon Monitoring and Research Center, Flagstaff, AZ.

Webb, R.H., Mehs, T.S., Griffiths, P.G., and J.C. Elliott. (1999). Downstream effects of Glen Canyon Dam on the Colorado River in Grand Canyon: a review. In R.H. Webb, J.C. Schmidt, G.R. Marzolf, and R.A. Valdez (Eds.), *The controlled flood of Grand Canyon*. Washinton, DC: American Geophysical Union.

Wood, R. (1984). *Whitewater boatman: the making of a river guide*. Berkeley, CA: Ten Speed Press.

Websites

Grand Canyon Private Boaters Association: www.gcpba.org
Grand Canyon River Outfitters Association: www.gcroa.org
National Park Service, Grand Canyone National Park, Colorado River Management
  Plan: www.nps.gov/grca/crmp

9

Kayaking

Simon Hudson and Paul Beedie

Overview

As Ray Rowe (1989) succinctly argues, paddling is "a primitive battle with a hostile environment" (p. 1) and, despite advances in building materials and a sophisticated understanding of hydrodynamics, this exploratory activity has not, he claims,
changed a great deal since ancient times. By paddling a range of canoes and kayaks,
humans have been able to navigate "the lakes, rivers, estuaries, coasts and oceans of
the world" (Rowe 1989, p. 1). Using this idea as a starting point, this chapter examines how paddling has become a part of tourism, sport, and recreation, and the
extent to which this claim can be supported. In particular, it develops a focus on
kayaking, which is technically a subsection of the collective term "canoeing."

According to Hutchinson (1999) a canoe is "a boat pointed at both ends, which is
suitable for being propelled by one or more forward facing paddlers, using paddles
without any rowlock or other fulcrum, and is light enough to be carried overland by
its crew" (p. ix). Within this broad definition, canoes are open craft, paddled by one
or more persons with a single-bladed paddle usually, or traditionally, from a kneeling position in the boat. These are often known as Canadian canoes, as their history
can be traced back to the native populations whose cultures settled the woods, lakes,
and rivers of the vast continent of North America. Kayaking has its historical origins
in Inuit cultures as "the skin boats of the Arctic" (Hutchinson 1999, p. ix). A kayak
is an enclosed boat paddled from a sitting position with a doubled-bladed paddle.

Canoes generally evolved for transport and economic purposes but have been
developed for recreation, sport (as in the Olympic Games), and tourism. The purpose of this chapter is to concentrate on kayaking and to discuss how kayaking
characteristically fits these categories today. It will show how Rowe is essentially
correct when he says paddling (re)engages with our atavistic past because it
retains an exploratory dimension, which is part of its appeal, yet it is not immune

---

Source: Sea Kayaking Milos, the Cyclades Islands, Greece (www.seakayak-greece.com)

to broader influences upon sport, recreation, and tourism today. Kayaking has, for example, fragmented into subsections, some of which emphasize exploration (e.g., sea kayaking and wilderness whitewater descents, and kayak camping), while others are closer to sport (slalom competition, river racing, and marathons such as the Devizes to Westminster race on the River Thames). Additionally, other activities, such as kayak surfing and play-boating, might be recreation or sport depending upon the location and the participants. Kayaking, then, is a generic term: it involves paddling a maneuverable boat in any of a range of water environments (e.g., sea, river, estuary, canal, and lake) for a variety of purposes (e.g., exploration, sporting competition, adventure and challenge, recreation, tourism, and outdoor education) by all sorts of people (e.g., male and female, young and old, able-bodied and disabled). The chapter, therefore, has a very broad potential remit.

The structure of the chapter will follow that of the rest of the book and will deal with theory, relevant issues, and other pertinent topics before concluding with a case study.

Our intention, then, becomes one of articulating the defining characteristics of kayaking within sport, recreation, and tourism by drawing upon examples from our own experiences and a host of supporting literature. The result is an emphasis upon understanding kayaking through a discussion of the theory and practice of paddling, illustrated by a range of selected examples, rather than a definitive study of this substantial area.

Background

There are a number of trends that can be identified within kayaking as sport, recreation, and tourism. The first is an exploratory or journeying dimension across a range of water environments based on lightness and maneuverability and linked to a kayaking history in the developed world. This can be traced back to the Victorian Age (1837 to 1901), explorers in general, and John Macgregor in particular. This remarkable man is credited as the founder of modern kayaking (Rowe 1989, pp. 1–2). Having observed kayaks in North America and Kamschatka, he persuaded the London-based boatbuilders Searles of Lambeth to build the clinker-constructed *Rob Roy*. This craft was then paddled by Macgregor all over the world, leading to a series of books that included *A Thousand Miles in the Rob Roy Canoe* (1867), *The Rob Roy on the Jordan* (1869), and *The Rob Roy on the Baltic* (1872). The written word was a powerful medium of dissemination in the late nineteenth century, as Riffenburgh (1993) has clearly shown. This led to a disproportionate representation from the "educated" classes in the emergent recreation and sport of kayaking.

As kayaking became established, further trends became evident. An important second trend concerns kayak design and manufacture. This began to evolve, and innovative technologies were applied to the production of kayaks and ancillary kits such as paddles, spray decks, and buoyancy aids. Each stage in this process emphasized the kayak's lightness and maneuverability while adding strength and robustness to the craft. For example, the original wooden *Rob Roy* weighed 90 lbs (41 kg), but the *Rob Roy II* weighed only 60 lbs (27 kg). Then the use of canvas over a wooden frame took the weight down significantly in the early- to mid-twentieth century. While good for touring and flat water, the canvas kayaks broke up on rapids. Fiberglass was the panacea for this problem. Light and strong as well as easily repaired, the kayak could now be paddled through whitewater and unpredictable seas. Mike Jones and a team famously paddled "down Everest" in their first descent of the Dudh Khosi river in Nepal in 1976 in fiberglass kayaks. Only two of the six kayaks completed the descent.

The late twentieth century has witnessed an unprecedented pace of development in kayak design, durability, maneuverability, and customized features. Plastic boats now dominate the market, but each subsection of kayaking has its own design and production direction: a "play-boat" is short and has built-in "rails" for fast turns (Whiting 2002), whereas a sea kayak looks like the original Inuit hunting craft. It sits low in the water but is long and has the ability to cut through waves and travel for long distances in a straight line with a minimum of paddling effort (Hutchinson 1999).

A third trend has been the gradual evolution of rules, regulations, and structures that have shaped kayaking as sport, recreation, and tourism. Evidence for this includes the long history of national governing bodies. In the United Kingdom, the British Canoe Association was formed as early as 1887, followed by an international federation known as the Internationalen Representation für Kanusport (IRK) of Austria, Germany, Denmark, and Sweden in 1924. The British Canoe Union (BCU) dates from 1936, although the coaching scheme did not emerge until the 1960s. Today, the BCU is a robust national body responsible for the plethora of coaching awards across kayaking (e.g., sea kayaking, inland flat and whitewater kayaking, and surf kayaking). Such a bureaucracy is a characteristic of modern sport and recreation. It is particularly important that kayaking is seen to operate responsibly, for example, with regard to environmental sensitivity and social contestation as well as the "correct" leadership of groups. One of the key lines of inquiry in the public investigation that followed the tragedy of Lyme Bay in 1993, when several children perished from hypothermia, uncovered the fact that the "instructors" of the group were not suitably qualified for sea kayaking—an outcome that led to the conviction and jail sentencing of the center manager who employed them. The case also led to the creation in the UK of the Adventure Activities Licensing Agency (AALA) and thus a further level of bureaucracy, a situation common to developed countries around the world.

A final trend concerns paddling environments. Commercial agendas such as those discussed above, combined with a restrictive social agenda to "contain and control" risk sports and recreations (such as the bureaucracies of licensing and certification schemes), have led to the creation of artificial water courses in and around urban centers (Beedie 2004). This is, in the UK, partly a result of access issues (to be explored later), along with technical developments in water control, the "controllability" of a potentially dangerous environment, and commercial expediency aligned to personal comfort. Thus, a number of factors have combined to lead to the logical progression from Augsburg 1972, when a whitewater slalom course was built for the Munich Olympics. In the UK, there are now a significant number of artificial whitewater kayaking sites on accessible rivers. These include the River Trent at Nottingham, the River Tees at Middlesbrough, the River Nene at Northampton, and the River Ouse at Bedford. In North America, mountain towns are rushing to build kayaking play parks. One of their models is the Clear Creek Whitewater Park in Golden, Colorado. The downtown kayaking park is 800 feet long, and from 2000 to 2003 had swelled city coffers by millions (Casimiro 2003).

These sites are accessible to large numbers of paddlers; water levels are controlled by sluice gates; there are car parks, changing rooms, and hot showers; and they provide a sport training or adventure recreation setting for a range of kayaking paddlers. This artificial paddling environment is popular and attractive to people who are willing to pay to paddle and/or watch. It remains very different from the spirit of Macgregor in his *Rob Roy,* but perhaps is closer to the zeitgeist of a time when performance, play, and identity construction are both more sought after and more ephemeral.

Market Profile

Kayaking as a sport has regional, national, and international competitions leading to world championships. For example, apart from the flat-water sprint disciplines of the Olympic Games, new international competitions have emerged in many kayaking activities. These include the World Freestyle Kayaking Championships (Whiting 2002); canoe sailing, where competition can be traced back to the New York Cup in 1886 (Rowe 1989); and whitewater slalom, where the first World Championships were held in Geneva in 1949 (Rowe 1989). Slalom became an Olympic sport in 1972 when, as another technical first, the artificial slalom course was constructed at Augsburg. The first World Championship Wild Water Race was held on the River Vezere in France in 1959; flat-water marathon racing has existed since 1920 with the internationally renowned Devizes to Westminster Race emerging in embryonic form in 1949. Surf kayaking had an unofficial World Championship in the USA in 1980, but the surfing of kayaks has been superseded at this level by the more specialized surf shoe (Rowe 1989). Each competition operates according to rules and regulations set out by the authorities responsible, and participants will train and perform at times and at places suitable for that kayaking activity. The "spectacle" of kayak sports can therefore contribute to tourism.

Kayaking as leisure/recreation operates across a full spectrum from hard to soft adventure and across a range of paddlers from novice to expert. The hard–soft model in Figure 9-1 is a useful reference point in understanding the above-mentioned trends in kayaking.

In this model, kayaking is viewed as a hard adventure activity. Technology, especially in kayak design, has paved the way for more extreme paddling—waterfall descents, for example, which are hard adventure. However, these remain the preserve of a few enthusiasts because the "controlling" dimensions of kayaking outlined above act to pull mainstream kayaking toward the realm of soft adventure. In this respect, kayaking really fits the "adventure dimension" between hard and soft found in other outdoor pursuits in which the ratio of participation is approximately 2:1 in favor of soft adventure. However, adventure as "uncertainty of outcome" (Mortlock 1984) is highly personalized so that, although the soft–hard model is useful, it needs to integrate a more flexible understanding of adventure in order to reflect the complex social circumstance that kayaking represents. For example, using specially adapted kayaks, disabled and physically handicapped groups have had successful kayaking experiences (Smedley 1995).

Kayaking can have a profound influence upon participants. Geoff Smedley (1995), for example, outlines supportive kayaking programs for people with

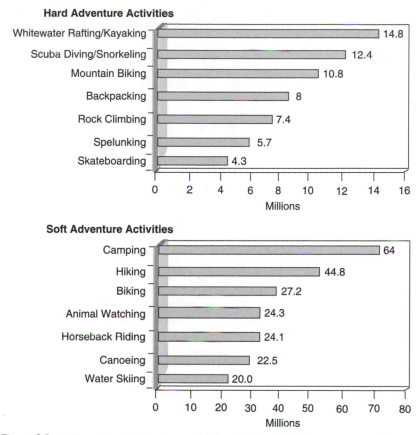

Hard Adventure Activities

Activity	Millions
Whitewater Rafting/Kayaking	14.8
Scuba Diving/Snorkeling	12.4
Mountain Biking	10.8
Backpacking	8
Rock Climbing	7.4
Spelunking	5.7
Skateboarding	4.3

Soft Adventure Activities

Activity	Millions
Camping	64
Hiking	44.8
Biking	27.2
Animal Watching	24.3
Horseback Riding	24.1
Canoeing	22.5
Water Skiing	20.0

Figure 9-1 Soft and hard adventure activities: Participation between 1993 and 1998. Source: Travel Industry Association of America (1998).

epilepsy, learning difficulties, and physical disabilities, which form an agenda of rehabilitation beyond the more primary aims of recreation (see also related comments in Chapters 2 and 8). Similarly, kayaking has been used as a form of catharsis by many across a range of settings. David Aaronovitch's (2000) journey around Britain and Maria Coffey's (1990) world tour with a "kayak in her baggage" are examples of how kayaking has been used as a medium for exploration and self-reflection leading to lifestyle changes. Walt Blackadar (Watters 1994, 2003) used wild water exploration throughout North America to extend his recreational kayaking into the realm of first paddling descents.

More conventionally, the popularity of kayaking around the world has never been greater. Many countries can absorb and cultivate this interest, and the links with tourism and other commercial possibilities become obvious. In the UK, however, Storry (1991) has shown that the huge increase in the numbers of people kayaking has not been "serviced" by a commensurate increase in access to paddling inland water. The fragmentation of kayaking into many sub-disciplines and the facility of improved kayak design and construction materials have opened up new paddling possibilities that have exacerbated access issues. Storry (1991) refers to the Seiont trespass of 1988 as such an example (see Impacts section later in this chapter).

Kayaking as tourism presents a complicated picture. There is no doubting the popularity of paddling activities, but commercial developments in kayaking face a problem not faced by charter sailing companies, for example. While a sailing boat can be hired with a skipper to actually sail the craft, a kayak must be paddled by its occupant—this requires some basic skills. When the risk assessment requirements commensurate with safety regulations in developed countries are added to a water-based tourist operation, it is easy to see why commercial paddling developments emerge as potentially problematic. This has a certain irony at a time when Mounet and Chifflet (2003, p. 269) argue that

As all outdoor sports activities, white-water sports have become extremely popular. The public demands contact with nature in an unconstrained atmosphere. The need for companionship within groups and a refusal of complicated instruction and specialization in sporting activities have fostered the development of commercial activity in this domain. The clientele freely buys and consumes a service designed by sports supervision professionals and accessible to the general public. (p. 269)

However, when the details of whitewater sports emerge, it becomes clear from their model (Mounet and Chifflet 2003, p. 274) that by introducing an axis of technical difficulty, the growth within the tourist sector is in less skill-demanding whitewater activities such as whitewater swimming, kayak rafting, raft tubing, and rafting. Indeed, Mounet and Chifflet's main conclusion is that, "confronted by a difficult milieu, white-water companies have thus created original products that allow their clients lacking specific technical training to access a white-water experience" (p. 276; see also related discussions in Chapter 8 of this volume).

There is, therefore, a growing tourist sector around the commodification of whitewater, but the commercial development of kayaking remains problematic because of the prerequisite of technical paddling skills that may exist for the casual "paddler as tourist." The invention of less technical alternatives acts against the promotion of kayaking as a commercially viable alternative to, for example, rafting. Kayaking is an individual activity for the most part (although kayak "doubles" do exist, as popularized by the Outward Bound movement for its teamwork agendas, and people do, of course, go paddling in groups). More importantly, it requires skill and experience to paddle a kayak, and fitness to sustain the endeavor over a long period of time. The evidence for such an observation is found in the prolific publication of "how-to" books. Examples for sea kayaking have been written by Nigel Foster (1991) and Derek Hutchinson (1999). Examples for whitewater river running and touring include Steven Krauzer's *Kayaking: White-Water and Touring Basics* (1995), and concerning where to paddle, Cassidy and Dunlap's (1999) *World White-Water: A Global Guide for River Runners*. The creative and expressive dimension of kayaking is fully explained by Eric Brymer, Tom Hughes, and Loel Collins 2000) in *The Art of Freestyle* and duplicated to some extent by Whiting's (2002) book *The Playboater's Handbook II: The Ultimate Guide to Freestyle Kayaking*.

There is a certain irony in the idea of the creative dimension of kayaking being set out as a series of maneuvers in a coaching manual, but this appears to reflect a growing commercial usurping of the idea of adventure. Additionally, it provides a source of income for professional paddlers who use the medium of manuals to consolidate their position as "experts" or "names" in the field. In a commercially driven world, celebrity matters. Here is what Shaun Baker, a professional adventure paddler, has to say about the *Art of Freestyle* book (in the forward, his singular "named" contribution) and the niche market it is targeting:

Freestyle is a thinking person's sport. The authors, the contributors, and the book's publisher have an unrivaled breadth of knowledge in the field, so let this book do some of the thinking for you. The full-color format and the emphasis on personal training and coaching make for a particularly easy read. (quoted in Brymer et al. 2000, p. 3)

Perhaps the most interesting point of analysis concerns the idea that creative kayaking can be reduced to a set of maneuvers and training regimes set out by self-appointed "experts" in the activity. Moreover, the manual is marketed as a visual stimulant (it is dominated by impressive, well-produced color photographs) that purports to fast-track potential "freestyle/play-boaters" into the realm of expert performer by letting the book "do the thinking." So, even in this most expressive dimension of kayaking, there are discursive agendas operating that illuminate the true nature of the sport, recreation, or tourism agendas operating.

Kayaking, then, cannot be entered into lightly because it makes demands upon people to perform a series of paddling strokes that must first be learned. Such paddling capital becomes a gateway to exploring the multitude of water environments, but at the same time excludes those who cannot paddle, or at least restricts their paddling to the safest and most accessible (and therefore controllable) water places, such as swimming pools and small, sheltered, and shallow lakes and rivers, for example. Kayaking has some tourism potential because it takes time and effort to learn how to paddle, and this is most easily achieved in the least exciting water environments such as canals. Whitewater rafting by comparison has huge commercial possibilities because it involves a guided descent of a series of rapids, which can be undertaken by groups of people who, with a minimum of preparation, can have the adventure of their lives (Swarbrooke, Beard, Leckie, and Pomfret 2003; see also Chapter 8 of this volume), at a cost. The foregoing discussion has suggested that kayaking as tourism has limited possibilities as mainstream tourism and is easily surpassed by other whitewater activities. However, there remains a more select group of people for whom "kayaking as adventure" remains important. These are people that aspire to be kayak paddlers, and see their chosen pursuit as a leisure career. Such people are catered to by commercial kayaking operators. The most challenging environment is the sea because it is the least controllable paddling environment, and it therefore demands the greatest application of skill and judgment.

According to Morgan (1998), sea kayakers can be classified into four groups: fearless thrill seekers, daring thrill seekers, ecotourists, and competence testers. Kayakers in the last group seek a high-level challenge in an expedition. The 1999 Greenland kayak and dog expedition, for example, covered 2,000 miles traveling halfway around Greenland. With a budget of US$400,000, Dupre and Hoelschre, who conducted the expedition, obtained support from 80 sponsors. Kayakers who conduct such expeditions, or even those participating in whitewater kayaking, can be considered to be engaging in serious leisure (Stebbins 2001). According to Stebbins, serious leisure is the systematic pursuit of an activity that is sufficiently rewarding despite the costs that participants find a career in the acquisition and expression of its special skills and knowledge. Serious leisure is exclusive of people who want a superficial "quick fix" sense of excitement. Serious paddlers use their knowledge, skills, and experiences as a point of distinction from those who may participate less frequently and who, when they do, are paddling under the umbrella of "tourism." Serious paddlers may also be better suited to the physical discomforts that are part of any sustained paddling experience.

Other studies of kayakers differentiate between those paddling with clubs, solo paddlers, and those who kayak with a guide (Schuett 1995). Club participants prefer larger kayaking groups, prefer comfort facilities on the river, and are not concerned about teaching or leading others. In fact, these participants would fit into a category that many in the outdoor recreation business are referring to as *bobos*: bourgeois bohemians. John Waibel, owner of the Vancouver Island–based Outfitter *Spirit of the West,* caters for these bobos. He says, "our guests are not experienced kayakers. Most tend to be between 35 and 55 and what they want is a chance to have an outdoor adventure without the risk of being uncomfortable" (Buhasz 2003, p. T5).

As for those kayaking alone, Schuett (1995) suggests that they prefer solitude, are highly skilled, paddle many times a year, kayak at a lower level of difficulty, are sensation seekers, and have a higher income than other groups. They are daring yet adept individuals who specifically want to be alone on the river seeking solitude and personal thrills. Finally, those kayakers who use a guide tend to be less skilled paddlers, do not feel kayaking is central to their lives, seek thrills, and like to kayak in larger kayaking groups. Even though these inexperienced individuals seek the use of guides or choose to take kayaking classes, an important outcome is apparently the need for thrills and excitement. Previous research has shown that kayakers may have positive experiences even when their abilities are exceeded by the difficulty of the river (Jones, Hollenhorst, Perna, and Salin 2000).

Kayak tourism, where it does exist, divides itself into two broad areas. First, there are "hire a kayak" companies who attract tourists who want to "mess around" in boats in relatively safe water. Generally, this means flat-water rivers such as most of the River Wye in the UK, the Dorgogne in France, and lakes such as Windermere in the English Lake District. At its most adventurous, such companies can be found concentrated at the access points to the relatively "safe" whitewater rivers of the warmer climates; a good example is the Ardeche Gorge in southern France.

Second, there are the "exotic" possibilities set up for experienced paddlers discussed above. This is water-based adventure tourism, and an in-depth example is included as a case study at the end of this chapter. However, it is worth noting here the increasing number of kayaking possibilities worldwide. North America and Central America dominate the scene, with 72 different destinations listed in 1996 (Cater and Cater 2000). For example, Newfoundland in Canada has 17,000 kilometers of coastline with 14 tour operators offering kayaking tours. However, there are an increasing number of operations in Europe, Oceania, and Asia. Kayakers are even flocking to China to indulge their passion, finding miles of virgin whitewater in the drainages of Sichuan province. However, there remains a huge gap between destinations such as the Pacific Northwest or Maine, where guided kayak trips are a mainstream tourist business, and Madagascar or Tierra del Fuego, where organized tours have been available for only a few years, and remain the province of one or two companies.

Prime sea kayaking destinations require lots of water interspersed at short intervals with interesting shapes of land—islands, inlets, coves, bays, cliffs, beaches, and other places to land the kayak. Ideally, some of the terrain will be exposed to open water, and some will be sheltered, and there will be a generous dose of inter-tidal life, and human or natural history (Johnson 2003). Most kayaking tours are guided. Guided trip costs tend to vary according to the length of the trip and the remoteness of the location, rather than the services provided, since the vast major-ity of kayak tours include all paddling equipment and food, to reduce logistical and packing problems for the guide. For example, in 2004, a 15-day escorted sea kayaking trip in Thailand was priced at CDN$3990 (US$3,594), whereas a 4-day tour of the Campbell River in British Columbia cost CDN$889 (US$800). British Columbia outfitter Rob Lyon has pioneered a new concept in guiding, "Guided Solo Trips" (Shuff 2003). For just over CDN$16,000 (US$14,410), clients of his Lyon Expeditions get to spend two months alone on the outer coast of Vancouver Island. Except for the guidance of Lyon's voice on the other end of a satellite con-nection, they are paddling solo.

Barriers to entry for a kayak tour operator are quite high. Unlike trekking, where anyone can buy a pack and become a guide, kayaking requires a substantial initial investment in equipment. According to Effeney (1999), in popular kayaking destina-tions, competition keeps everyone sharp, and in remote areas, the tour guides are there because they love it and enjoy sharing the experience. Either maintains a high service quality. He also suggests that a quality operator will have the best equipment, excellent food, and will involve the indigenous community as much as possible.

It should be noted that, although examples of such tourism can be found in the frontier countries of New Zealand and Canada, and despite substantial potential such as in China, developments in kayaking generally are not as pro-lific as in comparable adventure fields such as mountaineering (Beedie and Hudson 2003).

Advantages

A kayak is a small, relatively cheap boat that can be transported easily by car or via manageable trailers to a range of paddling locations. Its size also means that it can be carried by one person so that portages can be made around difficulties, across beaches, or to link river-canal-lake systems together, thus facilitating extended journeys. Most kayaks—except for short play-boats—can carry one per-son and a range of spare kit, food, and clothing. Sea kayaks have bulkheads to aid buoyancy and provide carrying space for multi-day or -week expeditions. Kayaks can be paddled on a range of water settings, from small ponds via rivers and lakes to open sea. Kayaking can be a solo experience, something that Colin Mortlock (1984, 2001) writes extensively about. Extended journeys are opportunities to reflect and, in Mortlock's case, to articulate life-defining philosophies. His longest solo Alaskan paddling journey led him to write, "reflecting further on the oceanic feeling, the implication was startling. Instead of accepting the fact that I was a part of nature, I now felt that, potentially, I was Nature" (Mortlock 2001, p. 55). This is Rowe's (1989) "primitivism" at its most powerful.

At the other end of the spectrum, freestyle play-boating involves little paddling of distance. Instead, the paddler aims to reach a site of usable waves. These may be produced at sea by tidal overflows such as "The Bitches" in Pembrokeshire, in England, or on whitewater rivers such as the Grand Tully rapids on the River Tay in Scotland. Additionally, such waves may be found on water regulation sites such as Duck Mill weir on the River Ouse or at full artificial whitewater sites such as Holmepierrepont on the River Trent. Once on the wave, the play-boater can explore the creative paddling opportunities afforded, often in the social setting provided by fellow paddlers who will understand the codes and etiquette operating (of waiting one's turn, for example). Such contemporary forms of kayaking are essentially social and popular for that reason, as Mounet and Chifflet (2003) suggest.

Finally, the act of kayaking, although difficult to learn in its differing forms, can provide great personal satisfaction as progress is achieved. Ken Whiting's (2002) rise from novice paddler at a kayaking school on the Ottowa River in 1989 to World Freestyle Kayaking Champion in 1997 may be exceptional, but it demonstrates what can be achieved. Even at a recreational level, it offers a route to fitness through physical endeavor, while on whitewater and at sea, high levels of technical competence are required through the challenge of these environments. Moreover, the range of paddling environments remains diverse. Developed countries have a variety of canal networks that, now that industrial usage for transportation is minimal, are gradually being reclaimed for recreation (refer to Chapter 3 for a similar comment). Water has always added an attractive potential to places, partly through human curiosity and partly through the potential it offers for sport, recreation, and tourism. For example, kayak races and slalom competitions (e.g., Duck Mill, Bedford, and the races of the biannual River Festival in the UK) are spectator friendly, as the River Ouse bisects Bedford town center, and creates a recreation setting that is also attractive for tourism.

Disadvantages

There are problems with water quality throughout developed countries. An example is the acute problem at the estuary of the River Mersey where at one stage there were no water life forms at all! This was a stimulus to the formation in the UK of the National Rivers Authority (NRA), which has begun to clean up UK rivers and canals.

In developed countries with concentrated populations and limited inland kayaking sites, access has become a major issue. This is particularly well demonstrated in the UK where there are two main access dimensions. The first is contested space and users; for example, fishing and kayaking have often been antagonistic sports/recreations (see also Chapter 3 regarding boating, fishing, and other user conflicts). This relationship has been exacerbated by a willingness by many angling clubs to pay for exclusive access rights and the obduracy of paddlers promoting an agenda of freedom and exploration in the spirit of adventure.

The second concerns land ownership, and in particular riparian owners (those owning river banks, often different people for each bank or shoreline) who are effectively the gatekeepers for access (getting on the water) and egress (getting off the water). In the UK, almost all navigable rivers require constant monitoring and bureaucracy as only a few (notably the Rivers Wye and Severn) have statutory rights of navigation. The BCU shoulders the significant burden of negotiating and setting up access agreements in England and Wales through its network of regional access officers. However, access comes at a price because paddling rights are not necessarily extended to those nonmembers of the BCU (membership requires a significant annual subscription); for example, all water craft using canals in the

UK must be licensed (this is part of the annual subscription to BCU). Thus, a complicated situation has emerged that, from one line of argument, suggests kayaking opportunities favor paddlers who can pay either directly or indirectly for their sport/recreation, a circumstance amply illustrated by the growth of commercial kayaking operators.

This is part of a bigger problem for the UK and other densely populated countries that have more paddlers than rivers to put them on (see also discussion in Chapter 8 regarding rafting and rafting numbers). There has been, for example, a huge increase in paddlers on the Dee Tour (upper River Dee; the interesting bit climaxing in the town falls at Llangollen is only open on certain days throughout the year), so that a quasi wilderness adventure paddle down some of the best white-water in Wales has become a "bumper-to-bumper" line of kayaks. Such experiences are less of a problem elsewhere in the world, such as in Canada and New Zealand, which have substantial areas of inland kayaking waters and relatively small populations. In New Zealand, there is an emerging section of commercial kayaking that uses helicopters to access remote rivers, just as heli-skiing has opened up exciting opportunities (for those who can afford to pay) in the wilds of Canada. Additionally, the underdeveloped possibilities in South America (e.g., Chile) and Asia (e.g., China) are beginning to emerge.

Impacts

These might be outlined under three headings: social, economic, and environmental. Mounet and Chifflet (2003) note the growing attractiveness of whitewater sports and recreations. These, they suggest, are part of an increasing popularity of rivers in general and whitewater runs in particular. There is, therefore, a social impact identifiable in a growing number of people interested in water sports; kayaking is a part of this trend. Socially, there has been a diversification of kayaking into subsections of activity usually associated with specific paddling environments; for example, sea kayaking is distinct from inland river paddling. However, paddling skills are transferable between craft and it is not uncommon to find play-boaters on the sea, on inland rivers, or at artificial sites. In water-based tourism, where arguably the greatest social impacts can be found, kayaking appears to be relatively benign. According to Jennings (2003), social impacts between hosts and guests are relatively small, as most expeditions venture into unpopulated areas. Invariably, there might be entries into cultural and indigenous locations that require prior approval.

Economic impacts cover a range of areas. Building and selling kayaks and kayaking equipment has become an industry in its own right (e.g., www.canoeking.com). This has been driven by (or is driving) kayaking specialization such as the different design features of play-boats and touring boats. Manuals, guidebooks, and videos are also increasingly available. Urban paddling, e.g., London Docklands and Bristol City Docks, is now more common. Further economic dimensions can be seen in the employment involved in constructing and maintaining waterways.

Sea kayaking is potentially the most environmentally friendly of all marine tourism (Cater and Cater 2000) because, providing waste is taken back, it is non-polluting. It is also less intrusive to wildlife: birds and animals tend to be curious rather than frightened (Figure 9-2). However, kayaks do still have an impact. Orams (1999) suggests that, for nature tourism in marine settings, initially developments were encouraged as "the impacts of tourism were largely viewed as positive." However, the individual success stories of cases of conservation, for example, must be offset against an increasing number of reports that "show that significant environmental, social, cultural, and even economic damage can result" (Orams 1999, p.57).

One such example came from Phang-Nga Bay in Thailand. Originally purported to be a model of ecotourism for Asia where small groups of kayakers were taken into the limestone sea caves, the caves became so popular that 1,000 kayakers were visiting them each day. Boats jammed the narrow passages, tourists snapped off stalactites for souvenirs, and their bellowing scared away gibbons, hornbills, and other wildlife (Gray 1999). What was once an exclusive nature experience "had become a nightmare" (Shepherd 2002, p. 313). There is some hope on the horizon for a less damaging approach. An association of kayak operators has since set a quota of 300 boats a day into the caves.

The UK offers many examples of problems created by increasing numbers of people paddling. Storry (1991) articulates the legal and political debate concerning paddlers and fishermen and -women that remains largely unresolved today. He says,

Out of a total of 19,144 kilometers on 656 rivers listed by Edwards in his book *Inland Waterways*, there were agreements covering 519 kilometers on 31 rivers. In other words anglers have agreed to share 2.7% of the available length of rivers in England and Wales with touring canoeists at some time of the year. (p. 39)

Such a circumstance has stimulated the growth of pressure groups such as the Campaign for River Access for Canoes and Kayaks (CRACK). A CRACK supported stance was taken over the River Seiont in North Wales when a clash

Figure 9-2   Kayakers at sunset with support boat, Great Keppel Island, Australia. Photographer: Gayle Jennings.

between anglers and paddlers left a capsized kayaker with fractures from rocks thrown at close range on October 10, 1987. CRACK organized a well-prepared mass kayak trespass in March 1988 on the Seiont, which achieved little other than alienating CRACK from the BCU. The relative lack of access to inland water in England and Wales remains a complex situation today with a clear political dimension. The circumstances described here suggest that kayaking as leisure, recreation, or tourism is a multifaceted and complex phenomenon that will continue to engage with agendas of commerce, risk management and control, human endeavor, and environmental conservation in ways that will demand investigative research for many years to come.

Case Study

Greece has the archetypal Mediterranean climate: warm summers and mild winters with some rainfall. This makes the area attractive for activity vacations because people feel comfortable. Greece is a country with a rich cultural and historical legacy. It also has an appealing rugged landscape and, more importantly, a huge archipelago of islands that create a diverse series of seascapes. This combination of climate, physical attractions (of beaches, bays, and rock features), and a timelessness brought about by a slow pace of life away from the mainland has made the country ripe for tourist development. The islands are well networked by small aircraft and, more commonly, ferries. This leaves some of the islands more accessible than others. Milos, a part of the Cyclades group, is situated 84 miles south of Athens. It has one port and one airport, which makes it reasonably easy to reach in the summer when airplanes fly in twice a week and ferries run daily, but leaves it more cut off in the winter when there are no airplanes and the ferries may be canceled due to strong winds and rough seas.

The capital of Milos is Plaka, which is a large village rather than a town. Nevertheless, because of its outlier of Adamas, this northern peninsula is where the greatest concentrations of tourist facilities (as in restaurants, hotels, guest houses, and gift shops) are found. Sea Kayak Milos is based in the village of Triovasalos on the less developed northeast coast of the island. There are a number of reasons for this, but prime among them is the need to be reasonably close to the point at which tourists will access the island (the port of Adamas) without losing the peace and quiet that appears to be an important attraction for the clients of the kayaking company. As with many adventure tourist developments around the world, there is a balance to be struck between keeping the clients happy and comfortable (as they are on vacation!) and providing an apparent exploratory experience through a series of sea kayaking journeys.

On Milos, the majority of the population lives on the east side, leaving the west of the island virtually uninhabited with access only possible by dirt roads, or by sea kayak. In 1992, deposits of perlite were discovered on the island, along with traces of gold. A geological expedition was set up to explore the possibilities of commercial mining. Rod Feldtmann was a part of this team. He was also a paddler, and he fell in love with the island in general and the daughter of a local businessman in particular. He decided that a kayak was the appropriate craft to facilitate geological exploration and the process led, over several years, to the accumulation of considerable local knowledge. He began to receive kayak rental offers from locals and from tourists. He was not slow to see the business potential of this situation and, in 2002, he launched Sea Kayak Milos and began sea kayaking tours.

The business took off in that first summer, although things slowed for the winter. Rod Feldtmann's wife owns properties that were developed as guest houses. These required some renovations and adjustments to bring them up to acceptable levels of accommodation for clients. The embryonic company then developed a website and began to take Internet bookings, which is when the business moved quickly forward.

Sea Kayaking Milos, then, offers a packaged sea kayaking vacation opportunity. Its strength is its exotic location, both accessible and remote at the same time. The clients that are attracted to the package will have some paddling experience. The vacation packages are family friendly and each paddling session (a half or a full day) can be negotiated depending upon the experience and ambitions of the group. It will always be a small business because it relies heavily upon the local knowledge and leadership/guiding on the sea by Rod Feldtmann. The attractions for clients include not having to supply any of the specialist kit (kayak, paddles, spray decks, buoyancy aids, etc.) and an opportunity to determine the location and duration of each session (although inevitably people will be heavily influenced by Rod Feldtmann's suggestions). Additionally, each package can be customized by the number of days or sessions, for example, and transport on the island, accommodation, and food as required are all supplied as part of the package.

Sea Kayaking Milos is still developing but does have a business plan. Profits are reinvested in buying more kayaks and refurbishing the "cafenio" to provide for clients and other tourists. Rod Feldtmann is also keen to offer longer sea journeys for experienced paddlers. He has considered the Milos–Crete crossing, for example, which is 70 kilometers of open sea.

This plan encapsulates the primary tension in developing adventure tourism companies such as this one. Business acumen requires a careful balance between conventional tourist activity (food, drink, gift shops, and accommodation), which may offer potential for growth and a steady income, and bringing in experienced paddlers as clients who may be attracted by the perceived "authenticity" of wilderness paddling. The latter trips, notably the open sea crossings, are sporadic. Even though the business can charge more for these more demanding excursions, the income may not be significant over a full year in business. This point is illustrated by the example of an English family who had a booking from July 22, 2003. The father is a commercial manager for Pyranha Boats, he is an experienced paddler, and his work involves kayak design. The mother and two teenage daughters were attracted by the sunshine, beaches, and the snorkeling opportunities as much as the paddling. Field notes taken when observing this group noted a male–female tension: the father was clear about wanting to be amidst "peace and quiet"; the females found this "Okay" up to a point but needed additional stimulation at times. When paddling as a group along the remote west coast of Milos, it was the father who became most agitated when a commercial charter yacht moored in a remote bay that the paddlers thought they had to themselves and unloaded a score of tourists onto the beach.

Sea Kayak Milos is currently profitable. There are a variety of half-day trips for the clients to select depending upon weather conditions, particularly wind speed and direction. The aim of each trip is to fit as many points of interest as possible into the journey; these include sea caves, rock formations, and snorkeling sites. The cost for a half day is 30 Euros (US$39), which includes all equipment hire, transport, and a fruit snack. Departures are usually at either 10 AM or 3 PM and last for about four hours. This itinerary is flexible but will usually consist of about two hours of actual paddling, an hour of "out-of-kayak exploring" (caves, beaches, and snorkeling sites, for example), and an hour's allowance for the group. Distances covered in a half day are usually between four and six miles. Full-day trips will depart at 10 AM and last about seven hours—about three hours of paddling and three hours of out-of-kayak exploring. Distances covered are between 9 and 15 miles, and the cost is 50 Euros (US$64). A 20% discount is given to groups of four or more.

Thus, within the limitations explored in this chapter concerning the relationship between kayaking and sport, leisure, recreation, and tourism, here is an example of a successful business built upon Rowe's (1989) principle of "engaging with a primitive and hostile environment." Today, for kayaking, the equipment is good, weather forecasts are detailed and accurate, experienced and qualified guides can lead groups, and manuals and guidebooks can teach us how to paddle, but ultimately, we still have to do it for ourselves.

References

Aaronovitch, D. (2000). *Paddling to Jerusalem*. London: Fourth Estate.

Beedie, P. (2004/forthcoming). The adventure of urban tourism. *The Journal of Travel and Tourism Marketing,* **18** (3), 37–48.

Beedie, P., and S. Hudson. (2003). Emergence of mountain based adventure tourism. *Annals of Tourism Research,* **30** (3), 625–643.

Brymer, E., Hughes, T., and L. Collins. (2000). *The art of freestyle*. Bangor, Wales: Pesda Press.

Buhasz, L. (2003, June 21). Pampered campers. *The Globe and Mail,* (pp. T5).

Casimiro, S. (2003). The leading edge. *Adventure,* **5** (10), 69.

Cassidy, J., and D. Dunlap. (1999). *World whitewater*. New York: Ragged Mountain Press-McGraw Hill.

Cater, C., and E. Cater. (2000). Marine environments. In D.B. Weaver (Ed.), *The encyclopedia of tourism*, (pp. 265–282). CAB International.

Coffey, M. (1994). *A boat in our baggage*. London: Little-Brown.

Effeney, G. (1999). *An introduction to sea kayaking in Queensland*. Ashgrove West, Australia: Gerard Effeney.

Foster, N. (1991). *Sea kayaking*. Brighton: Fernhurst Books.

Gray, D.D. (1999, July 9). Thailand's eco-tourism effort swamped by greed. *The Ottawa Citizen,* (pp. B8).

Hutchinson, D. (1999). *Sea kayaking*. London: A & C Black.

Jennings, G. (2003). Marine tourism. In S. Hudson (Ed.), *Sport & adventure tourism*. (pp. 125–164). London: The Haworth Press.

Johnson, R. (2003, April 2). Sea kayaking in the Alberni Valley. *Alberni Valley Times,* (pp. 11).

Jones, C.D., Hollenhorst, S.J., Perna, F., and S. Salin. (2000). Validation of the flow theory in an on-site whitewater kayaking setting. *Journal of Leisure*, **32** (2), 247–262.

Krauzer, S. (1995). *Kayaking*. London: W. W. Norton & Company.

Morgan, D. (1998). Adventure tourists on water: linking expectations, affect, achievement and enjoyment to the adventure. Working Paper number 1960/1998. Caulfield East, Australia: Monash University.

Mortlock, C. (1984). *The adventure alternative*. Milnthorpe: Cicerone Press.

Mortlock, C. (2001). *Beyond adventure*. Milnthorpe: Cicerone Press.

Mounet, J-P, and P. Chifflet. (2003). *Whitewater sports*. In R. Rinehart and S. Sydnor (Eds.), *To the extreme,* (pp. 267–277). Albany: SUNY Press.

Orams, M. (1999). *Marine tourism*. London: Routledge.

Riffenburgh, B. (1993). *The myth of the explorer*. London: Belhaven Press.

Rowe, R. (Ed.) (1989). *Canoeing handbook*. Guildford: Biddles Ltd.

Schuett, M.A. (1995). Predictors of social group participation in whitewater kayaking. *Journal of Park and Recreation Administration*, **13** (2), 42–54.

Shepherd, N. (2002). How ecotourism can go wrong: The cases of Sea Canoe and Siam Safari, Thailand. *Current Issues in Tourism*, **5** (3/4), 309–318.

Shuff, T. (2003, July 12). Me, myself and a guide. *The Globe and Mail,* (pp. T6).

Smedley, G. (1995). *Canoeing for disabled people*. Exeter: The British Canoe Union.

Stebbins, R.A. (2001). Serions leisure. *Society*, **38** (4), 53–57.

Storry, T. (1991). *British whitewater*. London: Constable.

Swarbrooke, J., Beard, C., Leckie, S., and G. Pomfret. (2003). *Adventure tourism: the new frontier*. London: Butterworth-Heinemann.

Travel Industry Association of America. (1998, February). *Adventure Travel Report*.

Watters, R. (1994). *Never turn back: the life of white water pioneer Walt Blackader*. Potacello, Idaho: Great Rift Press.

Watters, R. (2003). The wrong side of the thin edge. In: R. Rinehart and S. Sydnor (Eds.), *To the extreme.* (pp. 257–266). Albany: SUNY Press.

Whiting, K. (2002). *The playboater's handbook II*. Clayton, Canada: The Heliconia Press.

10

One-Day Boating Adventures

Gianna Moscardo

Overview

Change and Challenge

One of the most noteworthy and enduring features of tourism and recreation in all their forms and in all parts of the world is change. Change as a general concept represents a major challenge to tourism and recreation research and practice at a number of levels. First, despite its widely noted existence as a core feature of contemporary life, very little research in tourism or recreation has focused on the factors that contribute to, or the processes that underpin, change in the way people travel and recreate (Laws, Faulkner, and Moscardo 1998). This general avoidance of the topic is not peculiar to researchers; several authors have noted the tendency for managers and practitioners to also avoid explicit considerations of change (Hall 1995; Laws et al. 1998; Boniface 2001; Rayman-Bacchus and Molina 2001). In addition, despite a limited understanding of the processes of change in tourism and recreation, much government policy and discussion of sustainability advocates changes of various sorts, especially changes in tourism development styles and recreation patterns. One-day boating tours are a core component of coastal and marine tourism, which in turn is a very common form of tourism and recreation (Baum 1998; Giavelli 2001; Jennings 2003; Wilson and Garrod 2003), and as such it is a sector that offers an excellent opportunity to explore the effects of various predicted trends. This chapter will review what is known about commercial one-day boat tours and their markets, impacts, and management, guided by the theme of examining the extent to which various predictions and trends identified in tourism in general apply to this sector of marine tourism and recreation.

A broad definition of one-day boating adventures includes both commercial one-day boating tours as well as recreational activities undertaken on one-day boat trips. This latter category consists of many of the specific activities, such as fishing, sailing, diving, and motorboating, that are covered elsewhere in this book. To avoid repetition, this chapter will focus on the former category of one-day boat tours run as commercial tour operations. Although the focus is on one type of one-day boating adventure, many of the issues identified also apply to other forms.

Figure 10-1 provides a summary of the major trends that have been identified as already occurring in tourism or predicted to occur in tourism in the near future. Bergsma (2000) divides these into four main areas: changes in consumers, changes in the way we see the environment, changing technology, and changes in business practice. The first area covers the greatest set of predictions. These include increased job and time stress, which in turn raises concerns about health and quality of life. Together, these forces have supported a move away from long holidays and toward more frequent short breaks and an increased interest in using these breaks to relieve stress, improve health, and have meaningful leisure experiences (Matathia and Salzman 1998). These forces also coincide with rising standards of living and greater demand for personalized services and products. Tourists are therefore seeking to move away from traditional, larger-scale homogeneous products and toward more personal, individualized experiences (Bergsma 2000; Mok, Stutts, and Wong 2000; Moscardo, Faulker, and Laws 2001a). Visitors are also becoming more diverse, with more travelers from developing countries, especially from Asia (Boniface 2001; Moscardo et al. 2001a).

MOVING FROM THE OLD	TO THE NEW
• Established destinations	• Emerging destinations, especially in Asia-Pacific region
• Established markets	• New markets, especially from developing countries
• Separate, single activity focus	• Integrated multiple activity experiences
• Single long trips	• Multiple short breaks
• Regional competition	• Regional co-operation
• Price based competition	• Value based competition
• Environmental protection	• Environmental improvement
• Cultural intrusion	• Cultural awareness
• Mass production	• Mass customization
• Product dominance	• Customer dominance
• Inexperienced tourists	• Experienced travellers
• Passive consumers	• Active participants
• Meeting customer needs	• Exceeding customer expectations
• New investment	• Revenue enhancement
• Print media	• Information & computer technology
• Reality	• Virtual reality
• Sensitive environments	• Artificial environments

Figure 10-1   Key tourism and leisure trends. Adapted from: Jones (1998); Matathia and Salzman (1998); Bergsma (2000); Mok et al. (2000); Boniface (2001); and Moscardo et al. (2001a).

Tourists and recreationists are also becoming more experienced. Pearce and Moscardo (2001) provide a review of the literature on repeat visitation to tourism destinations. Their work offers evidence that for many destinations, the proportion of repeat visitors is increasing. This review plus the results of an analysis of repeat visitation to the Great Barrier Reef note substantial differences in the behaviors, motivations, and evaluations of repeat visitors. Some of the consistent findings of studies of repeat visitation include the following:

1. A move away from central to more peripheral parts of destinations
2. A move toward more specialized activities within the destination region.

Bergsma (2000) also describes changes in the way we see the environment. More specifically, there is evidence that consumers are becoming increasingly concerned about the environment and seeking more sustainable or green products and services. Greater travel experience combined with the increased environmental concern creates consumer pressure on operators and destination managers to engage in more sustainable tourism practices (Jones 1998; Bergsma 2000; Moscardo et al. 2001a).

The third major area of change is that of technology. Its rapid development, especially transport and information and computer technology, has a number of consequences for the tourism and recreation sectors. The first is that consumers have much greater access to a wider range of sources of information. For businesses that provide tourism and recreation services, this means more intense competition. More informed visitors also increase the pressure for sustainable operations. Second, changes in transport technology have allowed access to a wider range of environments, adding further to the increased competition for visitor attention. Technology can also be used to create artificial or "virtual reality" experiences that can act as another form of competition for tourism and recreation businesses. Virtual reality can, however, offer ways to provide access to places that could not sustain tourism and for groups of visitors who could not otherwise experience them. In a similar fashion, the Internet offers ways for small businesses to access visitors and assist them, making them competitive with large companies. Information technology also offers opportunities for destination managers to inform visitors about minimal-impact behaviors, and many other technologies can assist in the protection and enhancement of the environment (Buhalis 2001; Moscardo et al. 2001a).

Finally, there are changes in business practices. Most of these changes can be seen as responses to the forces outlined in the previous three paragraphs. More specifically, a number of authors have argued that tourism and recreation businesses need to become more customer oriented, more cooperative with other organizations in their destination regions, better informed about their clients and the environment they operate in, more focused on staff training and support, more concerned about the sustainability of their operations, and more flexible and creative in their ability to respond to change (Jones 1998; Matathia and Salzman 1998; Bergsma 2000; Mok et al. 2000; Boniface 2001; Moscardo et al. 2001a; see related discussion in Chapter 7 of this volume).

All of these predicted and actual changes provide a context for analyzing one-day boat tours by outlining a set of predictions about the patterns that should be observed in any review of one-day boat tours, and highlighting a set of challenges for the management of this form of tourism. For the purposes of this chapter, three kinds of managers are involved: commercial operators; managers of protected areas, which are often the main destination for these operations; and regional destination managers. The rest of this chapter will explore a broad range of examples and studies from a variety of locations around the world. The chapter will also explore one-day boat tours on the Great Barrier Reef because of the author's personal research experience with this destination, the amount of published material on this world heritage site, and the fact that this destination offers a number of lessons in the management of one-day boat tours (Newsome, Moore, and Dowling 2002; Jennings 2003; Wilson 2003).

Types of One-Day Boating Adventures—Diversity and Competition

This section will explore the range of one-day boat tours available at various international destinations. Three core themes derived from the previous predictions about tourism will guide this exploration:

1. Increasing diversity in the range of types of tours available, resulting in increasing competition and reflecting a demand for more specialized experiences
2. Increasing integration of multiple activities into a single tour experience
3. The use of new technologies to enhance visitor experiences and manage environmental impacts.

It is not possible to provide a comprehensive or exhaustive review of all the different types of one-day boat tours, as such tours exist in thousands of destinations around the world. Entering the phrase "one-day boat tours" into the Internet search engine for Microsoft Network (MSN), for example, produces more than 240,000 hits. Virtually all island and coastal destinations offer a variety of boat tours for visitors. The Great Barrier Reef region of Australia, for example, has more than 400 permitted tour operations, the majority of which are concerned with one-day boat tours of some sort. In addition, one-day boat tours are offered on many rivers, dams, canals, lakes, and in wetland areas (Figure 10-2).

Table 10-1 provides some examples to illustrate the diversity of one-day boat tours, organized by geographic region and by the main focus of the tour, which in turn is divided into the following three categories:

1. A boat tour as a way to relax and escape, with the environment as a pleasant backdrop
2. A boat tour that allows the participants to engage in a specific activity such as diving, fishing, or interacting with marine wildlife
3. A boat tour that provides access to special places such as coral reefs, glaciers, historical sites, or ethnic and indigenous communities.

The examples reported in Table 10-1 highlight the three themes identified at the start of this section. First, they emphasize the diversity of one-day boat tours with variety in locations, settings, types of boats, activities offered, and attractions advertised. Second, nearly all of these tours combine several attractions or activities, offering a destination-specific experience. Much attention is also paid in the

Figure 10-2 One-day boating opportunities exist along the Moselle River, Germany. Photographer: Ross Rynehart.

promotional material to the knowledge of the staff and interpretive elements. Finally, there is some evidence of new boat technology being used to offer enhanced access and experiences for visitors.

The literature on tourism development in coastal areas and in the realm of eco-tourism also provides support for the growing diversity of one-day boat operations and the expansion of new destinations offering one-day boat tours. A number of case studies of coastal tourism development include one-day boat tours as actual and potential areas of expansion. See Ballinger (1996) for a discussion of the South Wales coast; Berrow (2003) for whale watching in Ireland; Chakravarty (2003) for an example from India; Faulkner (1998) for central Java, Indonesia; Forbes (1998) for the Oregon coast; Hull (1998) for the Lower North Shore of Quebec, Canada; Kim and Kim (1996) for examples in South Korea; Lipscomb (1998) in the Solomon Islands; Payne, Johnston, and Twynam (2001) for development plans for the North Shore of Lake Superior; Speedie (2003) for a discussion of development in South Devon and Cornwall, England; and the World Tourism Organization (2000) for examples in the Seychelles.

Few published studies have examined changes over time in coastal and marine destinations, so it is difficult to provide examples of increasing specialization of tours. Two exceptions are Petreas's (2003) description of diving in Greece and studies of changes in tour operations over time on the Great Barrier Reef (Moscardo, Saltzer, Norris, and McCoy 2004). Petreas (2003) provides a history of the development of coastal and marine tourism in Greece. In this historical analysis, he offers evidence that the first three decades of development were based on large-scale coastal tourism products to support mass-package tourism. The analysis goes on to more recent government recognition of the importance of diversifying tourism products and activities to meet changing market demands. Within this context, Petreas reviews the development of diving as an alternative form of marine activity.

Table 10-1   Examples of One-Day Boat Tours

Type	Place and Example	Activities	Special Features	Operator Website
Coastal setting as a backdrop for relaxation and escape	U.S. Virgin Islands tour from St. Croix to Buck Island and Turtle Beach	Sailing Snorkeling Beach walks Beach barbeque	Glass-bottom sailing boat	Big Beard's Adventure Tours www.bigbeards. com/sailing. htm#full
Adventure activity— kayaking	North Carolina tour around Masonboro Island	Kayak tour Guided interpretive walks Swimming Picnic lunch	Rare, undeveloped barrier island	Kayak Carolina www.kayak-carolina.com/ masonboro-islandt.html
Adventure activity— diving	Michigan Shipwreck diving tour in Lake Superior	Diving on several shipwrecks Views of lake shore forests	Access to the shipwrecks and underwater rock formations	Shipwreck Tours www.shipwreck-tours.com
Adventure activity— fishing	Zanzibar, Africa	Fish with a local on a traditional boat	Experience of traditional fishing culture	Eco & Culture Tours Zanzibar www. ecoculture-zanzibar.org/ HTML/ e_daytours.htm
Wildlife viewing	Sisimiut, Greenland	Whale-watching Seals Visits to abandoned settlements	Wildlife Unique culture	Inuit Outfitting www.greenland-guide.gl/sisimiut/ tour-boat.htm
Access to a special place —historical significance	Lefkas, Greece	Historic sites Local villages, islands	Replica Greek war galleon	Odysseus www.lefkas.net/ odysseus.htm
Access to a special place —indigenous/ ethnic communities	Vietnam Namtha River	Traditional villages Rapids Bird watching	Access to several ethnic groups	Nam Ha Guides www.theboat-landing. laopdr.com/ dayboat.html
Access to special places— coral reefs	Puerto Vallarta, Mexico	Snorkeling Diving Islands Beaches	Marine wildlife Coral formations	Inside Vallarta Travel www.hypermex. com/html/ pv_act2.htm
Access to special places— island scenery	Skagafjordur, Iceland	Islands Seabirds Marine wildlife	Historical interpretation	Nonni Travel www.nonnitravel. is/iceland/N17-Boat_tour.htm
Access to special places— coastal scenery	Chesapeake Bay, USA	Tour around bay Museums Restaurants Shops Historic homes	Access to local arts studio	Watermark Cruises www.water. markcruises com/tours_ excursion.shtml
Access to special places —glaciers	Seward, Alaska	Glaciers Marine wildlife	Icebergs Limited numbers	Bear Glacier Tours Seward. net/kayakcamp/

The Great Barrier Reef (GBR) is a major tourist attraction for visitors coming to the coastal region along the northeast coast of Australia. This World Heritage area has been an attraction for tourists since 1900, but in the early 1980s, the introduction of large, high-speed catamarans greatly increased the range of reef sites that could be accessed by tour operators for day trips. Growth in reef tourism from that time was substantial, with an increase in annual visitor days from around 150,000 in the early 1980s to more than 1.5 million in the mid-1990s. In the early stages of this growth, the largest proportion of one-day boat trips were based in Cairns in the north of the region and were concentrated on large catamarans visiting pontoons moored on coral reefs or islands.

Moscardo et al. (2004) reported significant changes in this pattern in the period 1996 to 2000, with a major shift in visitor numbers away from the Cairns region to other ports along the coast adjacent to the GBR. A move from large pontoon–based day trips and island trips to a wider variety of smaller, more specialized operations is also apparent. Data presented in this article show that the number of larger boats (those carrying more than 100 passengers) expanded from 35 to 50 over a five-year period from 1996. The number of boats in the category of less than 16 passengers expanded from 261 to 443. The researchers identified three main factors as contributing to the changes in patterns of reef visitation. These were changes in transport modes and access points to the region, changes in the markets with fewer package tourists and more independent travelers, and an increasing proportion of repeat visitors.

Market Profiles

The Moscardo et al. (2004) study described two changes in one-day boat tour markets that correspond to the predictions listed in the introduction to this chapter: increasing travel experience and a move away from traditional forms of travel toward more individualized tour options. These results highlight the importance of understanding markets to tourism and recreation managers in all sectors. This section will review the available literature on the market profiles of one-day boat tours. The literature can be broken down into two categories: descriptions of specific one-day tour markets and research into the factors associated with visitors' satisfaction.

Descriptions of Specific One-Day Boat Tour Markets

Despite the large number and variety of one-day boat tour operations around the world, very little published research gives market profiles or details, and the few available studies are mostly concerned with diving and wildlife-viewing tours. In addition, many of these studies only include limited information on the markets. Galicia and Baldassarre (1996), for example, only provide information on the expenditure, length of stay, type of accommodation used, and usual place of residence for participants in boat tours to view flamingos in Mexico. Saltzer provides more details in a series of reports on marine wildlife-viewing day trips in the southern section of the GBR (2002a), to Kangaroo Island, off the South Australian coast (2002b), and cruises based in Dunedin in New Zealand (2003). These studies give details of motivations, expectations, and evaluations of the experiences as well as demographics and travel behavior variables. Jennings (2003) also provides more details in a review of different marine activities such as sailing, fishing, and diving. The review covers information about motivations as well as socio-demographics but does not distinguish between those who choose a one-day option versus visitors who select longer trips.

Tabata (1992) offers similar details for divers but further divides this type of marine tourist into groups based on their level of interest or experience in diving. Moscardo (2000, 2001a) also divides marine wildlife-viewing day trippers into groups based on their level of interest in this type of activity. These studies found that a number of variables, including preferences for interpretive activities, satisfaction with the provided services, and motivations, were related to different levels of interest in marine wildlife viewing. These results are consistent with studies in the area of recreational specialization (Martin 1997).

Factors Associated with Visitor Satisfaction

A study of river rafters in the Argentinean-Chilean Great Lakes region also divided the tourists into groups based on levels of specialization (Gonzalez and Otero 2003). Again, a number of differences were reported among the various levels of experience, including differences in motivation and service expectations. This study also looked at the factors that contributed to satisfaction with the experience (refer also to Chapter 8). Table 10-2 gives a summary of this and other similar studies.

Table 10-2   Factors Associated with Satisfaction with One-Day Boat Tours

Study	Place and Type of Tour	Key Factors
Gonzalez and Otero 2003	Rafting tours, Argentinean-Chilean Great Lakes	Difficulty level of the rapids experienced Perceived security of the operation
Orams 2000	Whale-watching tours, Queensland, Australia	Whale behavior Number of other passengers Ease of viewing of the whales Duration of the cruise Seasickness
Williams et al. 2000	Dive tours, Western Australia	Customer service focus of the tour operator Quality of the tour guide Interpretation
Saltzer 2002c	Reef day tours Great Barrier Reef, Australia	Perceived quality of the reef environment Visitor motivation, particularly interest in and experience with nature Number of activities undertaken
Moscardo 2001b	Wildlife viewing tours, Great Barrier Reef, Australia	Range of wildlife seen Amount visitors believed they learned on the tour How natural the visitors thought the encounter was How much the visitors perceived the wildlife to be responding to their presence

No consistent patterns appear to exist in the results reported in Table 10-2, except that the key factors associated with satisfaction are usually connected to the main focus of the tour. In other words, the markets and variables associated with satisfaction are as diverse as the range of tour operations available. The only factor mentioned in several studies was the importance of interpretation, which is consistent with the predicted trend toward more meaningful and interactive tour experiences.

Benefits and Challenges

One-day boating tours offer a number of benefits and challenges for both participants and the destination regions that host them. Cater (2003) offers a model of the key forces and interactions in marine ecotourism that can be used to organize a discussion of these benefits and challenges. An adaptation of this model is presented in Figure 10-3. The model suggests that sustainable marine ecotourism needs to be centered on environmental protection. This center is then supported by, and supportive of, four main factors: profitable tourist enterprises, enhanced economic conditions for the destination community, revenue and support for conservation, and quality tourist experiences.

The model in Figure 10-3 suggests that there are four main types of benefit or advantage of one-day tours. Profitable tourist enterprises are the most immediate beneficiaries of successful one-day boat tours. Tabata (1992) provides an example of the potential income that can be derived from one-day boat tours reporting an annual turnover of more than US$20 million for 47 dive shops in Hawaii. Maintaining a profitable business is not, however, easy in a dynamic and competitive world. Ryan's (1998) analysis of a wildlife-based boat tour company in New Zealand highlights the problems that small operators face from increasing competition and limits to growth. Shepherd (2003) offers a disturbing case study of competitive pressure that ultimately led to the failure of a sea kayaking business in Thailand that ran one-day tours (see also Chapter 9).

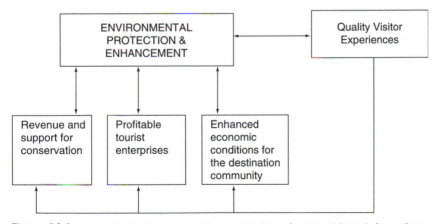

Figure 10-3 Key relationships in marine ecotourism. Source: Adapted from Cater (2003, p. 39).

Profitable tourism businesses in turn provide opportunities for enhancing the economic well-being of coastal and island destination communities. A number of authors provide case studies of the use of tourism development, including one-day boat tours, for enhancing regional economies:

1. Lipscomb (1998) describes an example of how one-day boat tours could be an alternative to logging and fishing for indigenous villagers in the Solomon islands.
2. Faulkner (1998) puts forward a similar argument proposing that local residents in central Java develop one-day fishing trips for visitors.
3. Forbes (1998) also argues for the development of wildlife-viewing day-trip boat tours as an alternative to forestry for communities along the Oregon Coast.
4. The World Tourism Organization (2000) provides similar examples of actual programs on the Egyptian Red Sea coast, whitewater rafting in Fiji, and day boat tours to seabird nesting sites in the Seychelles.

The challenge here is to ensure that the development of tourism is sustainable. In other words, the actual and potential negative impacts of one-day boat tours must be recognized and managed, a topic that will be given more consideration in the next section.

The third category of potential benefits from one-day boat tours is that of quality visitor experiences. Positive experiences have the potential to be very rewarding at the personal level for visitors, and to encourage them to support the conservation of the destination region. As with the other two categories, however, these benefits are also balanced by a number of challenges for the participants.

Three studies of barriers to participation in one-day boat tours to the Great Barrier Reef give some insights into the sorts of challenges that visitors can face (Moscardo and Woods 1998; Saltzer 2002d; Moscardo, Saltzer, Galletly, Burke, and Hildebrandt 2003). Although the studies were conducted at three different times using three different methodologies, there was a remarkable consistency in the results. Visitors to the coastal region under study who did *not* take a one-day boat tour to the Great Barrier Reef were more likely than those that did to be:

1. Repeat visitors to the region
2. Domestic rather than international visitors
3. Traveling in a family group
4. Looking for relaxation
5. Participating at low levels in a wide range of commercial tourist activities available in the region.

In addition, the latter two studies, which specifically examined reasons for not visiting the reef, found three major barriers to one-day boat tour participation: time, money, and concern over seasickness. These studies suggest that boat tours may present a physical challenge for some tourists.

Finally, there are benefits from one-day boat tours for the conservation of the region. These include direct revenue from fees and support for conservation. A number of authors have noted the actual and potential benefits of positive tourist experiences in providing revenue or political pressure for environmental conservation. Williams, O'Neill, and MacCarthy (2000), for example, provide evidence that tourists on one-day dive trips in Western Australia were particularly concerned about the environmental actions of the tour operators. In a similar fashion, Galicia and Baldassarre (1996) found that tourists on day boat trips to see flamingos in Mexico were prepared to pay for environmental conservation programs in the area. The World Tourism Organization (2000) also provides a set of examples of environmental initiatives funded and supported by one-day boat tourists.

Negative Impacts

Maintaining a sustainable one-day boat tour sector requires an understanding of the actual and potential negative impacts of this type of tourism. A number of authors have provided lists of potential negative impacts of tourism in general, many of which are applicable to one-day boat tours (see Archer and Cooper 1998; Pearce 1998; Newsome et al. 2002; refer also to Chapters 3 and 4 of this volume). The following is a list of some of the main impacts that have been identified from the boats and infrastructure associated with one-day boat tours and the activities of the tourists and tour operators.

1. Activities of tourists on one-day boat trips
   a. Coral damage from divers (Hawkins et al. 1998; Allen 1992; Tratalos and Austin 2001; Zakai and Chadwick-Furman 2001; Musa 2002)
   b. Stirring of sediment, which encourages algal growth (Tratalos and Austin 2001; Zakai and Chadwick-Furman 2001)
2. Activities of tour operators and boats
   a. Noise pollution (Holder 1991)
   b. Oil leakages (Holder 1991; Allen 1992)
   c. Anchor damage and damage from boat groundings (Allen 1992; Tratalos and Austin 2001)
   d. Feeding of wildlife, which can result in aggressive behavior, poor health, and detrimental changes to the wildlife population structures (Hawkins et al. 1998; Tratalos and Austin 2001; Mann and Kemps 2003)
   e. Disturbance to wildlife, including collisions with wildlife (Galicia and Baldassarre 1996; Weber, Horak, and Mikacic 2001; Kousis 2001; Bejder and Samuels 2003; Kirkwood et al. 2003; Samuels, Bejder, Constantine, and Heinrich 2003).
3. A range of negative impacts associated with the coastal and island development that often accompanies activities such as one-day boat tours include erosion, water pollution, overfishing, visual pollution, socio-cultural impacts, conflicts with local residents, and damage to ecosystems (Holder 1991; Ballinger 1996; Priestley 1996; Cocossis and Parpairis 1996; Payne et al. 2001).

Future Directions

There are two major pressures on the managers of one-day boat tours. The first of these is the need to improve the ecological sustainability of these operations to meet the demands of both consumers and destination residents. The second pressure is to respond to increasing competition (Moscardo, Green, and Greenwood

197

2001b). A number of different tools and strategies have been proposed to assist marine tourism managers in responding to these pressures. The most commonly cited tool for improving sustainability and enhancing competitive advantage is the provision of interpretive activities (Crabtree 1995; Williams et al. 2000; World Tourism Organization 2000; Moscardo et al. 2001b; Newsome et al. 2002; Samuels et al. 2003). A number of technological solutions have also been proposed to manage waste and resource use (World Tourism Organization 2000), to minimize anchor damage (Allen 1992), and to provide alternative experiences to ease pressure (Zakai and Chadwick-Furman 2001). Other tools include the development of monitoring systems (Moscardo and Ormsby 2003), strategic alliances among tour operators (Buhalis and Cooper 1998), and better staff training (World Tourism Organization 2000).

Emerging Concerns

Two newly emerging concerns can be identified for one-day boat tour managers. The first of these is the emergence of safety and security as key visitor concerns after the various terrorist attacks of the last five years and the SARS crisis in Asia in 2003. Wilks and Page (2003) note that, while the events of 2001 brought media attention to the issue of tourist safety and security, these issues were already becoming important for tourism managers, with increased consumer demand for better standards as well as increasing litigation. The second emerging concern is a shift in attention away from the potential impacts of tourism on the environment to the potential impacts of the environment on tourism. Harriott's (2002) review of the literature notes that the major threats to the Great Barrier Reef are "declining inshore water quality, outbreaks of crown-of-thorns starfish, effects of trawling on reef benthos, effects of line fishing, and threat of oil spills from shipping" (p. 18). In addition, she reports the recent appearance of a phenomenon referred to as coral bleaching, which appears to be linked to global warming. Each of these impacts and the consequent negative environmental conditions pose threats to reef tourism.

Understanding Change in One-Day Boat Tour Participants on the Great Barrier Reef

A number of themes were identified in the introductory section of this chapter. These included increasing consumer demand for smaller, more specialized tour options; greater travel experience among consumers; more interest in participatory activities; and a greater concern about the environment. Very few longitudinal studies have been conducted in tourism, and so it can be difficult to find evidence to support these predicted trends. However, the Cooperative Research Center (CRC), Reef Research Center Australia, has funded a 10-year research program to profile and analyze tourists to the Great Barrier Reef. This section will provide an analysis of data available from this research program, particularly focusing on change over time in the characteristics of one-day reef tour participants.

These analyses are an extension of work reported in Moscardo et al. (2004), which examined differences between 1996 and 2000 and focused on exploring the reasons for changes in reef tour participation rates in different locations and for different types of boat tours. That study found evidence of a shift in tourist interest away from larger boats to more specialized tour options, and a move away from Cairns toward the Whitsunday region as the major departure point for reef boat tours in Queensland. The present study extends these analyses by examining a longer time period, from 1996 to 2002. The present study also concentrates on the characteristics of participants on one-day reef boat trips and examines differences pre- and post-September 11, 2001.

Tables 10-3 and 10-4 provide a summary of those characteristics that differed significantly across time for the two main reef tour departure points. Across both areas, a number of consumer trends are confirmed. The results reveal an increasing concern for escape, novelty, and physical activity in the desired benefits of a reef day trip. The predicted rise in the use of the Internet for information is also confirmed in these results. Both regions also experienced a change in the proportion of reef tour participants with previous reef travel experiences.

This kind of longitudinal research provides evidence to support the major theme of this chapter in that one-day boat tours, like the rest of tourism, are changing, and research can be insightful in describing and anticipating these changes.

Table 10-3   Significant Differences Between 1998, 2001, and 2002 GBR Day Trip Visitors in the Whitsunday Region (*)

Characteristics	1998	2001	2002	Characteristics	1998	2001	2002
Usual place of residence:				**Motivations for travel[a]:**			
International	**32%**	**56%**	**33%**	To be close to family and friends	3.08	1.85	2.10
UK/Ireland	12%	11%	4%	To rest and relax	3.43	3.34	3.58
Other European	8%	23%	12%	To experience the beauty of nature	3.36	3.88	3.87
USA/Canada	6%	17%	12%				
Asia	2%	3%	2%	To have some excitement	3.05	3.44	3.52
Other	4%	2%	4%	To escape normal routine	3.25	3.42	3.71
Australia	**68%**	**44%**	**67%**	To experience something new and different	3.43	3.79	3.82
Resident of the GBR region	14%	4%	6%	To be physically active	2.99	3.02	3.18
Other Queensland visitor	22%	10%	31%				
Interstate visitor	32%	29%	29%				
Age group:				**Information sources:**			
<21 years	11%	11%	14%	Family and friends	48%	39%	39%
21–30	40%	35%	26%	Travel agent	24%	14%	20%
31–40	21%	17%	26%	Been before	27%	18%	21%
41–50	13%	14%	24%	Books/library	20%	29%	25%
51–60	11%	13%	7%	Brochures picked up outside the region	25%	19%	24%
>60 years	5%	11%	4%	Internet	1%	11%	19%

Continued

Table 10-3   Cont'd

Characteristics	1998	2001	2002	Characteristics	1998	2001	2002
Travel party size:				**Total stay in region:**			
1 person	10%	8%	7%	1–4 days	10%	39%	33%
2 people	47%	43%	5%	5–7 days	29%	35%	33%
3–5	28%	31%	55%	8–14 days	33%	20%	29%
6–10	7%	8%	23%	15–21 days	12%	2%	3%
More than 10 people	9%	10%	10%	More than 21 days	16%	5%	2%
Travel party:				**Time away from home on this vacation:**			
Alone	11%	8%	6%	Up to 1 week	22%	26%	31%
Spouse/Couple	57%	33%	32%	>1 week–2 weeks	22%	17%	30%
Family	18%	28%	33%	>2 weeks–3 weeks	12%	13%	9%
Family and friends	4%	6%	6%	>3 weeks–4 weeks	4%	6%	6%
Friends	27%	17%	10%	>1 month–6 months	27%	31%	17%
				>6 months	13%	7%	8%
Been to GBR before:	44%	40%	55%	**Activities:**			
				Swimming	75%	58%	73%
Been to other reefs before:				Snorkeling	57%	77%	86%
Other Australian reefs	13%	5%	9%	Glass bottom boat and/or semi-sub	35%	16%	23%
Caribbean	3%	13%	7%	**Overall Satisfaction[b]:**	8.43	8.74	8.97
South East Asia	3%	9%	7%				
South Pacific	7%	7%	13%				

[a] Mean on a scale where 1 = not at all important, 2 = not very important, 3 = somewhat important, 4 = very important.
[b] Mean on a scale where 0 = not at all, 10 = very much.
*Chi-square or T-Test significant at the $p<.05$ level.

Table 10-4   Significant Differences Between 1996, 2001, and 2002 GBR Day Trip Visitors in the Cairns Region*

Characteristics	1996	2001	2002	Characteristics	1996	2001	2002
Usual place of residence:				**Motivations for travel[a]:**			
International	**75%**	**57%**	**54%**	To be close to family and friends	2.79	2.02	2.05
UK/Ireland	10%	15%	19%	To experience the beauty of nature	3.39	3.89	3.87
Other European	9%	8%	10%	To have some excitement	2.98	3.45	3.54
USA/Canada	11%	20%	17%	To rest and relax	3.09	3.45	3.48
Asia	45%	4%	3%	To escape normal routine	2.83	3.42	3.55
Other	<1%	10%	4%	To experience something new and different	3.34	3.84	3.81
Australia	**25%**	**43%**	**46%**	To be physically active	2.85	2.94	3.05
Queensland	8%	11%	12%				
NSW/ACT	7%	14%	19%				
Victoria	4%	11%	11%				
Other Australia	6%	6%	4%				

Age group:				Information sources:			
<21 years	7%	7%	8%	Travel agent	49%	21%	18%
21–30	33%	27%	29%	Been before	42%	25%	21%
31–40	25%	18%	22%	Brochures picked up	20%	16%	19%
41–50	18%	17%	19%	outside the region			
51–60	11%	16%	11%	Tour operator/company	11%	20%	19%
61–70	7%	9%	8%	Articles in newspapers/			
>70 years	<1%	6%	3%	magazines	20%	27%	25%
				Books/library	17%	14%	19%
				Brochures picked up			
				inside the region	21%	30%	31%
				Internet	0%	14%	17%
Travel party size:				**Total stay in region:**			
1 person	7%	9%	1%	1–2 days	13%	5%	8%
2 people	39%	44%	7%	3–7 days	64%	62%	53%
3–5	18%	24%	47%	>1 week–2 weeks	18%	24%	32%
6–10	5%	7%	33%	>2 weeks	5%	9%	8%
More than 10 people	31%	16%	12%				
Travel party:				**Time away from home on this vacation:**			
Spouse/Couple	53%	40%	29%	Up to 1 week	35%	23%	22%
Family	18%	22%	26%	>1 week–2 weeks	35%	29%	29%
Family and friends	2%	6%	6%	>2 weeks–3 weeks	11%	20%	12%
Friends	19%	14%	16%	>3 weeks–4 weeks	3%	9%	11%
				>4 weeks	16%	19%	26%
Been to GBR before:	21%	29%	38%				
Been to other reefs before:	45%	39%	40%	**Activities:**			
Caribbean	4%	11%	12%	Swimming	64%	47%	61%
South East Asia	10%	7%	11%	Snorkeling	66%	65%	76%
South Pacific	4%	12%	13%	Glass-bottom boat	55%	40%	31%
				Sailing	11%	2%	4%
Number of times been to the region:				**Overall Satisfaction[b]:**	8.15%	8.72%	8.71%
None	68%	73%	71%	**Recommendations:**			
				No	1%	2%	3%
Once	22%	13%	14%	Don't know	7%	3%	3%
Twice	4%	5%	6%	Probably	30%	17%	24%
More than twice	6%	8%	9%	Definitely	62%	79%	70%

[a] Mean on a scale where 1 = not at all important, 2 = not very important, 3 = somewhat important, 4 = very important.

[b] Mean on a scale where 0 = not at all, 10 = very much.

[*] Chi-square or T-Test significant at the p<.05 level.

References

Allen, W.H. (1992). Increased dangers to Caribbean marine ecosystems. *Bioscience*, **42**(5), 330–335.

Archer, B., and C. Cooper. (1998). The positive and negative impacts of tourism. In W. F. Theobald (Ed.), *Global tourism*. (2nd ed., pp. 63–81). Oxford, UK: Butterworth-Heinemann.

Ballinger, R. C. (1996). Recreation and tourism management in an area of high conservation value: the Gower Peninsula, South Wales. In G. K. Priestley, J. A. Edwards, and H. Coccossis (Eds.), *Sustainable tourism? European experiences.* (pp. 35–53). Wallingford, UK: CAB International.

Baum, T. (1998). Tourism marketing and the small island environment: cases from the periphery. In E. Laws, B. Faulkner, and G. Moscardo (Eds.), *Embracing and managing change in tourism.* (pp. 116–137). London: Routledge.

Bejder, L., and A. Samuels. (2003). Evaluating the effects of nature-based tourism on cetaceans. In N. Gales, M. Hindell, and R. Kirkwood (Eds.), *Marine mammals. fisheries, tourism and management issues* (pp. 229–256). Collingwood, Victoria, Australia: CSIRO Publishing.

Bergsma, M. (2000). The future of tourism and hospitality. *Tourism and Hospitality Research*, **2** (1), 76–79.

Berrow, S.D. (2003). Developing sustainable whale watching in the Shannon Estuary. In B. Garrod and J. C. Wilson (Eds.), *Marine ecotourism: issues and experiences.* (pp. 198–203). Clevedon, UK: Channel View Publications.

Boniface, P. (2001). *Dynamic tourism.* Clevedon, UK: Channel View Publications.

Buhalis, D. (2001). Tourism in an era of information technology. In B. Faulkner, G. Moscardo, and E. Laws (Eds.), *Tourism in the twenty–first century.* (pp. 163–180). London: Continuum.

Buhalis, D., and C. Cooper. (1998). Competition or co-operation? Small and medium sized tourism enterprises at the destination. In E. Laws, B. Faulkner, and G. Moscardo (Eds.), *Embracing and managing change in tourism.* (pp. 324–346). London: Routledge.

Cater, E. (2003). Between the devil and the deep blue sea: Dilemmas for marine ecotourism. In B. Garrod and J.C. Wilson (Eds.), *Marine ecotourism: issues and experiences.* (pp. 37–47). Clevedon, UK: Channel View Publications.

Chakravarty, I. (2003). Marine ecotourism and regional development: A case study of the Marine Park Project, Malvan, Maharashta, India. In B. Garrod and J.C. Wilson (Eds.), *Marine ecotourism: issues and experiences.* (pp. 177–197). Clevedon, UK: Channel View Publications.

Coccossis, H., and A. Parpairis. (1996). Tourism and carrying capacity in coastal areas: Mykonos, Greece. In G.K. Priestley, J.A. Edwards and H. Coccossis (Eds.), *Sustainable tourism? European experiences.* (pp. 153–175). Wallingford, UK: CAB International.

Crabtree, A. (1995). Quicksilver connections. In R. Harris and N. Leiper (Eds.), *Sustainable tourism. An Australian perspective.* (pp. 145–154). Chatswood, NSW, Australia: Butterworth-Heinemann.

Faulkner, B. (1998). Tourism development options in Indonesia and the case of agro-tourism in central Java. In E. Laws, B. Faulkner, and G. Moscardo (Eds.), *Embracing and managing change in tourism.* (pp. 202–221). London: Routledge.

Forbes, B. (1998). Curry county sustainable nature-based tourism project. In C.M. Hall and A.A. Lew (Eds.), *Sustainable tourism: A geographical perspective.* (pp. 119–131). New York: Addison-Wesley Longman.

Galicia, E., and G.A. Baldassarre. (1996). Effects of motorized tour boats on the behavior of nonbreeding American Flamingos in Yucatan, Mexico. *Conservation Biology*, **11** (5), 1159–1165.

Giavelli, G. (2001). Tourism development and sustainability in the Aeolian Islands. In D. Ioannides, Y. Apostolopoulos, and S. Sonmez (Eds.), *Mediterranean islands and sustainable tourism development.* (pp. 127–142). London: Continuum.

Gonzalez, R., and A. Otero. (2003). Alternative tourism activities management in the Argentinean-Chilean Great Lakes Corridor. In M. Luck and T. Kirstges (Eds.), *Global ecotourism policies and case studies.* (pp. 21–35). Clevedon, UK: Channel View Publications.

Hall, C.M. (1995). In search of common ground: Reflections on sustainability, complexity, and process in tourism systems. *Journal of Sustainable Tourism, 3* (2), 99–105.

Harriott, V.J. (2002). *Marine tourism impacts and their management on the Great Barrier Reef.* (CRC Reef Research Center Technical Report No. 46). Townsville, Queensland, Australia: CRC Reef Research Center.

Hawkins, J.P., Roberts, C.M., Van't Hof, T., De Meyer, K., Tratalos, J., and C. Aldam. (1998). Effects of recreational scuba diving on Caribbean coral and fish communities. *Conservation Biology, 13* (4), 888–897.

Holder, J.S. (1991). Pattern and impact of tourism on the environment of the Caribbean. In S. Medlik (Ed.), *Managing tourism.* Oxford, UK: Butterworth-Heinemann.

Hull, J. (1998). Market segmentation and ecotourism development on the Lower North Shore of Quebec. In C.M. Hall and A.A. Lew (Eds.), *Sustainable tourism: A geographical perspective.* (pp. 146–158). New York: Addison-Wesley Longman.

Jennings, G. (2003). Marine tourism. In S. Hudson (Ed.), *Sport and adventure tourism.* (pp. 125–164). New York: Haworth Hospitality Press.

Jones, C.B. (1998). *The new tourism and leisure environment.* San Francisco: Economic Research Associates.

Kim, S., and Y. J. Kim. (1996). Overview of coastal and marine tourism in Korea. *Journal of Tourism Studies, 7* (2), 46–53.

Kirkwood, R., Boren, L., Shaughnessy, P., Szteren, D., Mawson, P., Huckstadt, L., et al. (2003). Pinniped-focused tourism in the Southern Hemisphere: a review of the industry. In N. Gales, M. Hindell, and R. Kirkwood (Eds.), *Marine mammals: fisheries, tourism and management issues.* (pp. 257–276). Collingwood, Victoria, Australia: CSIRO Publishing.

Kousis, M. (2001). Tourism and the environment in Corsica, Sardinia, Sicily, and Crete. In D. Ioannides, Y. Apostolopoulos, and S. Sonmez (Eds.), *Mediterranean islands and sustainable tourism development.* (pp. 214–233). London: Continuum.

Laws, E., Faulkner, B., and G. Moscardo. (1998). Embracing and managing change in tourism. In E. Laws, B. Faulkner, and G. Moscardo (Eds.), *Embracing and managing change in tourism: international case studies.* (pp. 1–12). London: Routledge.

Lipscomb, A.J.H. (1998). Village-based tourism in the Solomon Islands: impediments and impacts. In E. Laws, B. Faulkner, and G. Moscardo (Eds.), *Embracing and managing change in tourism.* (pp. 185–201). London: Routledge.

Mann, J., and C. Kemps. (2003). The effects of provisioning on maternal care in wild bottlenose dolphins, Shark Bay, Australia. In N. Gales, M. Hindell, and R. Kirkwood (Eds.), *Marine mammals: fisheries, tourism and management issues.* (pp. 304–317). Collingwood, Victoria, Australia: CSIRO Publishing.

Martin, S. (1997). Specialization and differences in setting preferences among wildlife viewers. *Human Dimensions of Wildlife, 2* (1), 1–18.

Matathia, I., and M. Salzman. (1998). *Next: trends for the future.* Sydney, Australia: MacMillan.

Mok, C., Stutts, A.T., and L. Wong. (2000, June). Mass customization in the hospitality industry: Concepts and applications. Paper presented at the Tourism in Southeast Asia and IndoChina Conference, ChiangMia.

Moscardo, G. (2000). Understanding wildlife tourism market segments: an Australian marine study. *Human Dimensions of Wildlife*, **5** (2), 36–53.

Moscardo, G. (2001a, June). *Understanding visitor–wildlife interactions: profiling markets.* (Project B2.3 Data Summary Report). Townsville, Queensland, Australia: CRC Reef Research Center.

Moscardo, G. (2001b, June). *Understanding visitor–wildlife interactions: factors influencing satisfaction.* (Project B2.3 Data Summary Report). Townsville, Queensland, Australia: CRC Reef Research Center.

Moscardo, G., Faulkner, B., and E. Laws. (2001a). Introduction: moving ahead and looking back. In B. Faulkner, G. Moscardo, and E. Laws (Eds.), *Tourism into the twenty-first century.* (pp. xviii–xxxii). London: Continuum.

Moscardo, G., Green, D., and T. Greenwood. (2001b). How great is the Great Barrier Reef? Tourists' knowledge and understanding of the world heritage status of the Great Barrier Reef. *Tourism Recreation Research*, **26** (1), 19–26.

Moscardo, G., and J. Ormsby. (2003). *A social indicators monitoring system for tourist and recreational use of the Great Barrier Reef.* (Technical Report No. 50). Townsville, Queensland, Australia: Great Barrier Reef Marine Park Authority.

Moscardo, G., Saltzer, R., Galletly, A., Burke, A., and A. Hildebrandt. (2003). *Changing patterns of reef tourism.* (Technical Report No. 49). Townsville, Queensland, Australia: CRC Reef Research Center.

Moscardo, G., Saltzer, R., Norris, A., and A. McCoy. (2004). Changing patterns of regional tourism: implications for tourism on the Great Barrier Reef. *Journal of Tourism Studies* **15** (1), 34–50.

Moscardo, G., and D. Woods. (1998, August 18–21). Travel patterns of coastal and marine tourists: An Australian case study. In *Proceedings of the Fourth Asia Pacific Tourism Association Conference,* Korea.

Musa, G. (2002). Sipadan: a SCUBA-diving paradise: an analysis of tourism impact, diver satisfaction, and tourism management. *Tourism Geographies*, **4** (2), 195–209.

Newsome, D., Moore, S. A., and R. K. Dowling. (2002). *Natural area tourism: ecology, impacts, and management.* Clevedon, UK: Channel View Publications.

Orams, M.B. (2000). Tourists getting close to whales: is it what whale-watching is all about? *Tourism Management*, **21**, 561–569.

Payne, R.J., Johnston, M.E., and G.D. Twynam. (2001). Tourism, sustainability, and the social milieux in Lake Superior's north shore and islands. In S.F. McCool and R. N. Moisey (Eds.), *Tourism, recreation, and sustainability: Linking culture and the environment.* (pp. 315–342). Wallingford, UK: CABI Publishing.

Pearce, P. L. (1998). The relationship between residents and tourists: The research literature and management directions. In W. F. Theobald (Ed.), *Global tourism.* (2nd ed., pp. 129–149). Oxford, UK: Butterworth-Heinemann.

Pearce, P.L., and G. Moscardo. (2001). "Been already and done it before": Understanding visitors repeating trips to the Great Barrier Reef. In C. Pforr and B. Janeczko (Eds.), *CAUTHE 2001: Capitalizing on research.* (pp. 268–280). Canberra, Australia: University of Canberra.

Petreas, C.P. (2003). Scuba diving: An alternative form of coastal tourism for Greece? In B. Garrod and J.C. Wilson (Eds.), *Marine ecotourism: issues and experiences.* (pp. 215–232). Clevedon, UK: Channel View Publications.

Priestley, G.K. (1996). Structural dynamics of tourism and recreation-related development: The Catalan coast. In G.K. Priestley, J. A. Edwards, and H. Coccossis (Eds.), *Sustainable tourism? European experiences.* (pp. 99–119). Wallingford, UK: CAB International.

Rayman-Bacchus, L., and A. Molina. (2001). Internet-based tourism services: business issues and trends. *Futures*, **33** (7), 589–609.

Ryan, C. (1998). Dolphins, canoes, and marae: ecotourism products in New Zealand. In E. Laws, B. Faulkner, and G. Moscardo (Eds.), *Embracing and managing change in tourism.* (pp. 285–306). London: Routledge.

Saltzer, R. (2002a, July). *Understanding visitor–wildlife interactions: Lady Musgrave Island and Lady Elliot Island.* (Project B2.3 Data Summary Report). Townsville, Queensland, Australia: CRC Reef Research Center.

Saltzer, R. (2002b, August). *Understanding visitor–wildlife interactions: Kangaroo Island.* (Project B2.3 Data Summary Report). Townsville, Queensland, Australia: CRC Reef Research Center.

Saltzer, R. (2002c, August). *Understanding Great Barrier Reef visitors: factors that contribute to visitor satisfaction.* (Project B2.1.1 Data Summary Report). Townsville, Queensland, Australia: CRC Reef Research Center.

Saltzer, R. (2002d, August). *Understanding Great Barrier Reef visitors: profile of repeat visitors.* (Project B2.1.1 Data Summary Report). Townsville, Queensland, Australia: CRC Reef Research Center.

Saltzer, R. (2003, March). *Understanding visitor–wildlife interactions: a case study of Monarch Wildlife Cruises, Otago Peninsula, New Zealand.* (Project B2.3 Data Summary Report). Townsville, Queensland, Australia: CRC Reef Research Center.

Samuels, A., Bejder, L., Constantine, R., and S. Heinrich. (2003). Swimming with wild cetaceans, with a special focus on the Southern Hemisphere. In N. Gales, M. Hindell, and R. Kirkwood (Eds.), *Marine mammals: fisheries, tourism, and management issues.* (pp. 277–303). Collingwood, Victoria, Australia: CSIRO Publishing.

Shepherd, N. (2003). How ecotourism can go wrong: the cases of SeaCanoe and Siam Safari, Thailand. In M. Luck and T. Kirstges (Eds.), *Global ecotourism policies and case studies.* (pp. 137–146). Clevedon, UK: Channel View Publications.

Speedie, C.D. (2003). Marine ecotourism potential in the waters of South Devon and Cornwall. In B. Garrod and J.C. Wilson (Eds.), *Marine ecotourism: issues and experiences.* (pp. 204–214). Clevedon, UK: Channel View Publications.

Tabata, R.S. (1992). Scuba diving holidays. In B. Weiler and C. M. Hall (Eds.), *Special interest tourism.* (pp. 171–184). New York: Belhaven Press.

Tratalos, J.A., and T.J. Austin. (2001). Impacts of recreational SCUBA diving on coral communities of the Caribbean island of Grand Cayman. *Biological Conservation*, **102**, 67–75.

Weber, S., Horak, S., and V. Mikacic. (2001). Tourism development in the Croatian Adriatic islands. In D. Ioannides, Y. Apostolopoulos, and S. Sonmez (Eds.), *Mediterranean islands and sustainable tourism development.* (pp. 171–192). London: Continuum.

Wilks, J., and S.J. Page. (2003). Current status of tourist health and safety. In J. Wilks and S. J. Page (Eds.), *Managing tourist health and safety in the new millennium.* (pp. 3–18). Amsterdam: Pergamon.

Williams, P., O'Neill, M., and M. MacCarthy. (2000, June 28–July 1). *Consumption issues in dive tourism: an exploratory study.* Paper presented at the Sixth Asia Pacific Tourism Association Annual Conference. Phuket, Thailand.

Wilson, J.C. (2003). Planning policy issues for marine ecotourism. In B. Garrod and J.C. Wilson (Eds.), *Marine ecotourism: issues and experiences.* (pp. 48–65). Clevedon, UK: Channel View Publications.

Wilson, J.C., and B. Garrod. (2003). Introduction. In B. Garrod and J.C. Wilson (Eds.), *Marine ecotourism: issues and experiences.* (pp. 1–16). Clevedon, UK: Channel View Publications.

World Tourism Organization. (2000). *Sustainable development of tourism. A compilation of good practices*. Madrid: World Tourism Organization.

Zakai, D., and N.E. Chadwick-Furman. (2001). Impacts of intensive recreational diving on reef corals at Eilat, northern Red Sea. *Biological Conservation*, **105**, 179–187.

Websites

Bear Glacier Tours: seward.net/kayakcamp/
Big Beard's Adventure Tours: www.bigbeards.com/sailing.htm#full
CRC Reef Research Center: www.reef.crc.org.au
Eco and Culture Tours, Zanzibar: www.ecoculture-anzibar.org/HTML/e_daytours.htm
Great Barrier Reef Marine Park Authority: www.gbrmpa.gov.au
Inside Vallarta Travel: www.hypermex.com/html/pv_act2.htm
Inuit Outfitting: www.greenland–guide.gl/sisimiut/tour–boat.htm
Kayak Carolina: www.kayakcarolina.com/masonboroislandt.html
Nam Ha Guides: www.the boatlanding.laopdr.com/dayboat.html
Nonni Travel: www.nonnitravel.is/iceland/N17–Boat_tour.htm
Odysseus: www.lefkas.net/odysseus.htm
Shipwreck Tours: www.shipwrecktours.com
Watermark Cruises: www.watermarkcruises.com/tours_excursion.shtml

Note

Research on one-day boat tours to the Great Barrier Reef reported in this chapter was supported by research funding from the CRC Reef Research Center. Research on one-day wildlife-viewing boat tours was supported by funding from the CRC Reef Research Center and the CRC for Sustainable Tourism.

11

Sail Training Adventures

Gary Easthope

A small, 68-year-old woman jumped off the side of the ship into the cold waters of the dock in Hobart, Tasmania. There she joined other fully dressed "crew members" of the *Endeavour* clad in sneakers, shirts, and trousers and wearing life jackets. They treaded water and huddled around one person in the center. At a command, another person moved to the center and the other person moved out to maintain the circle.

What I was observing was part of the practice emergency drill carried out by those who were about to sail on the *Endeavour* around the Horn of Africa to England. They could expect cold weather, gales, and seasickness. The woman and her 71-year-old husband were paying approximately 200 pounds (US$377) a day to sail on the *Endeavour* as "supernumeraries." They did not have to stand "watches" if they did not wish it (a watch is a shift system on ships in which a team works together for four hours, then is off duty for four hours or eight hours, depending on the number of watches). Other passengers called "voyage crew" paid between 75 (US$141) and 95 pounds (US$179) per day and acted as full crew members. They were allocated to a watch and were expected to be fully involved in all sail handling and other crew duties. In addition to voyage crew and supernumeraries, the *Endeavour*, like most tall ships, has an experienced, paid crew (some tall ships also have experienced but unpaid crew).

The *Endeavour* clearly markets itself as engaged in "adventure sailing." On their Website, www.barkendeavour.com.au, they state,

This is not a leisure cruise. It is hard work and you will have very little free time. It is also a great adventure and worth every minute on board. You will have a lot of fun and a life experience on a unique ship that you will never forget.

The *Endeavour* is one of the most famous ships offering such an adventure, but there are many others around the world.

In this chapter, I describe the different types of sail training adventures offered. I then try to analyze the motivations of some of the people who are prepared to pay money to jump into a cold dock and take watches in the dead of night. To achieve this, I draw upon the theoretical literature on tourism, as well as interviews with and surveys of participants. I am aided in understanding these motivations by the fact that I am a volunteer crew member on a tall ship, the *Lady Nelson*, and can draw on my own experience. In addition, this chapter includes a case study in which the *Lady Nelson* provides an example of "serious leisure" (Stebbins 1982, 1993). I also look at the social, economic, and environmental impacts of adventure sailing before concluding with an attempt to examine the future of this form of tourism.

Types of Sail Training Adventures

Although one can learn to sail in courses run by many yacht clubs, the term sail training implies learning to sail a "tall ship." The epithet "tall" does not refer to the height of the masts. A tall ship is any large sailing vessel. People usually think of square-rigged ships, but the term also includes schooners and other ships with fore and aft rigging.

There is a huge variety of such ships. Not all of them offer sail training. Many merely offer "trips around the harbor," such as on the *Bounty* in Sydney, Australia. There is also a small number of tall ships whose primary business does not involve sail training; for example, *Square Sail* of Cornwall, England, specializes in providing tall ships for the film/television industry. Finally, there are museum ships, maintained or built to illustrate a particular era. Most museum ships rarely if ever sail, and if they do, it is with an experienced crew, not with trainees on board. One example of such a ship is the *USS Constitution* in Boston (Easthope 2001).

Tall ships are expensive to maintain; the joke is that they are a hole in the water surrounded by wood or metal into which one throws money, so most owners of such ships are happy to charter for many purposes. Consequently, no categorization of tall ships can be rigid. For example, as well as providing ships for films, *Square Sail* offers sail training up to able seaman level as well as voyages for management training. The *Endeavour* is a museum ship that provides sail training adventures.

Despite the overlaps, I argue that sail training adventure as a form of tourism or recreation can be distinguished from other forms of sailing in that it:

1. Is normally not competitive (The aim of most voyages is not to beat competitors to a finish line, except when engaged in tall ship races.)
2. Takes people away on overnight voyages
3. Requires passengers to participate in the sailing of the ship
4. Offers an adventure experience.

Market Profile

This section considers sail training offerings as an experience as well as motivations for participation. Relatedly, as the general market for adventure tourism is discussed extensively by Swarbrooke, Beard, Leckie, and Pomfret (2003), it will not be repeated here, but note that there is no discussion of the market for sail training in that work.

So what is the attraction of sail training?

What Does Sail Training Offer?

The majority of tall ships that offer sail training do so as a form of personal development. Typically, but not exclusively, it is aimed at young people (see, for example, The Tall Ships Youth Trust in the UK [www.sta.oruk] and Tall Ship Adventures in Canada [www.tallshipadventures.on.ca/sail_training.htm]). The preference for young people is also expressed in the rules for all tall ship races, which stipulate that at least half the crew must be between 18 and 25 years of age. However, there are also specialist ships catering to people with disabilities (see, for example, the Jubilee Sailing Trust [www.jst.org.uk]), and not all tall ships require that the sail trainees be young.

The emphasis on personal development is central to sail training:

Sail training opens the hatch to seamanship and unforgettable adventure. . . . Strange as it seems, the main aim of sail training is not to turn out fine sailors. . . . [It] is all about old fashioned notions like self-discovery, character building, team-work, self reliance and self-discipline. (Hamilton 1988)

Sail training is about living, working, and playing with people you haven't met before; about becoming a member of a team, about taking responsibility, giving and taking orders, pushing yourself physically and mentally. Being cold, wet, weary, perhaps sick, often frightened—and looking back on it as the most wonderful experience of your life. (Horwarth, cited on www.windbound@south.com.au)

This is true not just for trainings geared to young people, but also for the corporate training offered by many tall ships. Here the emphasis is often as much on team building as on personal development. For example,

Enterprize specializes in providing a range of corporate training and incentive reward programs to help build a more productive, cohesive, and competitive workforce for your organization. These programs have been specifically designed to address skills and issues within organizations such as delegation, team building, and management. (*Enterprize* Website: www.enterprize.com.au)

Such voyages can also be offered as a break from routine:

Adventure voyages are aimed at adults but are open to all those over the age of 15 years. Anyone who can imagine escaping the armchair, television, and normal day-to-day routines will really enjoy participating in a lifestyle that has changed little in 200 years. (One and All Website: www.oneandall.org.au)

Many sail training vessels are sponsored by governments and run by naval officers—for example, the *Young Endeavour* in Australia. However, there are also many that operate with a combination of government grants, charitable donations, volunteer labor, and private business (e.g., in Australia: *Windeward Bound, Svanen, Enterprize, Duyfken, Lady Nelson, James Craig, Lieuwen*).

Finally, there are those that operate solely as a business. In Australia, these tend to be in Queensland, specially the Whitsundays (e.g., *Solway Lass*). They usually only sail for a few days, and unlike the other operators of tall ships, they do not appeal on the basis of personal development but rather an historical mystique, as in this example describing the schooner *Friendship*: "Originally built as a training vessel, her gracious timber lines reflect a bygone era of elagant [sic] sailing. This prestigious and romantic vessel . . ." and so forth (www.whitsundays-sailing.com/whitsunday-sailing-holiday/classic-sailing).

The large fleet of such ships in the Whitsundays are at the luxury end of the "hard work" promised by most sail training, as here the work is optional and presented as a pleasant holiday diversion. For example, *Windjammer* (the misnomer of a schooner) offers what it calls sailing adventures, but

Windjammer is fully crewed with a captain, cook/hostess, and deckhand, however guests are encouraged to take the wheel, tend the sheets, or for the more adventurous, climb the ratlines and fine tune the canvas 70 feet above the deck. Whether it's an active or relaxing holiday you're after, the professional attentive crew will ensure you enjoy a memorable holiday in the Whitsunday Islands. (www.seethewhitsundays.com/opp/tours/bc/windjammer)

What Motivates People to Undertake Sail Training Adventures?

All the ships are offering adventure and a break from routine, and some are offering relaxation. What, however, are the trainees getting out of it? Why are they choosing this form of tourism?

Early work on tourism (e.g., MacCannell 1976) saw tourists seeking an escape from the monotony of everyday work; mass tourism provided a counterpoint to the drab lives of the workers. For a brief period, they could escape routine, relax, and enjoy life. Later work, drawing on Foucault's writings, developed the notion of the "tourist gaze," i.e., the idea that tourists were trained to appreciate certain landmarks, in particular vistas that, derived from the Romantic tradition, were "wild" and "untamed" (Urry 2002). They also gazed at the "authentic" at heritage sites (what constitutes the authentic is considered in detail by MacCannell 1992, 2001).

The concept of the tourist gaze is criticized (by Franklin 2003, for example) as being too limiting a notion of tourist experience. Tourists do not just gaze; they participate. They participate, in particular, in consumption. Franklin has argued that the mass tourism of places such as Blackpool in England in the 1930s was an escape into vibrant consumption; shopping is still a major feature of the tourist experience. Participation in consumption did not just involve gazing at consumer goods, but also consuming them. It was not just the eyes that were satisfied but all the bodily senses.

The body becomes even more central to the tourist experience when we examine adventure tourism. Here the experimental bodily aspect of the tourist experience comes to center stage. As Cater (2000) states, "adventure tourism is fundamentally about active recreation participation and it demands new metaphors based more on 'being, doing, touching, seeing' rather than just seeing."

Work on this aspect of tourism experience uses the concept of "peak experience" (Maslow 1976) or Csikszentmihalyi's concept of "flow" (see, for example, Stranger 1999):

Flow refers to the holistic sensation present when we act with total involvement. It is a kind of feeling after which one nostalgically says "that was fun," or "that was enjoyable." It is the state in which action follows upon action according to an internal logic which seems to need no conscious intervention on our part. We experience it as a unified flowing from one moment to the next in which we are in control of our actions, and in which there is little distinction between self and environment; between stimulus and response; or between past, present, and future. (Csikszentmihalyi 1974, p. 5)

Finally, there is a small but growing literature that draws upon the work of Victor Turner (1969) on liminality. This harkens back to the early work on tourism that sees it as an escape from everyday life. In this literature, tourist journeys are seen as having some of the aspects of a pilgrimage (Turner and Turner 1978) in that they are outside normal space and time and participants can experience "slow time"(Hylland Eriksen 2001), time not dominated by the calendar and the clock.

Another aspect of tourism largely neglected in the literature can also be derived from the Turners' work. Pilgrims and tourists frequently travel as groups. This group travel may change the experience of the individual. In certain circumstances, the travelers may experience "*communitas*" (Turner and Turner 1978), i.e., the social experience of traveling together that creates a camaraderie in which all are, during the journey, equal pilgrims. Distinctions of class and rank are left behind, and the sole and important status is that of pilgrim and group member.

To try and understand the tourist experience as belonging solely to the individual is to ignore the fact that most tourist experience is communal. Even apparently individualistic experiences such as surfing involve induction into a surfing culture that specifies dress, demeanor, language, and behavior and considerable social interaction while sitting waiting for "the wave" (Stranger 2001).

Consideration of these various conceptualizations of the tourist experience underlay my own research into sail training adventures. These ships are offering adventure. Is that what attracts voyage crew (sail trainees)? Is sail training sought because it is a break from routine? Is viewing wild, untamed nature one of the attractions of sail training? Are participants looking for authenticity? Do participants experience "flow"? Are sail training ships liminal spaces—spaces outside normal time during which participants experience "slow time"? Do trainees experience *communitas*? Is there a subculture of sail training that shapes and develops the experience of participants?

To answer these questions, I draw upon several data sets. The first comes from a re-analysis of questionnaires distributed for marketing purposes to voyage crew on the *Lady Nelson* who chose an Adult Education weekend activity of "sailing on a tall ship" (76 voyage crew over 11 trips between March 2000 and April 2003). Participants were asked why they were attracted to the trip and were given five categories from which they could select (adventure, escape, being on the ocean, sailing on a square-rigger, and sailing on a replica). The second set of data comes from a questionnaire, developed for this chapter, distributed to all members of the Tasmanian Sail Training Association (TSTA).[1] Respondents were given seven categories to rank as attractions of the *Lady Nelson* (sense of adventure, escape from routine, learning about square-riggers, being on the ocean, meeting people, helping preserve history, and physical challenge). They were also asked to respond to a question designed to measure "flow."[2] This question was asked in the following way:

Here is a description of one kind of experience people sometimes have:

---

[1] An exact count of members is difficult. Questionnaires were sent to 157 households, but of those, 56 had family membership and many of those memberships included young children. The "estimated" response rate was approximately 60%. All figures in the text refer to percentage of the total 114 returned questionnaires or, where appropriate, to the 102 questionnaires of those who sail.

[2] This is a modified version of a question developed with others to measure flow for the Catholic Church Life Survey. Permission to use it was kindly granted by its developer, Dr. Michael Mason.

"You get totally absorbed in what you are doing and you forget yourself and your thoughts, and don't notice time going by. Playing your part seems to come almost automatically and you feel intense pleasure and satisfaction."

Have you ever had this experience when sailing aboard the *Lady Nelson*?

How often have you had this experience?

Never

Rarely

Often

Nearly always

In both surveys, participants were also given the opportunity to write what they most enjoyed about sailing on the *Lady Nelson*.

These surveys are supplemented by detailed interviews carried out with crew and voyage crew on the *Lady Nelson*, the *Enterprize,* and the *Endeavour* that also asked about motivation and flow. The interpretation of these data sets is informed by my own participation as a member of a sail training association undertaking adventure voyages on the *Lady Nelson* (Figure 11-1).

The results demonstrate that adventure is a major attraction for participants. In the marketing survey, it was the option chosen by most people (74%). Among the TSTA respondents, it was ranked second[3] after learning to sail a square-rigger. By

Figure 11-1　Sail-training vessel. Photographer: Gary Easthope.

---

[3] Ranking was calculated by averaging the responses. The mean ranks were sense of adventure (3.2), escape from routine (4.8), learning about square-riggers (2.9), being on the ocean (3.3), meeting people (4.6), helping preserve history (3.9), and physical challenge (4.7).

contrast, fewer participants in the marketing survey were seeking an escape from routine (45%), and it was ranked last as an option for TSTA respondents.

To elicit responses regarding wild nature, the option "being on the ocean" was used as an indicator. Among those in the marketing survey, 65% selected this option, and 22% in the open response section of the questionnaire stated the best part of the trip was the scenery. Among the TSTA respondents, this was the third ranked item, and several expanded on it using such phrases as "getting back to nature," and "the beauty of being on the water."

Authenticity is a contentious concept and it was not explored in the marketing survey. However, it was broached in interviews. The responses fell into two clear and opposing categories. Some respondents saw authenticity as unattainable and unimportant. For others it was "critically important" and they saw "no point in being here if she's not authentic." Among TSTA respondents, "helping preserve history" was the fourth ranked motivation and some waxed lyrical: "There are moments when with very little imagination I can escape into the past; into a word of creaking timbers, the flapping of canvas, and the beautiful motion of a square-rigger under sail."

The experience of flow was remarkably common. Among the sailing members of the TSTA (n = 102), 77% reported experiencing it with 86% of those reporting experiencing it often or always. The experience of flow was related to the extent and type of sailing experience: 79% of those who had done day sails reported it compared with 94% of those who had done overnight sails and 96% of those who had undertaken open sea passages. In the detailed interviews, the description of the experience provided some respondents with words to articulate something they had not been able to express before, and they responded with an emphatic "yes" or "certainly." Others were content to just agree they had had the experience, while a few felt the description did not capture their experience fully and provided comments such as "agree with a lot but it doesn't quite sum up the experience." For a few respondents, the experience created a total loss of self-consciousness:

You go off your normal type of thinking. For me an unusual thing to happen. You go "out of it" so to speak. Not just out of day-to-day stuff but off the ship into another feeling—you and the elements. (*Enterprize*)

Things just seem to fall away. The moment becomes the very focus; the very place of being. (*Lady Nelson*)

Forget the cold, forget why you are here and where you are. (*Endeavour*)

The liminality of tall ships as sites for "slow time" was not explored in either survey, but in interviews and in open responses, this feature of tall ship sailing was expressed. It was notable, for example, that very few of the people interviewed on the ships after a voyage knew the date (which had to be put on informed consent forms). As one said on commencement of the interview, "when you go sailing you forget what day it is and certainly what date it is. A total turnoff from your normal life" (*Enterprize*)—a response echoed by several others who made statements such as "once you sail away . . . [you] cut the ties that bind and that gives a feeling of timelessness" (*Enterprize*) and "you forget time, what day it is. Days blend in" (*Lady Nelson*). Some of the TSTA respondents also reported this, e.g., "a chance to lose myself among the water and history. It's as though I forget everything else when I step aboard" and [I experience a] "sense of timelessness."

In an article summarizing much of the literature on heritage, Ravenscroft (1999) states, heritage effectively seeks to subjugate individual authority over time by breaking down the demarcation between past and present: by inviting the audience both to step back in time, as well as welcome the past into the present, heritage challenges linear constructions of time. In the place of linear time is "timelessness," the outcome of boarding a "time machine" in which the past and present enmesh to de-center the individual. (p. 73)

Tall ships are particularly effective as "heritage time machines," as the voyagers are literally as well as figuratively transported out of normal time for the duration of the voyage. Such transportation is aided by the fact that voyagers on such vessels are expected to crew. They not only experience the "heritage site" through eyes and ears and through kinesthetic senses, but are also participants in its operation.

Communitas was experienced by some voyagers. My own experience of sailing on the *Lady Nelson* on a four-day voyage from Hobart to Devonport was that a form of weak communitas was created. Certainly, the important distinctions did not relate to land-based hierarchies but rather to abilities to fulfill duties and to skill in sailing. The experience was best described by a woman who was a voyage crew member on the *Enterprize*'s crossing of Bass Strait: "Amazing camaraderie. Usually strangers at the outset and at the end you are not friendly but have got something in common." Most respondents were not so articulate in expressing this aspect of sailing but many used the words "comradeship" or "camaraderie" to describe their experience. This was the most frequent response to the question in the TSTA questionnaire that asked respondents what they most enjoyed about sailing on the *Lady Nelson,* with 30% of respondents using phrases such as "being part of a team," "the camaraderie," "a very good form of mateship," "the outside world stops and you become an integral part of the *Lady Nelson*'s crew."

With such camaraderie, it is not surprising that there is a strong subculture among those who sail on the *Lady Nelson*. One of its key features, which relates to communitas, is that there is a studied attempt to disregard crew members' lives outside the ship. Crew members are rarely asked about their occupation, or their former occupation in the case of the many retired members, and first names are used rather than surnames. Skills in sailing or maintaining the ship are the prime concern. Conversation after relaxed evening meals, when moored during overnight passages, consists of anecdotes of former voyages or discussions of sailing feats in the past by other ships or sailors. Talk of seasickness experiences, frequently as an amusing anecdote, is a common theme in the conversations. Experiencing seasickness, yet continuing to sail on future voyages, appears to be an important element in acceptance as a long-time crew member.

Summary of Motivations

Although tall ships are offering personal development, a break from routine, and, in some cases, an appeal to history, these are not major motivations for those undertaking sail training adventures. Instead they are motivated by a positive search for adventure rather than the negative escape from routine. Likewise, although history is important to them, it is not a major motivation.

What the surveys and interviews demonstrate is that it is the experiential aspects of sail training adventures that are central for participants. They enjoy gazing upon nature. They report the experience of "flow" and "slow time." They find the camaraderie of sailing to be a major attraction, and the subculture they create has aspects of communitas in which hierarchical distinctions between participants relate to sailing skills rather than those of the land.

Impacts

Tall ships are frequently built and/or maintained by political entities. These are sometimes nation states as with the *Young Endeavour* in Australia. They can also be state governments as with the *One and All,* which is subsidized by the South Australian government. This means they can come to symbolize the nation or, less frequently, the state.

The symbolic value of such tall ships is important. It can be a positive factor when, after tall ships races, the ships take part in a parade of sail and the crews of such ships parade through cities. Like the Olympic Games, such parades can be a means to increase peaceful relations between countries. However, also like the Olympic Games, the symbolic nature of these ships make them an attractive target for terrorism. In 2003, I visited the *USS Constitution* in Boston, which symbolizes early U.S. victories in the war against England. To board the ship, I had to go through a rigorous security screening similar to those now common at American airports. In Tasmania, the *Lady Nelson* replica is a symbol of white invasion to surviving Aborigines. The original ship landed the first settlers in Risdon Cove in 1803. Shortly thereafter, several Aborigines were killed by the white settlers. Risdon Cove is now under Aboriginal jurisdiction. Consequently, to avoid Aboriginal protests that could damage the ship or put crew and passenger lives in danger, in the bicentenary year 2003, commemorative historical sailings did not go to Risdon Cove.

Tall ships are tourist attractions in themselves. They frequently feature prominently in tourist brochures (e.g., Sydney's weekly guide often features the *James Craig* on its cover) and are used to sell property or tourist accommodation (as noted in the case study of the *Lady Nelson* later in this chapter). One apocryphal tale is of a tall ship being paid to moor before a block of waterfront apartments for three days. Pictures were taken to advertise the apartments, and the ship then returned to its usual mooring.

Tall ships in large numbers attract considerable tourist interest. In 1992, visitors spent an estimated US$315 million in Boston to see the start of the tall ships race, and over 2 million spectators came to see them on arrival in Liverpool (Easthope 2001).

Environmentally, tall ships create a minimal impact. Part of the attraction of such ships is the opportunity they provide for passengers to view the natural environment. Consequently, both commercial and noncommercial ships attempt to minimize their environmental impact. Precautions are taken when refueling engines to avoid spillage; most now have "grey water" tanks for storage of waste water and sullage tanks for sewage. More and more ports are providing facilities to pump sewage ashore for treatment and requiring their use. However, sewage is also often discharged overboard in open sea. Despite this, modern tall ships probably make less environmental impact than their historical predecessors, whose sailors deposited all their waste into the sea and brought their diseases to the indigenous inhabitants of the lands they visited.

Future Directions

Tall ships are very expensive to maintain. Their physical fabric is under constant attack from salt water—for example, salt crystals ruin ropes and rust metals. Wood rots and, if in tropical waters, is attacked by the torredo worm. Most tall ships are consequently like the grandfather's axe—all their parts have been replaced but they remain the same. The *Alma Doepel* of Melbourne, for example, was declared unseaworthy and, at the time of writing, was being repaired and prepared for sea by volunteers at Port Macquarie. Such constant maintenance is, however, costly in both money and time. At some stage in their life, active sailing ships have to become museum ships or rotting hulks.

Senior crew must be skilled in navigation and ship handling and such skills are scarce, especially for square-rig sailing. Ordinary crew, both paid and trainees, are easier to train and, of course, people pay to undergo sail training. The original square-riggers were designed to be operated by crews who may never have been to sea before and may, in navy crews, even have been forcibly recruited via the press gang. Consequently, the skills needed are simple although arduous.

Other major costs associated with sail training are the linked costs of safety and insurance. Adventure by definition contains an element of danger. To reduce that danger to a minimum requires present-day tall ships, unlike the historical originals, to have safety harnesses for people when they are aloft, as well as provide lifeboats, flares, and other safety devices. These are not just expensive to purchase; they must also be checked, maintained, and replaced at regular intervals if a ship is to remain "under survey" and able to carry passengers. Finally, there is the high cost of insurance. Public liability insurance is mandatory and, in Australia, has increased exponentially in the past few years.

The size of such ships means there is a limit to the number of passengers they can carry at a price acceptable to the people they wish to attract, especially if they aim to attract young people. As a consequence, they can rarely be a completely economical proposition. Some ships, faced by these costs, rely on entirely voluntary labor (e.g., *Lady Nelson*, *Alma Doepel*) or, more frequently, sponsorship from a government (e.g., *Young Endeavour*).

Despite all these problems, it is likely that sail training adventures will thrive. The tall ships races were started in 1956 by a London lawyer as a last magnificent display of these disappearing machines. Rather than being the last such race, it triggered interest in the ships. As of this writing, 20 nations now maintain such ships, as do numerous nongovernmental associations. If adventure tourism becomes more popular, it is likely that tall ships will continue to be maintained to fill a niche in that market, as well as provide adventure for people on ships that are symbolic of a nation or state.

Lady Nelson: A Case Study in Serious Leisure

The original *Lady Nelson* was built in Deptford in 1798 to undertake survey work in the new colony of New South Wales, Australia. She was a brig built to a radical design with a very shallow draft to enable her to enter and survey coastal inlets, but with drop keels in order to, it was hoped, give her good sailing characteristics in the open ocean. She was a small ship, less than 60 feet long (about 16 meters), with a beam of less than 18 feet (about 6 meters). Historically, her importance lies in being the first vessel to sail eastward through Bass Strait, the first to enter Port Phillip Bay (on which Melbourne now stands), as well as the fact that, along with other ships, she was the first to bring Europeans to settle both in Tasmania and in Northern Australia.

The replica is built to the same size and is also rigged as a brig, with the same sail plan as the original. However, she has a full keel, a motor, and modern safety equipment. The Tasmanian Sail Training Association (TSTA) was established as a limited company in 1983 to build and sail the replica vessel for Australia's bicentennial celebration. She was built locally of local timbers (Tasmanian blue gum keel and frames, celery top pine decking, with masts of Oregon pine grown locally). Launched in 1988, she took part in the tall ships race to Sydney from Hobart. In 1990, she was sent to the mainland with paid crew and a marketing specialist to generate income from corporate sponsorship. The timing was disastrous, as the 1980s economic boom collapsed in corporate scandals. By 1995, the ship was AU$250,000 (US$185,452) in debt. In 1996, it was proposed that the ship be sold to clear the debt. In response, a small group of enthusiasts calling themselves the "Friends of the Lady Nelson" managed to raise collateral from an abalone diver's license and persuade creditors to forego closure. The ship returned to Tasmania and began operating using solely volunteer labor. Through offering six harbor sails each weekend (originally at AU$5 [US$4] for 90 minutes, now AU$6 [US$4.50]) and chartering (for parties, weddings, scattering of ashes, and historical celebrations in Victoria), the debt, which was at one time accruing interest of AU$87 per day (US$65), was paid off in January 2001.

The TSTA is a small business operation. It costs approximately AU$50,000 (US$38,000) a year to keep the *Lady Nelson* operating. This is without any labor costs, as all labor is voluntary. This is a clear example of what Stebbins (1982, 1993) has called "serious leisure,"

the systematic pursuit of an amateur, hobbyist, or volunteer activity sufficiently substantial and interesting for the participant to find a career there in the acquisition and expression of a combination of its special skills, knowledge, and experience. (Stebbins 1993, p. 23)

There are two arms of this leisure. One is the Board and the office of the TSTA. The other is sailing and maintaining the ship. The Board is an elected body of directors with a chairperson, treasurer, secretary, and so forth, that meets at least once monthly. The Board runs an office, open every weekday between 10 AM and 3 PM, which takes bookings and keeps records of members and other documentation. The Board operates like any commercial board of management and under the same regulations. To sail the vessel requires a qualified captain and engineer as well as crew in training. Of the four captains currently involved with the *Lady Nelson,* two "came up through the ranks" at their own expense. They have attended courses at the Australian Maritime College, which is by good fortune located in Tasmania, to gain their certification. Several members have also trained as marine engineers using the same facilities. Recently, new regulations have required that some crew must have first-aid certificates and qualifications in elements of shipboard safety. Several members, including myself, have undertaken these courses at the Australian Maritime College, which include practical experience in entering and righting life rafts. Further, a few volunteers meet every Thursday to perform routine maintenance, and once a year the ship is taken into a slip, for a week or more, for major work.

A clear career path within the Tasmanian Sail Training Association has been developing since 2000. This path has now been formalized with a training manual produced by one of the members at the request of the Board. The manual specifies the skills needed to become progressively a deckhand, senior deckhand, and bosun or uncertified watchkeeper. Higher levels of skill require formal professional certification through the Maritime College.

In the responses to the TSTA survey, learning to sail on a square-rigger was the first-ranked attraction for members, and one in five members (19%) said learning new skills was one of the things he or she most enjoyed about sailing on the *Lady Nelson*. The production of a manual is unusual on tall ships and is a function of the entirely voluntary nature of the TSTA. Normally, tall ships have at least one paid captain who can order crew to undertake certain tasks. The entirely voluntary nature of the TSTA means no one can be "required" to do anything. Consequently, there are members who, although in all other respects are competent deck crew never go aloft because of disability or fear of heights. The voluntary nature of the TSTA also means that, unlike many sail training vessels, there is no upper age limit to participation. The oldest active sailing member in 2004 was 76, and of the four captains, three are retired from full-time employment. Although some members of the TSTA no longer sail because of age, there is a very wide age span, from 15 to over 80 (Table 11-1).

This age structure is slightly older than that reported by Swarbrooke and colleagues (2003) for trekking adventure holidays. There are more male than female members (65% male, 35% female) in the TSTA, and males are more likely than females to be in senior positions onboard ship—for example, all captains are male. However, tasks are not gendered, with both men and women climbing rigging and cleaning toilets, and the Board has five male and four female directors. The social background of members is difficult to estimate because half the members are not in the workforce, most of whom are retired, but if we take highest level of education as a surrogate measure, 27% have only completed secondary school, 20% have trade qualifications, and 53% have a university degree.

Although in this case study I have stressed the aspects of the operation of the *Lady Nelson* that illustrate its role as a vehicle for serious leisure, this does not preclude it fulfilling other functions. The vessel is clearly also a tourist attraction. The hotel and the cafes behind its mooring use its presence as part of the ambience they are marketing. In 2003, its harbor sails were a feature of a segment of the television holiday program *Getaway*, leading to increased tourist interest in sailing on her. She has played a central role in bicentennial celebrations in Mt. Gambier, Victoria (which was named from the deck of the original), and Port Phillip Bay, and in the year 2004, fulfilled a similar role in the bicentennial celebrations for Hobart town.

For more details of the *Lady Nelson,* see her Website, www.tased.edu.au/tasonline/ladynel.

Table 11-1   Age of Tasmanian Sailing Training Association (TSTA) Members (n = 114)

Age	Under 18	18–25	26–35	36–45	46–55	56–65	Over 65
Percentage	1.8%	5.4%	5.4%	10.8%	24.3%	25.2%	27.0%

Glossary of Nautical Terms

Brig: a ship that has two masts, both of which are square-rigged, and also a fore and aft gaff rig behind the main mast.

Drop keels: sometimes called boards-boards or dagger boards, these are boards lowered through the bottom of a ship to provide a keel that can be adjusted according to water depth and sailing conditions.

Fore and aft: front and back.

Fore and aft sail(s): sails that are used parallel to the ship's sides. They are normally triangular in shape.

Gaff rig: a fore and aft sail configuration where the upper part of the sail is held by a pole (gaff) attached to a mast and the lower part by a pole (boom) attached to the same mast.

Schooner: a ship with fore and aft sails on two masts, one mast, the main mast, being taller than the other.

Square sail(s): sails that are used across the ship and are square to the mast. They are normally rectangular, not square.

Windjammer: originally a large, square-rigged trading ship, usually with hull and masts of iron. The name is now frequently used for any large, square-rigged ship with at least three masts.

References

Cater, C. (2000). Can I play too? Inclusion and exclusion in adventure tourism. *The Northwest Geographer,* **3**, 49–59.

Csikszentmihalyi, M. (1974). *Flow: studies in enjoyment.* PHS Grant Report N ROH1HM 22883-02.

Easthope, G. (2001). Heritage sailing in Australia: a preliminary schema. *International Journal of Heritage Studies,* **7**, (2) 185–190.

Franklin, A. (2003). *Tourism: an introduction.* London: Sage.

Hamilton, J. (1988). Open the hatch to adventure. In *Tall Ships Australia 1988.* (A Bulletin/Australian Bicentennial Authority Official Publication.).

Hylland Eriksen, T. (2001). *Tyranny of the moment.* London: Pluto.

MacCannell, D. (1976). *The tourist: a new theory of the leisure class.* New York: Schocken.

MacCannell, D. (1992). *Empty meeting grounds: the tourist papers.* London: Routledge.

MacCannell, D. (2001). Tourist agency. *Tourist Studies,* **1** (1), 23–38.

Maslow, A.H. (1976). *The farther reaches of human nature.* Harmondsworth, UK: Penguin.

Ravenscroft, N. (1999). Editorial: the created environment of heritage as leisure. *International Journal of Heritage Studies,* **5** (2), 68–74.

Stebbins, R.A. (1982). Serious leisure; a conceptual statement. *Pacific Sociological Review,* **25** (2), 251–272.

Stebbins, R.A. (1993). Social world, life-style, and serious leisure: toward a meso structural analysis. *World Leisure and Recreation,* **35** (1) 23.

Stranger, M. (1999). The aesthetics of risk: a study of surfing. *International Review for the Sociology of Sport,* **33** (3), 256–276.

Stranger, M. (2001). *Risk taking and postmodernity: commodification and the ecstatic in leisure lifestyles.* Unpublished doctoral thesis, Hobart: University of Tasmania,

Swarbrooke, J., Beard, C., Leckie, S., and G. Pomfret. (2003). *Adventure tourism: the new frontier*. Oxford, UK: Butterworth-Heinemann.

Turner, V. (1969). *The ritual process*. Chicago: Aldine.

Turner, V., and E. Turner. (1978). *Image and pilgrimage in Christian culture: anthropological perspectives*. Oxford, UK: Oxford University Press.

Urry, J. (2002). *The tourist gaze*. London: Sage.

Websites

For an extensive list of tall ships, see www.schoonerman.com

One of the best Websites of a tall ship is that of the Endeavour: www. barkendeavour.com.au

Notes

My thanks to Claire Ellis, my colleague and tourism lecturer, who directed me to work on adventure tourism and gave helpful comments on my text.

I wish to express my thanks to all those who responded to my questions but, in particular, the Board and members of the T.S.T.A. who facilitated my research.

IV

Sustainability

The three previous sections have served to organize discussion of each of the water-based experiences presented in this book. Such groupings are just one interpretation of possible clusters. Of course, sailing and boating could equally have been positioned in adventure, and readers will have other ways of generating clusters. However, the defining characteristic that positioned a water-based experience to one section and not another was based on everyday-life social constructions, discourses, and dialogues pertaining to each. Consequently, the first section is explicitly about boats. The second section, based on promotion, advertising, and written discourses, is about "sport-associated" experiences. The third section focused on adventures. In the preceding sections, each of the chapters has provided background information, market profiles, advantages of the specific water-based experience over others, impacts associated with the respective experience, and future directions.

In this fourth section, a synthesis of the advantages, and in some instances disadvantages, of a number of the water-based experiences, their impacts, and future directions will be undertaken. In generating this synthesis, the concept of sustainability will be applied. As a starting point for this discussion, Chapter 12 proposes that "sustainability" is a socially constructed term and one that is subject to change. The changes bear the marks of (re)presentation and (re)interpretation of the social and cultural values and political agendas of their times and those of the definition or concept makers. The chapter proffers that sustainability of each of the water-based experiences in this book is under constant negotiation and is dependent on the attitudes, values, and behaviors of the participants, the providers, the host communities, and government agencies, as well as a variety of stakeholder groups at any given time. Constant dialogue, consultation, and wide stakeholder involvement in planning and decision making, as well as education, are imperative for these water-based experiences to endure. External to this human element are acts of nature and environmental change, which can impact on the short-, medium-, and long-term sustainability of these experiences. Over some of these acts, humans have no control and so must be prepared for informed decision making with a suite of responsive strategies and actions. The chapter concludes that the sustainability of water-based experiences is linked to the quality of the settings, support providers, facilities, infrastructure, the behavior of self as well as others, and the perceptions of the overall quality of the experience by the various participants and stakeholder groups. In the end, both the sustainability and quality of the respective water-based experiences comes down to the actions of individuals, regardless of their constituency affiliation.

12

Sustainability and Future Directions

Gayle Jennings

Reflections on Sustainable Tourism, Sport, Leisure, and Recreation

Sustainability is a term that has drawn the attention of numerous researchers, practitioners, community members, stakeholder groups, and government agencies at the local, regional, state, national, and international levels. However, despite much talking and writing, a definitive meaning has yet to be embraced by all possible users. One of the earliest frames for consideration of "sustainability" originated from the work of Meadows and Meadows (1972). This frame emphasized the finite capacity of resources and subsequent "limits to growth." Another early set of frames was constructed by the International Union for the Conservation of Nature and Natural Resources (IUCN), the World Wildlife Fund (WWF), and the United Nations Environment Program (UNEP) in 1980. This set encompassed notions of "sustainable utilization" and "sustainable development."

Later, in 1987, the landmark sustainability text, the Brundtland Report, otherwise known as *Our Common Future,* advocated that sustainable development was "development that meets the needs of the present without compromising the ability of future generations to meet their own needs" (World Commission on Environment and Development [WCED] 1987). The intent of this concept of sustainable development was reaffirmed at the Rio Summit in 1992 and called Agenda 21.

As a result of the Brundtland Report and the Rio Summit, the earlier discussion of sustainable utilization and sustainable development (IUCN, WWF, and UNEP 1980) was replaced by "sustainability" discourses. Accordingly, such discourses served to move the concept of sustainability toward negotiated or accepted definitions/constructions/interpretations (see Row 1 in Table 12-1). However, just as the term seemed to be definable, discourses arose to query whether sustainability was

Table 12-1   Overview of Discourses Related to Sustainability, and Examples of Representative Academic Texts (in Reverse Chronological Order)

Discourse Topic	Examples of Representative Academic Texts
Definitions and discussions of sustainability, sustainable development	Berke and Conroy 2000; International Institute for Sustainable Development 1997; Gunn 1994; van den Bergh and van der Straaten 1994; United Nations Development Program 1992; Redclift 1987; World Commission on Economic Development 1987
Concept of sustainable tourism	McCool et al. 2001; Font and Tribe 2000; Twining-Ward 1999; Swarbrooke 1999; Middleton 1998; Mowforth and Munt 1998; Hall and Lew 1998; Clarke 1997; France 1997; Stabler 1997; Wahab and Pigram 1997; Priestley et al. 1996; Briguglio et al. 1996; Coccossis and Nijkamp 1995; Goulet 1995; Hughes 1995; Hunter and Green 1995; McCool and Watson 1995; Miecczkowski 1995; World Conference on Sustainable Tourism 1995; Gale and Corday 1994; Hunter 1995; Murphy 1994; Bramwell and Lane 1993; Butler 1993; MacGregor 1993; Nelson et al. 1993; De Kadt 1992; Eber 1992; Innskeep 1991; Butler 1991; Farrell and Runyan 1991; Slater 1991; Barbier 1987; Edington and Edington 1986; Budowski 1976
Queries and critiques of sustainability and sustainable tourism	Buhalis and Diamantis 2001; Kousis 2001; Bossel 1999; Butler 1999; Honey 1999; McCool and Stankey 1999; Sautter and Leisen 1999; Twining-Ward 1999; Garrod and Fyall 1998; Rothman 1998; Butler 1997; McLaren 1997; Wahab and Pigram 1997; Wall 1997a; Campbell 1996; Coccossis 1996; Burr 1995; Hunter and Green 1995; McCool 1995; Cater and Lowman 1994; Butler 1993; Cater and Goodall 1992; Butler 1991; Innskeep 1991; Shumway 1991; Barbier 1987
(Re)constructing and (re)interpreting sustainability	McCool et al. 2001; Payne et al. 1999; Bramwell and Lane 1999; Hunter 1997; Potts and Harrill 1997; McCool 1995; Cater and Lowman 1994
Sustainability and community/stakeholder participation	Bricker and Kerstetter 2005; Bramwell and Sharman 1999; Burns 1999; Hall 1999; McCool and Stankey 1999; Ritchie 1999; Sautter and Leisen 1999; Robinson 1999; Timothy 1999; Marien and Pizam 1997; Gartner 1997; Shindler and Neburka 1997; Pearce et al. 1996; Hughes 1995; Shamai 1991; Stokowski 1991; Court, 1990
Sustainability tourism and ethics	Caalders 1997; Ewert and Shultis 1997; Potts and Harrill 1997; Zeigler and McDonald 1997; Dovers et al. 1996; Fennell and Malloy 1995; Hughes 1995; Hultsman 1995; Orams 1995; Walsh and Matthews 1995; Gale and Corday 1994; D'Amore 1992; Butler 1991; Court 1990; Shearman 1990
Tourism growth and transformations, as well as sustainability indicators	McCool et al. 2001; Bossel 1999; McCool and Stankey 1999; Cooper 1997; Moldan et al. 1997; Manning 1996; Butler and Waldbrook 1991; Debbage 1990; Cooper and Jackson 1989; Stankey and McCool 1984; Gormsen 1981; Butler 1980; Stansfield 1978; Miossec 1976; Plog 1973; Christaller 1963

indeed achievable, and especially if tourism, as well as leisure and recreation experiences, could support sustainability principles. Table 12-1 provides an overview of sustainability discourses with particular regard to tourism. Why? Because in the sustainability literature related to this book, there is a plethora of academic texts concerning sustainable tourism, but not so for sustainable sport, leisure, and recreation. Granted that the distinguishing lines between tourism, sport, leisure, and recreation may at times be blurred, the discourses are emblematic rather than representative.

The skepticism of discourses regarding the achievability of sustainable development has proven to be warranted, as Table 12-1 portrays in relation to tourism. Ten years after the Rio Summit, it would seem that sustainability and sustainable development are as elusive as ever. Specifically, it was noted at the World Summit on Sustainable Development, the 2002 Johannesburg Summit, that "progress in implementing sustainable development has been extremely disappointing . . . with poverty deepening and environmental degradation worsening" (United Nations Department of Economic and Social Affairs 2002).

As Table 12-1 demonstrates, and as Pigram (2000) has stated, "[s]ustainability is multifaceted and any tendency to view sustainability as an unidimensional state ignores the several dimensions of the concept as it applies to human activity and development"(p. 373). Also as noted in Table 12-1, the conceptualization of "sustainability" is extended further by dialogues relating to community and stakeholder participation, ethics and ethical practices, tourism growth within sustainable practices, and the development of sustainability indictors. Just as tourism is a multifaceted phenomenon, so the discourses have proved about sustainability.

Interpretations of sustainability, however, are not just twentieth-century, developed world–led constructions. Concepts of stewardship of the land, resources, and interconnectivity of all things—that is, sustainable practices—have informed indigenous peoples' ways of life for hundreds of years.

One of the key issues in attempting to achieve a definitive term is the way individuals, collectives, and societies frame and construct reality. As a consequence, definitions are always tentative—the passage of time, changing values and mores, political agendas, social discourses, and interpersonal interactions constantly construct and reconstruct meaning. In turn, meaning making (Dunn 1998; Schwandt 2000) and sense making (Weick 1995) are influenced by everyday lived experiences, and these experiences also shape and reshape meaning making and sense making. In particular,

[w]e continually and actively build and rebuild our worlds not just through language, but through language used in tandem with actions, interactions, non-linguistic symbol systems, objects, tools, technologies, and distinctive ways of thinking, valuing, feeling, and believing. (Gee 1999, p. 11)

Thus, meaning making is in a constant state of flux. No wonder there is no unifying definition of sustainability but a plethora of textual scripts addressing the concept (see again Table 12-1). As Gee (1999) further notes, "language-in-use" is everywhere and always "political" (p. 1). Such a political agenda in relation to sustainability resonates, for example, in the writings of Shumway (1991), Pearce (1992), Butler (1993), Burr (1995), McCool (1995), Mowforth and Munt (1998), Garrod and Fyall (1998), Butler (1999), McCool and Stankey (1999), Sautter and Leisen (1999), Evans (2001), Kousis (2001), McCool and Moisey (2001), and Ioannides (2003). These commentators explicitly address the nature of definitions of sustainability and sustainable tourism as being dependent on who is doing the constructing and interpretation and their vested interests. Moreover, a political agenda is reflected in the past (and at times present) "silencing" of indigenous voices regarding stewardship of the land as a result of Western-centric hegemony of dialogues associated with sustainability and sustainable development.

Table 12-2 illustrates the "language-in-use" concept in relation to sustainable development reflected in discourses resulting from various symposia, conferences, research papers, technical papers, and research. It also implicitly demonstrates the political nature of texts—compare, for example, the definitions presented in Table 12-2.

Table 12-2   Sustainable Development Counterpointed Against Sustainable Tourism, Sport, Leisure, and Recreation Definitions

	Sustainable Development
Definition Source and Date	*Example of a Definition*
World Commission on Environment and Development, the Brundtland Report 1987, p. 43	Sustainable development is "development that meets the needs of the present without compromising the ability of future generations to meet their own needs."

	Sustainable Tourism
Definition Source and Date	*Examples of Some Definitions*
Eber 1992, p. 3	"Tourism and associated infrastructure that, both now and in the future operate within natural capacities for the regeneration and future productivity of natural resources, recognize the contribution that people and communities, customs and lifestyles make to the tourism experience, accept that these people must have an equitable share in the economic benefits of tourism, and are guided by the wishes of local people and communities in the local area."
Butler 1993, p. 29 (Sector-specific orientation)	"[T]ourism which is in a form which can maintain its viability in an area for an indefinite period of time."
Butler 1993, p. 29 (Holistic definition recognizing the multiplicity of interactions related to tourism)	"[T]ourism which is developed and maintained in an area (community, environment) in such a manner and at such a scale that it remains viable over an indefinite period and does not degrade or alter the environment (human and physical) in which it exists to such a degree that it prohibits the successful development and wellbeing of other activities and processes."
World Travel and Tourism Council (WTTC), World Tourism Organization (WTO), and Earth Council (EC) 1995	". . . meets the needs of present tourists and host regions while protecting and enhancing opportunity for the future."
Swarbrooke 1999, p. 241	"[T]ourism which is economically viable but does not destroy the resources on which the future of tourism will depend, notably the physical environment and social fabric of the host community."

Flint and Danner 2001	There are three elements of sustainability: ecological integrity, social equity, and economic vitality.
Global Development Research Centre 2005	"Sustainable tourism in its purest sense, is an industry which attempts to make a low impact on the environment and local culture, while helping to generate income, employment, and the conservation of local ecosystems. It is responsible tourism which is both ecologically and culturally sensitive."
Sustainable Tourism— Cooperative Research Center 2005	"**OUR MISSION** is the development and management of intellectual property (IP) to deliver innovation to business, community and government enhancing the environmental, economic and social sustainability of tourism—one of the world's largest, fastest growing industries."

Sustainable Sport, Leisure, and Recreation

Definition Source and Date	*Examples of Some Definitions*
Sustainable sport (Green and Gold, Inc. 2001)	"Sport is sustainable when it meets the needs of today's sports community while contributing to the improvement of future sports opportunities for all and the integrity of the natural environment on which it depends."
	Principles for sustainable sport include conservation, steward ship, eco-efficiency, partnership, leadership, quality, responsibility/accountability, democratization, investing in the future, equality and access, diversity, active living.
Sustainable leisure (Wigan Council n.d.)	"Sustainable leisure and culture.
	Objective 16.1: To ensure that high quality leisure and cultural activities are available to all and that such activities are managed sustainably."
	"There needs to be a vision, which we can all share, of how we want our Borough to develop in the future. That vision has to be based on the principles of 'sustainable development' namely:
	Making sure that everyone has access to good quality of life
	Raising people's aspirations for themselves, their communities and their world
	Giving people more control over their own lives, and a greater sense of responsibility towards others
	Protecting the long term interests of the environment and society
	Taking account of the links between one course of action and another"
Sustainable recreation (Department of Natural Resources and Environment 2002)	"To achieve Ecological Sustainable Development the natural and cultural values of public land must be conserved to ensure that the benefits of outdoor recreation and nature based tourism areas remain available in the long term." (p. 6)
	"To ensure that quality recreation and tourism opportunities remain available in the future, our public land must be managed wisely by the State's land management agencies in partnership with the recreation and tourism industry and the community." (p. 12)

Given such a background and diversity of literature, the purpose of this introduction to the chapter has not been to determine a singular definition that could be applied to a consideration of the water-based experiences in this book. That would have been an improbable task, and one that would have privileged one stakeholder's definition over another. Therefore, rather than privilege one position, this chapter recognizes the multiplicity of definitions and the socially constructed nature of our discourses, that is, that living language does and should change over time.

So, given the previous discussion, are sustainable water-based tourism experiences attainable? The following two sections, which address first, the advantages and disadvantages of water-based experiences, and second, the impacts of these experiences, will move us to some final reflections on that question. Additionally, those reflections will incorporate contemplation of literature presented in the introduction of this chapter.

Advantages and Disadvantages

Each of the chapters in this book has commented on advantages and disadvantages of different types of water-based experiences. This section presents an overview of those advantages and disadvantages as well as a composite summary of them. This overview and summary are presented in tabular form for easy reference and comparative purposes.

Drawing on the text from Table 12-3, a number of key advantages of water-based experiences are proposed, namely, their ability to:

- Potentially enable participants to access "back areas," wilderness, remote settings, or engage with nature
- Develop a sense of "communitas" with like-minded participants or with family and friends
- Offer participants personal challenges, self-actualization, adventure
- Benefit from regulation in regard to safety and amenity management.

Again drawing on Table 12-3, the following key disadvantages of water-based experiences are tendered. Those disadvantages are connected with:

- Limited resource settings in which to undertake the water-based experiences
- Loss of amenity for residents or other users also associating with water-based settings
- Conflict between multiple users of water-based settings
- Perceptions of over-regulation of water-based experiences
- Limitations on participation based on cost, time, accessibility of sites, or training requirements.

Having addressed the advantages and disadvantages, the next section will focus on various impacts of the water-based experiences discussed in this book.

Impacts

The discussion regarding impacts of water-based experiences will be organized using the following categories: environmental, economic, and socio-cultural. This section will apply a similar style to the preceding section and will utilize tabular

Table 12-3   Advantages and Disadvantages of Water-Based Tourism, Sport, Leisure, and Recreation Experiences

Water-Based Experiences	Advantages	Disadvantages
Sailing (See Chapter 2, Jennings)	Visiting the backs of regions Increased host–guest interaction Taking your home with you Luggage not a problem Accessing own cooking and water facilities diminishes health and hygiene issues Unmediated experiences Own decision making	Change of plans difficult Visiting the edges of destinations Sometimes limited interaction with locals Safety of boat when unattended Cruisers become "gazed upon" "Environmental bubble"/ "comfort capsule" can be broken by visitors and protocols Seasickness Adverse resident reactions— unwelcoming "hosts"
Motorboating (See Chapter 3, Jennings)	Activity suitable for family and friends and individuals Speed of access to sites Improved facilities and site access Rules and regulations to enhance participation behaviors and practices Security from regulatory presence Recreate with similar-minded people Travel to other locations and participate in other water-based experiences	Costs of fuel, storage issues Weather dependency for usage Safety issues and accidents Conflict between users Storage facility access and cost Time involved in traveling from home to storage to site Perception of too much regulation Maintenance costs and time out from boating time to participate Insufficient infrastructure and facility support Congestion and crowding
Motorized water sports (See Chapter 4, Richins)	Economic benefits for local community Adding to leisure base for locals Sense of adventure enjoyment in outdoor water sports Affordability Ease of handling and use, maneuverability Feelings of exhilaration and excitement Element of risk, challenge, and fun	These are primarily associated with the negative impacts associated with environmental degradation, loss of social amenity Refer to impacts section for further details
Surfing and windsurfing (See Chapter 5, Ryan)	Union with nature Less noisy than motorized experiences Less polluting Less intrusive Exhilaration "Flow" experiences	Conflict with other users Conflict with political agendas Political advocacy organizes unorganized "sport"

Continued

229

Table 12-3   Cont'd

Water-Based Experiences	Advantages	Disadvantages
Sport fishing and big game fishing (See Chapter 6, Killion)	Destination development International competitions Establishment of organizations and professionalization contribute to scientific knowledge, certification of captains, and observers, resource management and policy input	Support for one form alienates other forms Seasonality of experiences
Scuba diving, snorkeling, and free diving (See Chapter7, Dimmock)	Scuba: Longer bottom time than snorkeling and free diving Basic skill development Education Snorkeling and free diving: Use less equipment than scuba	Scuba more expensive than snorkeling and free diving Requires training and health checks May have loss of amenity because of crowding
Whitewater rafting (See Chapter 8, Jonas)	Wilderness experience Escape daily routines Challenge, learn new skills People with special needs are accommodated Rafts provide space and potential for more luxury items than kayaking, for example, because of space issues Being with family and friends Meeting new people Developing an adventurer identity	Made to move on if no space available Time for permit access to occur Limited amount of water resources for activity Seasonality influences
Kayaking (See Chapter 9, Hudson and Beedie)	Easy to transport Relatively cheap Being part of nature Individual or group activity Testing oneself on rapids Fitness	Difficult to learn Water quality Limited access points Land ownership and riparian owners Popular sites become congested
One-day boating adventures (See Chapter10, Moscardo)	Tourist enterprises Access that would not otherwise be available Conservation— environmental management charges	Ensuring sustainability Related to negative impacts (see below)
Sail training adventures (See Chapter11, Easthope)	Belonging to a subculture Relaxed evening times Sense of belonging together *Communitas* Travel back in time "Flow" experiences	Seasickness

Source: Chapters 2 to 11.

form to facilitate ease of reference and comparison. This representation, however, is not meant to be a definitive listing of all environmental, economic, and socio-cultural impacts. Rather, it constitutes a synthesis of resonating themes noted in the chapters. There is also some degree of connectivity to the previously identified advantages and disadvantages of water-based experiences. This serves to iterate their influence and scope for multiple interpretations.

Environmental Impacts

In Chapters 2 to 11, environmental impacts were identified and categorized as either positive or negative in nature. These categories are presented in Table 12-4. Readers will note that there is a certain amount of overlap regarding impacts associated with the various water-based experiences.

Accordingly, based on a synthesis of Table 12-4 content, common positive impacts involve educative practices, development of codes of conduct/practice, and management strategies to support sustainable practices. Potential negative impacts include creation of an imbalance in ecosystems, demonstrative physical effects to biodiversity and specific species, changes to water quality, as well as various forms of pollution.

Economic Impacts

Economic impacts of water-based experiences may be classified according to their potential positioning as either positive or negative (see Table 12-5). They are also reported in Chapters 2 to 11 as having a range of impacts, from the local to the international level.

To summarize Table 12-5, some of the common positive economic impacts of water-based experiences are implementation of user pay systems, income and revenue generation, market expansion and diversification, and income and employment multiplier effects. A number of potential negative economic impacts include leakages, small business issues and local disadvantages related to increased prices, and possible seasonality in employment opportunities.

Socio-Cultural Impacts

Socio-cultural impacts arise before, during, and after engagement in water-based experiences for participants, for hosting communities, and vicariously for various stakeholder groups. As with the previous two subsections, the impacts are separated into positive and negative frames (see Table 12-6).

Water-based experiences are associated with a number of positive socio-cultural impacts, and these comprise benefits to self-identity and esteem through the pursuit of fun, adventure, challenge, fulfillment of belonging needs, and membership in a subculture. Some of the negative impacts include onsite issues such as crowding and congestion; loss of amenity; pollution; cultural commodification; demonstration effect; conflicts between stakeholders; and associated management issues such as social and physical carrying capacity, zoning, development, and review of resource management strategies.

Table 12-4 Overview of Various Environmental Impacts of Water-Based Experiences

Water-Based Experiences	Positive Environmental Impacts	Negative Environmental Impacts
Sailing (See Chapter 2, Jennings)	Development of knowledge of sustainable principles Education for sustainability —"leave only footprints" ethos	Anchor damage to "floor/bed" of the water setting Coral damage Marina construction and other water-based infrastructure developments changing ecosystem patterns and systems Waste pollution Marine animal hits
Motorboating (See Chapter 3, Jennings)	Development of knowledge of sustainable principles Education for sustainability See also commentary for Chapter 4 in the next cell	Anchor damage to "floor/bed" of water setting Coral damage Marina construction and other water-based infrastructure developments changing ecosystem patterns and systems Waste pollution Marine animal hits See commentary for Chapter 4 in the next cell
Motorized water sports (See Chapter 4, Richins)	Development of regulations and management practices to ameliorate negative environmental impacts	Physical stress on aquatic organisms Biological effects of pollutants Negative impacts on physical environment
Surfing and windsurfing (See Chapter 5, Ryan)	Water quality advocacy Politicizing environmental issues	Minimal damage: debris from broken boards, foot straps, broken masts, litter from equipment failure May be environmental disturbance related to difficult site access points from land entry—trampling of vegetation, habitat disturbance, possible littering
Sport fishing and big game fishing (See Chapter 6, Killion)	Alleged low impact because of tag-and-release program or tagging	Technology used to participate can cause impacts, for example, pollution Marina, jetty, wharf developments impact on natural ecosystems Waste discharge Anchor practices may cause damage Litter
Scuba diving, snorkeling, and free diving (See Chapter 7, Dimmock)	Training and education practices Codes of conduct Increased preservation values over extractive use	Damage resulting from infrastructure developments, marinas, jetties, pontoons Slow-moving water, buildup of pollutants Propeller action on animals and vegetation Stress on animals Fin and tank damage Anchoring practices damage Holding and standing on coral Stirring up sediment
Whitewater rafting (See Chapter 8, Jonas)	Appreciation of environmental values	Management of campsites—campfires, human waste, rubbish, damage to soils and vegetation, trail building, destruction of prehistoric sites

Kayaking (See Chapter 9, Hudson and Beedie)	Less intrusive activity than a number of other water-based experiences Nonpolluting activity in itself	Concerns regarding access issues and water quality issues
One-day boating adventures (See Chapter 10, Moscardo)	See cell entries for Chapters 3, 4, and 7	See cell entries for Chapters 3, 4, and 7
Sail training adventures (See Chapter 11, Easthope)	Sail training adventures try to minimize environmental impacts due to practices in place during refueling engines and waste water storage	Marina construction and other water-based infrastructure developments changing ecosystem patterns and systems Waste pollution

Source: Chapters 2 to 11.

Table 12-5   Overview of Various Economic Impacts of Water-Based Experiences

Water-Based Experiences	Positive Economic Impacts	Negative Economic Impacts
Sailing (See Chapter 2, Jennings)	User pays—permits and access Significant contribution across a number of sporting fronts: club sailing and racing, independent casual sailing, cruising Increased income generation in host communities Income and employment multiplier effects	Leakages in developing nations due to the nature of sailing technology and its sophistication and resultant sourcing of equipment and materials elsewhere
Motorboating (See Chapter 3, Jennings)	User pays—permits and access fees Significant contribution across a number of fronts: club membership, competitions, motorboating expenditure Increased income generation in host communities Income and employment multiplier effects	Leakage effects from goods, services, and experiences purchased elsewhere
Motorized water sports (See Chapter 4, Richins)	Local and regional benefits for local communities in regard to expenditures, equipment, maintenance, and repair Daily expenditures associated with outings	Leakages

Continued

Table 12-5   Cont'd

Water-Based Experiences	Positive Economic Impacts	Negative Economic Impacts
Surfing and windsurfing (See Chapter 5, Ryan)	Market expansions—extreme sports Clothing and other related sport equipment, franchises	Cost of technology research and development and innovation Competition practices
Sport fishing and big game fishing (See Chapter 6, Killion)	Marine tourism contributes to economies, for example, marine tourism in GBR contributes $1.5 m AUS (US1.13m) to Australian economy	Big game fishing is high cost, leakage is uncertain and not determined Socioeconomic distance emphasized between hosts and guests
Scuba diving, snorkeling, and free diving (See Chapter 7, Dimmock)	Support local communities Develop infrastructure Increase social services Generate foreign exchange Job creation Entry fees—user pays Market competition	Small business issues Price inflation for locals
Whitewater rafting (See Chapter 8, Jonas)	User pays Income and employment generation from tours Income generation from self-organized experiences	Leakages especially from self-organized experiences
Kayaking (See Chapter 9, Hudson and Beedie)	Increased revenue generation from associated media production, books, manuals, videos, guides Industry in its own right with equipment and clothing production associated with the outdoors Employment in construction and maintenance of waterways	Refer to entries for Chapters 5 and 8.
One-day boating adventures (See Chapter 10, Moscardo)	Profitable tourist enterprises Revenue and support for conservation Enhanced economic conditions in the host destination (Cater 2003)	Refer to entries for Chapters 2, 3, 4, 6, and 7.
Sail training adventures (See Chapter 11, Easthope)	Income and revenue generation from reenactment Races as special events can inject revenue into local economies	Possible leakages Employment being short-term

Source: Chapters 2 to 11.

Future Directions

The writers of chapters 2 to 11 proffered a number of reflections in regard to the future of the various water-based experiences presented in this book. These reflections included thoughts about participation numbers, nature of the experience, and management issues. In addition, embedded within their texts were comments on the overall sustainability of each of the water-based experiences. These are summarized and presented here.

In Section I, Chapters 2 and 3, Jennings commented that sailing and motorboating would continue to grow as water-based experiences. This was due in part to technological advances, increased affordability of participation due to diversity in the range of participation choices, increased and improved accessibility for public participation via clubs and sponsorship, school education, and public programs. Continued growth was also linked to societal changes and increased leisure

Table 12-6   Overview of Various Socio-Cultural Impacts of Water-Based Experiences

Water-Based Experiences	Positive Socio-Cultural Impacts	Negative Socio-Cultural Impacts
Sailing (See Chapter 2, Jennings)	Opportunity to increase understanding between peoples Cultural exchanges Opportunity to be with like-minded people, family, and friends Positive feelings about self Opportunities for minority group participation via club, public, and not-for-profit organization programs	Development of social pathologies Cultural commodification Gendered nature of participation and potential for marginalization Overcrowding User conflicts
Motorboating (See Chapter 3, Jennings)	*Communitas* Fulfillment of self	Past gendered nature of participation and potential for marginalization Loss of amenity User conflicts Resident antagonism
Motorized water sports (See Chapter 4, Richins)	Pursuit of fun, adventure, challenge Self-fulfillment	Loss of amenity Noise Crowding Safety issues Conflict among user groups
Surfing and windsurfing (See Chapter 5, Ryan)	Demonstration of a counter-culture Individualism Pursuit of adventure, extreme sport	Spatial conflict and social carrying capacity perceptions, e.g., the Pass at Byron Bay, Australia, is a good place for surfing but also a site for launching dive boats as well as swimming
Sport fishing and big game fishing (See Chapter 6, Killion)	Self-esteem and ego-enhancement	Spatial conflict and user conflict Demonstration effect and social distancing Exacerbation of haves and have nots Souveniring and lack of respect for sacred sites

Continued

Table 12-6   Cont'd

Water-Based Experiences	Positive Socio-Cultural Impacts	Negative Socio-Cultural Impacts
Scuba diving, snorkeling, and free diving (See Chapter 7, Dimmock)	Promotion of in-group values and attitudes regarding ethics and behavior—subcultural values	Demonstration effect—haves and have nots participate in activities Loss of amenity Variations in perceptions of social carrying capacity Crowding Congestion and inconvenience
Whitewater rafting (See Chapter 8, Jonas)	Development of *communitas* Development of subcultural traits Self-fulfillment Fun, adventure, and challenge	Crowding Loss of amenity Perception of mediated authenticity and loss in authenticity values when mediation of experience occurs Souveniring and lack of respect for sacred sites
Kayaking (See Chapter 9, Hudson and Beedie)	Participants usually access wilderness areas so impacts are relatively small for expeditions	Site carrying capacity can be an issue Social carrying capacity issues User conflicts between paddlers and fisherpeople Conflicts with residents, e.g., riparian owners
One-day boating adventures (See Chapter 10, Moscardo)	Quality tourist experiences due to interpretation (Cater 2003)	Resident conflicts Visual pollution (Cater 2003)
Sail training adventures (See Chapter 11, Easthope)	National ownership can elicit nationalism or pride in statehood	Associated reenactment and special events may be insulting to indigenous peoples

Source: Chapters 2 to 11.

options. Additionally, it was recognized that legislation and regulation in relation to safety and security issues and management of amenity have served to increase or maintain participation levels.

To enhance the sustainability of sailing and motorboating, development of multiple use of sites, management plans and international charters, agendas and listings regarding sustainability, as well as education and codes of conduct have been utilized. These are strategies that past practice indicates are useful for consideration or incorporation as future management strategies. However, the future and the sustainability of sailing and motorboating will be influenced by participant behaviors and actions, the consequences of increasing legislation and regulation developed in response to the former, and ongoing monitoring of numbers in relation to physical and social carrying capacity.

In Chapter 4, the first of the four chapters addressing water-based experiences classified as sport and extreme sport, Richins commented on a decline in motorized water sports toward the beginning of the twenty-first century in some nations. However, given the overcoming of challenges in regard to best practice, and the ensuring of participant enjoyment via germane conflict management, participation should continue to remain static if not increase.

Sustainability issues for motorized water sports are strongly related to participant behaviors, codes of conduct, education, and the amelioration of negative environmental impacts. As Holland, Pybas, and Sanders (1992) noted, "Personal watercraft users should be encouraged at the very least to be aware of the fours 'Cs': common sense, courtesy, communication to other users, and conservation of natural resources" (p. 56). This same note may be applied to all the water-based experiences presented in this book.

Ryan, in Chapter 5, situated surfing and windsurfing as being in the mature stages of their experience life cycles, although both are undergoing rejuvenation due to younger people becoming interested. Also contributing to an increase in participation levels are advances in technology that enable aging participants to continue to pursue these water-based experiences. In addition, Ryan highlighted shifts in the nature of gender participation. In particular, women's participation has increased due to commercial sponsorship; the establishment and development of role models; as well as changing social attitudes regarding gender, identity, and ways embodied beings may act and be.

Ironically, as noted in Chapter 5, while surfing and windsurfing are strongly aligned with a quest for freedom, these water-based experiences are becoming bureaucratized as a result of sporting organization and commercial interests. In their endeavors to ensure the sustainability of surfing and windsurfing, participants have become politicized beings and constituted bodies as demonstrated in the case study in Chapter 5. This has served to expand the repertoire of activities associated with surfing and windsurfing and simultaneously runs somewhat counter to the original ethos of freedom and individualism. Moreover, as other water-based experiences multiply and participation numbers increase, conflicts between users for setting access and use will increase, and this may serve to restrict participation numbers for surfing and windsurfing as well as other water-based experiences.

Ryan advocated that, compared to other water-based experiences, surfing and windsurfing tended to involve more sustainable usages of water settings due to the nature of the experiences and minimal equipment requirements. The future, however, is keenly linked to management of user conflicts, water quality issues, and possible changing tastes of participants and potential participants.

In Chapter 6, Killion identified that seasonality was a substantive issue for sport and big game fishing as a water-based experience. However, while it is possible for participants to travel around the world to pursue these experiences, this tends to position sport and big game fishing at the higher, more costly end of the market. Ways to facilitate the sustainability of sport and big game fishing have been achieved via certification as well as development and implementation of ethical practices—codes of conduct by operators and participants alike. Further, the use of catch and release or tagging are important strategies for sustainability as long as everyone embraces these principles, which the case study in Chapter 6 demonstrated does not always occur.

Additionally, to assist with maintaining a future for sport and big game fishing, increasing knowledge, educating participants across sectors, and involving professional bodies should ensure that numbers do not "exceed threshold levels." Further, by managing spaces and user conflicts, the quality of the experiences should also be sustained. In terms of numbers, sport and big game fishing is not anticipated to become a mass market since, as previously mentioned, its high cost limits those who can participate.

Killion indicates that resource management is the key for the future, particularly legislation of tag-and-release practices that are linked to government data collection in order to monitor resource stocks and thereby simultaneously monitor sustainability of sport and big game fishing.

According to Dimmock in Chapter 7, the popularity of scuba diving, snorkeling, and free diving will continue. This is founded on the basis that training and education must continue so that diver skills and knowledge are maintained if not enhanced. This is particularly necessary as the market diversifies further. Accordingly, with greater market diversification, the regular monitoring of dive sites to check impacts must be continued from environmental, social, and economic perspectives. Management of social amenity is also a necessity. Along with future technological development and innovation in these water-based activities, improvements in transportation technology will increase access to scuba, snorkeling, and free diving sites and thereby increase consideration of sustainability issues for all users of routes and related sites.

As with the previously discussed water-based experiences, the future and sustainability of scuba diving, snorkeling, and free diving is strongly related to behaviors, practices, and attitudes; knowledge and education; and management practices.

In Chapter 8, the first of the chapters focusing on adventure in Section III, Jonas proposed that growth in the pursuit of whitewater rafting as a water-based experience is expected to continue. Intertwined with the future of whitewater rafting are participant dispersion issues as well as seasonality issues and site number capping, which tends to relocate pressure to other locations. Regarding the future of whitewater rafting, carrying capacity is a real issue. One way of ameliorating issues associated with increasing participation numbers is to distribute demand beyond usual summer seasons into winter seasons.

Sustainability of whitewater rafting is a concern, given increasing participation numbers, which is compounded by some of the impacts associated with onshore activities, such as damage to cultural heritage sites, souveniring of materials, and maintenance of authenticity—"value for money" and "being scared." Capping usage and controlling numbers via permits is a current strategy; however, this has impacts on the quality of rafters' and potential rafters' experiences. Education, compliance with codes of conduct, and site management are critical.

Similar future and sustainability issues for whitewater rafting resonated in Chapter 9, in which Hudson and Beedie indicated that participation numbers for kayaking would continue to grow. Such growth has also resulted in an increase in commercial enterprises associated with kayaking. Already, sustainability issues are at a critical point, with the key issues being the meeting of increased demand, access to suitable sites, and water quality. Crowding, congestion, and conflict with other users and "owners" of waters are impacting on the nature of the experience and the resource settings in which kayaking is occurring. In response, management strategies are constantly under review. Construction and manufacture of kayaking runs are struggling to meet demand in some locations. However, authenticity of experience is questionable and may diminish satisfaction with overall kayaking experiences since they are occurring in a contrived/human-built setting. This mirrors concerns noted in Chapter 8 concerning whitewater rafting. Additionally, as demand increases and carrying capacities are exceeded, access will continue to have limits set. With restrictions and regulation of site access, participants become increasingly concerned with water quality, and, like surfers and windsurfers, kayakers have also engaged in lobbying and political activities to address sustainability of the water-based experience. Hudson and Beedie indicated, as did Ryan in the case of surfing and windsurfing, that kayaking as a water-based experience is primarily a nonpolluting activity in itself.

The future for kayaking will be partially dependent on suitable balances being established among risk management and control, provision of sites for human challenge, and environmental conservation and appropriate management strategies involving stakeholder participation. Moreover, to ensure a sustainable future, Hudson and Beedie emphasized the need for research to enable informed planning and management of kayaking as a water-based experience.

Moscardo in Chapter 10 considered the present and future of one-day boating adventures by linking to the work of Bergsma (2000). Levels of participation were found to be particularly aligned and responsive to changes in consumers, changes in perceptions regarding the environment, technology changes, and changes in business practices. More broadly, Moscardo stated that the sustainability issues for one-day boating adventures were similar to those for tourism in general. These included strategies to ensure ecological sustainability and address impacts from increasing competition, inclusion of education via interpretive activities as part of overall tourist experiences, and attention to improving strategies for management of waste. Ways forward included resource use plans, monitoring systems, strategic alliances between operators, and better staff training. In addition, the sustainability of tourism and water-based experiences requires that safety and security issues be addressed. Moscardo also indicated a rebalancing of the sustainability focus on the part of businesses, from "impacts of tourism on the environment" to "impact of the environment on tourism."

In the final chapter in Section III, Easthope in Chapter 11 noted that participation levels and interest in sail training adventures have burgeoned. From what was to have been a nostalgic farewell to old sailing ships in the 1950s, a renaissance of interest and revival of historic "tall ships" has occurred into the late twentieth to early twenty-first century. When compared to some other water-based experiences, the participation numbers are not large. However, people from various socioeconomic backgrounds are able to participate, more than in higher-cost activities such as sport and big game fishing.

The future of sail training adventures as a lived experience as opposed to a static and landlocked experience lies in the continued maintenance and support of these vessels. Should governments, benefactors, and public support diminish, funding for some of the vessels would disappear. Further, as a number of vessels and their operations rely on volunteerism, without that support, vessels would fall into disrepair and operations would cease. In addition, maintenance of these vessels tends to be costly, especially when there is a strong degree of authenticity required of ship materials and equipment.

Essentially, the sustainability of sail training adventures is dependent on maintaining a market, government funding, sponsorship, benefactors, and the continued transference of work skills and knowledge sets.

In summary, there are a number of reoccurring themes regarding the future of the various water-based experiences. These are changing social circumstances, technological advancements, user conflicts arising from competition for water resource usage, suites of management strategies, and experience quality. Each of these will now be considered in turn.

Due to changing social circumstances in developed nations, such as improvements in health, sanitation, diet, education, disposable incomes, social justice programs, and support mechanisms, as well as changes in hours of work, hours of leisure time, number of work careers, breaks between careers, and long periods of post-work "retirement" time, the potential for participation levels to increase and for market segments to multiply is highly probable. Additionally, changing attitudes toward gender; age; and physical, mental, and emotional ability levels have afforded many people increased opportunity to become or continue to be water-based experience participants.

Moreover, technological advances have reduced costs for equipment, lengthened the periods of time that people may participate in sports, and increased opportunities for people with special needs to be involved in water-based experiences. These technological advances have both served to ensure the sustainability of water-based experiences and to work against their sustainability. Technologies, for example, have assisted in dealing with waste management as well as creating constructed water resource sites. However, they have also, through increased participation levels, increased the opportunity for pollution and change to ecosystems and biodiversity.

As noted in various chapters, conflict between users is almost a certainty due to resource base sharing, limits to water resource access, differences in attitudes and behaviors between participants in the various water-based experiences, and the nature of those experiences. As Friedmann (1973) notes, action requires individuals to operate collectively. To reduce user conflicts as well as to contribute to the sustainability of the water-based experiences, collective action is therefore required. Education and codes of conduct, ethics, and behavior come some way to address these conflicts; however, if these methods do not work, more formal management practices and strategies would be required.

An array of management strategies is available to water resource managers, planners, and stakeholders: resource inventories, tourism and recreational opportunity spectra, zoning maps, management plans, public participation, permits, codes of practice, education, the precautionary principle, research, and enforcement (Jennings 2002). Each of these strategies is considered briefly in turn before considering aspects of quality related to water-based experiences.

Resource inventories list assets based on their historical, cultural, natural, and/or aesthetic value and are used to develop management plans, as well as to assist with long-term monitoring of usage impacts. In addition, tourism opportunity spectra (TOS) (Butler and Waldbrook 1991) and recreational opportunity spectra (ROS) (Stankey and Wood 1982) are management tools that provide for a variety of tourism and recreation experiences across resource settings ranging from urban-based to wilderness (Driver 1989, cited in Watson 1989). One application of these tools has been developed to consider an indigenous people's cultural opportunity spectrum for tourism (IPCOST) (Sofield and Birtles 1996). The intent of resource inventories is to assist with auditing, monitoring, and planning.

There are a number of types of plans, such as zoning and management. Zoning plans specify an activity or range of activities appropriate for various locations within sections that have been classified in a resource setting. Usage usually ranges from general use where most activities are allowed, to non-use areas classified as preservation zones. Zoning attempts to keep apart conflicting use and activities while also protecting environmental quality of settings. Other zoning strategies are discussed by Meganck (1991) and Stewart (1993). After zoning plans are prepared for a section, management plans are devised for various areas within each of the sections. Zoning plans tend to organize users and activities on a macro scale, while management plans organize them on a micro scale. Additionally, representative and site-specific area plans may also be utilized to manage activities and resources.

Aligned with zoning and management plan development is public participation. This involves various stakeholders in determination of management practices. However, there are differing types of participation used in resource and activity planning, ranging from lip service to full participatory involvement in decision making. See, for example, Arnstein (1969) as well as Krumpe and McCool (1997) and McCool, Guthrie, and Kapler-Smith (2000) for discussions regarding consensus building.

Another management strategy is associated with permits. Permits regulate the type and number of users in specific areas as well as the period of time (see Claridge 1994). The permit system is a tool that is used to respond to carrying capacity issues as well as monitor and manage impacts. Stankey and McCool (1984) suggest that carrying capacity triggers the question, "How many is too many?" However, there are critiques of carrying capacity—refer to discussions by Lindberg, McCool, and Stankey (1997); Butler (1996); and Getz (1982). As would be expected, the issuing of permits is also linked to management plans where those plans specify the number of permitted users at or visitors to a specific site (Alder 1993).

Other means to minimize user conflict and environmental damage are previously mentioned best practice codes, which identify experience and operation protocols for participants and providers. Essentially, codes serve to raise users' awareness, educate users, and complement other sustainable management practices (Mason 1996) and are linked to voluntary compliance. Relatedly, and also mentioned earlier as a management strategy, education is used by resource managers to facilitate ecologically sustainable practices by increasing the knowledge and awareness of user groups and individual users.

Science, both the presence and the lack of it, informs management practices. The use of science can be associated with ongoing monitoring and evaluation. When there is little or no research, the precautionary principle may be applied in which conservative and precautionary strategies and management practices are put into play until relevant scientific data is available. Research enables resource managers to determine the status of resources, effects of usage, and quality of management practices. Additionally, in association with the previous examples, legal measures can be applied to ensure conformity with regulations and guidelines. Nonconformity may result in fines, equipment confiscation, or imprisonment.

The final theme to be considered is "experience quality" or quality of water-based experiences. Throughout *Water-Based Tourism, Sport, Leisure, and Recreation Experiences*, quality has been a consistently used term. Chapter 2 commented on "quality of experiences" relating to sailing. Chapter 3 mentioned the "quality and nature of facilities," "quality of participants," "perception of quality of experience," "quality of boating experience," and the fact that quality relates to price in regard to motorboating. In Chapter 4, one of the motorized sports' case studies discussed river setting quality and water quality. In Chapter 5, quality control of boards was discussed, as well as quality of the environment and water quality. Chapter 6 emphasized the nature of experience as well as particular experiences connected to sport and big game fishing, with implicit connections to quality.

Quality was an important issue in Chapter 7 for scuba diving, snorkeling, and free diving. Statements were made about the quality of dive and snorkel opportunities, diving conditions, diver experience, marine environments, and sites. In addition, references were made to "environmental and ecological quality," "high-quality marine biodiversity," the need to "rehabilitate to improve quality," and "quality experience." For Chapter 8, quality was associated with "quality time with family and friends" and the "quality of recreation experiences." Similarly to Chapter 7, Chapter 9 spoke of "high service quality," "quality operator," and "water quality." Chapter 10 imported quality on one-day boating adventures with "quality of life," "quality of tour guide interpretation," "perceived quality of reef environment," "quality tourist experiences," "quality visitor experiences," and "water quality." Chapter 11, like Chapter 6, commented on "life experience" and "nature of experience," with implicit connections to quality of experience. Obviously, then, from an industry perspective, quality and nature of experience are significant elements of water-based experiences that warrant further consideration if not research.

Furthermore, regarding quality and nature of experiences for participants, a comment previously made by Lipscombe (1996) in the context of adventure tourists is germane for industry providers. It is paraphrased and expanded upon here. Participants in water-based experiences:

- Are sophisticated (see Weiler and Hall 1992)
- Demand choice due to diverse lifestyle needs (see Martin and Mason 1987)
- Quest for novel experiences that incorporate varying perceptions of "adventure" (see Fay, McCure, and Begin 1987).

In addition, participants:

- Prefer experiences with customer tailoring (see Schwaninger 1987)
- Expect value for money (Lipscombe 1996).

Additionally, as indicated in this book and elsewhere by Berno, Moore, Simmons, and Hart (1996), water-based experiences are not the purview of youth only. Internationally, the baby boomers are potential participants of water-based experiences if they are not already participants.

Thus, issues and areas for research for industry providers are associated with provision of choice through multiplicity and flexibility in products; customization of experiences; inclusion of learning components; competency of operators, guides, leaders, and participants; as well as issues associated with legal responsibilities and safety issues (Jennings 2002).

The nature of quality, then, is inherently linked to management practices. These in turn can be affected by conflicting usage of water resources resulting from increasing participation levels due to technological advances and changing socio-cultural circumstances, attitudes, and processes.

The introduction to this chapter indicated that further reflection on the literature would occur. Although no one definition or concept of sustainability has been promulgated, the inferred application is comparable to the Brundtland Report definition, that is, being able to "meet . . . the needs of the present without compromising the ability of future generations to meet their own needs." Table 12-1 provided a thematic overview of discourses related to sustainability. The chapter in its structure and content has engaged in questioning sustainability of water-based experiences. It has iterated that sustainability and quality are constructed and reconstructed, interpreted and reinterpreted; that community and stakeholder involvement is vital; and that ethical standards of practice and codes of conduct are necessary, as is a consideration of growth in water-based experiences and concomitant sustainability issues for the present and the future. To return to the focus of this section, future directions for water-based experiences, a concluding commentary follows.

The future and sustainability of sailing; motorboating; motorized sports; surfing and windsurfing; sport and big game fishing; scuba diving, snorkeling, and free diving; whitewater rafting; kayaking; one-day boating adventures; and sail training adventures are a continuous socio-cultural, economic, environmental, and political negotiation. Their futures are reliant on and responsive to the attitudes, values, and behaviors of the participants, providers, hosting communities, and various levels of governments and their departments in addition to a diversity of other stakeholders at any particular time. Continuous dialogue and engagement of wide stakeholder representation in planning, decision making, and education are critical for the future of these water-based experiences. Beyond these human actions, to ensure futures and sustainability, are acts of nature and environmental change. These acts are able to immediately and dramatically influence the short-, medium-, and long-term future and sustainability of these water-based experiences. Such dialogue will also need to address related issues of climate change and peak oil issues. The changes, however, may be more subtle and take longer in presenting their influence. While humans may have no control over some of these acts and changes, preparedness for informed decision making related to a suite of responsive strategies and actions is necessary. Ways to achieve that are numerous in the related literature (see, for example, Fink 1986; Roberts 1994; Pizam and Mansfield 1996; World Tourism Organization 1999; Faulkner 2001; Bierman 2003; Glaesser 2003; Ritchie 2004; and Tarlow 2005).

Finally, the future of water-based experiences is linked to the quality of the resource settings, providers, facilities, infrastructure, and equipment, along with host communities, and the behavior of self as well as others. The determination of quality is also founded on the overall quality of the water-based experiences as interpreted and perceived by the various participants and stakeholder groups. Ultimately, the future, sustainability, and quality of water-based tourism, sport, leisure, and recreation experiences are dependent on the actions of individuals, both singly and collectively, irrespective of stakeholder representation or affiliation.

References

Alder, J. (1993). Permits, an evolving tool for day-to-day management of the Carins Section of the Great Barrier Reef Marine Park. *Coastal Management.* **21**, 25–36.

Arnstein, S.R. (1969). A ladder of citizen participation. *Journal of the American Institute of Planners*, **35**, 216–224.

Barbier, E.B. (1987). The concept of sustainable economic development. *Environmental Conservation*, **14** (2), 101–110.

Bergsma, M. (2000). The future of tourism and hospitality. *Tourism and Hospitality Research*, **2** (1), 76–79.

Berke, P.R., and M.M. Conroy. (2000). Are we planning for sustainable development: an evaluation of 30 comprehensive plans. *Journal of the American Planning Association*, **66** (1), 21–33.

Berno, T., Moore, K., Simmons, D., and V. Hart. (1996, June). The nature of the adventure tourism experience in Queenstown, New Zealand. *Australian Leisure*, **7** (2), 21– 25.

Bierman, D. (2003). *Restoring tourism destinations in crisis*. Crows Nest, Australia: Allen and Unwin.

Bossel, H. (1999). *Indicators for sustainable development: theory, method, applications*. Winnipeg, Manitoba, Canada: International Institute for Sustainable Development.

Bramwell, B., and B. Lane. (1993). Sustainable tourism: an evolving global approach. *Journal of Sustainable Tourism*, **1**, 1–5.

Bramwell, B., and A. Sharam. (1999). Collaboration in local tourism policymaking. *Annals of Tourism Research*, **26** (2), 392–415.

Bricker, K., and D. Kerstetter. (2005). Saravanua ni vanua: exploring sense of place in rural highlands of Fiji. In G. Jennings and N. Nickerson (Eds.), *Quality tourism experiences*. (pp. 99–111). Burlington, MA: Elsevier.

Briguglio, L., Archer, B., Jafari, J., and G. Wall. (Eds.). (1996). *Sustainable tourism in islands and island states—issues and policies*. London: Pinter.

Budowski, G. (1976). Tourism and environmental conservation: conflict, coexistence, or symbiosis? *Environmental Conservation*, **3** (1), 27–31.

Buhalis, D., and D. Diamantis. (2001). Tourism development and sustainability in the Greek Archipelagos. In D. Ioannides, Y. Apostolopoulos, and S. Sonmez (Eds.), *Mediterranean islands and sustainable tourism development*. London: Cassell.

Burns, P. (1999). Paradoxes in planning: tourism elitism or brutalism? *Annals of Tourism Research*, **26** (2), 329–348.

Burr, S.W. (1995). What research says about sustainable tourism development. *Parks and Recreation*, **30** (9), 12–14, 21–26.

Butler, R.W. (1980). The concept of a tourist area cycle of evolution: implications for management of resources. *Canadian Geographer,* **29,** 5–12.

Butler, R.W. (1991). Tourism, environment, and sustainable development. *Environmental Conservation,* **18** (3), 201–207.

Butler, R.W. (1993). Tourism—an evolutionary perspective. In *Tourism and sustainable development: monitoring, planning, managing*. (Department of Geography Publications Series number 37). Waterloo, Ontario, Canada: University of Waterloo, pp. 27–44.

Butler, R.W. (1996). The concept of carrying capacity for tourist destinations: dead or merely buried? *Progress in Tourism and Hospitality Research,* **2**, 283–292.

Butler, R.W. (1997). Modeling tourism development: evolution, growth, and decline. In S. Wahab and J. J. Pigram (Eds.), *Tourism development and growth: the challenge of sustainability*. (pp. 109–125). New York: Routledge.

Butler, R.W. (1999). Sustainable tourism: a state of the art review. *Tourism Geographies*, **1** (1), 7–25.

Butler, R.W., and L.A. Waldbrook. (1991, May). A new planning tool: the Tourism Opportunity Spectrum. *Journal of Tourism Studies,* **2**(1), 2–14.

Caalders, J. (1997). Managing the transition from agriculture to tourism: analysis of tourism networks in Auvergne. *Managing Leisure*, **2**, 127–142.

Campbell, S. (1996). Green cities, growing cities, just cities? Urban planning and the contradictions of sustainable development. *Journal of the American Planning Association*, **62** (3), 296–312.

Cater, E. (2003). Between the devil and the deep blue sea: dilemmas for marine ecotourism. In B. Garrod and J.C. Wilson (Eds.), *Marine ecotourism: issues and experiences*. (pp. 37–47). Clevedon, UK: Channel View Publications.

Cater, E., and B. Goodall. (1992). Must tourism destroy its resource base? In A.M. Mannion and S. R. Bowlby (Eds.), *Environmental issues in the 1990s* (pp. 309–323). Chichester, UK: Wiley.

Cater, E., and G. Lowman. (Eds.). (1994). *Ecotourism: a sustainable option?* Chichester, UK: Wiley.

Christaller, W. (1963). Some considerations of tourism location in Europe. *Paper of the Regional Science Association*, **12**, 95–105.

Claridge, G. (1994). *Managing roving tourist program operations, a review of approaches in the Great Barrier Reef Marine Park*, October 1994, Townsville: Great Barrier Reef Marine Park Authority.

Clarke, J. (1997). A framework of approaches to sustainable tourism. *Journal of Sustainable Tourism*, **5**, 224–243.

Coccossis, H. (1996). Tourism and sustainability: perspective and implications. In G.K. Priestley, J.A Edwards, and H. Coccossis (Eds.), *Sustainable tourism? European Experiences*. (p. 21). Wallingford, Oxon, UK: CABI.

Coccossis, H., and P. Nijkamp. (Eds.). (1995). *Sustainable tourism development*. Aldershot, Hampshire, UK: Ashgate.

Cooper, C. (1997). The contribution of life cycle analysis and strategic planning to sustainable tourism. In S. Wahab and J. J. Pigram. (Eds.), *Tourism development and growth: the challenge of sustainability*. (pp. 78–94). London: Routledge.

Cooper, C., and S. Jackson. (1989). Destination life cycle: the Isle of Man case study. *Annals of Tourism Research*, **16** (3) 377–98.

Court, T. (1990). *Beyond Brundtland: green development in the 1990s*. London: Zed Books.

D'Amore, L.J. (1992). Promoting sustainable tourism—the Canadian approach. *Tourism Management*, **13** (3), 12–18.

Debbage, K.G. (1990). Oligopoly and the resort cycle in the Bahamas. *Annals of Tourism Resarch*, **17**, 513–527.

De Kadt. E. (1992). Making the alternative sustainable: lessons from development for tourism. In V. Smith and W. R. Eadington (Eds.), *Tourism alternatives: potentials and problems in the development of tourism*. (pp. 47–75). Philadelphia: University of Pennsylvania Press.

Department of Natural Resources and Environment. (2002). *Sustainable recreation and tourism on Victoria's public lands*. Melbourne, Australia: State Government of Victoria, Department of Natural Resources and Environment.

Dovers, S.R., Norton, T.W, and J.W. Handmer. (1996). Uncertainty, ecology, sustainability, and policy. *Biodiversity and Conservation*, **5**, 1143–1167.

Dunn, D.R. (1998). *Home truths from aboard: Television representations of the tourist destination*. Unpublished thesis, University of Birmingham, England.

Eber, S. (Ed.). (1992). Beyond the green horizon. Principles of sustainable tourism: a discussion paper. London: World Tourism Concern and Wide Fund for Nature.

Edington, J.M., and M.A. Edington. (1986). *Ecology, recreation, and tourism*. Cambridge, UK: Cambridge University Press.

Ewert, A., and J. Shultis. (1997). Resource-based tourism: an emerging trend in tourism experiences. *Parks and Recreation*, **32** (9), 94–105.

Farrell, B.H., and D. Runyan. (1991). Ecology and tourism. *Annals of Tourism Research*, **18**, 26–40.

Faulkner, B. (2001). Towards a framework for tourism disaster management. *Tourism Management*, **22** (2), 135–147.

Fay C.H., McCure, J.T., and J.P. Begin. (1987). The setting for continuing and education in the year 2000. *New Directions for Continuing Education,* **36** (Winter), 15–27.

Fennell, D.A., and D.C. Malloy. (1995). Ethics and ecotourism: a comprehensive ethical model. *Journal of Applied Recreation Research,* **20** (3), 163–183.

Fink, S. (1986). *Crisis management: Planning for the inevitable.* New York: American Association of Management.

Flint, W.R. and M.J.E. Danner. (2001). The nexus of sustainability and social equity: Virginia's Eastern shore (USA) as a local example of global issues. *International Journal of Economic Development,* **3** (2), 1–30.

Font, X., and J. Tribe. (Eds.). (2000). *Forest tourism and recreation: case studies in environmental management.* Wallingford, Oxon, UK: CAB International.

France, L. (Ed.). (1997). *The earthscan reader in sustainable tourism.* London: Earthscan Publications.

Friedmann, J. (1973). *Retracking America.* Garden City, NY: Anchor Press/Doubleday.

Gale, R.P., and S.M. Corday. (1994). Making sense of sustainability: nine answers to "what should be sustained?" *Rural Sociology,* **59,** 314–332.

Garrod, B., and A. Fyall. (1998). Beyond the rhetoric of sustainable tourism? *Tourism Management,* **19** (3), 199–212.

Gartner, W. (1997). Image and sustainable tourism systems. In S. Wahab and J.J. Pigram (Eds.), *Tourism development and growth: the challenge of sustainability.* (pp. 179–196). London: Routledge.

Gee, J. P. (1999). *An introduction to discourse analysis: theory and method.* London: Routledge.

Getz, D. (1982). A rationale and methodology for assessing capacity to absorb tourism. *Ontario Geography,* **19,** 92–102.

Glaesser, D. (2003). *Crisis management in the tourism industry.* London: Butterworth-Heinemann.

Global Development Research Center. (2005). Sustainable tourism. Accessed December 24, 2005, from http://www.gdrc.org/uem/eco-tour/eco-tour.html

Gormsen, E. (1981). The spatio-temporal development of international tourism: attempt at center periphery model. *La Consommation D'Espace par le Tourisme et sa Preservation.* Aix-en-Provence, France: Centres des Hautes Etudes to Tourisme.

Goulet, D. (1995). Authentic development: is it sustainable? In T.C. Trzyna. (Ed.), *A sustainable world: defining and measuring sustainable development.* (pp. 45–59). Sacramento, CA: International Center for the Environment and Public Policy.

Green and Gold, Inc. (2001). *Defining the principles of sustainable sport.* Accessed January 27, 2006, from http://www.greengold.on.ca/issues/index.html

Gunn, C.A. (1994). *Tourism planning.* New York: Taylor and Francis.

Hall, C.M. (1999). Rethinking collaboration and partnership: a public policy perspective. *Journal of Sustainable Tourism,* **7,** 274–289.

Hall, C.M., and A.A. Lew. (Eds.). (1998). *Sustainable tourism: a geographical perspective.* Harlow, Essex, UK: Addison-Wesley Longman.

Hamdi, H. (1995, July). "Take the plunge!" *PATA Travel News*: Asia/Pacific edition, pp. 6–8.

Holland, S., Pybas, D., and A. Sanders. (1992, November). Personal watercrafts: fun, speed—and conflict. *Parks and Recreation,* pp. 52–56.

Honey, M. (1999). *Ecotourism and sustainable development: Who owns paradise?* Washington, DC: Island Press.

Hughes, G. (1995). The cultural construction of sustainable tourism. *Tourism Management,* **16** (1), 49–59.

Hultsman, J. (1995). Just tourism: an ethical framework. *Annals of Tourism Research,* **22** (3), 553–567.

Hunter, C. (1995). On the need to re-conceptualize sustainable tourism development. *Journal of Sustainable Tourism,* **3,** 155–165.

Hunter, C. (1997). Sustainable tourism as an adaptive paradigm. *Annals of Tourism Research,* **24** (2), 850–867.

Hunter, C., and H. Green. (1995). *Tourism and the environment. A sustainable relationship?* London: Routledge.

Innskeep, E. (1991). *Tourism planning: an integrated and sustainable development approach.* London: Routledge.

International Institute for Sustainable Development. (1997). *Bellagio principles.* Available online at http: www.iisd1.iisd.ca/measure/compindex.asp

International Union for the Conservation of Nature and Natural Resources, the World Wildlife Fund, and the United Nations Environment Program. (1980). *World conservation strategy for sustainability.* Gland, Switzerland: IUCN.

International Union for the Conservation of Nature and Natural Resources, the World Wildlife Fund, and the United Nations Environment Program. (1990). *Caring for the world: a strategy for sustainability.* (2nd draft). Gland, Switzerland: IUCN.

Ioannides, D. (2003). Economics of tourism in host communities. In S. Singh, D.J. Timothy, and R.K. Dowling (Eds.), *Tourism in destination communities.* (pp. 37–54). Wallingford, Oxon, UK: CABI.

Jennings, G.R. (2002). Marine tourism. In S. Hudson (Ed.), *Sport and adventure tourism.* Binghamton, NY: Haworth Press.

Kousis, M. (2001). Tourism and the environment in Corsica, Sardinia, Sicily, and Crete. In D. Ioannides, Y. Apostolopoulos, and S. Sonmez (Eds.). *Mediterranean islands and sustainable tourism development.* London: Cassell.

Krumpe, E., and S.F. McCool. (1997). Role of public involvement in the Limits of Acceptable Change wilderness planning system. In S.F. McCool and D.N. Cole (Eds.), *Limits of Acceptable Change and related planning processes: progress and future directions.* (pp. 16–20). Missoula, MT: USDA Forest Service, Intermountain Research Station.

Lindberg, K., McCool, S.F., and G. Stankey. (1997). Rethinking carrying capacity. *Annals of Tourism Research,* **24** (2), 461–464.

Lipscombe, N. (1996, September). The aged and adventure: a perfect match. *Australian Leisure,* **7** (3), 38–41.

MacGregor, J.R. (1993). Sustainable tourism development. In M.A. Khan, M.D. Olsen, and T. Var (Eds.), *Encyclopedia of hospitality and tourism.* (pp. 781–789). New York: Van Nostrand Reinhold.

Manning, E. (1996, Spring). Tourism: where are the limits? *Ecodecision,* 35–39.

Marien, C., and A. Pizam. (1997). Implementing sustainable tourism development through citizen participation planning process. In S. Wabab and J.J. Pigram (Eds.), *Tourism development and growth: the challenges of sustainability.* (pp. 164–178). London: Routledge.

Martin, W.H., and S. Mason. (1987). Social trends and tourism futures. *Tourism Managment,* **8** (2), 112–114.

Mason, P. (1996). Codes of conduct in tourism. *Progress in Hospitality Research,* **2:** 151–167.

McCool, S.F. (1995). Linking tourism, the environment, and concepts of sustainability: setting the stage. In S. F. McCool and A. E. Watson (Eds.), *Linking tourism, the environment, and sustainability.* (General Technical Report INT-GTR-323). Ogden, UT: U.S. Department of Agriculture and Forest Service, Intermountain Research Station.

McCool, S.F., Guthrie, K. and J. Kapler-Smith. (2000). *Building consensus: Legitimate hope or seductive paradox?* Ft. Collins, CO: U.S. Department of Agriculture and Forest Service, Rocky Mountain Research Station.

McCool, S.F. and R.N. Moisey. (2001). Introduction: pathways and pitfalls in the search for sustainable tourism. In S.F. McCool and R.N. Moisey (Eds.), *Tourism, recreation and sustainability: linking culture and the environment.* Wallingford, Oxon, UK: CABI.

McCool, S.F., Moisey, R.N., and N. Nickerson. (2001). What should tourism sustain? Industry perceptions of useful indicators. *Journal of Travel Research,* **40** (4), 124–131.

McCool, S.F., and G.H. Stankey. (1999). *Searching for meaning and purpose in the quest for sustainability.* Missoula, MT: School of Forestry.

McCool, S.F., and A.E. Watson. (Eds.). (1995). *Linking tourism, the environment, and sustainability.* (General Technical Report INT-GTR-323). Ogden, UT: U.S. Department of Agriculture and Forest Service, Intermountain Research Station.

McLaren, D. (1997). *Rethinking tourism and ecotravel: the paving of paradise and what you can do to stop it.* West Hartford, CT: Kumerian Press.

Meadows, D., and D. Meadows. (1972). *Limits to growth.* New York: Universe Books.

Meganck, R. (1991). Coastal parks as development catalysts: a Caribbean example. *Ocean and Shoreline Management,* **15,** 25–36.

Middleton, V.T.C. (1998). *Sustainable tourism: a marketing perspective.* Oxford, UK: Butterworth-Heinemann.

Mieczkowski, Z. (1995). *Environmental issues of tourism and recreation.* Lanham, MD: University Press of America.

Miossec, J.M. (1977). Un modèle de l'éspace touristique. *L'Espace Géographique,* **6** (1), 41–48.

Moldan, B., Billharz, S., and R. Matravers. (Eds.). (1997). *SCOPE 58 Sustainability indicators: a report on the project on indicators of sustainable development.* Chichester, UK: Wiley.

Mowforth, M., and I. Munt. (1998). *Tourism and sustainability: new tourism in the Third World.* London: Routledge.

Murphy, P.E. (1994). Tourism and sustainable development. In W. Theobald (Ed.), *Global tourism: the next decade.* (pp. 274–290). Oxford, UK: Butterworth-Heinemann.

Nelson, J.G., Butler, R., and G. Wall. (1993). *Tourism and sustainable development: monitoring, planning, managing.* Waterloo, Ontario, Canada: University of Waterloo.

Orams, M.B. (1995). Towards a more desirable form of ecotourism. *Tourism Management,* **16** (1), 3–8.

Payne, R.J., Twynam, G.D., and M.E. Johnston. (1999). Tourism and sustainability in Northern Ontario. In J.G. Nelson, R. Butler, and G. Wall (Eds.), *Tourism and sustainable development: monitoring, planning, managing, decision making: a civic approach.* (pp. 237–266). Waterloo, Ontario, Canada: University of Waterloo, Department of Geography.

Pearce, D.G. (1992). Alterative tourism: concepts, classifications, and questions. In V. L. Smith and W. R. Eadington (Eds.), *Tourism alternatives: potentials and problems in the development of tourism.* Chichester, UK: Wiley.

Pearce, P.L., Moscardo, G., and G.F. Ross. (1996). *Tourism community relationships*. Oxford, UK: Pergamon Press.

Pigram, J.J. (2000). Tourism and sustainability: a positive trend. In Gartner, W. C., and D. W. Lime (Eds.), *Trends in outdoor recreation, leisure and tourism*. (pp. 373–382). Wallingford, Oxon, UK: CABI.

Pizam, A., and Y. Mansfield. (Eds.). (1996). *Tourism, crime, and international security issues*. New York: Wiley.

Plog, S.C. (1974). Why destination areas rise and fall in popularity. *Cornell Hotel and Restaurant Administration Quarterly*, **14**, 55–58.

Potts, T.D., and R. Harrill. (1997). In search of a travel ecology paradigm. *The evolution of tourism: adapting to change*. Proceedings of the 28th Annual Travel and Tourism Research Association Conference, Norfolk, VA, pp. 186–208.

Priestley, G.K., Edwards, J. A. and H. Coccossis. (Eds.). (1996). *Sustainable tourism? European experiences*. Wallingford, Oxon, UK: CAB International.

Redclift, M. (1987). *Sustainable development: exploring contradictions*. London: Routledge.

Ritchie, B.W. (2004). Chaos, crises, and disasters: a strategic approach to crisis management in the tourism industry. *Tourism Management*, **25**, 669–683.

Ritchie, J.R.B. (1999). Interest-based formulation of tourism policy for environmentally sensitive destinations. *Journal of Sustainable Tourism*, **7**, 206–239.

Roberts, V. (1994) Flood management: Bradford paper. *Disaster Prevention and Management*, **3** (3), 44–60.

Robinson, M. (1999). Collaboration and cultural consent: refocusing sustainable tourism. *Journal of Sustainable Tourism*, **7**, 379–397.

Rothman, H.K. (1998). *Devil's bargains: tourism in the twentieth century American West*. Lawrence: University Press of Kansas.

Sautter, E.T., and B. Leisen. (1999). Managing stakeholders: a tourism planning model. *Annals of Tourism Research*, **26** (2), 312–328.

Schwandt, T.A. (2000). Three epistemological stances for qualitative inquiry: Interpretivism, hermeneutics, and social constructionism. In N. K. Denzin and Y. S. Lincoln (Eds.), *Handbook of Qualitative Research*. (2nd ed., pp. 189–213). Thousand Oaks, CA: Sage.

Schwaninger, M. (1989). Trends in leisure and tourism for 2000–2010. Scenario with consequences for planners. In S.F. Witt and L. Moutinho (Eds.), *Tourism marketing and management handbook*. New York: Prentice Hall.

Shamai, S. (1991). Sense of place: an empirical measurement. *Geoforum,* **22** (3), 347–358.

Shearman, R. (1990). The meaning and ethics of sustainability. *Management*, **14** (1), 1–8.

Shindler, B., and J. Neburka. (1997). Public participation in forest planning—8 attributes of success. *Journal of Forestry*, **95**, 17–19.

Shumway, N. (1991). *The invention of Argentina*. Berkeley: University of California Press.

Slater, R.W. (1991). Understanding the relationship between tourism, environment, and sustainable development. In L. J. Reid (Ed.), *Tourism—environment—sustainable development: an agenda for research*. (pp. 10–13). Proceedings of the Travel and Tourism Research Association, Quebec, Canada.

Sofield, T.H.B., and R.A. Birtles. (1996). Indigenous peoples' cultural opportunity spectrum for tourism (IPCOST). In R. Butler and T. Hinch (Eds.), *Tourism and indigenous peoples*. (pp. 396–433). London: International Thomson Business Press.

Stabler, M.J. (Ed.). (1997). *Tourism and sustainability: from principles to practice.* Wallingford, Oxon, UK: CABI.

Stankey, G.H., and S.F. McCool. (1984). Carrying capacity in recreational settings: evolution, appraisal, and application. *Leisure Sciences,* **6**, 453–473.

Stansfield, C. (1996). Reservations and gambling: Native Americans and the diffusion of gaming. In D. Butler and T. D. Hinch (Eds.), *Tourism and indigenous peoples.* London: International Thomson Business Press.

Stewart, M.C. (1993). Sustainable tourism development and marine conservation regimes. *Ocean and Coastal Management,* **20**, 201–217.

Stokowski, P.A. (1991). *"Sense of place" as a social construct.* Paper presented at the 1991 National Recreation and Parks Association Research Symposium, Baltimore, MD.

Sustainable Tourism, Cooperative Research Center. (2005). *About STCRC.* Accessed December 23, 2005, from http://www.crctourism.com.au/page.aspx?page_id=42

Swarbrooke, J. (1999). *Sustainable tourism management.* Wallingford, Oxon, UK: CABI.

Tarlow, P. (2005, Fall). The second battle for New Orleans. *TTR Association News,* pp. 3 and 11.

Timothy, D.J. (1999). Participatory planning: a view of tourism in Indonesia. *Annals of Tourism Research,* **26** (2), 371–391.

Twining-Ward, L. (1999). Towards sustainable tourism development: observations from a distance. *Tourism Management,* **20**, 187–188.

United Nations Department of Economic and Social Affairs. (2002). *Johannesburg Summit 2002.* New York: United Nations Department of Economic and Social Affairs.

United Nations Development Program. (1992, June 3–14). *Report of the United Nations Conference on Environment and Development,* Rio de Janeiro.

Van den Bergh, J., and J. Van der Straaten. (1994). *Towards sustainable development: concepts, methods, and policy.* Washington, DC: Island Press.

Wahab, S., and J.J. Pigram. (Eds.). (1997). *Tourism development and growth: the challenge of sustainability.* London: Routledge.

Wall, G. (1997a). Is ecotourism sustainable? *Environmental Management,* 21, 483–491.

Wall, G. (1997b). Sustainable development—unsustainable development. In S. Wahab and J.J. Pigram (Eds.), *Tourism development and growth: the challenge of sustainability.* (pp. 33–49). London: Routledge.

Walsh, J.A., and B. E. Matthews. (1995). The interplay between ethics and sustainable rural tourism. *Proceedings of the 1995 Northeastern Recreation Research Symposium,* State Parks Management and Research Institute, Saratoga Springs, NY, pp. 125–130.

Watson, M. (1989). *Recreational planning: a seminar and discussion of the ROS and LAC models.* A report submitted to the Great Barrier Reef Marine Park Authority. Townsville, Queensland, Australia: Great Barrier Reef Marine Park Authority.

Weick, K.E. (1995). *Sensemaking in organizations.* Thousand Oaks, CA: Sage.

Weiler, B., and C.M. Hall. (1992). *Special interest tourism.* London: Belhaven.

Wigan Council. (n.d.) *The Agenda 21 Plan for the Metropolitan Borough of Wigan, Executive Summary.* Wigan, UK: Wigan Council.

Wilks, J. and T. Atherton. (1994). Health and safety in Australian marine tourism: a social, medical, and legal appraisal. *Journal of Tourism Studies,* **5** (2), 2–16.

World Commission on Environment and Development. (1987). *Our common future.* Oxford, UK: Oxford University Press.

World Conference on Sustainable Tourism. (1995, April). *Charter for sustainable tourism*. Lanzarote, Canary Islands, Spain. Available online at http://www.insula.org/carturi.pdf

World Tourism Organization. (1999). *Handbook of Disaster Reduction in Tourism Areas*. Geneva, Switzerland: World Tourism Organization.

World Travel and Tourism Council, World Tourism Organization, and Earth Council. (1995). *Agenda 21 for the Travel and Tourism Industry: towards environmentally sustainable development*. London: World Travel and Tourism Council.

Zeiger, J.B., and D. McDonald. (1997). Ecotourism: wave of the future. *Parks and Recreation*, **32** (9), 84–92.

Index